# 美国文学

# American literature

范翠华　胡新建／主编

贵州大学出版社
Guizhou University Press

**图书在版编目（CIP）数据**

美国文学 / 范翠华，胡新建主编. -- 贵阳 : 贵州大学出版社，2023.9

ISBN 978-7-5691-0534-6

Ⅰ. ①美… Ⅱ. ①范… ②胡… Ⅲ. ①英语—阅读教学—高等学校—教材 Ⅳ. ①H319.4：I

中国国家版本馆 CIP 数据核字（2023）第 145081 号

# 美国文学

MEIGUO WENXUE

主　　编：范翠华　胡新建

出 版 人：闵　军

责任编辑：高佩佩

装帧设计：陈　艺　方国进

出版发行：贵州大学出版社有限责任公司

地址：贵阳市花溪区贵州大学东校区出版大楼

邮编：550025　电话：0851-88291180

印　　刷：贵州思捷华彩印刷有限公司

开　　本：889 毫米×1194 毫米　1/32

印　　张：18.5

字　　数：466千字

版　　次：2023年9月第1版

印　　次：2023年9月第1次印刷

书　　号：ISBN 978-7-5691-0534-6

定　　价：52.50元

# 总　序

人文学科对发展国家经济文化、增强民族凝聚力不可或缺。在经济快速发展、社会不断进步、对外交流日益频繁的时代背景下，国家提出了发展“新文科”的要求。新文科的“新”，是更新与创新，更新传承传统文科的优势，创新文科发展的路径。对人文学科的教育者而言，不仅是要运用新技术，更要使用新理念、新方法，为培养社会主义强国的建设者贡献力量。如今科学技术迅猛发展，互联网、大数据、人工智能、虚拟技术广泛进入社会生活的各个方面，互联网对教育的影响颇为深远，对教师教学、学生学习都产生了深刻的影响，学科之间的交叉变得越来越广泛，要求我们要更新教育理念和教学方法。文科发展需适合国情发展需要，体现中国特色，彰显文化自信，培养的人才要适应新时代复合型人才的要求，培养外语人才也不例外。

贵州大学外国语学院作为贵州省重要的外语人才培养基地，以培养高质量复合型外语人才为目标，注重培养学生扎实的语言技能、宽广的知识面、开阔的国际视野以及朴素的爱国情怀，让学生成为通晓世界文化，谙熟跨文化沟通，能讲述中国故事，服务于社会主义经济建设的高素质综合型优秀人才。而目标的实现，依靠的是广大教师对学生日常的教育，具体体现在教师每一堂课的准备与实施、对学生每一项任务的设计、对教学科研的探讨上。在国家大力提倡建设“新文科”的背景下，结合教育部一流本科专业建设要求，我们努力建设高水平本科教育，全面提高人才培养水平，以建设面向未来、适应需求、引领发展、理念先进、保障有力的一流专业为抓手，夯实教学和科研。

作为教育部首批国家级一流本科专业和首批新文科研究与改革实践项目的建设单位，贵州大学外国语学院极为注重师资队伍建设和教学成果建设，鼓励广大教师开展教学和科研创新，凝练教学科研成果并付诸出版。我们组织长期扎根一线教学和科研的中青年教师，将他们在英语阅读、翻译、英美文学及专业能力测评等方面的教学科研成果与新文科背景相结合，集结出版本丛书，以期让更多的学生、同行及读者得到进一步的学习与交流。

在编写过程中，本丛书得到了贵州大学教务处向嵩处长、贵州大学出版社闵军社长、龚晓康副社长的关心和指导，贵州大学出版社教材编辑室主任葛静萍女士等提出了很好的意见和建议，在此一并致谢。

由于编者水平有限，本丛书在设计和编写上肯定还有不足和不当之处，恳请广大读者批评指正。

丛书编委会

2022 年 11 月

# 序　言

美国建国历史短，所以美国文学的历史也不长，但其经济发展迅猛，文学发展也比较快速。20世纪以来，美国文学取得了举世瞩目的成就。美国文学的影响遍及全球，迄今为止共有12位作家获得了诺贝尔文学奖。了解和学习美国文学，目的就在于通过文学的阅读了解他们的文化，借以促进与美国人民的交流、沟通和理解，同时也丰富我们的知识，提高文化修养。再者，“美国文学”课程是高校英语专业学生的必修课，编写本书也可供这门课教学之用。

我国著名的外国文学学者陆建德曾说过：“文学史上没有地理学上的海岸线和分水岭，历史的变化缓慢而不易察觉，它绵延不断，没有结合处和固定形体，因此文学史上的分期、分界线需要时时修订，如能统统去掉或许更好。”所以，尽管已有众多关于美国文学的教材，新编一本美国文学教材也无连篇累牍之嫌；再者，根据笔者多年的教学经验，考虑到学生的知识储备及外语水平，编写这套教材一来更方便教师制定教学计划，二来所选的经典文本详略得当，简繁相宜，更有利于学生们的深入学习。

本书按时间先后排序，共有六个部分，每个部分涵盖三个大的知识点：社会历史背景、文学特征及代表作家作品。众所周知，要在一本书中对每一个时期的每一个作家作品进行介绍和学习是不可能的，所以本书在具体内容编排及每一个时期作家、作品的遴选上，遵循了以下几个原则。

第一，每个部分首先按照时间顺序介绍这一时期所发生的历史大事，对当时文学发展产生巨大影响的历史事件尽可能详细而又重点地进行介绍。

第二，每个部分所选的作家及作品均是业界公认相当优秀且具有文学、社会价值的。

第三，每个部分有1~2篇精选文本的赏析，每个文本都有较为详细的注释和介绍；在每个精选文本的后面设有2个思考题，这些思考题或与文本相关，或与中国文学进行对比赏析，它们都是开放性的，没有标准答案。老师们可引导学生查阅相关资料，为今后进一步的学习打下基础。

第四，第一部分至第三部分编写比较容易。二战后的美国文学流派纷呈，作家众多，有些小说家不止于只写小说，有些诗人也不限于只写诗歌，因此在编写时把这些跨界作家罗列在他们成就最大的领域。

第五，本书的使用建议按照以下学时进行：第一、第二部分各4个学时，第三、第四部分各6个学时，第五、六部分各8个学时。这样编写主要基于高校每个学期授课18周，每周2个学时的教学量。当然，也可根据各个学校的开设周期进行教学，或长或短，自由灵活。

本书的编写从筹划到定稿所经历的困难和艰辛不言而喻，所幸一直有真诚、善良的贵州大学外国语学院英美文学教研组同仁——宁梅老师、胡新建老师、陈思老师、陈恒娇老师和陶晓莉老师长久的陪伴、莫大的鼓励及无私的支持。在此，要特别感谢贵州大学国际教育学院院长、贵州大学外国语学院教授宁梅老师。从课题申报到教材体例的敲定再到每个关键点的撰写和修改都有宁梅老师积极的参与和无私的付出。胡新建老师除编写内容庞杂的第五部分外，还负责联系外教修订文本，对整本书的格式进行调整。感谢胡新建老师的辛苦付出！在此也真诚感谢外教Mark Bynum先生百忙之中对本书每部分的第一、第二知识点的审阅。最后还要感谢我的研究生莫露、史运雪、严晓茵、简雪姣和袁燕，感谢她们认真地收集与梳理资料！

最后需强调的是，胡新建老师和我在编写本书的过程中虽然百思千虑，但该书定然会有疏漏失误之处，恳请各位专家、读者不吝指正！

范翠华

2023年1月4日

# 目　录

# Part I The Colonial Period (1492—1750)

## 1. Historical Background

When Christopher Columbus reached North America in 1492, the continent was already populated, though sparsely, by several hundred Native American tribes, however, Europeans did not encounter these tribes all at one time. Explorers from different nations came into contact with them at different times. As we now know, the widely dispersed tribes of Native Americans differed greatly from one to another in language, government, social organization, customs, housing, and methods of survival.

No one knows for certain when or how the first Americans arrived in what is now the United States. It may have been as recently as 12,000 years ago or as long ago as 70,000 years ago. Even if the shorter estimate is correct, Native Americans have been on the continent 30 times longer than the Europeans. Colonists from Europe did not begin arriving on the east coast of North America until the late 1500s. Additionally, no written story of Native Americans exists. Archaeologists have deduced a great deal from artifacts, however, and folklorists have recorded a rich variety of songs, legends, and myths.

What we do know is that Native Americans usually, but by no

means always, greeted the earliest European settlements as friends. They instructed the newcomers in their agriculture and woodcraft, and introduced them to maize, beans, squash, maple sugar, snow shoes, toboggans, and birch bark canoes. Indeed, many more of the European settlers would have succumbed to the bitter Northeastern winters had it not been for the help of these first Americans.

In 1620, a small group of Europeans sailed from England on the Mayflower,with many being passengers that were religious reformers—Puritans who were critical of the Church of England. Having given up hope of purifying the church from within, they chose instead to withdraw from the church. This action earned them the name Separatists, and end eventually referred to themselves as Pilgrims. The initial group set down on the raw Massachusetts shore in November in 1620. They landed in North America and established a settlement at what is now Plymouth Massachusetts. With the help from friendly tribes of Native Americans, the Plymouth settlement managed to survive the rigors of North America. Much larger at the start was the well-financed effort that brought a contingent of Puritans under John Winthrop to Massachusetts Bay, not far north of Plymouth, in 1630.

Like the Plymouth colony, the Massachusetts Colony was also founded by religious reformers. These reformers, however, did not withdraw from the Church of England. Unlike the Separatists, they were Puritans who intended instead to reform the church from within. In America, the Puritans hoped to establish a model community guided in all aspects by the Bible. Their form of government would be a theocracy, a state under the immediate guidance of God!

The Puritans' central beliefs were as follows:

(1) They believe that all human beings exist for the glory of God and that the Bible is the sole expression of God's will.

(2) They also hold that their destiny is dictated by God, and he has already decided who will achieve salvation and who will not, like what John Calvin believed.

(3) The Puritans felt that they could accomplish good only through continual hard work and self-discipline. When people today speak of the "Puritan Work Ethic," that is what they mean.

(4) Unsurprisingly, the Puritans held to the strictest requirements regarding communion, or, as they preferred to call it, the Lord's Supper.

Puritanism was in decline throughout New England by the early 1700's, as more liberal Protestant congregations attracted followers. Puritan ideals of hard work, fragility, self-improvement, and self-reliance are still regarded as basic American virtues.

The Southern Colonies differed from New England in various aspects: climate, crops, social organization, and religion. Prosperous coastal cities grew up in the south, just as in the North, but beyond the Southern cities were their large plantations, not small farms. Despite its romantic image, the plantation was, in fact, a large scale agricultural enterprise and a center of commerce. However, many of the people enslaved might live and work on a single plantation.

The first black slaves were brought to Virginia in 1619, a year before the Pilgrims landed at Plymouth. Most of the plantation owners were Church of England members who regarded themselves as aristocrats. The first generation of owners were men that established great plantations and were quite ambitious, energetic, self-disciplined, and resourceful, just as the Puritans were. The way of life on most plantations, however, was more sociable and elegant than that of any Puritan.

## 2. Literature of the Period

Generally speaking, indeed, much of the literature that the colonists read was not produced in the colonies—it came from England. Yet, by 1750, there were the very beginnings of natively produced literature that would one day be honored throughout the English speaking world.

For a long time, Native American literature was viewed by many as folklore. The consequence was that song lyrics, hero tales, migration legends, and accounts of creation beliefs were studied more for their content than for their literary qualities. In an oral tradition, the telling of a tale has no fixed or singular version like in literary works. The use of words and language in Native American lyrics and narratives that have been captured in writing are often poetic and moving. Therefore, oration was much prized among Native Americans. The names of certain orators, such as Logan and Red Jacket, were widely known.

Just as religion dominated the lives of the Puritans, it also dominated their writings—most of which would not be considered literary works by modern standards. Typically, the Puritans wrote theological studies, histories, biographies, and autobiographies. Because the Puritans regarded both fiction and drama as sinful, most of the literary works are narrative. Among all the Puritan writers, William Bradford (1590—1657) comes first. The first "Pilgrims" (a word Bradford himself used to describe the community of believers who sailed from Southampton, England, on the Mayflower and settled in Plymouth, Massachusetts, in 1620) epitomizes the spirit of determination and self-sacrifice. He was tolerant, intelligent, and courageous, which were important factors while surviving in North America. Shortly after their arrival, Bradford was elected governor and was reelected thirty times. During his tenure, he organized the repayment of debts to financial backers, encouraged new immigration, and established good relations with the Native Americans. Without his help, the colony would have never survived. In 1630, Bradford began writing *Of Plymouth Plantation*, a firsthand account of the pilgrims' struggle to endure, sustained only by courage and unbending faith. The work written in the simple language known as Puritan Plain Style, was not published until 1856. Bradford's own life provides a model of the life of the community as a whole. He later joined the "Separatists" movement in about 1606. Bradford was a self-educated man, deeply committed to the Puritan cause. In his *Ecclesiastical History of New England*, Cotton Mather describes him as, "...a person for study as well as action; and hence notwithstanding the difficulties which he passed in his youth, he attained unto a notable skill in languages...But the Hebrew he most of all studied, because, he said, he would see with his own eyes the ancient oracles of God in their native beauty...The crown of all his life was his holy, prayerful, watchful and fruitful walk with God, wherein he was exemplary."

Another important Puritan writer is John Winthrop (1588—1649). His father was a lawyer and his mother was a daughter of a tradesman. He went to Cambridge University for two years (1603—1605). It was probably at Cambridge University that Winthrop was exposed to Puritan ideas. Unlike Bradford and the Pilgrims, however, Winthrop was not a Separatist; that is, he wished to reform the national church from within. In March of 1629, a group of enterprising merchants, all sympathetic believers, were able to get a charter from the Council for New England for land in the New World. They called themselves "The Company of Massachusetts Bay in New England." From four candidates, Winthrop was chosen governor in October 1629; for the next twenty years most of the responsibility for the colony rested in his hands. Either just before departing from England or on the high seas, Winthrop delivered his sermon *A Model of Christian Charity*. It set out clearly and eloquently the ideals of a harmonious Christian community and reminded all those on board that they would stand as an example to the world, either in triumph or failure of this Christian enterprise. He began to keep a journal on the Bay colonists' voyage to Massachusetts aboard the ship Arbella in 1630. He maintained this practice for the rest of his life. Parts of his journal were first published in 1790, with the complete work printed in 1825 under the title *The History of New England from 1632 to1649*. Other papers of his exist, but the journal remains his chief work. His work is notable for its candid simplicity and honesty, and each account attained literary excellence.

Then, Jonathan Edwards (1703—1758) should also be talked

about. He is regarded as the great American theologian and powerful puritan preacher. He became a leader of the Great Awakening, a religious revival that swept the colony in the 1730s and 1740s. Edward's highly emotional sermon *Sinners in the Hands of an Angry God* is by far his most famous work. It was delivered to a congregation in Enfield, Connecticut, in 1741, and it is said to have caused listeners to rise from their seats in the stated of history.

One of the first books printed in the colonies was *The Bay Psalm Book*, the standard hymnal of the time. Increase Mather, one of the book's three authors, was also the author of some 130 books. *Cases of Conscience Concerning Evil Spirits* published in 1693 was a discourse on the Salem witchcraft trials of the previous year. The trials conducted in the atmosphere of hysteria resulted in the hanging of 20 people as witches. Increase's eldest son, Cotton Mather (1663—1728), far succeeded his father's literary output, publishing at least 400 works in his lifetime. Still, Cotton Mather was one of the most learned man of his time, a power within the state and notable works. His theory of writing was simple: the more information a work contains the better its style

The Puritans did write poetry, however, as a vehicle of spiritual enlightenment, although they were less concerned with their poetry's literary form than with its message. Some writers were more naturally gifted than others. A few excellent Puritan poets emerged in the 1600s, among them Anne Bradstreet (c.1612—1758), and Edward Taylor (c.1642—1729). Anne Bradstreet's moving, personal voice and Edward Taylor's devotional intensity shine through the conventional puritanism of their sins. The puritans had a strong belief in education for both men and women. In 1636, they founded Harvard College to ensure a well-educated ministry. Two years later, they set up the first printing press in the colonies.

In fact, the Puritans in general had a theory of literary style. They believed in a plain style of writing—one in which clear statements is the highest goal. An ornate or clever style would be a sign of vanity and, as such, would not be in accordance with God's will. Despite the restrictions built into their life and literature, the Puritans succeeded in producing a small body of excellent writing.

Comparatively, there are only a few notable southern writers that appeared prior to 1750. As in Puritan New England, those who were educated produced a substantial amount of writing, but it was mostly of a practical nature. For example, John Smith, the leader of the settlement at Jamestown, Virginia, wrote the *General History of Virginia* to describe his experiences for Europeans. In addition to accounts like Smith, letters written by southern planters also provide insight into this time period. Unlike the Puritans, southerners did not oppose fiction or drama, and the first theatre in America opened in Williamsburg, Virginia, in 1716.

## 3. Representative Writers' Works

### (1) John Smith (1580—1631)

Adventurer, poet, mapmaker, and egotist are just a few of the labels that apply to Smith, who was one of England's most famous explorers. Following a 10-year career as a soldier (1596—1606),

Smith led a group of colonists to this continent, where they landed in Virginia in 1607 and founded Jamestown, the first successful English colony in America. As president of the colony from 1608 to 1609, Smith helped to obtain food, enforce discipline, and deal with the local Native Americans. Even though Smith returned to England in 1609, he made two more voyages to America to explore the New England coast.

Born into a farmer's family in Lincolnshire, he was apprenticed at fifteen to a shopkeeper near his home. But tales of exploration, piracy, and military adventure already had stirred his imagination. In 1596, he went to the Netherlands as a volunteer soldier to fight for the Dutch in their long war of independence from Philip II. Smith next joined the Austrian army in its continuing war (1593—1606) against the Turks. Then, suffering much, Smith returned to England in the winter of 1604—1605. Many of these details come to us only through Smith's own, at times garbled, narratives, most of them penned long after the events.

In the fall of 1607, he was elected president of the council—in effect, the colony's governor—and in 1608, after a series of wide-ranging explorations that made him the most knowledgeable of the settlers regarding the new land. The explorations also led to his imprisonment at the hands of Powhatan, overlord of the Chesapeake Bay Indians, from whom he claimed (much later) that the king's young daughter, Pocahontas, rescued him. This becomes the source for the story of his rescue by Pocahontas. On his return to Jamestown from Powhatan's village, he was charged with the loss of two soldiers and would have been hanged had a fleet with much-needed supplies not arrived from England. He left Virginia in 1609 (never to return).

He published several works during the course of his life. The first of his publications, *A True Relation of Such Occurrences and Accidents of Note as Hath Happened in Virginia* (1608), was a letter he had sent back from the colony without intending that it be published. Then a work to which many colonists, including Smith, contributed, *A Map of Virginia: with a Description of the Country*...[and] *The Proceedings of those Colonies* (1612) was published. Some years later, Smith enlarged this book by adding more texts by other hands, expanding his own prose, and extending its geographical range and chronological coverage. More its editor than its author, Smith published the resulting *General History of Virginia, New England, and the Summer Isles*[1] (that is, Bermuda) in 1624. During his life, Smith published more works on New England than on Virginia (*A Description of New England*, 1616; *New England's Trials*, 1620 and 1622; and *Advertisements for the Inexperienced Planters of New England, or Anywhere*, 1631).

Smith and his works form an important bridge between the first two permanent English colonies in North America. Some scholars argued that Smith's America was not the geographical realm about which he had entertained such bright hopes for at the century's start, but, rather, the verbal domain he continued to explore in his later writings. When he closed the Virginia part of his *General History* by writing, "Thus far have I travelled in this Wilderness of Virginia," he was revealing how much like a country of his mind Virginia had become. Long gone was he from that still-struggling colony by then, but he had internalized it so well that he helped to make it a permanent part of the English— and the Anglo-American—imagination.

The following excerpts are from Philip L. Barbour (1986) edited *The Complete Works of Captain John Smith: General History of Virginia, New England, and the Summer Isles'*(the Third Book) The following passages are mainly about the descriptions of John Smith's hardships when they made the expeditions, and how he who was captured by the Indians befriended with the Indians.

## CHAPTER 2. WHAT HAPPENED TILL THE FIRST SUPPLY

Being thus left to our fortunes, it fortuned[2] that within ten days, scarce ten amongst us could either go or well stand, such extreme weakness and sickness oppressed us. And there at none need marvel if they consider the cause and reason which was this: While the ships stayed, our allowance was somewhat bettered by a daily proportion of biscuit which the sailors would pilfer to sell, give, or exchange with us for money, sassafras[3], furs, or love. But when they departed, there remained neither tavern, beer-house, nor place of relief but the common kettle[4]. Had we been as free from all sins as [we were free from] gluttony and drunkenness we might have been canonized for saints, but our President would never have been admitted for engrossing to his private, oatmeal, sack, oil, aqua vitae, beef, eggs, or what not but the Kettle[5]; that indeed he allowed equally to be distributed, and that was half a pint of wheat and as much barley boiled with water for a man a day, and this, having fried some twenty-six weeks in the ship's hold, contained as many worms as grains so that we might truly call it rather so much bran than corn; our drink was water[6],our lodgings castles in the air.

With this lodging and diet, our extreme toil in bearing and planting palisades so strained and bruised us and our continual labor in the extremity of the heat had so weakened us, as were cause sufficient to have mad e us as miserable in our native country or any other place in the world.

From May to September, those that escaped lived upon sturgeon and sea crabs. Fifty in this time we buried; the rest seeing the[7] projects to escape these miseries in our pinnace by flight (who all this time had neither felt want nor sickness) so moved our dead spirits as we deposed him and established Ratcliffe in his place (Gosnold being dead), Kendall deposed. Smith newly recovered, Martin[8] and Ratcliffe were by his care preserved and relieved, and the most of the soldiers recovered with the skillful diligence of Master Thomas Wotton our surgeon general.

But now was all our provision spent, the sturgeon gone, all helps abandoned, each hour expecting the fury of the savages, when God, the patron of all good endeavors, in that desperate extremity so changed the hearts of the savages that they brought such plenty of their fruits and provision as no man wanted[9].

And now where some affirmed it was ill done of the Council to send forth men so badly provided, this in contradictable reason will show them plainly they are too ill advised to nourish such ill conceits: First, the fault of our going was our own; what could be thought fitting or necessary we had, but what we should find, or want, or where we should be, we were all ignorant and supposing to make our passage in two months, with victual to live and the advantage of the spring to work; we were at sea five months where we both spent our victual and lost the opportunity of the time and season to plant, by the unskillful presumption of our ignorant transporters that understood not at all what they undertook.

Such actions have ever since the world's beginning been subject to such accidents, and everything of worth is found full of difficulties, but nothing [is] so difficult as to establish a commonwealth so far remote from men and means and where men's minds are so untoward[10] as neither do well themselves nor suffer others. But to proceed.

The new President and Martin, being little beloved, of weak judgment in dangers, and less industry in peace, committed the managing of all things Abroad[11] to Captain Smith, who, by his own example, good words, and fair promises, set some to mow, others to bind thatch, some to build houses, others to thatch them, himself always bearing the greatest task for his own share, so that in short time he provided most of them lodgings, neglecting any for himself.

……

Smith little dreaming of that accident, being got to the marshes at the river's head twenty miles in the desert[12], had his two men slain (as is supposed) sleeping by the canoe, while himself by fowling sought them victual, who finding he was beset with 200 savages, two of them he slew, still defending himself with the aid of a savage his guide, whom he bound to his arm with his garters and used him as a buckler[13], yet he was shot in his thigh a little, and had many arrows that stuck in his clothes but no great hurt, till at last they took him prisoner.

When this news came to Jamestown, much was their sorrow for his loss, few expecting what ensued.

Six or seven weeks those barbarians kept him prisoner, many strange triumphs and conjurations they mad e of him, yet he so demeaned[14] himself amongst them, as he not only diverted them from surprising the fort, but procured his own liberty, and got himself and his company such estimation amongst them, that those savages admired him more than their own Quiyoughkasoucks.

The manner how they used and delivered him is as followeth:

The savages having drawn from George Cassen whither Captain Smith was gone, prosecuting that opportunity they followed him with 300 bowmen, conducted by the King of Pamunkey, who in divisions searching the turnings of the river found Robinson and Emry[15] by the fireside; those they shot full of arrows and slew. Then finding the Captain, as is said, that used the savage that was his guide as his shield (three of them being slain and divers others so galled[16]), all the rest would not com e near him. Thinking thus to have returned to his boat, regarding them, as he marched, more than his way, [he] slipped up to the middle in an oozy creek and his savage with him, yet dared they not com e to him till being near dead with cold he threw away his arms. Then according to their composition[17] they drew him forth and led him to the fire where his men were slain. Diligently they chafed his benumbed limbs.

He demanding for their captain, they showed him Opechancanough[18], King of Pamunkey, to whom he gave a round ivory double compass dial. Mu h they marveled at the playing of the fly[19] and needle, which they could see so plainly and yet not touch it because of the glass that covered them. But when he demonstrated by that globe-like jewel the roundness of the earth and skies, the sphere of the sun, moon, and stars, and how the sun did chase the night round about the world continually, the greatness of the land and sea,the diversity of nations, variety of complexions, and how we were to them antipodes[20] and many other such like matters, they all stood as amazed with admiration.

Notwithstanding, within an hour after, they tied him to a tree, and as many as could stand about him prepared to shoot him, but the King holding up the compass in his hand, they all laid down their bows and arrows and in a triumphant manner led him to Orapaks[21] where he was after their mannes kindly feasted and well used.

Their order in conducting him was thus: Drawing themselves all in file, the King in the midst had all their pieces and swords borne before him. Captain Smith was led after him by three great savages holding him fast by each arm, and on each side six went in file with their arrows nocked[22]. But arriving at the town (which was but only thirty or forty hunting house s made of mats, which they remove a s they please, as we our tents), all the women and children staring to behold him, the soldiers first all in file performed the form of a bissom[23] so well as could be, and on each flank, officers as sergeants to see them keep their orders. A good time they continued this exercise and then cast themselves in a ring, dancing in such several posture s and singing and yelling out such hellish notes and screeches; being strangely painted, every one [had] his quiver of arrows and at his back a club, on his arm a fox or an otter's skin or some such matter for his vambrace, their heads and shoulders painted red with oil and pocones mingled together, which scarlet like color made an exceeding handsome show, his bow in his hand and the skin of a bird with her wings abroad,[24] dried, tied on his head, a piece of copper, a white shell, a long feather with a small rattle growing at the tails of their snakes tied to it, or some such like toy. All this while, Smith and the King stood in the midst, guarded as before is said, and after three dances they all departed. Smith they conducted to a long house where thirty or forty tall fellows did guard him, and ere long more bread and venison was brought him than would have served twenty men. I think his stomach at that time was not very good; what he left they put in baskets and tied over his head. About midnight they set the meat again before him; all this time not one of them would eat a bit with him, till the next morning they brought him as much more, and then did they eat all the old and reserved the new as they had done the other, which made him think they would fat him to eat him. Yet in this desperate estate, to defend him from the cold, one Maocassater brought him his gown in requital[25]of some beads and toys Smith had given him at his first arrival in Virginia.

Two days after, a man would have slain him (but that the guard prevented it) for the death of his son, to whom they conducted him to recover the poor man then breathing his last. Smith told them that at Jamestown he had a water would do it, if they would let him fetch it, but they would not permit that, but made all the preparations they could to assault Jamestown, craving his advice, and for recompence he should have life, liberty, land, and women. In part of a table book[26] he wrote his mind to them at the fort, what wasintended, how they should follow that direction to affright the messengers, and without fail send him such things as he wrote for. And an inventory with them. The difficulty and danger, he told the savages, of the mines, great guns, and other engines[27] exceedingly affrighted them, yet according to his request they went to Jamestown in as bitter weather as could be of frost and snow, and within three days returned with an answer.

But when they came to Jamestown, seeing men sally out as he had told them they would, they fled, yet in the night they cam e again to the same place where he had told them they should receive an answer and such things as he had promised them, which they found accordingly, and with which they returned with no small expedition to the wonder of them all that heard it, that he could either divine[28] or the paper could speak.

Then they led him to the Youghtanunds, the Mattapanients, the Piankatanks, the Nantaughtacunds, and Onawmanients[29]upon the rivers of Rappahannock and Potomac, over all those rivers and back again by divers other several nation[30], to the King's habitation at Pamunkey where they entertained him with most strange and fearful conjurations: [31]

As if near led to hell
Amongst the devils to dwell.

Opitchapam, the King's brother[32], invited him to his house, where, with as many platters of bread, fowl, and wild beasts as did environ him, he bid him welcome, but not any of them would eat a bit with him but put up all the remainder in baskets.

At his return to Opechancanough's, all the King's women and their children flocked about him for their parts[33], as a due by custom, to be merry with such fragments:

> But his waking mind in hideous dreams did
> 
> oft see wondrous shapes,
> 
> Of bodies strange, and huge in growth, and
> 
> of stupendous makes.[34]

At last they brought him to Werowocomoco[35], where was Powhatan, their Emperor. Here more than two hundred of those grim courtiers stood wondering at him, as [if] he had been a monster, till Powhatan and his train had put themselves in their greatest braveries[36]. Before a fire upon a seat like a bedstead, he sat covered with a great robe made of raccoon skins and all the tails hanging by. On either hand did sit a young wench of sixteen or eighteen years and along on each side [of] the house, two rows of men and behind them as many women, with all their heads and shoulders painted red, many of their heads bedecked with the white down of birds, but every one with something, and a great chain of white beads about their necks.

At his entrance before the King, all the people gave a great shout. The Queen of Appomattoc[37] was appointed to bring him water to wash his hands, and another brought him a bunch of feathers, instead of a towel, to dry them; having feasted him after their best barbarous manner they could, a long consultation was held, but the conclusion was, two great stones were brought before Powhatan; then as many as could, laid hands on him, dragged him to them, and thereon laid his head and being ready with their clubs to beat out his brains, Pocahontas[38], the King's dearest daughter, when no entreaty could prevail, got his head in her arms and laid her own upon his to save him from death, whereat the Emperor was contented he should live to make him hatchets, and her bells, beads, and copper, for they thought him a s well of all occupations as themselves[39]. For the King himself will make his own robes, shoes, bows, arrows, pots; plant, hunt, or do anything so well as the rest.

> They say he bore a pleasant show,
> But sure his heart was sad.
> For who can pleasant be, and rest,
> That lives in fear and dread:
> And having life suspected, doth
> It still suspected lead.[40]

Two days after, Powhatan, having disguised himself in the most fearfulest manner he could, caused Captain Smith to be brought forth to a great house in the woods and there upon a mat by the fire to be left alone. Not long after, from behind a mat that divided the house, was made the most dolefulest noise he ever heard; then Powhatan more like a devil than a man, with some two hundred more as black as himself, came unto him and told him now they were friends, and presently he should go to Jamestown to send him two great guns and a grindstone for which he would give him the country of Capahowasic and forever esteem him as his son Nantaquoud.[41]

So to Jamestown with twelve guides Powhatan sent him. That night they quartered in the woods, he still expecting (as he had done all this long time of his imprisonment) every hour to be put to one death or other, for all their feasting. But almighty God (by His divine providence) had mollified the hearts of those stern barbarians with compassion. The next morning betimes they came to the fort, where Smith having used the savages with what kindness he could, he showed Rawhunt, Powhatan's trusty servant, two demiculverins [42]and a millstone to carry [to] Powhatan; they found them somewhat too heavy, but when they did see him discharge them, being loaded with stones, among the boughs of a great tree loaded with icicles, the ice and branches came so tumbling down that the poor savages ran away half dead with fear. But at last we regained some conference with them and gave them such toys and sent to Powhatan, his women, and children such presents as gave them in general full content.

Now in Jamestown they were all in combustion, the strongest preparing once more to run away with the pinnace; which, with the hazard of his life, with saker falcon[43] and musket shot, Smith forced now the third time to stay or sink.

Some, no better than they should be, had plotted with the President the next day to have him put to death by the Levitical law[44], for the lives of Robinson and Emry; pretending the fault was his that had led them to their ends; but he quickly took such order with such lawyers that he laid them by the heels till he sent some of them prisoners for England.

Now every once in four or five days, Pocahontas with her attendants brought him so much provision that saved many of their lives, that else for all this had starved with hunger.

Thus from numb death our good God sent relief,
The sweet assuager of all other grief.[45]

His relation of the plenty he had seen, especially at Werowocomoco, and of the state and bounty of Powhatan (which till that time was unknown), so revived their dead spirits (especially the love of Pocahontas)[46] as all men's fear was abandoned.

Thus you may see what difficulties still crossed any good endeavor; and the good success of the business being thus oft brought to the very period of destruction; yet you see by what strange means God hath still delivered it.

## Notes

1. The Bermuda Islands. The Third Book is titled "The Proceedings and Accidents of the English Colony in Virginia" and is derived from Smith's *Virginia* book of 1612. The bulk of this chapter, which opens with an account of the sickness whose dire results were chronicled by George Percy, may have been written by John Smith himself, although

at its publication in 1612 it was credited solely to Thomas Studley, chief storekeeper of the colony. In 1624, Smith added to Studley's signature at the end of this section of the text not only his own initials but also the names of Robert Fenton and Edward Harrington as part authors. According to Percy, Studley died early in the first year, on August 28, 1607, four days after Harrington, so neither could have written much of what is in part attributed to them. Of Robert Fenton nothing is known.

2. By the end of June 1607, after Captain Christopher Newport (d.1617) left to fetch new supplies from England. "Fortuned": happened.

3. The bark of the sassafras tree, sold for its supposed medicinal qualities, was a valuable commodity in London.

4. The communal resources.

5. I.e., President Edward Maria Wingfield (c.1560 — 1613), a man of high connections in England, would not have been canonized as a saint because he diverted many supplies (everything except the contents of the common kettle) for his own use, including sack (wine) and aqua vitae (brandy).

6. It was more customary to drink wine or beer. "Corn": grain.

7. I.e., Wingfield.

8. Captain John Martin (c.1567 — 1632?) was a colonist best known for his contentiousness. "Captain John Ratcliffe" was an alias of John Sicklemore, master of one ol the vessels on the voyage over and a member of the local council. The most enigmatic figure in Jamestown, he was elected president of the council in September 1607, but later fell out with Smith. Captain Bartholomew Gosnold (c.1572 — 1607), who had explored NewEngland before the first Jamestown voyage,

probably had been responsible for Smith's recruitment to the venture. Captain George Kendall (d.1607) was executed for mutiny later in the year.

9. I.e., was in want.

10. Intractable.

11. I.e., outside the palisade.

12. Wilderness.

13. Shield. "Garters": laces used for tying clothing.

14. Behaved.

15. The two men mentioned above as having been killed while they slept. Thomas Emry was a carpenter. John Robinson was a "gentleman."

16. Wounded.

17. Agreement for surrender.

18. Powhatan's younger half-brother and Smith's captor, Opechancanough (d.1644) was to lead the Indian Confederacy's attack on the colonists in 1622 and as late as1644 attempted one last time to expel them from the country.

19. Compass card.

20. On the opposite side of the globe.

21. A village located farther inland, later the residence of Powhatan.

22. Notched; i.e.. with their arrows fitted on the bowstring ready to use.

23. From an Italian term denoting a snakelike formation.

24. Outspread. "Vambrace": forearm protection. "Pocones": a dye of vegetative origin.

25. Payment.

26. A notebook.

27. Weaponry.

28. Perform magic. “Expedition”: speed.

29. These groups were part of the confederacy that was under the rule of Powhatan.

30. Other Algonquian-speaking groups.

31. Incantations; but the following couplet Smith derived from a translation of Seneca published by Bishop Martin Fotherby in his Atheomastix (1622).

32. Actually the chiefs half-brother; he succeeded Powhatan in 1618.

33. Gifts.

34. From a translation of Lucretius by Fotherby.

35. Powhatan’s village on the north shore of the York River, almost due north of Jamestown.

36. Finery; i.e., costumes.

37. Opossunoquonuske was the weroansqua, or leader, of a small village (Appamatuck) near the future site of Petersburg, Virginia. In 1610, she was killed by the English in retaliation for the deaths of fourteen settlers.

38. Daughter of Powhatan (c.1591 — 1617), she was mentioned in Smith’s earlier versions of his captivity narrative, but first emerged as its heroine only in the History, which was published seven years after her death in England.

39. I.e., they thought him as variously skilled as themselves.

40. Derived from a translation of Euripides by Fotherby.

41. I.e., Powhatan would esteem him as highly as his own son Nantaquoud. Capahowasic was along the York River near where Smith was held prisoner.

42. Large cannons.

43. Small falcon.

44. "And he that killeth any man shall surely be put to death" (Leviticus 24.17).

45. Apparently the first line is Smith's own, based on Fotherby, but the second is borrowed directly from Fotherby's translation from a quotation of Euripides found in Plutarch.

46. I.e., the evident affection of Pocahontas for Smith and the English was instrumental in reviving the colonists' spirits.

## Questions

1. How much help had the colonists got from the Indians in this passage? What kind of attitude did Smith take towards the Indians?

2. Try to compare *The Travels of Xu Xiake* by Chinese writer Xu Xiake (Ming Dynasty) with this excerpt and then illustrate why John Smith took so many risks.

### (2) Anne Bradstreet (1612—1672)

Anne Bradstreet was very much the apple of her father's, Thomas Dudley's, eye, who was the manager of the country estate of the Puritan earl of Lincoln. Therefore, she received an education superior to that of most young women of the time. When she was only sixteen she married the young Simon Bradstreet, a talented and capable young man. Both her father and her husband were Governor of the Bay Colony. In 1630, the Bradstreets and the Dudleys sailed with Winthrop's fleet.

We know very little of Bradstreet's daily life, except that it was a hard existence.

Her husband was busy as secretary for the company, then and in the future. Obviously, she had to take most of the responsibility for the family. And like any good Puritan, she added to the care of daily life the examination of her conscience, which is well presented in her poems.

She is the first in a long line of American poets who took their consolation not from theology but from the "wondrous works".

When Bradstreet was a young girl, she had written poems to please her father, and he made much of their reading them together. After her marriage she continued writing. Quite unknown to her, her brother-in-law, John Woodbridge, pastor of the Andover church, brought with him to London a manuscript collection of her poetry and had it printed there in 1650. The Tenth Muse Lately Sprung Up in America was the first published volume of poems written by a resident in the New World and was widely read. The second edition of Bradstreet's poems was published in 1678. Although she herself probably took the greatest pride in her long meditative poems on the ages of humankind and on the seasons. Her poems that have attracted present-day readers are the more intimate ones, which reflect her concern for her family and home, and the pleasures she took in everyday life rather than in the life to come. Nevertheless, Bradstreet was an ambitious poet whose imagination was firmly grounded in

English religious, political, and cultural history; and she was a firm believer in the Puritan experiment in America.

The following text is from the Works of Anne Bradstreet, edited by Jeannine Hensley (1967).

## Contemplations

### 1

Some time now past in the autumnal tide,
When Phoebu[1] wanted but one hour to bed,
The trees all richly clad, yet void of pride,
Were gilded o'er by his rich golden head.
Their leaves and fruits seemed painted, but was true,
Of green, of red, of yellow, mixed hue ;
Rapt were my senses at this delectable view.

### 2

I wist not what to wish, yet sure thought I,
If so much excellence abide below.
How excellent is He that dwells on high,
Whose power and beauty by His works we know?
Sure He is goodness, wisdom, glory, light,
That hath this under world so richly dight[2]
More heaven than earth was here, no winter and no night.

**3**

Then on a stately oak I cast mine eye,
Whose ruffling top the clouds seemed to aspire;
How long since thou wast in thine infancy?
Thy strength, and stature, more thy years admire,
Hath hundred winters past since thou wast born?
Or thousand since thou brakest thy shell of horn?
If so, all these as nought, eternity doth scorn.

**4**

Then higher on the glistering Sun I gazed.
Whose beams was shaded by the leafy tree;
The more I looked, the more I grew amazed,
And softly said, "What glory's like to thee?"
Soul of this world, this universe's eye,
No wonder some made thee a deity;
Had I not better known, alas, the same had I.

**5**

Thou as a bridegroom from thy chamber rushes.
And as a strong man, joys to run a race; [3]
The morn doth usher thee with smiles and blushes;
The Earth reflects her glance s in thy face.
Birds, insects, animals with vegative,
Thy heat from death and dullness doth revive,
And in the darksome womb of fruitful nature dive.

**6**

Thy swift annual and diurnal[4] course,
Thy daily straight and yearly oblique[5] path.
Thy pleasing fervor and thy scorching force,
All mortals here the feeling knowledge hath.
Thy presence make s it day, thy absence night,
Quaternal[6] seasons caused by thy might:
Hail creature, full of sweetness, beauty, and delight.

## Notes

1. Apollo, the sun god.

2. furnished, adorned.

3. The sun "is as a bridegroom coming out of his chamber, and rejoiceth as a strong man to run a race" (Psalm 19.5).

4. It means happening or active during the daytime.

5. Sloping at an angle.

6. Quaternate in American English,adj. arranged in or consisting of four parts, as the leaves of certain plants.

## To My Dear and Loving Husband

If ever two were one, then surely we.
If ever man were loved by wife, then thee;
If ever wife was happy in a man,
Compare with me, ye women, if you can.

I prize thy love more than whole mines of gold
Or all the riches that the East cloth hold.
My love is such that rivers cannot quench,
Nor ought but love from thee, give recompense.
Thy love is such I can no way repay,
The heavens reward thee manifold, I pray.
Then while we live, in love let's so persevere
That when we live no more, we may live ever.

1678

## Questions

1. Anne Bradstreet is a pious Puritan. What and how is her belief expressed in her above poems?

2. Try to paraphrase the second poem and see how many messages have you gained or lost by paraphrasing.

# Part II The Revolutionary and Independent Period (1765—1799)

## 1. Historical Background

If religion occupied many colonists in the first half of the 18th century, after 1763, when Great Britain had consolidated its empire in the New World with victory over the French in Canada, politics dominated its second half.

Until the 1730s, there were 13 colonies along the Atlantic, mainly from England. By 1750, there were fourth and fifth generation Americans of European descent living in Virginia and New England. These people were English subjects and, on the whole, they were all satisfied with that status. In fact, as late as the early 1760s, few Americans had given much thought to the prospect of independence.

Between the mid-1760s and the mid-1770s, King George III and Parliament imposed a lot of regulations that threatened the liberties of the colonists. With each succeeding measure, the outrage in America grew and finally erupted into war. The American Revolution (1775—1783) was a ripe upheaval, and the groundwork for it had been made by European writers and thinkers, as well as by the English King and Parliament. The British government, wanting to raise revenue from companies to pay its debt, passed the Stamp Act in 1765, which required the buying and affixing of stamps to each of 54 ordinary items. Colonial reaction to it was swift and bitter. Stamps were burned. Stamps distributors were beaten and their shops destroyed. Eventually, the Stamp Act was repealed. In 1767 the Townshend Acts was passed, which taxed paper, paint, glass, lead, and tea. When the colonists organized a boycott, the British dissolved the Massachusetts legislature and sent two regiments of British troops to Boston. In 1770, the Boston Massacre further inflamed colonial passions. The Tea Act stirred the fury of the Bostonians, and they dumped a shipment of tea into Boston harbor. Then as punishment for this “Boston Tea Party,” the English Parliament passed the Coercive Acts. Because they shut down the port of Boston and insisted that British troops could be housed in colonists’ homes, colonists immediately dubbed these laws the Intolerable Acts. In September 1774, Colonial leaders met in Philadelphia for the first Continental Congress. And on April 19, 1775, British troops met the colonists on the Lexington green. A musket shot was fired. The encounters at Lexington and Concord, Massachusetts, a landmark in American history, have been referred to as “the shot heard round the world.” The American Revolution had begun. After six years of fighting, the war came to an end in 1783.

After the revolution, the Federal constitution was ratified only after a long fight, and then later a Bill of Rights was added to placate those who feared the centralization of power that the Constitution conferred. George Washington became the first president of the United State, and John Adams, signer of the Declaration of Independence, succeeded him in that office. Then in 1800, Americans elected Thomas Jefferson, the brilliant statesman who had drafted the Declaration, as their president.

## 2. Literature of the Period

The 18th century saw enormous changes—economic, social, philosophical, and scientific—that inevitably affected the influence and authority of clergymen like Mather, and transformed the ways in which they understood the world. By the early 18th century, scientists and philosophers had posed great challenges to 17th-century beliefs. The 19th century is often characterized as The Enlightenment or the Age of Reason. This was spurred by the work of many 17th-century thinkers—such as scientists Galileo (1564—1642) and Sir Isaac Newton (1642—1727), philosophers Voltaire (1694—1778), and Jean Jacques Rousseau (1712—1778), and political theorist John Locke (1632—1704)—who held that the mind is rather like a blank wax tablet on which experiences are inscribed; they qualified traditional belief and suggested that the more that we understood and sympathized with our fellow men and women, the richer our social and spiritual lives would be. The writers and thinkers of the Enlightenment valued reason over faith. Unlike the Puritans, they have little interest in the hereafter, believing instead in the power of reason and science to further human progress. They spoke of a social contract, which forms the basis of government. Above all, they believed that people are by nature, good, not evil. A perfect society seemed to them to be more than just an idle dream.

The American statesmen of the Revolutionary period were themselves figures of the Enlightenment. Benjamin Franklin (1706—1790), Thomas Paine (1737—1809), and Thomas Jefferson (1743—1826) not only expressed the ideas of the Age of Reason, but they also helped to put them spectacularly into practice.

In contrast to the private soul-searching of the Puritans of New England, much of what was produced during the Revolutionary period was public writing. By the time of the war for independence, nearly 50 newspapers had been established in the coastal cities. At the time of Washington's inauguration, there were nearly 40 magazines. Almanacs were in fashion from Massachusetts to Georgia. Journalists and printers provided a forum for the expression of political ideas after 1763. These ideas were increasingly focused on relations with Great Britain and, more broadly, on the nature of government. The writings of prominent importance from the revolutionary era is mostly political. The increase in population alone helps account for the greater diversity of opinion in religious as well as in political life that marked it and its literature.

Patrick Henry was a spellbinding orator whose speech against the Stamp Act brought cries of "treason." Ten years later, his electrifying speech to the Virginia Convention expressed the rising sentiment for independence. Thomas Paine was perhaps more influential than any other in swaying public opinion in favor of independence. His pamphlet titled Common Sense, published in January 1776, swept the colonies. In December 1776, when Washington's troops were at their most demoralized, it was, again, Paine's first Crisis paper—popularly called The American Crisis—that was read to all the regiments and was said to have inspired their future success. The Declaration of

Independence was first drafted by Thomas Jefferson in June 1776. The finished document was largely his work, although others, including Benjamin Franklin, were involved in its creation. This document, despite some exaggerated charges against King George III, is one of the most influential political statements ever made. Another revolutionary period document is the Constitution of the United States, drafted in 1787. The Americans hoped that the Constitution would last at least a generation. It still survives, amended only 27 times, as the political foundation of the 50 states.

While politics dominated the literature of the revolutionary period, not every writer of note was a statesman. Verse appeared in most of the newspapers. Joel Barlow (1754—1812) and Philis Wheatley (c.1753—1784) were prominent among them. Barlow, a 1778 Yale graduate, is best remembered for The Hasty Pudding, a mock-heroic tribute to cornmeal mush. Philis Wheatley, born in Africa and brought to Boston in childhood as a slave, showed early signs of literary genius. A collection of her poems was published in England while she was still a young woman. Philip Freneau (1752—1832), the "Poet of the American Revolution," succeeded first as a writer of satires of the British, and later wrote impassioned verse in support of the American Revolution. He turned all his rhetorical gifts against anyone thought to be in sympathy with the British monarchy. He became renowned after the publishing of his Poems Written Chiefly during the Late War (1786).

Perhaps the best in writing of that period, outside the field of politics, was done by Benjamin Franklin. His Poor Richard's Almanack became familiar to most households in the colonies. His autobiography, covering only his early years, is regarded as one of the finest autobiographies in any language. It marks the beginning of a new sense of national identity as colonists from greatly different backgrounds and of varied nationalities now found reasons to call themselves "Americans."

By the early 1800s, America could boast a small body of national literature. The Native Americans had contributed haunting poetry and legends through their own traditions. The Puritans had written a number of powerful, inward-looking works. The statesmen of the Revolutionary period had produced political documents for the ages. A few poets and essayists had made a permanent mark on the literature of the young republic. There were, however, no American novels or plays of importance, and the modern short story had yet to be invented. As the 18th century came to a close, however, the raw materials for a great national literature were at hand, wishing to be used. The nation stood on the threshold of a territorial and population explosion unique in the history of the world. The colonial age ended with few works of memorable literature. The 19th century would close with a library of works that formed a major part of the American literary heritage.

## 3. Representative Writers' Works

### (1) Benjamin Franklin (1706—1790)

A statesman, printer, author, inventor, and scientist, Franklin was a true son of the Enlightenment. Although he never received a formal education, Franklin made important contributions in a variety of fields, including literature, journalism, science, diplomacy, education, and philosophy. As one of seventeen children, he was born to a big family in Boston. After leaving school at the age of 10, he spent two years working for his father before becoming an apprentice to his older brother, who was a printer. When he was 17, Franklin left Boston and traveled to Philadelphia, hoping to open his own print shop. Once he established himself as a printer, Franklin began producing a newspaper and an annual publication called *Poor Richard's Almanack*, in which contained information, observations, and divine advice. *Poor Richard's Almanack*, published from 1732 through 1757, was very popular and earned Franklin a reputation as a talented writer.

When Franklin turned 40, he retired from the printing business to devote himself to science. He proved to be a successful scientist. Over the course of his lifetime, Franklin was responsible for inventing the lightning rod, bifocals, and a new type of stove; these led to the confirmation of the laws of electricity and contributions to the scientific understanding of earthquakes and ocean currents. In spite of all these achievements, Franklin is best remembered for his career in politics. He played an important role in crafting the Declaration of Independence, enlisting French support during the American Revolutionary War, negotiating a peace treaty with Britain, and drafting the Constitution of the United States. In his late life, he was an ambassador, first to England and then to France. He was considered a "father of his country."

Franklin wrote the first section of his autobiography in 1771 at the age of 65. At the urging of friends, he wrote three more sections—the last shortly before his death—but succeeded only in scribing the account of his life between the years of 1757 to 1759. *The Autobiography of Benjamin Franklin* describes his desire to improve himself. He writes of his ambition to help others follow in his path. It set the standard for what was then a new genre. Though never completed, his autobiography, filled with opinions and suggestions, provides not only a record of his achievements but also an understanding of his character. In many ways, Franklin represents the new American.

An autobiography is a person's account of his or her life, generally presented in the first person with the author using the word "I." Autobiographies present life events as the writer viewed them. In addition to providing inside details about the writer's life, autobiographies also offer insights into the beliefs and perceptions of the author. They offer a glimpse of what it was like to live in the author's time period. Autobiographies often provide a view of historic events that you won't find in history books.

The following reading is from part 2 (something is omitted from the original text), mainly talking about how "I" carried on the "project of arriving at moral perfection," during which "I" seems contrived some ways.

## The Autobiography [Part Two]

It was about this time that I conceiv'd the bold and arduous Project of arriving at moral Perfection. I wish'd to live without committing any Fault at anytime; I would conquer all that either Natural Inclination, Custom, or Company might lead me into. As

I knew, or thought I knew, what was right and wrong, I did not see why I might not always do the one and avoid the other. But I soon found I had undertaken a Task of more Difficulty than I had imagined: While my Care was employ'd in guarding against one Fault, I was often surpris'd by another. Habit took the Advantage of Inattention. Inclination was sometimes too strong for Reason. I concluded at length, that the mere speculative Conviction that it was our Interest to be completely virtuous, was not sufficient to prevent our Slipping, and that the contrary Habits must be broken and good Ones acquired and established, before we can have any Dependence on a steady uniform Rectitude of Conduct. For this purpose I therefore contriv'd the following Method.

In the various Enumerations of the moral Virtues I had met with in my Reading, I found the Catalog more or less numerous, as different Writers included more or fewer Ideas under the same Name. Temperance, for Example, was by some confin'd to Eating and Drinking, while by others it was extended to mean the moderating every other Pleasure, Appetite, Inclination or Passion, bodily or mental, even to our Avarice and Ambition. I propos'd to myself, for the sake of Clearness, to use rather more Names with fewer Ideas annex'd to each, than a few Names with more Ideas; and I included after Thirteen Names of Virtues all that at that time occurr'd to me as necessary or desirable, and annex'd to each a short Precept, which fully express'd the Extent I gave to its Meaning.

These Name s of Virtues with their Precepts were

1. TEMPERANCE.

Eat not to Dullness. Drink not to Elevation.

2. SILENCE.

Speak not but what may benefit others or yourself. Avoiding trifling Conversation.

3. ORDER.

Let all your Things have their Places. Let each Part of your Business have its Time.

4. RESOLUTION.

Resolve to perform what you ought. Perform without fail what you resolve.

5. FRUGALITY.

Make no Expense but to do good to others or yourself: i.e., Waste nothing.

6. INDUSTRY.

Lose no Time. Be always employ'd in something useful. Cut off all unnecessary Actions.

7. SINCERITY.

Use no hurtful Deceit. Think innocently and justly; and, if you speak; speak accordingly.

8. JUSTICE.

Wrong none, by doing Injuries or omitting the Benefits that are your Duty.

9. MODERATION.

Avoid Extremes. Forbear resenting Injuries so much as you think they deserve.

10. CLEANLINESS.

Tolerate no Uncleanness in Body, Clothes or Habitation.

11. TRANQUILITY.

Be not disturbed at Trifles, or Accidents common or unavoidable.

12. CHASTITY.

Rarely use Venery but for Health or Offspring; Never to Dullness, Weakness, or the Injury of your own or another's Peace or Reputation.

13. HUMILITY.

Imitate Jesus and Socrates.

My intention being to acquire the Habitude[1] of all these Virtues, I judg'd it would be well not to distract my Attention by attempting the whole at once, but to fix it on one of them at a time, and when I should be Master of that, then to proceed to another, and so on till I should have gone thro' the thirteen. And as the previous Acquisition of some might facilitate the Acquisition of certain others, I arrang'd them with that View as they stand above. *Temperance* first, as it tends to procure that Coolness and Clearness of Head, which is so necessary where constant Vigilance was to be kept up, and Guard maintained, against the unremitting Attraction of ancient Habits, and the Force of perpetual Temptations. This being acquir'd and establish'd, *Silence* would be more easy, and my Desire being to gain Knowledge at the same time that I improv'd in Virtue, and considering that in Conversation it was obtain'd rather by the Use of the Ears than of the Tongue, and therefore wishing to break a Habit I was getting into of Prattling, Punning and Joking, which only made me acceptable to trifling Company, I gave Silence the second Place. This, and the next, *Order*,

I expected would allow me more Time for attending to my Project and my studies; RESOLUTION once become habitual, would keep me firm in my Endeavors to obtain all the subsequent Virtues; *Frugality* and *Industry*, by freeing me from my remaining Debt, and producing Affluence and Independence would make more easy the *Practice* of *Sincerity* and *Justice*, etc., etc. Conceiving then that agreeable to the Advice of Pythagoras[2] in his Golden Verses, daily Examination would be necessary, I contriv'd the following Method for conducting that Examination.

I made a little Book in which I allotted a Page for each of the Virtues. I rul'd each Page with red Ink so as to have seven Columns, one for each Day of the Week, marking each Column with a Letter for the Day. I cross'd these Columns with thirteen red Lines, marking the Beginning of each Line with the first Letter of one of the Virtues, on which Line and in its proper Column I might mark by a little black Spot every Fault I found upon Examination, to have been committed respecting that Virtue upon that Day.

I determined to give a Week's strict Attention to each of the Virtues successively. Thus in the first Week my great Guard was to avoid every the least Offence against Temperance, leaving the other Virtues to their ordinary Chance, only marking every Evening the Faults of the Day. Thus if in the first Week I could keep my first Line marked T clear of Spots, I suppos'd the Habit of that Virtue so much strengthen'd and its opposite weaken'd, that I might venture extending my Attention to include the next, and for the following Week keep both Lines clear of Spots. Proceeding thus to the last, I could go thro' a Course complete in Thirteen Weeks, and four Courses in a Year. And like him who having a Garden to weed, does not attempt to eradicate all the bad Herbs at once, which would exceed his Reach and his Strength, but works on one of the Beds at a time, and having accomplish'd the first proceeds to a second; so I should have, (I hoped) the encouraging Pleasure of seeing on my Pages the Progress I made in Virtue, by clearing successively my Lines of their Spots, till in the End by a Number of Courses, I should be happy in viewing a clean Book after a thirteen Weeks' daily Examination....

## Notes

1. I.e., making these virtues an integral part of his nature.

2. Pythagoras (6th century B.C.E.) was a Greek philosopher and mathematician. Franklin added a note here: "Insert those Lines that direct it in a Note," and wished to include verses translated: "Let sleep not close your eyes till you have thrice examined the transactions of the day: where have 1 strayed, what have I done, what good have I omitted?"

## Questions

1. Do you think the life of this kind of mode presented in this passage is the one which people living at the time of the American Revolution wanted to create? Why or why not?

2. Try to compare Franklin's "Virtues with their Precepts" with the ideas of Chinese Confucius as far as the view of Virtue is concerned.

### （2）Philip Freneau (1752—1832)

Philip Freneau was the most significant poet of 18th-century America. Some of his themes and imagination anticipated the works of such 19th-century American Romantic writers as Cooper, Emerson, Poe, and Melville.

He was born in New York in 1752. In 1767, he entered the College of New Jersey (now Princeton University). There he became fast friends with his roommate, James Madison, a future president, and a classmate, Hugh Henry Brackenridge, who became a successful novelist. While still an undergraduate, he wrote in collaboration with H. H. Brackenridge a poem entitled The Rising Glory of America, which establishes early in Freneau's career his recurrent vision of a glorious future in which America would fulfill the collective hope of humankind. In 1776, he was offered a position as secretary on a plantation in the West Indies and he remained there for almost three years. It was on that island that Freneau wrote some of his most sensuous lyrics, which included abundant discussions about the slaves' poverty and misery. In 1778, he attended the War of Independence and was captured by the British army in 1780. After being released, he published The British Prison Ship in 1781. In the same year, he published To the Memory of the Brave Americans. He moved to Philadelphia after spending 10 more years of his life at sea. It was in Philadelphia that he gained his reputation as a satirist, journalist, and poet. As editor of the Freeman's Journal, Freneau wrote impassioned verse in support of the American Revolution and turned all his rhetorical gifts against anyone thought to be in sympathy with the

British monarchy. It was during this period in his life that he became identified as the "Poet of the American Revolution." But after 50 years old, he entered a life of poverty, and at last he died in a blizzard.

There is no doubt that he did much to pave the way for the later writers. His obsession with the beautiful, transient things of nature and the conflict in his art between the sensuous and the didactic are central to the concerns of American poetry.

The following texts used are from *The Norton Anthology of American Literature*(6th edition).

## On the Emigration to America and Peopling the Western Country

**1**

To western woods, and lonely plains,
Palemon[1] from the crowd departs,
Where Nature's wildest genius reigns,
To tame the soil, and plant the arts—
What wonders there shall freedom show,
What mighty states successive grow!

**2**

From Europe's proud, despotic shores
Hither the stranger takes his way,
And in our new found world explores
A happier soil, a milder sway,

Where no proud despot holds him down,
No slaves insult him with a crown.

**3**

What charming scenes attract the eye,
On wild Ohio's savage stream!
There Nature reigns, whose works outvie
The boldest pattern art can frame;
There ages past have rolled away,
And forests bloomed but to decay.

**4**

From these fair plains, these rural seats,
So long concealed, so lately known,
The unsocial Indian far retreats,
To make some other clime his own,
Where other streams, less pleasing flow,
And darker forests round him grow.

**5**

Great sire[2] of floods! whose varied wave
Through climes and countries takes its way,
To whom creating Nature gave
Ten thousand streams to swell thy sway!
No longer shall they useless prove,
Nor idly through the forests rove;

**6**

Nor longer shall your princely flood
From distant lakes be swelled in vain,
Nor longer through a darksome wood
Advance, unnoticed, to the main,[3]
Far other ends, the heavens decree—
And commerce plans new freights for thee.

**7**

While virtue warms the generous breast,
There heaven-born freedom shall reside,
Nor shall the voice of war molest,
Nor Europe's all-aspiring pride—
There Reason shall new laws devise,
And order from confusion rise.

**8**

Forsaking kings and regal state,
With all their pomp and fancied bliss,
The traveler owns,[4] convinced though late,
No realm so free, so blessed as this—
The east is half to slaves consigned,
Where kings and priests enchain the mind.

**9**

O come the time, and haste the day,

When man shall man no longer crush,
When Reason shall enforce her sway,
Nor these fair regions raise our blush,
Where still the African complains,
And mourns his yet unbroken chains.

**10**

Far brighter scenes a future age,
The muse predicts, these states will hail,
Whose genius may the world engage,
Whose deeds may over death prevail,
And happier systems bring to view,
Than all the eastern sages knew.

## Notes

1. Conventionally, any young man setting out on a journey. Palamon appears in Chaucer's "*Knight's Tale*", an adaptation of Boccaccio's *Teseide*.

2. Mississippi [Freneau's note].

3. Ocean.

4. Admits.

### On the Religion of Nature

**1**

The power, that gives with liberal hand
The blessings man enjoys, while here,

And scatters through a smiling land
Abundant products of the year;
That power of nature, ever blessed,
Bestowed religion with the rest.

**2**

Born with ourselves, her early sway
Inclines the tender mind to take
The path of right, fair virtue's way
Its own felicity to make.
This universally extends
And leads to no mysterious ends.

**3**

Religion, such as nature taught,
With all divine perfection suits;
Had all mankind this system sought
Sophists[1] would cease their vain disputes,
And from this source would nations know
All that can make their heaven below.

**4**

This deals not curses on mankind,
Or dooms them to perpetual grief,
If from its aid no joys they find,
It damns them not for unbelief;

Upon a more exalted plan
Creatress nature dealt with man—

**5**

Joy to the day, when all agree
On such grand systems to proceed,
From fraud, design, and error free,
And which to truth and goodness lead:
Then persecution will retreat
And man's religion be complete.

## Notes

1. Eachers of philosophy.

## Questions

1. For the piece *On the Emigration to America and Peopling the Western Country*, does the speaker make any direct statements to readers that help establish his r identity or character?

2. In *On the Religion of Nature*, what attitude is conveyed and how?

# Part III The Age of Romanticism (1800—1865)

## 1. Historical Background

America in the 19th century, as throughout its history, generated expectations and passions that often conflicted with a reality that was more mundane and more complex. The young nation's size and diversity defied easy generalization and invited contradiction: America was both a freedom-loving and slave-holding society, a nation of expansive and primitive frontiers, and a society with cities built on growing commerce and industrialization.

In 1800, the United States consisted of 16 states clustered near the east coast. In 1803, Thomas Jefferson doubled the nation's size by signing the Louisiana Purchase, which would become the nation's heartland and one of the world's great granaries. The rapid growth of the nation inspired an upsurge in national pride and self-awareness, with the American people were expecting further change.

By the end of the 18th century, many educated Americans no longer professed traditional Christian beliefs in reaction to the secularism of the age, a religious revival spread westward in the first half of the 19th century. This second great religious revival in

American history consisted of several kinds of activities, distinguished by locale and expression of religious commitment. In contrast to the great awakening of the 1730s, the revivals in the east were notable for the absence of hysteria and open emotion. The Second Great Awakening exercised a profound impact on American history. The numerical strength of the Baptist and Methodist rose relatively to quickly to that of other denominations in the colonial period—the Anglicans, Presbyterians and Congregationalists. America was becoming a more diverse nation in the early to mid-19th century, and the growing differences within American Protestantism reflected and contributed to this diversity.

As the nation expanded, Americans began to take more direct control of their government. The 1828 election of Andrew Jackson, "the people's president" ushered in the year of the common man, as property requirements for voting began to be eliminated. The democratic advances of the time, however, were confined to white males. Scant political attention was paid to women, and most African Americans remained enslaved. One of the most tragic policies of this period was "Indian removal," the forced westward migration of Native Americans from confiscated tribal lands—as in the 1838 *Trail of Tears* in which 4000 of 15000 Cherokee perished on the trek from Georgia to Oklahoma.

The War of 1812 with Britain was, in a sense, a second war of independence. Commerce was cementing national unity. The prospect of peace, prosperity, and social progress opened before the nation.

During the opening decades of the 19th century, Central and

South America turned to revolution. In the Monroe Doctrine of 1823, President James Monroe (1817—1825) declared the country's refusal to tolerate any further extension of European domination in the Americas. In the 1830s, the United States became embroiled in the conflict involving the secession of Texas from Mexico; in 1836, the Mexican army made its famous assault on the Alamo, in which every Texan defender was killed. When Texas was admitted to the union in 1845, the resulting war with Mexico (1846—1848) ended in a U.S. victory, which added more territory to the nation, including California. Soon after, the Gold Rush of 1849 drew hundreds of thousands to this new land of promise.

By 1850, the national territory stretched over forests, plains, and mountains. Within these far-flung limits dwelt 23 million people in a union comprised of 31 states. In the East, industry boomed. In the Mid-West and the South, agriculture flourished. New England and the middle-Atlantic states were the main centers of manufacturing, commerce, and finance. The South from the Atlantic to the Mississippi River and beyond, was a relatively compact political unit featuring an economy centered on agriculture. The Mid-West, with its boundless prairies and swiftly growing population, flourished. An important stimulus to western prosperity was the great improvement in transportation facilities. In the 1850s, the "iron horse," or the railroad, began to dominate long distance American travel. By 1869, rail lines link east and west coasts. Advances in technologies spurred on social change. Factories sprang up all over the northwest. The steel plow and reaper encouraged frontier settlement by making farming practical on the vast, sod-covered grasslands. The telegraph facilitated almost instant communication across great distances.

It was evident to even the most cheerful observer that the United States during the mid-century faced troubles as well as bright promises, for the new prosperity unleashed fierce competition. Child labor and unsafe working conditions were common. In 1840, most women could not vote or file a lawsuit. The awakening of women began with a visit to America by France Wright, a Scottish lecturer and journalist. By the 1840s, a group of American women emerged who would be the first women's rights movement. Foremost in this distinguished group was Elizabeth Cady Stanton. In 1869, the National Woman Suffrage Association (NWSA) was founded by Susan B. Anthony and Elizabeth Cady Stanton, which advocated a constitutional amendment for women's right to the vote.

As far back as 1836, sectional lines had been steadily hardening on the slavery question. In some areas bordered by the sea, slavery, by 1850, was well over 200 years old. Slavery was inherently a system of brutality and coercion in which beatings and the breakup of families through the sale of individuals were commonplace. In the end, however, the most trenchant criticism of slavery was not the behavior of individual masters and overseers toward the slaves, but slavery as a fundamental violation of every human being's inalienable right to be free.

In the presidential election of 1860, the Republican Party nominated Abraham Lincoln as its candidate. Party spirit soared as leaders declared that slavery could spread no further. On April 12,

1861, the American Civil War broke out over a number of unresolvable state disagreements, and it would also set the path for the removal of the slavery practice. On April 9, 1865. In December of 1865, Congress ratified the 13th Amendment to the U.S. Constitution which abolished slavery. Slaves were granted their freedom but still had many years before reaching actual equality.

## 2. Literature of the Period

At the beginning of the 19th century, the United States came to the stage of the world as an independent nation. The writers of this period would define the American voice—personal, idiosyncratic, bold—its primary theme: the quest of the individual to define him or herself.

The writings of the early 19th century can all be described as Romanticism. Romanticism is an artistic movement that dominated Europe and America during the 19th century. Romantic writers elevated the imagination over reason, and intuition over fact. The Romanticists in America imitated the writers of England, but the subject matter focused on America, such as the story about the frontiers and pioneers. Among them, Washington Irving (1783—1859), James Fenimore Cooper (1789—1851), William Cullen Bryant (2794—1878), and Edgar Allan Poe (1809—1849) are most famous.

Washington Irving with his *The Sketch Book* (1851) made him the first American to achieve an international literary reputation. James Fenimore Cooper, the first successful American novelist, was noted for his frontier saga, *The Leatherstocking Tales* (1827—1854), which consists of five books. In the order of events, not the order in which they were written, the novels are *The Deerslayer* (1841), *The Last of the Mohicans* (1826), *The Pathfinder* (1840), *The Pioneers* (1823), and *The Prairie* (1827). With Natty Bumppo, an aged hunter and the central figure in the novels, who goes by the various names of Leatherstocking, Deerslayer, Pathfinder, and Hawkeye, he had created one of the most popular characters in world literature. Besides the frontier saga, Cooper's sea adventure tale and historical romance are also well-known. *The Spy* (1821) is the first important historical romance of the Revolutionary War; the virtual creation of the sea novel *The Pilot* was started in 1824. Not until the 1920s did scholars begin to see Cooper's value as the country's first great social critic. What most appeals to modern readers are his profoundly ambivalent dramatizations of such enduring American conflicts as natural rights versus legal rights, order versus change, and primeval wilderness versus civilization.

William Cullen Bryant is best remembered for his *Thanatopsis* (view of death) which was first published in 1813 or 1814. Since his early teens, Bryant had been influenced by British "graveyard poets" of the previous decades, then in 1810 or soon afterward Bryant read *Lyrical Ballads* and responded strongly to Wordsworth's near pantheistic view of nature. *Thanatopsis* won Bryant immediate acknowledgment in 1817 and is non-doctrinally meditative. The fuller version of 1821 concludes with a fervent injunction to trust in something or someone who remains unspecified. His short poems, such as *To a Waterfowl* (1818) and *The Yellow Violet* (1815), are typically full of romanticism.

Edgar Allan Poe's detective stories and haunting poems have remained extremely popular among generations of American people.

From Jackson's inauguration to the Civil War, American romantic literature came into its heyday. An impressive burst of literary activity took place in and around Boston between 1840 and 1855. This "flowering of England" would produce an array of great writers and enduring literature. This is often called the "New England Renaissance," the first flowering in American literature.

Most, if not all, of these writers were influenced by the transcendental philosophy originally expressed by the German Emmanuel Kant. In his *Critique of Practical Reason* (1788), Kant defines transcendentalism as the understanding a person gains intuitively. Closely associated with Emerson, American transcendentalism drew on other thinkers as well: the Greek philosopher Plato, the French mathematician Pascal, the Swedish mystic and scientist Swedenborg, and the anti-materialism of Buddhist thought. The Transcendentalists believed that the most fundamental truth lies outside the experience of the senses, residing instead in the "Oversoul," an all-pervading power for goodness from which all things come and of which all things are a part.

The most influential expression of transcendental philosophy came from Emerson and his young friend and protégé Henry David Thoreau, who withdrew from society to live by himself on the shores of Walden pond. In poetry, the "Fireside Poets" were made up of Henry Wadsworth Longfellow (1807—1882), Oliver Wendell Holmes (1809—1894), James Russell Lowell (1801—1891), and John

Greenleaf Whittier, and they became prominent among the American reading public. All of them were born into noble families and were all well-educated, but, by no means, were they all innovative and unsophisticated.

Henry Wadsworth Longfellow's greatest virtue is that he made poetry seem worth reading and worth writing. He domesticated European meters, such as in his adaptation of classical Greek meters to tell the story of Evangeline Bellefontaine, set in the recent North American past, or in his use of Finnish folk meter in his celebration of American Indian legends in *Hiawatha*. Longfellow's *A Psalm of Life* (1838) was translated into Chinese in the 1970s.

Writer, doctor, and educator, Oliver Wendell Holmes Sr., was a brilliant and innovative doctor who was well known for his witty lectures at Harvard. Holmes's nationally acclaimed prose series *The Autocrat of the Breakfast Table* first appeared in the *Atlantic Monthly* in its inaugural issue in 1857. A year later, it was published as a book, which also included some of his most memorable poetry. Holmes's other books include *The Poet of the Breakfast-Table* (1872), *The Professor of the Breakfast-Table* (1860), and the novels *A Mortal Antipathy* (1885), *The Guardian Angel* (1867), and *Elsie Venner* (1861).

The most versatile of the New Englanders during the middle of the 19th-century, James Russell Lowell, was a vital force and thought in the history of American literature during his lifetime. His range and perspicacity in literary criticism are unequalled in 19th century America. He did more than anyone before Mark Twain in elevating the vernacular to a medium of serious artistic expression, and *The Biglow*

*Papers* (1848) ranks among the finest political satires in American literature. His public odes expressed a mind and an outlook that drew the praise of Henry Brooks Adams, William James, and William Dean Howells. His personal charm made him both an effective diplomat during the emergence of the United States as a world power and one of its finest letter writers.

In the 30-year struggle to abolish slavery, John Greenleaf Whittier played an important role as a poet, as a politician, and as a moral force. His collected poetry includes a core of excellent work, at the head of which stands his masterpiece *Snow-Bound: A Winter Idyl* (1866), a lovingly imaginative recreation of the good life in rural New England. This work—together with *Telling the Bees*, *Ichabod*, *Massachusetts to Virginia*, *Skipper Ireson's Ride*, *The Rendition*, *The Double-Headed Snake of Newbury*, and a dozen or so others, suggests that not only was New England a source of Whittier's finest achievements but also the predominant appeal for folk material that influenced his imagination.

Walt Whitman (1819—1892) is America's world poet—a latter-day successor to Homer, Virgil, Dante, and Shakespeare. In *Leaves of Grass* (1855, 1891—1892), he celebrated democracy, nature, love, and friendship. This monumental work chanted praises to the body as well as to the soul, and found beauty and reassurance even in death. Along with Emily Dickinson (1830—1886), Whitman is regarded as one of America's most significant 19th-century poets and would influence many later poets, including Ezra Pound, William Carlos Williams, Allen Ginsberg, Simon Ortiz, C. K. Williams, and Martín Espada.

Emily Dickinson is one of America's greatest and most original poets of all time. She took definition as her province and challenged the existing definitions of poetry and the poet's work. Like writers such as Ralph Waldo Emerson, Henry David Thoreau, and Walt Whitman, she experimented with expression in order to free it from conventional restraints.

Not everyone shared the transcendentalists' optimistic views, Nathaniel Hawthorne (1804—1864) and Herman Melville (1819—1891) expressed the darker vision of those. Hawthorne chose mainly American materials, drawing especially on the history of colonial New England and his native Salem in the time of his early American ancestors. His masterpiece, *The Scarlet Letter* (1850), set in Boston in the 17th century, deals with sin, concealed guilt, hypocrisy, and humanity.

Herman Melville, novelist, short story writer, and poet, is best known for his novels of the sea, especially *Moby-Dick* (1851). Born in 1819 to a merchant family in New York City, Melville's formal education was often interrupted due to lack of funds for tuition. Melville's experiences at sea informed much of his fiction. His first published works, *Typee: A Peep at Polynesia Life* (1846) and *Omoo* (1847), were based on a momentous journey aboard the whaling ship *Acushnet*. *Typee* portrayed Melville's enduring interests in cross-cultural difference and exchange, and began his life-long critique of Western imperialism. Melville was deeply influenced by Hawthorne, and his *Moby-Dick*, now considered one of the greatest works in the English language, was dedicated to Hawthorne. This book is infused with energy and insights the two developed through letters and conversation. Undoubtedly, in *Moby-Dick*, there is a mighty theme: the rebellious struggle of Captain Ahab against the overwhelming mysterious vastness of the universe and its awesome, sometimes merciless forces. The fitting symbol for his theme was the "gliding great demon of the seas of life," the white whale. Ahab's ship, the Pequod, was like a world in miniature form, with the characters ranging from the observer and narrator Ishmael to the savage harpooners and the motley crew.

In 1831, De Tocqueville wrote, "America has produced very few writers of distinction...The literature of England still darts its rays into the forests of the New world." By 1870, America had produced many writers of distinction. All of them eventually shone their unmistakably American light into and far beyond "the forests of the New world." The following excerpts are from these distinguished writers' works.

## 3. Representative Writers' Work

### (1) Washington Irving (1783—1859)

Washington Irving, the first American to achieve an international literary reputation, was born into a wealthy family and began studying at the age of 16. Though he had planned to be a lawyer, he found he was more interested in travel and writing. He spent much time traveling throughout Europe and New York's Hudson Valley and reading widely in English literature at home. He modeled his early prose on the graceful Spectator papers by Joseph Addison, but was also delighted by many other writers, including Shakespeare, Oliver Goldsmith, and Laurence Sterne.

When Irving was 24, he and his brother began publishing a magazine anonymously, which carried humorous sketches and essays about New York society. In 1809, he published his first major work, *A History of New York from the Beginning of the World to the End of the Dutch Dynasty*, using the pseudonym Diedrich Knickerbocker. The book, a humorous examination of New York during colonial times, was well received and made Irving famous. From 1815 to 1832, Irving lived in Europe. There he traveled extensively and learned about European customs, traditions, and folk lore. Inspired by the European folk heritage, In 1819 Irving began sending The Sketch Book to the United States for publication in installments. When the full version was printed in England the next year, it increased Irving's fame and brought him the friendship of many of the leading British writers of the time. His new pseudonym, Geoffrey Crayon, became universally recognized, and over the next years selections from The Sketch Book entered the classroom as models of English prose just as selections from Addison had long been used. Irving's next book, *Bracebridge Hall* (1822), a worshipful tribute to old-fashioned English country life, was, as the author realized, a feeble follow-up, and *Tales of a Traveller* (1824) was widely taken as a sign that he had written himself out. Irving worked intensely and in 1828 published *The Life and Voyages of Christopher Columbus*, not a translation of Navarrete (though the Spaniard's volume supplied most of the facts) but a biography of Irving's own, shaped by his skill at evocative re-creation of history. Out of these Spanish years came also *Tire Conquest of Granada* (1829), *Voyages and Discoveries of the Companions of Columbus* (1831), and

*The Alhambra* (1832), which became known as the "Spanish Sketch Book".

Decades before his death, Irving had achieved the status of a classic writer; in his own country he had no rival as a stylist. His works are usually based in England. There are romantic legends, descriptions of America manners and customs, and travel diaries. His realistic details of rural life in America could be worked memorably into fiction. Most of his works are informal essay and short story. From the 18th century to the 19th century, Washington Irving's works reflected the American literature's transformation from rationalism to romanticism. To some extent, Washington Irving is the "father of the American literature."

The following is the story of *Rip Van Winkle*.

Rip Van Winkle, a villager of Dutch descent, lives in a nice village at the foot of New York's Catskill Mountains. An amiable man whose home and farm suffer from his lazy neglect, he is loved by all but his wife. One autumn day he escapes his nagging wife by wandering up the mountains. After encountering strangely dressed men who are playing nine-pin, and after drinking some of their liquor, he settles down under a shady tree and falls asleep. He wakes up twenty years later and returns to his village. He finds out that his wife is dead and his close friends have died in a war or gone somewhere else. He immediately gets into trouble when he hails himself a loyal subject of King George III, not knowing that in the meantime the American Revolution has taken place. An old local recognizes him, however, and Rip's now grown daughter eventually puts him up. As Rip resumes his habit of idleness in the village, and his tale is solemnly believed by the old Dutch settlers, certain hen-pecked husbands especially wish they shared Rip's luck.

From the beginning, Americans identified with Rip as a counter-hero, an anti-Franklinian, who made a success of failure, and successive generations have responded profoundly to Irving's pervasive theme of mutability, especially the focus of his portrayal on the bewildering and destructive rapidity of change in American life.

## Rip Van Winkle

Writing of Diedrich Knickerbocker
By Woden, God of Saxons,
From whence comes Wensday, that is Wodensday,
Truth is a thing that ever I will keep
Unto thylke day in which I creep into My sepulchre—
—CARTWRIGHT[1]

Whoever has made a voyage up the Hudson, must remember the Kaatskill mountains. They are a dismembered branch of the great Appalachian family, and are seen away to the west of the river, swelling up to a noble height, and lording it over the surrounding country. Every change of season, every change of weather, indeed, every hour of the day, produce s some change in the magical hue s and shape s of these mountains, and they are regarded by all the good wives, far and near, as perfect barometers. When the weather is fair and settled, they are clothed in blue and purple, and print their bold outlines on the clear evening sky; but some times, when the rest of the landscape is cloudless, they will gather a hood of gray vapours about their summits, which, in the last rays of the setting sun, will glow and light up like a crown of glory.

At the foot of these fairy mountains, the voyager may have descried the light smoke curling up from a village, whose shingle roofs gleam among the trees, just where the blue tints of the upland melt away into the fresh green of the nearer landscape. It is a little village of great antiquity, having been founded by some of the Dutch colonists, in the early times of the province, just about the beginning of the government of the good Peter Stuyvesant[2], (may he rest in peace!) and there were some of the house s of the original settlers standing within a few years, with lattice windows, gable fronts surmounted with weathercocks, and built of small yellow bricks brought from Holland.

In that same village, and in one of these very houses, (which, to tell the precise truth, was sadly time worn and weather beaten,) there lived many years since, while the country was yet a province of Great Britain, a simple good natured fellow, of the name of Rip Van Winkle. He was a descendant of the Van Winkles who figured so gallantly in the chivalrous days of Peter Stuyvesant, and accompanied him to the siege of Fort Christina. He inherited, however, but little of the martial character of his ancestors. I have observed that he was a simple good natured man; he was moreover a kind neighbour, and an obedient, henpecked husband. Indeed, to the latter circumstance might be owing that meekness of spirit which gained him such universal popularity; for those men are most apt to be obsequious and conciliating abroad, who are under the discipline of shrews at home. Their tempers, doubtless, are rendered pliant and malleable in the fiery furnace of domestic tribulation, and a curtain lecture[3] is worth all the sermons in the world for teaching the virtues of patience and long suffering. A termagant wife may, therefore, in some respects, be considered a tolerable blessing; and if so, Rip Van Winkle was thrice blessed.

Certain it is, that he was a great favourite among all the good wives of the village, who, as usual with the amiable sex, took his part in all family squabbles, and never failed, whenever they talked those matters over in their evening gossippings, to lay all the blame on Dam e Van Winkle. The children of the village, too, would shout with joy whenever he approached. He assisted at their sports, mad e their playthings, taught them to fly kites and shoot marbles, and told them long stories of ghosts, witches, and Indians. Whenever he went dodging about the village, he was surrounded by a troop of them, hanging on his skirts, clambering on his back, and playing a thousand tricks on him with impunity; and not a dog would bark at him throughout the neighbourhood.

The great error in Rip's composition was an insuperable aversion to all kinds of profitable labour. It could not be for the want of assiduity or perseverance; for he would sit on a wet rock, with a rod as long and heavy as a Tartar's lance, and fish all day without a murmur, even though he should not be encouraged by a single nibble. He would carry a fowling piece on his shoulder, for hours together, trudging through woods and swamps, and up hill and down dale, to shoot a few squirrels or wild pigeons. He would never even refuse to assist a neighbour in the roughest toil, and was a foremost man at all country frolicks for husking Indian corn, or building stone fences; the women of the village, too, used to employ him to run their errands, and to do such little odd job s as their less obliging husbands would not do for them; —in a word, Rip was ready to attend to any body's business but his own; but as to doing family duty, and keeping his farm in order, it was impossible.

In fact, he declared it was no us e to work on his farm; it was the most pestilent little piece of ground in the whole country; every thing about it went wrong, and would go wrong, in spite of him. His fences were continually falling to pieces; his cow would either go astray, or get among the cabbages; weeds were sure to grow quicker in his fields than any where else; the rain always made a point of setting in just as he had some out-door work to do. So that though his patrimonial estate had dwindled away under his management, acre by acre, until there was little more left than a mere patch of Indian corn and potatoes, yet it was the worst conditioned farm in the neighbourhood.

His children, too, were as ragged and wild as if they belonged to nobody. His son Rip, an urchin begotten in his own likeness, promised to inherit the habits, with the old clothes of his father. He was generally seen trooping like a colt at his mother's heels, equipped in a pair of his father's cast-off galligaskins[4], which he had much ado to hold up with one hand, as a fine lady does her train in bad weather.

Rip Van Winkle, however, was one of those happy mortals, of

foolish, well-oiled dispositions, who take the world easy, eat white bread or brown, which ever can be got with least thought or trouble, and would rather starve on a penny than work for a pound. If left to himself, he would have whistled life away, in perfect contentment; but his wife kept continually dinning in his ears about his idleness, his carelessness, and the ruin he was bringing on his family. Morning, noon, and night, her tongue was incessantly going, and every thing he said or did was sure to produce a torrent of household eloquence. Rip had but one way of replying to all lectures of the kind, and that, by frequent use, had grown into a habit. He shrugged his shoulders, shook his head, cast up his eyes, but said nothing. This, however, always provoked a fresh volley from his wife, so that he was fain to draw off his forces, and take to the outside of the house—the only side which, in truth, belongs to a henpecked husband.

Rip's sole domestic adherent was his dog Wolf, who was as much henpecked as his master; for Dam e Van Winkle regarded them as companions in idleness, and even looked upon Wolf with an evil eye, as the cause of his master's so often going astray. True it is, in all points of spirit befitting an honourable dog, he was as courageous an animal as ever scoured the woods—but what courage can withstand the ever-during and all-besetting terrors of a woman's tongue? The moment Wolf entered the house, his crest fell, his tail drooped to the ground, or curled between his legs, he sneaked about with a gallows air, casting many a sidelong glance at Dam e Van Winkle, and at the least flourish of a broomstick or ladle, would fly to the door with yelping precipitation.

Times grew worse and worse with Rip Van Winkle as years of matrimony rolled on; a tart temper never mellows with age, and a sharp tongue is the only edge tool that grows keener by constant use. For a long while he used to console himself, when driven from home, by frequenting a kind of perpetual club of the sages, philosophers, and other idle personage s of the village, that held its sessions on a bench before a small inn, designated by a rubicund portrait of his majesty George the Third. Here they used to sit in the shade, of a long lazy summer's day, talk listlessly over village gossip, or tell endless sleepy stories about nothing. But it would have been worth any statesman's money to have heard the profound discussions that sometime s took place, when by chance an old newspaper fell into their hands, from some passing traveller. How solemnly they would listen to the contents, as drawled out by Derrick Van Bummel, the schoolmaster, a dapper learned little man, who was not to be daunted by the most gigantic word in the dictionary; and how sagely they would deliberate upon public events some months after they had taken place.

The opinions of this junto[5] were completely controlled by Nicholas Vedder, a patriarch of the village, and landlord of the inn, at the door of which he took his seat from morning till night, just moving sufficiently to avoid the sun, and keep in the shade of a large tree; so that the neighbours could tell the hour by his movements as accurately as by a sun dial. It is true, he was rarely heard to speak, but smoked his pipe incessantly. His adherents, however, (for every great man has his adherents,) perfectly understood him, and knew how to gather his opinions. When any thing that was read or related displeased him, he was observed to smoke his pipe vehemently, and send forth short, frequent, and angry puffs; but when pleased, he would inhale the smoke slowly and tranquilly, and emit it in light and placid clouds, and sometime s taking the pipe from his mouth, and letting the fragrant vapour curl about his nose, would gravely nod his head in token of perfect approbation.

From even this strong hold the unlucky Rip was at length routed by his termagant wife, who would suddenly break in upon the tranquility of the assemblage, call the members all to nought, nor was that august personage, Nicholas Vedder himself, sacred from the daring tongue of this terrible virago, who charged him outright with encouraging her husband in habits of idleness.

Poor Rip was at last reduced almost to despair; and his only alternative to escape from the labour of the farm and the clamour of his wife, was to take gun in hand, and stroll away into the woods. Here he would sometime s seat himself at the foot of a tree, and share the contents of his wallet[6] with Wolf, with whom he sympathised as a fellow sufferer in persecution. "Poor Wolf," he would say, "thy mistress leads thee a dogs' life of it; but never mind, my lad, while I live thou shalt never want a friend to stand by thee!" Wolf would wag his tail, look wistfully in his master's face, and if dogs can feel pity, I verily believe he reciprocated the sentiment with all his heart.

In a long ramble of the kind on a fine autumnal day, Rip had unconsciously scrambled to one of the highest parts of the Kaatskill mountains. He was after his favourite sport of squirrel shooting, and the still solitudes had echoed and re-echoed with the reports of his gun. Panting and fatigued, he threw himself, late in the afternoon, on a green knoll, covered with mountain herbage, that crowned the brow of a precipice. From an opening between the trees, he could overlook all the lower country for many a mile of rich woodland. He saw at a distance the lordly Hudson, far, far below him, moving on its silent but majestic course, the reflection of a purple cloud, or the sail of a lagging bark, here and there sleeping on its glassy bosom, and at last losing itself in the blue highlands.

On the other side he looked down into a deep mountain glen, wild, lonely, and shagged, the bottom filled with fragments from the impending cliffs, and scarcely lighted by the reflected rays of the setting sun. For some time Rip lay musing on this scene, evening was gradually advancing, the mountains began to throw their long blue shadows over the valleys, he saw that it would be dark long before he could reach the village, and he heaved a heavy sigh when he thought of encountering the terrors of Dame Van Winkle.

As he was about to descend, he heard a voice from a distance, hallooing, "Rip Van Winkle! Rip Van Winkle!" He looked around, but could see nothing but a crow winging its solitary flight across the mountain. He thought his fancy must have deceived him, and turned again to descend, when he heard the same cry ring through the still evening air; "Rip Van Winkle! Rip Van Winkle!"—at the same time Wolf bristled up his back, and giving a low growl, skulked to his master's side, looking fearfully down into the glen. Rip now felt a vague apprehension stealing over him; he looked anxiously in the same direction, and perceived a strange figure slowly tojling up the rocks, and bending under the weight of something he carried on his back. He was surprised to see any human being in this lonely and unfrequented place, but supposing it to be some one of the neighbourhood in need of his assistance, he hastened down to yield it.

On nearer approach, he was still more surprised at the singularity of the stranger's appearance. He was a short square built old fellow, with thick bushy hair, and a grizzled beard. His dress was of the antique Dutch fashion—a cloth jerkin[7] strapped round the waist—several pair of breeches, the outer one of ample volume, decorated with rows of buttons down the sides, and bunches at the knees. He bore on his shoulder a stout keg, that seemed full of liquor, and made signs for Rip to approach and assist him with the load. Though rather shy and distrustful of this new acquaintance, Rip complied with his usual alacrity, and mutually relieving each other, they clambered up a narrow gully, apparently the dry bed of a mountain torrent. As they ascended, Rip every now and then heard long rolling peals, like distant thunder, that seemed to issue out of a deep ravine, or rather cleft between lofty rocks, toward which their rugged path conducted. He pause d for an instant, but supposing it to be the muttering of one of those transient thunder showers which often take place in mountain heights, he proceeded. Passing through the ravine, they came to a hollow, like a small amphitheatre, surrounded by perpendicular precipices, over the brinks of which impending trees shot their branches, so that you only caught glimpses of the azure sky, and the bright evening cloud. During the whole time, Rip and his companion had laboured on in silence; for though the former marvelled greatly what could be the object of carrying a keg of liquor up this wild mountain, yet there was something strange and incomprehensible about the unknown, that inspired awe, and checked familiarity.

On entering the amphitheatre, new objects of wonder presented themselves. On a level spot in the centre was a company of odd-looking personages playing at nine-pins. They were dressed in a quaint, outlandish fashion: some wore short doublets[8], others jerkins, with long knives in their belts, and most had enormous breeches, of similar style with that of the guide's. Their visages, too, were peculiar: one had a large head, broad face, and small piggish eyes; the face of another seemed to consist entirely of nose, and was surmounted by a white sugar loaf hat, set off with a little red cockstail. They all had beards, of various shapes and colours. There was one who seemed to be the commander. He was a stout old gentleman, with a weather-beaten countenance; he wore a laced doublet, broad belt and hanger[9], high crowned hat and feather, red stockings, and high heeled shoes, with roses in them. The whole group reminded Rip of the figures in an old Flemish painting, in the parlour of Dominie[10] Van Schaick, the village parson, and which had been brought over from Holland at the time of the settlement.

What seemed particularly odd to Rip, was, that though these folks were evidently amusing themselves, yet they maintained the gravest faces, the most mysterious silence, and were, withal, the most melancholy party of pleasure he had ever witnessed. Nothing interrupted the stillness of the scene, but the noise of the balls, which, whenever they were rolled, echoed along the mountains like rumbling peals of thunder.

As Rip and his companion approached them, they suddenly desisted from their play, and stared at him with such fixed statue-like gaze, and such strange, uncouth, lack lustre countenances, that his heart turned within him, and his knees smote together. His companion now emptied the contents of the keg into large flagons, and made signs to him to wait upon the company. He obeyed with fear and trembling; they quaffed the liquor in profound silence, and then returned to their game.

By degrees, Rip's awe and apprehension subsided. He even ventured, when no eye was fixed upon him, to taste the beverage, which he found had much of the flavour of excellent Hollands[11]. He was naturally a thirsty soul, and was soon tempted to repeat the draught. One taste provoked another, and he reiterated his visits to the flagon so often, that at length his senses were overpowered, his eyes swam in his head, his head gradually declined, and he fell into a deep sleep.

On awaking, he found himself on the green knoll from whence he had first seen the old man of the glen. He rubbed his eyes—it was a bright sunny morning. The birds were hopping and twittering among the bushes, and the eagle was wheeling aloft, and breasting the pure mountain breeze. "Surely," thought Rip, "I have not slept here all night." He recalled the occurrence s before he fell asleep. The strange man with the keg of liquor—the mountain ravine—the wild retreat among the rocks—the wo-begone party at ninepins—the flagon—"Oh!

that flagon! that wicked flagon!" thought Rip— "what excuse shall I make to Dam e Van Winkle?"

He looked round for his gun, but in place of the clean well-oiled fowling piece, he found an old firelock lying by him, the barrel encrusted with rust, the lock falling off, and the stock worm-eaten. He now suspected that the graver oysters of the mountain had put a trick upon him, and having dosed him with liquor, had robbed him of his gun. Wolf, too, had disappeared, but he might have strayed away after a squirrel or partridge. He whistled after him, shouted his name, but all in vain; the echoes repeated his whistle and shout, but no dog was to be seen.

He determined to revisit the scene of the last evening's gambol, and if he met with any of the party, to demand his dog and gun. As he arose to walk he found himself stiff in the joints, and wanting in his usual activity. "These mountain beds do not agree with me," thought Rip, "and if this frolick should lay me up with a fit of the rheumatism, I shall have a blessed time with Dam e Van Winkle." With some difficulty he got down into the glen: he found the gully up which he and his companion had ascended the preceding evening, but to his astonishment a mountain stream was now foaming down it, leaping from rock to rock, and filling the glen with babbling murmurs. He, however, made shift to scramble up its sides, working his toilsome way through thickets of birch, sassafras, and witch hazle, and sometime s tripped up or entangled by the wild grape vines that twisted their coils and tendrils from tree to tree, and spread a kind of network in his path.

At length he reached to where the ravine had opened through the cliffs, to the amphitheatre; but no traces of such opening remained. The rocks presented a high impenetrable wall, over which the torrent cam e tumbling in a sheet of feathery foam, and fell into a broad deep basin, black from the shadows of the surrounding forest. Here, then, poor Rip was brought to a stand. He again called and whistled after his dog; he was only answered by the cawing of a flock of idle crows, sporting high in air about a dry tree that overhung a sunny precipice; and who, secure in their elevation, seemed to look down and scoff at the poor man's perplexities. What was to be done? The morning was passing away, and Rip felt famished for his breakfast. He grieved to give up his dog and gun: he dreaded to meet his wife; but it would not do to starve among the mountains. He shook his head, shouldered the rusty firelock, and, with a heart full of trouble and anxiety, turned his steps homeward.

As he approached the village, he met a number of people, but none that he knew, which somewhat surprised him, for he had thought himself acquainted with every one in the country round. Their dress, too, was of a different fashion from that to which he was accustomed. They all stared at him with equal marks of surprise, and whenever they cast eyes upon him, invariably stroked their chins, the constant recurrence of this gesture, induced Rip, involuntarily, to do the same, when, to his astonishment, he found his beard had grown a foot long!

He had now entered the skirts of the village. A troop of strange children ran at his heels, hooting after him, and pointing at his gray beard. The dogs, too, not one of which he recognized for his old acquaintances, barked at him as he passed. The very village seemed altered: it was larger and more populous. There were rows of house s which he had never seen before, and those which had been his familiar haunts had disappeared. Strange names were over the doors—strange faces at the windows—every thing was strange. His mind now began to misgive him, that both he and the world around him were bewitched. Surely this was his native village, which he had left but the day before. There stood the Kaatskill mountains—there ran the silver Hudson at a distance—there was every hill and dale precisely as it had always been—Rip was sorely perplexed—"That flagon last night," thought he, "has addled my poor head sadly!"

It was with some difficulty he found the way to his own house, which he approached with silent awe, expecting every moment to hear the shrill voice of Dame Van Winkle. He found the house gone to decay—the roof fallen in, the windows shattered, and the doors off the hinges. A half starved dog, that looked like Wolf, was skulking about it. Rip called him by name, but the cur snarled, showed his teeth, and passed on. This was an unkind cut indeed— "My very dog," sighed poor Rip, "has forgotten me!"[12]

He entered the house, which, to tell the truth, Dam e Van Winkle had always kept in neat order. It was empty, forlorn, and_apparently abandoned. This desolateness overcame all his connubial fears—he called loudly for his wife and children—the lonely chambers rung for a moment with his voice, and then all again was silence.

He now hurried forth, and hastened to his old resort, the little village inn— but it too was gone. A large rickety wooden building stood in its place, with great gaping windows, some of them broken, and mended with old hats and petticoats, and over the door was painted, "The Union Hotel, by Jonathan Doolittle." Instead of the great tree that used to shelter the quiet little Dutch inn of yore, there now was reared a tall naked pole, with something on top that looked like a red night caps[13] and from it was fluttering a flag, on which was a singular assemblage of stars and stripes—all this was strange and incomprehensible. He recognised on the sign, however, the ruby face of King George, under which he had smoked so many a peaceful pipe, but even this "was singularly metamorphosed; the red coat was changed for one of blue and buff[14] a sword was stuck in the hand instead of sceptre, the dead was decorated with a cocked hat, and underneath was painted in large characters, GENERAL WASHINGTON.

There was, as usual, a crowd of folk about the door, but none that Rip recollected. The very character of the people seemed changed. There was a busy, bustling, disputatious tone about it, instead of the accustomed phlegm and drowsy tranquility. He looked in vain for the sage Nicholas Vedder, with his broad face, double chin, and fair long pipe, uttering clouds of tobacco smoke instead of idle speeches; or Van Bummel, the schoolmaster, doling forth the contents of an ancient newspaper. In place of these, a lean bilious looking fellow, with his pockets full of handbills, was haranguing vehemently about rights of citizens—election—members of congress—liberty—Bunker's hill—herpes of seventy-six—and other words, that were a perfect Babylonish jargon1 to the bewildered Van Winkle.

The appearance of Rip, with his long grizzled beard, his rusty fowling piece, his uncouth dress, and the army of women and children that had gathered at his heels, soon attracted the attention of the tavern politicians. They crowded around him, eyeing him from head to foot, with great curiosity. The orator bustled up to him, and drawing him partly aside, inquired "which side he voted?" Rip stared in yacant stupidity. Another short but busy little fellow pulled him by the arm, and raising on tiptoe, inquired in his ear, "whether he was Federal or Democrat."[15] Rip was equally at a loss to comprehend the question; when a knowing, self-important old gentleman, in a sharp cocked hat, made his way through the crowd, putting them to the right and left with his elbows as he passed, and planting himself before Van Winkle, with one arm akimbo, the other resting on his cane, his keen eyes and sharp hat penetrating, as it were, into his very soul, demanded, in an austere tone, "what brought him to the election with a gun on his shoulder, and a mob at his heels, and whether he meant to breed a riot in the village?" "Alas! gentlemen," cried Rip, somewhat dismayed, "I am a poor quiet man, a native of the place, and a loyal subject of the King, God bless him!"

Here a general shout burst from the bystanders—"A tory! a tory! a spy! a refugee! hustle him! away with him!" It was with great difficulty that the self important man in the cocked hat restored order; and having assumed a tenfold austerity of brow, demanded again of the unknown culprit, what he came there for, and whom he was seeking. The poor man humbly assured them that he meant no harm; but merely cam e there in search of some of his neighbours, who used to keep about the tavern.

"Well—who are they? —name them."

Rip bethought himself a moment, and inquired, "where's Nicholas Vedder?"

There was a silence for a little while, when an old man replied, in a thin piping voice, "Nicholas Vedder? why he is dead and gone these eighteen years! There was a wooden tombstone in the church yard that used to tell all about him, but that's rotted and gone too."

"Where's Brom Dutcher?"

"Oh he went offtn 'be army in the beginning nf the war: some say he was killed at the battle of Stoney-Poinf—others say he was drowned in a squall, at the foot of Antony's Nose[16]. I don't know—he never came back again." "Where s Van Bummel, the schoolmaster?"

"He went off to the wars too, was a great militia general, and is now in Congress."

Rip's heart died away, at hearing of these sad change s in his home and friends, and finding himself thus alone in the world. Every answer puzzled him, too, by treating of such enormous lapses of time, and of matters which he could not-Onderstand: war—congress—Stoney-Point; —he had no courage to ask after any more friends, but cried out in despair, "doe s nobody here know Rip Van Winkle?"

"Oh, Rip Van Winkle!" exclaimed two or three, "Oh, to be sure! that's Rip Van Winkle, yonder, leaning against the tree."

Rip looked, and beheld a precise counterpart of himself, as he went up the mountain: apparently as lazy, and certainly as ragged. The poor fellow was now completely confounded. He doubted his own identity, and whether he was himself or another man. In the midst of his bewilderment, the man in the cocked hat demanded who he was, and what was his name?

"God knows," exclaimed he, at his wit's end; "I'm not myself—I'm some - body else—that's me yonder—no—that's somebody else, got into my shoes— I was myself last night, but I fell asleep on the mountain, and they've changed my gun, and every thing's changed, and I'm changed, and I can't tell what's my name, or who I am!"

The bystanders began now to look at each other, nod, wink significantly, and tap their fingers against their foreheads. There was a whisper, also, about securing the gun, and keeping the old fellow from doing mischief. At the very suggestion of which, the self-important man in the cocked hat retired with some precipitation. At this critical moment a fresh likely woman pressed through the throng to get a peep at the graybearded man. She had a chubby child in her arms, which, frightened at his looks, began to cry. "Hush, Rip," cried she, "hush, you little fool, the old man wont hurt you." The name of the child, the air of the mother, the tone of her voice, all awakened a train of recollections in his mind.

"What is your name, my good woman?" asked he.

"ludith Gardenier,"

"And your father's name?"

"Ah, poor man, his name was Rip Van Winkle; it's twenty years since he went away from home with his gun, and never has been heard of since—his dog cam e home without him; but whether he shot himself, or was carried away by the Indians, nobody can tell. I was then but a little girl."

Rip had but one question mor e to ask; but he put it with a faltering voice:

"Where's your mother?"

Oh, she too had died but a short time since; she broke a blood vessel in a fit of passions at a New-England pedlar.

There was a drop of comfort, at least, in this intelligence. The honest man could contain himself no longer. —He caught his daughter and her child in his arms. —"I am your father!" cried he—"Young Rip Van Winkle once—-old Rip Van Winkle now!—Does nobody know poor Rip Van Winkle!"

All stood amazed, until an old woman, tottering out from among the crowd, put her hand to her brow, and peering under it in his face for a moment, exclaimed, "Sure enough! it is Rip Van Winkle—it is himself. Welcome home again, old neighbour—Why, where have you been these twenty long years?"

Rip's story was soon told, for the whole twenty years had been to him but as one night. The neighbours stared when they heard it; some were seen to wink at each other, and put their tongue s in their cheeks; and the selfimportant man in the cocked hat, who, when the alarm was over, had returned to the field, screwed down the corners of his mouth, and shook his head—upon which there was a general shaking of the head throughout the assemblage.

It was determined, however, to take the opinion of old Peter Vanderdonk, who was seen slowly advancing up the road. He was a descendant of the historian of that name[17]," I who wrote one of the earliest accounts of the province. Peter was the most ancient inhabitant of the village, and well versed in all the wonderful events and traditions of the neighbourhood. He recollected Rip at once, and corroborated his story in the most satisfactory manner. He assured the company that it was a fact, handed down from his ancestor the historian, that the Kaatskill mountains had always been haunted by strange beings. That it was affirmed that the great Hendrick Hudson, the first discoverer of the river and country, kept a kind of vigil there every twenty years, with his crew of the Half-moon, being permitted in this way to revisit the scene s of his enterprize, and keep a guardian eye upon the river, and the great city[18] called by his name. That his father had once seen them in their old Dutch dresses playing at nine pins in a hollow of the mountain; and that he himself had heard, one summer afternoon, the sound of their balls, like long peals of thunder.

To make a long story short, the company broke up, and returned to the more important concerns of the election. Rip's daughter took him home to live with her; she had a snug, well-furnished house, and a stout cheery farmer for a husband, whom Rip recollected for one of the urchins that used to climb upon his back. As to Rip's son and heir, who was the ditto of himself, seen leaning against the tree, he was employed to work on the farm; but evinced an hereditary disposition to attend to any thing else but his business.

Rip now resumed his old walks and habits; he soon found many of his former cronies, though all rather the worse for the wear and tear of time; and preferred making friends among the rising generation, with whom he soon grew into great favour.

Having nothing to do at home, and being arrived at that happy age when a man can do nothing with impunity, he took his place once more on the bench, at the inn door, and was reverenced as one of the patriarchs of the village, and a chronicle of the old times "before the war." It was some time before he could get into the regular track of gossip, or could be mad e to comprehend the strange events that had taken place during his torpor. How that there had been a revolutionary war—that the country had thrown off the voke of old England—and that instead of being a subject of his Majesty George the Third, he was now a free citizen of the United States. Rip, in fact, was no politician; the change s of states and empires made but little impression on him. But there was one species of despotism under which he had long groaned, and that was—petticoat government. Happily, that wag.at an end; he had got his neck nut of the yoke of matrimony, and could go in and out whenever he pleased, without dreading the tyranny of Dame Van Winkle. Whenever her name was mentioned, however, he shook his head, shrugged his shoulders, and cast up his eyes; which might pass either for an expression of resignation to his fate, or joy at his deliverance.

He used to tell his story to every stranger that arrived at Mr.Doolittle's hotel. He was observed, at first, to vary on some points every time he told it, which was, doubtless, owing to his having so recently awaked. It at last settled down precisely to the tale I have related, and not a man, woman, or child in the neighbourhood, but knew it by heart. Some always pretended to doubt the reality of it, and insisted that Rip had been out of his head, and that this was one point on which he always remained flighty. The old Dutch inhabitants, however, almost universally gave it full credit. Even to this day they never hear a thunder storm of a summer afternoon, about the Kaatskill, but they say Hendrick Hudson and his crew are at their game of nine pins; and it is a common wish of all henpecked husbands in the neighbourhood, when life hangs heavy on their hands, that they might have a quieting draught out of Rip Van Winkle's flagon.

NOTE

The foregoing tale, one would suspect, had been suggested to Mr.Knickerbocker by a little German superstition about Charles V[19]. and the Kypphauser mountain; the subjoined note, however, which he had appended to the tale, shows that it is an absolute fact, narrated with his usual fidelity:

"The story of Rip Van Winkle may seem incredible to many, but nevertheless I give it my full belief, for I know the vicinity of our old Dutch settlements to have been very subject to marvellous events and appearances. Indeed, I have heard many stranger stories than this, in the villages along the Hudson; all of which were too well authenticated to admit of a doubt. I have even talked with Rip Van Winkle myself, who, when last I saw him, was a very venerable old man, and so perfectly rational and consistent on every other point, that I think no conscientious person could refuse to take this into the bargain; nay, I have seen a certificate on the subject taken before a country justice, and signed with a cross, in the justice's own hand writing. The story, therefore, is beyond the possibility of doubt. D.K."

## Notes

1. In this quotation from The Ordinary, 3.1.1050 - 54, a play by the English writer William Cartwright (1611 — 1643), the speaker is a pedant named Moth. Woden was the Norse god of war.

2. Last governor of the Dutch province of New Netherlands (1592 — 1672), in 1655 (as mentioned below) defeated Swedish colonists at Fort Christina, near what is now Wilmington, Delaware.

3. Tirade delivered by a wife after the curtains around the four-poster bed have been drawn for the night.

4. Loose, wide breeches.

5. Ruling committee (Spanish).

6. Knapsack.

7. Jacket fitted tightly at the waist. thighs, where it hooked to hose.

8. Male garment covering from neck to upper.

9. Short, curved sword.

10. Minister.

11. Kind of gin.

12. Cf. Genesis 11.1 — 9, Babel being confused with Babylon.

13. Limp, close-fitting cap adopted during the French Revolution as a symbol of liberty. The pole is a "liberty pole" — i.e., a tall flagstaff topped by a liberty cap.

14. Colors of the Revolutionary uniform. Irving's joke is that the new proprietor, being a Yankee, is so parsimonious that he will only touch up the sign, not replace it with a true portrait of Wash.

15. Political parties that developed in the Washington

administrations, Alexander Hamilton leading the Federalists and Thomas Jefferson, the Democrats.

16. A mountain near West Point. Stoney Point, on the west hank of the Hudson south of West Point, was captured by General Anthony Wayne (1745 — 1796) during the Revolution.

17. Adriaen Van der Donck (1620 — 1655?) wrote a history of New Netherlands (1655).

18. Henry Hudson (d.1611). English navigator in the service of the Dutch. "Great city" is ironic, for the town named for him on the east bank of the Hudson River was flourishing but not a metropolis.

19. Later Irving changed "Charles V." (Holy Roman emperor, 1519 — 56) to "The Emperor Fredericktfer Rothbart" (i.e.. Frederick Barbarossa: Holy Roman emperor.1152-90). ("Rothbart" and "Barbarossa" both mean "redbeard".) In either form, the allusion is a red herring, a disarming way of suggesting indebtedness to a German source while concealing the most specific source, the story of Peter Klaus in the folktales of J.C.C.N. Otmar.

## Questions

1. "He is one of those happy mortals, who take the world easy, eat white bread or brown, whichever can be got with least thought or trouble, and would rather starve on a penny than work for a pound." Try to explain the character of Rip according to the above statements. Do you believe the story that Rip had been asleep for 20-year? Is there any metaphor?

2. Comparing with《桃花源记》by Tao Yuanming(陶渊明),

are there any similarities between the two work? Try to find them out.

### (2) Edgar Allan Poe (1809—1849)

Edgar Allan Poe's stature as a major figure in world literature is primarily based on his ingenious and profound short stories, poems, and critical theories, which established a highly influential rationale for the short form in both poetry and fiction. Regarded in literary histories and handbooks as the architect of the modern short story, Poe was also the principal forerunner of the "art for art's sake" movement in 19th-century European literature. Whereas earlier critics predominantly concerned themselves with moral or ideological generalities, Poe focused his criticism on the specifics of style and construction that contributed to a work's effectiveness or failure.

His life story is by no means happy. Before Poe was three years old both of his parents died, and he was raised in the home of John Allan, a prosperous exporter from Richmond, Virginia, who never legally adopted his foster son. The young man was forced to leave the school when his stepfather refused to pay Poe's large gambling debts at the University of Virginia. In 1827, soon after Poe left for Boston, he enlisted in the army and also published his first poetry collection, *Tamerlane, and Other Poems*. The volume went unnoticed by readers and reviewers, and a second collection, *Al Aaraaf, Tamerlane, and Minor Poems*, received only slightly more attention when it appeared in 1829. That same year Poe was admitted into the United States Military Academy at West Point. However, soon after, he gained a dismissal for ignoring his duties and violating regulations. He subsequently went to New York City, where *Poems*, his third collection of verse, was published in 1831.

During the second half his short life Paul pursued a small career in New York, Richmond, Philadelphia, and Baltimore, primarily supporting himself by writing and working as an editor for several magazines. After the third volume of *Poems* (1831) failed to bring him money or acclaim, he turned to fiction and literary criticism. Five of his short stories were published in newspapers in 1832, and in 1838 published his only novel, *The Narrative of Arthur Gordon Pym*. Even though his short stories gained him some recognition and his poem, *The Ravern* (1845), was greeted with enthusiasm, he could never escape from poverty. In 1849, two years after the day his beloved wife Virginia passed away, Poe died in Baltimore alone and unhappy.

He is widely known as the inventor of the detective story and his psychological thrillers have been imitated by scores of modern writers. His psychological stories—which include *The Black Cat*, *The Cask of Amontillado*, and *The Tell-Tale Heart*—are often told by a first-person narrator, and through this voice Poe probes the workings of a character's psyche. In his Gothic tales, Poe also employed an essentially symbolic, almost allegorical, method which gives such works as *The Fall of the House of Usher, The Masque of the Red Death*, and *Ligeia* an enigmatic quality that accounts for their enduring interest and links them with the symbolical works of Nathaniel Hawthorne and Herman Melville. In addition to his achievement as a creator of the modern horror tale, Poe is also credited with parenting two other popular genres: science fiction and the detective story. In such works as *The Unparalleled Adventure of Hans Pfaall and Von Kempelen and His Discovery*, Poe took advantage of the fascination for science and technology that emerged in the early 19th century to produce speculative and fantastic narratives which anticipate a type of literature that did not become widely practiced until the 20th century.

Similarly, Poe's three tales of ratiocination—*The Murders in the Rue Morgue*, *The Purloined Letter*, and *The Mystery of Marie Roget*—are recognized as the models which established the major characters and literary conventions of detective fiction, specifically the amateur sleuth who solves a crime that has confounded the authorities and whose feats of deductive reasoning are documented by an admiring associate. Poe's theory of literary creation is also noted.

While his works were not conspicuously acclaimed during his lifetime, today, Poe is recognized as one of the foremost progenitors of modern literature, both in its popular forms, such as horror and detective fiction, and in its more complex and self-conscious forms, which represent the essential artistic manner of the 20th century.

The following story *The Tell-Tale Heart* (1843) is one of a number of Poe's stories that focus on an obsessed protagonist/narrator. Indeed, what holds the story together and holds the attention of the reader is the single minded voice of the madman, who even as he denies his madness, tells a story that confirms it. The narrator decided to kill the old man with whom he seems to be living together, for he could not be facing the old man's eye. He wanted to rid himself of the eye forever. For seven nights he managed to sneak into the old man's room to kill him, but he found that the eyes were always closed. Upon the eighth night, he finally committed the murder of the old man with his "evil eye" open, after which he cut off the head, the arms, and the legs and deposited them under the floor. When the policemen came, the narrator took them all over the house and even to the old man's room. Everything was fine and he felt very proud of his wisdom. As the narrator sat with the police, he began to hear a sound in his ears, "...a low, dull, quick sound—much such a sound as a watch makes when enveloped in cotton." The narrator's tell-tale heart caused him to convict himself.

Here, Poe's use of a first person narrator obsessively recounting the past event is an important element in his contribution to the short story form as a highly unified aesthetic entity. The narrator is obsessively concerned with his irrational desire to kill the old man because of the old man's eye and by his rational method of proceeding, which exemplified Poe's theory that every element in the short story should contribute to its overall effect. Although there are two characters involved in the story, an old man and the younger man who lives with him, it is really about a single character. An examination of the nature of the narrator's obsession shows how Poe sets up this story about a split psyche. Therefore, reading this story is like trying to solve a mystery story. In this case, the mystery is the motivation of the killer.

## The Tell-Tale Heart[1]

Art is long and Time is fleeting,
And our hearts, though stout and brave.
Still, like muffled drums, are beating
Funeral marches to the grave.( Longfellow)[2]

True! —nervous—very, very dreadfully nervous I had been, and am; but why will you say that I am mad? The disease had sharpened my senses—not destroyed—not dulled them. Above all was the sense of hearing acute. I heard all things in the heaven and in the earth. I heard many things in hell. How, then, am I mad? Harken! and observe how healthily—how calmly I can tell you the whole story.

It is impossible to say how first the idea entered my brain; but, once conceived, it haunted me day and night. Object there was none. Passion there was none. I loved the old man. He had never wronged me. He had never given me insult. For his gold I had no desire. I think it was his eye! —yes, it was this! He had the eye of a vulture—a pale blue eye, with a film over it. Whenever it fell upon me, my blood ran cold; and so, by degrees—very gradually—I made up my mind to take the life of the old man, and thus rid myself of the eye forever.

Now this is the point. You fancy me mad. Madmen know nothing. But you should have seen me. You should have seen how wisely I proceeded—with what caution—with what foresight—with what dissimulation I went to work! I was never kinder to the old man than during the whole week before I killed him. And every night, about midnight, I turned the latch of his door and opened it—oh so gently! And then, when I had made an opening sufficient for my head, I first put in a dark lantern[3], all closed, closed, so that no light shone out, and then I thrust in my head. Oh, you would have laughed to see how cunningly I thrust it in! I moved it slowly—very, very slowly, so that I might not disturb the old man's sleep. It took me an hour to place my whole head within the opening so far that I could see the old man a s he lay upon his bed. Ha! —would a madman have been so wise as this? And then, when my head was well in the room, I undid the lantern cautiously—oh, so cautiously (for the hinges creaked)—I undid it just so much that a single thin ray fell upon the vulture eye. And this I did for seven long nights—every night just at midnight—but I found the eye always closed; and so it was impossible to do the work; for it was not the old man who vexed me, but his Evil Eye. And every morning, when the day broke, I went boldly into his chamber, and spoke courageously to him, calling him by name in a hearty tone, and inquiring how he had passed the night. So you see he would have been a very profound old man, indeed, to suspect that every night, just at twelve, I looked in upon him while he slept.

Upon the eighth night I was more than usually cautious in opening the door. A watch's minute-hand moves more quickly than did mine. Never, before that night, had I felt the extent of my own powers—of my sagacity. I could scarcely contain my feelings of triumph. To think that there I was, opening the door, little by little, and the old man not even to dream of my secret deeds or thoughts. I fairly chuckled at the idea. And perhaps the old man heard me; for he moved in the bed suddenly, as if startled. Now you may think that I drew back—but no. His room was as black as pitch with the thick darkness, (for the shutters were close fastened, through fear of robbers,) and so I knew that he could not see the opening of the door, and I kept on pushing it steadily, steadily.

I had got my head in, and was about to open the lantern, when my thumb slipped upon the tin fastening, and the old man sprang up in the bed, crying out—"Who's there?"

I kept quite still and said nothing. For another hour I did not move a muscle, and in the meantime I did not hear the old man lie down. He was still sitting up in the bed, listening; —just as I have done, night after night, hearkening to the death-watches[4] in the wall.

Presently I heard a slight groan, and I knew that it was the groan of mortal terror. It was not a groan of pain, or of grief—oh, no! —it was the low, stifled sound that arises from the bottom of the soul when overcharged with awe. I knew the sound well. Many a night, just at midnight, when all the world slept, it has welled up from my own bosom, deepening, with its dreadful echo, the terrors that distracted me. I say I knew it well. I knew what the old man felt, and pitied him, although I chuckled at heart. I knew that he had been lying awake ever since the first slight noise, when he had turned in the bed. His fears had been, ever since, growing upon him. He had been trying to fancy them causeless, but could not. He had been saying to himself—"It is nothing but the wind in the chimney—it is only a mouse crossing the floor," or "it is merely a cricket which has made a single chirp." Yes, he had been trying to comfort himself with these suppositions; but he had found all in vain. All in vain; because death, in approaching the old man, had stalked with his black shadow before him, and the shadow had now reached and enveloped the victim[5]. And it was the mournful influence of the unperceived shadow that caused him to feel—although he neither saw nor heard me — to feel the presence of my head within the room.

When I had waited a long time, very patiently, without hearing the old man lie down, I resolved to open a little—a very, very little crevice in the lantern. So I opened it—you cannot imagine how stealthily, stealthily—until, at length, a single dim ray, like the thread of the spider, shot from out the crevice and fell full upon the vulture eye.

It was open—wide, wide open—and I grew furious as I gazed upon it. I saw it with perfect distinctness—all a dull blue, with a hideous veil over it that chilled the very marrow in my bones; but I could see nothing else of the old man's face or person; for I had directed the ray, as if by instinct, precisely upon the damned spot.

And now—have I not told you that what you mistake for madness is but over acuteness of the senses? —now, I say, there cam e to my ears a low, dull, quick sound—much such a sound as a watch makes when enveloped in cotton. I knew that sound well, too. It was the beating of the old man's heart. It increased my fury, as the beating of a drum stimulates the soldier into courage.

But even yet I refrained and kept still. I scarcely breathed. I held the lantern motionless. I tried how steadily I could maintain the ray upon the eye. Meantime the hellish tattoo[6] of the heart increased. It grew quicker, and louder and louder every instant. The old man's terror must have been extreme! It grew louder, I say, louder every moment: —do you mark me well? I have told you that I am nervous: —so I am. And now, at the dead hour of night, and amid the dreadful silence of that old house, so strange a noise as this excited me to uncontrollable wrath[7]. Yet, for some minute s longer, I refrained and kept still. But the beating grew louder, louder! I thought the heart must burst! And now a new anxiety seized me—the sound would be heard by a neighbor! The old man's hour had come! With a loud yell, I threw open the lantern and leaped into the room. He shrieked once—once only. In an instant I dragged him to the floor, and pulled the heavy bed over him. I then sat upon the bed[8] and smiled gaily, to find the deed so far done. But, for many minutes, the heart beat on, with a muffled sound. This, however, did not vex me; it would not be heard through the walls. At length it ceased. The old man was dead. I removed the bed and examined the corpse. Yes, he was stone, stone dead. I placed my hand upon the heart and held it there many minutes. There was no pulsation. The old man was stone dead. His eye would trouble me no more.

If, still, you think me mad, you will think so no longer when I describe the wise precautions I took for the concealment of the body. The night waned, and I worked hastily, but in silence. First of all I dismembered the corpse. I cut off the head and the arms and the legs. I then took up three planks from the flooring of the chamber, and deposited all between the scantlings[9]. I then replaced the boards so cleverly, so cunningly, that no human eye—not even his—could have detected anything wrong. There was nothing to wash out— no stain of any kind—no blood-spot whatever. I had been too wary for that. A tub had caught all—ha ! ha!

When I had made an end of these labors, it was four o'clock—still dark as midnight. As the bell sounded the hour, there came a knocking at the street door. I went down to open it with a light heart, —for what had I now to fear? There entered three men, who introduced themselves, with perfect suavity, as officers of the police. A shriek had been heard by a neighbor during the night; suspicion of foul play had been aroused; information had been lodged at the police-office, and they (the officers) had been deputed to search the premises.

I smiled, —for what had I to fear? I bade the gentlemen welcome. The shriek, I said, was my own in a dream. The old man, I mentioned, was absent in the country. I took my visitors all over the house. I bade them search— search well. I led them, at length, to his chamber. I showed them his treasures, secure, undisturbed. In the enthusiasm of my confidence, I brought chairs into the room, and desired them here to rest from their fatigues; while I myself, in the wild audacity of my perfect triumph, placed my own seat upon the very spot beneath which reposed the corpse of the victim.

The officers were satisfied. My manner had convinced them. I was singularly at ease. They sat, and, while I answered cheerily, they chatted of familiar things. But, ere long, I felt myself getting pal e and wished them gone. My head ached, and I fancied a ringing in my ears: but still they sat and still chatted. The ringing became more distinct: I talked more freely, to get rid of the feeling; but it continued and gained definitiveness—until, at length, I found that the noise was wot within my ears.

No doubt I now grew very pale; —but I talked more fluently, and with a heightened voice. Yet the sound increased—and what could I do? It was a low, dull, quick sound—much such a sound as a watch makes when enveloped in cotton. I gasped for breath—and yet the officers heard it not. I talked more quickly—more vehemently; —but the noise steadily increased. I arose, and argued about trifles, in a high key and with violent gesticulations; —but the noise steadily increased. Why woidd they not be gone? I paced the floor to and fro, with heavy strides, as if excited to fury by the observations of the men; —but the noise steadily increased. Oh God! what could I do? I foamed—I raved—I swore! I swung the chair upon which I had sat, and grated it upon the boards; —but the noise arose over all and continually increased. It grew louder—louder—louder! And still the men chatted pleasantly, and smiled. Was it possible they heard not? Almighty God! no, no! They heard! — they suspected! —they knew!—they were making a mockery of my horror!— this I thought, and this I think. But anything better than this agony! Anything was more tolerable than this derision! I could bear those hypocritical smiles no longer! I felt that I must scream or die! —and now—again! —hark! louder! louder! louder! louder! —

"Villains!" I shrieked, "dissemble no more! I admit the deed! —tear up the planks! —here, here! —it is the beating of his hideous heart!"

## Notes

1. First published in The pioneer (January 1843), the source of

the present text. Poe very likely made a few of the changes for the reprinting in the Broadway Journal (August 23, 1845) (such a s changing the old man to "he" or "him" a few times), but the Broadway Journal compositor dropped some necessary words (footnoted in the text), misprinted others, and bungled the punctuation (including the use of italics) throughout. Most modern reprintings derive from the corrupt 1845 text that Rufus Griswold reprinted in the first volume of Poe's posthumous Works (1850).

2. Henry Wadsworth Longfellow's (1807 — 1882) "A Psalm of Life," lines 13-16.

3. One with panes that can be covered.

4. Beetles that make a hollow clicking sound by striking their heads against the wood into which they burrow

5. The 1845 text reads: "All in vain; because Death, in approaching him had stalked with his black shadow before him, and enveloped the victim."

6. Drumbeat.

7. The 1845 text replaces wrath with "terror".

8. The 1845 text lacks the grisly detail of sitting on the bed while smiling gaily ("I the n smiled gaily, to find the deed so far done.").

9. Small planks.

## Questions

1. The narrator insists from the very beginning of the story that he is not insane. What features does he say prove his sanity? What characteristics suggest his manners instead? Why is the

narrator so concerned with a time, such as watches, clocks, time passing etc. which are presented in the story?

2. Try to compare the story with one of the stories in《洗冤录》by Song Ci of China.

### （3）Walt Whitman (1819—1892)

Born into a working-class family, son of a carpenter on Long Island, New York, Whitman grew up in Brooklyn and only had five years of schooling. He tried various jobs including office boy, printer, schoolmaster, editor of eight successive newspapers, and journalist. At the age of twenty-two, he turned to journalism as a full-time career. At the age of twenty-seven he was editor of the Brooklyn Eagle. During the Civil War, Whitman worked as a volunteer nurse, a "wound dresser" in military hospitals. These experiences led to the poems in his 1865 publication Drum-Taps, which includes *When Lilacs Last in the Dooryard Bloom'd*, Whitman's eulogy for President Lincoln.

In 1842, he published his first novel *Franklin Evans*. In 1855, Whitman published the first edition of *Leaves of Grass* with his own money, which consisted of twelve untitled poems and a preface. Emerson himself declared the first edition was "the most extraordinary piece of wit and wisdom that America has yet contributed". In 1856, Whitman released a second edition of the book, containing thirty-three poems. After suffering a serious stroke in 1873, Whitman moved to his brother's home in Camden, New Jersey. While his poetry failed to garner popular attention from his American readership during his lifetime, over 1,000 people came to view his funeral. And as the first writer of truly American poetry, Whitman's legacy endures.

Of all the poets of the time period between 1800 and 1870, Whitman would have the most lasting effect on American literature—despite the fact that the first edition of *Leaves of Grass* sold fewer than 20 copies. Along with Emily Dickinson, Whitman is regarded as one of America's most significant 19th-century poets and would influence later many poets, including Ezra Pound, William Carlos Williams, Allen Ginsberg, Simon Ortiz, C. K. Williams, and Martín Espada.

His *Leaves of Grass* (1855, 1891—1892)was inspired in part by his travels through the American frontier and by his admiration for Ralph Waldo Emerson. This important publication underwent eight subsequent editions during his lifetime as Whitman expanded and revised the poetry and added more to the original collection of 12 poems. In *Leaves of Grass*, he celebrated democracy, nature, love, and friendship. This monumental work chanted praises to the body as well as to the soul, and found beauty and reassurance even in death. Whitman's originality lies first in his use of the poetic form free verse (i.e. poetry without a fixed beat or regular rhyme scheme). His poems are filled with optimistic expectation and enthusiasm about new things and a new epoch.

The following poems are given in their final form: that of the 1881 edition of *Leaves of Grass*.

## Song of Myself (1881)

### 1

I celebrate myself, and sing myself,
And what I assume you shall assume,
For every atom belonging to me as good belongs to you.
I loafe and invite my soul,
I lean and loafe at my ease observing a spear of summer grass.

My tongue, every atom of my blood, form'd from this soil, this air,
Born here of parents born here from parents the same, and their parents the same,
I, now thirty-seven years old in perfect health begin,
Hoping to cease not till death.

Creeds and schools in abeyance,
Retiring back a while sufficed at what they are, but never forgotten,
I harbor for good or bad, I permit to speak at every hazard,
Nature without check with original energy.

### 2

House s and rooms are full of perfumes, the shelves are crowded with perfumes,
1 breathe the fragrance myself and know it and like it,

The distillation would intoxicate me also, but I shall not let it.

The atmosphere is not a perfume, it has no taste of the distillation, it is odorless,
It is for my mouth forever, I am in love with it,
I will go to the bank by the wood and become undisguised and naked, I am mad for it to be in contact with me.

The smoke of my own breath,
Echoes, ripples, buzz'd whispers, love-root, silk-thread, crotch and vine,
My respiration and inspiration, the beating of my heart, the passing of blood and air through my lungs,
The sniff of green leaves and dry leaves, and of the shore and dark-color'd sea-rocks, and of hay in the barn,
The sound of the belch'd words of my voice loos'd to the eddies of the wind,

A few light kisses, a few embraces, a reaching around of arms,
The play of shine and shade on the trees as the supple boughs wag,
The delight alone or in the rush of the streets, or along the fields and hillsides,
The feeling of health, the full-noon trill, the song of me rising from bed and meeting the sun.

Have you reckon'd a thousand acres much? have you reckon'd the earth much?
Have you practis'd so long to learn to read?
Have you felt so proud to get at the meaning of poems?
Stop this day and night with me and you shall possess the origin of all poems,
You shall possess the good of the earth and sun, (there are millions of suns left,)
You shall no longer take things at second or third hand, nor look through the eyes of the dead, nor feed on the spectres in books,
You shall not look through my eyes either, nor take things from me,
You shall listen to all sides and filter them from your self.

**3**

I have heard what the talkers were talking, the talk of the beginning and the end,
But I do not talk of the beginning or the end.
There was never any more inception than there is now,
Nor any more youth or age than there is now,
And will never be any more perfection than there is now,
Nor any more heaven or hell than there is now.
Urge and urge and urge,
Always the procreant urge of the world.
Out of the dimness opposite equals advance, always substance and increase, always sex,
Always a knit of identity, always distinction, always a breed of life.

To elaborate is no avail, learn'd and unlearn'd feel that it is so.
Sure as the most certain sure, plumb in the uprights, well entretied[1], braced in the beams,
Stout as a horse, affectionate, haughty, electrical,
I and this mystery here we stand.
Clear and sweet is my soul, and clear and sweet is all that is not my soul.
Lack one lacks both, and the unseen is proved by the seen,
Till that become s unseen and receives proof in its turn.
Showing the best and dividing it from the worst age vexes age,
Knowing the perfect fitness and equanimity of things, while they discuss I am silent, and go bathe and admire myself.
Welcome is every organ and attribute of me, and of any man hearty and clean,
Not an inch nor a particle of an inch is vile, and none shall be less familiar than the rest.
I am satisfied—I see, dance, laugh, sing;
As the hugging and loving bed-fellow sleeps at my side through the night, and withdraws at the peep of the day with stealthy tread,

Leaving me baskets cover'd with white towels swelling the house with their plenty,
Shall I postpone my acceptation and realization and scream at my eyes,
That they turn from gazing after and down the road.
And forthwith cipher[2] and show me to a cent,
Exactly the value of one and exactly the value of two, and which

is ahead?

## Notes

1. Cross-braced.

2. Calculate.

## Questions

1. In the first stanza, who is the "I" and who is the "you"? try to explain their relationship on the basis of the poem.

2. Try to find a piece of poetry written by Guo Moruo( 郭沫若 ), which is the same theme as Whitman's and compare them.

### (4) Emily Dickinson (1830—1886)

Emily Elizabeth Dickinson was born in Amherst, Massachusetts, on December 10, 1830, to Edward and Emily Dickinson. To some extent, she lived in a quite wealthy family. Her father, Edward Dickinson was a very wealthy, successful, and prominent lawyer and politician. She was educated at Amherst Academy and Mt. Holyoke Female Seminary (1847—1948), in South Hadley, Massachusetts, for only one year due to health problems. Dressed in white and avoiding visitors as much as possible in her later life, she stayed almost all her life in the same house and the same yard, except for a visit for a few weeks to Washington, DC.

Around 1850, she began writing poetry. Her first poems were traditional and followed established form, but as time passed, she began producing huge amounts of poetry. Dickinson began experimenting during her lifetime. She wrote 1,775 poems in 1886, with only seven of which appeared in print in her lifetime. Her best work was read in the four year period from 1858 to 1862.

Dickinson's poems are usually based on her own experiences, her sorrows, and joys, but within her little lyrics, Dickinson addresses those issues that concern the human beings which includes religion, death, immortality, love and nature. Her poems are without titles, so in place of that, numbers or the first line are used to identify her poems. Many capital letters are also in her poems. The expressions are very direct and brave, the rhythm is a kind of musical device to create cadence. Her poems are always short, many of which are about two stanzas. And many rhetoric techniques are used, such as personification. There are also many dashes within her poems.

Emily Dickinson is one of America's greatest and most original poets of all time. She took definition as her province and challenged the existing definitions of poetry and the poet's work. Like writers such as Ralph Waldo Emerson, Henry David Thoreau, and Walt Whitman, she experimented with expression in order to free it from conventional restraints. Like writers such as Charlotte Brontë and Elizabeth Barrett Browning, she crafted a new type of persona for the first person. The speakers in Dickinson's poetry, like those in Brontë's and Browning's works, are sharp-sighted observers who see the inescapable limitations of their societies as well as their imagined and imaginable escapes. To make the abstract tangible, to define meaning without confining it, to inhabit a house that never became a prison, Dickinson created in her writing a distinctively elliptical language for expressing what was possible but not yet realized. Like the Concord Transcendentalists whose works she knew well, she saw poetry as a double-edged sword. While it liberated the individual, it as readily left him ungrounded. When the first volume of her poetry was published in 1890, four years after her death, it met with stunning success. Going through 11 editions in less than two years, the poems eventually extended far beyond their first household audiences. Dickinson is now known as one of the most important American poets, and her poetry is widely read among people of all ages and interests.

The following poems are from *The Norton Anthology of American Literature* (shorter 6th edition).

## "I never lost as much but twice"

### 49

I never lost as much but twice,
And that was in the sod.
Twice have I stood a beggar
Before the door of God!
Angels—twice descending

Reimbursed my store—
Burglar! Banker—Father!
I am poor once more!

## "This is my letter to the World"

### 441

This is my letter to the World
That never wrote to Me —
The simple News that Nature told—
With tender Majesty
Her Message is committed

To Hands I cannot see —
For love of Her—Sweet—countrymen
Judge tenderly—of Me

## "I cannot live with You—"

### 640

I cannot live with You—
It would be Life—
And Life is over there—
Behind the Shelf
The Sexton[1] keeps the Key to —

Putting up

Our Life—His Porcelain—
Like a Cup —
Discarded of the Housewife—
Quaint—or Broke—

A newer Sevres[2] pleases—
Old Ones crack—
I could not die—with You—
For One must wait
To shut the Other's Gaze down— is

You—could not—
And I—Could I stand by
And see You—freeze—
Without my Right of Frost—
Death's privilege?

## Notes

1. Church officer or employee who is custodian of church property, bellringer, and grave digger.

2. Fine, often elaborately decorated French porcelain.

## Questions

1. Paraphrase the three poems.

2. What are the figures of speech used in each poem?

### (5) Henry Wadsworth Longfellow (1807—1882)

Henry Wadsworth Longfellow was born on February 27, 1807, in Portland (while Maine was still a part of Massachusetts). One of his grandfathers was a State Senator and the other grandfather had been a Revolutionary War general and a congressman. Following his graduation in 1826 from Bowdoin College, where he was a classmate of Nathaniel Hawthorne, he went to Europe to study. When he returned to the United States three years later, he taught European languages first at Bowdoin and then at Harvard. After eighteen years of teaching at Harvard, he resigned his position because he felt it interfered with his writing. During the last years of his life, Longfellow received many honors, including honorary degrees from Cambridge and Oxford universities in England.

His poetic style is pure, and his lines are musical, direct, and sentimental, which are often written in a simple and gentle tone. His poetic technique is very traditional and the major theme of his poetry is an idealized vision of the world and life.

Henry Wadsworth Longfellow was one of the most widely known and best-loved American poets of the 19th century. He achieved a level of national and international prominence previously unequaled in the literary history of the United States and is one of the few American writers honored in the Poets' Corner of Westminster Abbey—in fact, he is believed to be the first as his bust was installed there in 1884. Poems such as *Paul Revere's Ride*, *Evangeline*, *A Tale of Acadie* (1847), and *A Psalm of Life* were mainstays of primary and secondary school curricula, long remembered by generations of readers who studied them as children. Longfellow's achievements are in fictional and non-fictional prose, in a striking variety of poetic forms and modes, and in translation from many European languages, resulting in a remarkably productive and influential literary career. His celebrity in his own time, however, has yielded to changing literary tastes and to reactions against the genteel tradition of authorship he represented. Even if time has proved him something less than the master poet he never claimed to be, Longfellow made pioneering contributions to American literary life by exemplifying the possibility of a successful authorial career, by linking American poetry to European traditions beyond England, and by developing a surprisingly wide readership for Romantic poetry.

The following poem is from *The Norton Anthology of American Literature* (shorter 6th edition).

## The Slave's Dream[1]

Beside the ungathered rice he lay,
His sickle in his hand;
His breast was bare, his matted hair
Was buried in the sand.
Again, in the mist and shadow of sleep,
He saw his Native Land.

Wide through the landscape of his dreams
The lordly Niger 2 flowed;

Beneath the palm-trees on the plain
Once more a king he strode;
And heard the tinkling caravans
Descend the mountain-road.

He saw once more his dark-eyed queen
Among her children stand;
They clasped his neck, they kissed his cheeks,
They held him by the hand!—
A tear burst from the sleeper's lids
And fell into the sand.

And then at furious speed he rode
Along the Niger[2] bank;
His bridle-reins were golden chains,
And, with a martial clank,
At each leap he could feel his scabbard of steel
Smiting his stallion's flank.

Before him, like a blood-red flag,
The bright flamingoes flew;
From morn till night he followed their flight,
O'er plains where the tamarind grew,
Till he saw the roofs of Caffre[3] huts,
And the ocean rose to view.

At night he heard the lion roar,
And the hyena scream,
And the river-horse[4], as he crushed the reeds
Beside some hidden stream;
And it passed, like a glorious roll of drums,
Through the triumph of his dream.

The forests, with their myriad tongues,
Shouted of liberty;
And the Blast of the Desert cried aloud,
With a voice so wild and free,
That he started in his sleep and smiled
At their tempestuous glee.

He did not feel the driver's whip,
Nor the burning heat of day;
For Death had illumined the Land of Sleep,
And his lifeless body lay
A worn-out fetter, that the soul
Had broken and thrown away!

## Notes

1. From the first printing, in *Poems on Slavery* (1842), a little volume that marked the high point of Longfellow's public concern over slavery in the United States. Longfellow's contemporaries reacted variously. Whittier thought the poems had been "of important service"

to the cause of abolitionism, while a more objective observer found them "perfect dish water" compared with Whittier's own poems against slavery. The majority, North and South, deplored the publication of the poems.

2. Great African river.

3. Kaffir, used here to mean non-Muslim Africans.

4. Hippopotamus.

## Questions

1. What kind of person is the speaker of this poem?

2. To what extent do you agree that this is a poem about abolitionism?

### (6) Nathaniel Hawthorne (1804—1864)

New England writer Nathaniel Hawthorne was born in 1804 in Salem, Massachusetts, where his paternal ancestors had been prominent since the founding generation (who then spelled their last name Hathorn). In his early teens he lived three years as free as "a bird of the air" at Sebago Lake, in Maine (then still a part of Massachusetts), acquiring a love of tramping, which he always kept. By his mid-teens he was reading 18th-century novelists like Henry Fielding, Tobias Smollett, and Horace Walpole, as well as contemporary writers like William Godwin and Sir Walter Scott, forming an ambition to be a writer himself. At Bowdoin College, his classmates were many of the important literary and political figures of the day, such as Horatio Bridge, later a famous writer, Franklin Pierce, later president, and became lifelong friends; Longfellow was also another classmate of his. These prominent friends supplied Hawthorne with government employment in the lean times, allowing him time to bloom as an author.

Like James Fenimore Cooper, Hawthorne was extremely concerned with the conventionality. His first pseudonymously published short stories imitated Sir Walt Scott, as did his 1828 self-published Fanshawe. He later formally withdrew most of his early work, discounting it as the work of inexperienced youth. From 1836 to 1854, the Boston-centered transcendentalism movement led by Ralph Waldo Emerson was an important force in New England intellectual circles. Hawthorne's later works show some transcendentalist influence, including a belief in individual choice and consequence, and an emphasis on symbolism. As America's first true psychological novel, *The Scarlet Letter* (1850) would convey these ideals, contrasting Puritan morality with passion and individualism.

While attending Bowdoin College, Hawthorne began writing tales or a romance, or both. His stories and novels, including Young *Goodman Brown* (1835), *Twice-Told Tales* (1837), *Ethan Brand* (1850), *The Scarlet Letter* (1850), *The House of the Seven Gables* (1851), and *The Blithedale Romance* (1852), are outstanding among his contemporaries.

In sketches, tales, and romances published in towards the middle of the 19th century, Hawthorne chose mainly American materials, drawing especially on the history of colonial New England and his native Salem in the time of his early American ancestors. Heir to the

Puritan tradition and alert to the transcendental thought prominent in his region and time, he injected both his skeptical, questioning scrutiny into morality and psychological probing into his writing that is characteristic of his fictional works. Considering guilt—actual or imagined, revealed or concealed—to be a universal human experience, he traced out in his characters the types and the effects of guilt. The seriousness of his literary purpose, his independence of mind, and his intellectual and artistic integrity were recognized by Herman Melville and others of his contemporaries.

He created a number of memorable characters and scenes in world literature; he was a master of the prose style that is individual, simple, and direct, and yet richly varied. Hawthorne's writing influenced Melville, who dedicated *Moby Dick* (1851) to Hawthorne, as well as Henry James and William Faulkner; they were drawn particularly by his symbolic method and his attention to the dark elements in the human experience. Through both direct statements and examples, he helped define for his age the literary sketch, the tale, and long fiction that fuses romance and psychological realism. *The Scarlet Letter* has been held both as the first symbolic novel and the first psychological novel in America. With the publication of this novel in 1850, Hawthorne's reputation as a major American author has been on the rise ever since.

The story describes the illicit love affair of Hester Prynne with the Reverend Arthur Dimmesdale. Hester is a young married woman whose husband Chillingworth was presumed to have been lost at the sea during a journey. She begins a secret adulterous relationship with

Dimmesdale, and becomes pregnant with a daughter, whom she names Pearl.

Then she is publicly vilified and forced to wear the scarlet letter on her clothing to identify her as an adulteress, but she refuses to reveal the identity of her lover. She accepts the punishment with grace and refuses to be defeated by the shame inflicted upon her by society. Eventually, Dimmesdale publicly admits his part in the adultery and dies in her arms.

*The Scarlet Letter* represents the height of Hawthorne's literary genius, dense with terse descriptions, and it remains relevant for its philosophical and psychological depth and continues to be read as a classic tale with universal themes.

The following excerpts are from the fifth Chapter of *The Scarlet Letter*.

## Chapter 5 HESTER AT HER NEEDLE

HESTER PRYNNE'S term of confinement was now at an end. Her prison-door was thrown open, and she came forth into the sunshine, which, falling on all alike, seemed, to her sick and morbid heart, as if meant for no other purpose than to reveal the scarlet letter on her breast. Perhaps there was a more real torture in her first unattended footsteps from the threshold of the prison, than even in the procession and spectacle that have been described, where she was made the common infamy, at which all mankind was summoned to point its finger. Then, she was supported by an unnatural tension of the nerves, and by all the combative energy of her character, which enabled her to convert the scene into a kind of lurid[1] triumph. It was, moreover, a separate and insulated event, to occur but once in her lifetime, and to meet which, therefore, reckless of economy, she might call up the vital strength that would have sufficed for many quiet years. The very law that condemned her—a giant of stern features, but with vigour to support, as well as to annihilate, in his iron arm—had held her up, through the terrible ordeal[2] of her ignominy. But now, with this unattended walk from her prison-door, began the daily custom; and she must either sustain and carry it forward by the ordinary resources of her nature, or sink beneath it. She could no longer borrow from the future to help her through the present grief. Tomorrow would bring its own trial with it; so would the next day, and so would the next; each its own trial, and yet the very same that was now so unutterably grievous to be borne. The days of the far-off future would toil onward, still with the same burden for her to take up, and bear along with her, but never to fling down; for the accumulating days, and added years, would pile up their misery upon the heap of shame. Throughout them all, giving up her individuality, she would become the general symbol at which the preacher and moralist might point, and in which they might vivify and embody their images of woman's frailty and sinful passion. Thus the young and pure would be taught to look at her, with the scarlet letter flaming on her breast—at her, the child of honourable parents—at her, the mother of a babe, that would hereafter be a woman—at her, who had once been innocent—as the figure, the body, the reality of sin. And over her grave, the infamy that she must carry thither would be her only monument.

It may seem marvellous, that, with the world before her—kept by no restrictive clause of her condemnation within the limits of the Puritan settlement, so remote and so obscure—free to return to her birthplace, or to any other European land, and there hide her character and identity under a new exterior, as completely as if emerging into another state of being- and having also the passes of the dark, inscrutable forest open to her, where the wildness of her nature might assimilate itself with a people whose customs and life were alien from the law that had condemned her—it may seem marvellous, that this woman should still call that place her home, where, and where only, she must needs be the type of shame. But there is a fatality, a feeling so irresistible and inevitable that it has the force of doom, which almost invariably compels human beings to linger around and haunt, ghost-like, the spot where some great and marked event has given the colour to their lifetime; and still the more irresistibly, the darker the tinge that saddens it. Her sin, her ignominy, were the roots which she had struck into the soil. It was as if a new birth, with stronger assimilations than the first, had converted the forest-land, still so uncongenial to every other pilgrim and wanderer, into Hester Prynne's wild and dreary, but life-long home. All other scenes of earth—even that village of rural England, where happy infancy and stainless maidenhood seemed yet to be in her mother's keeping, like garments put off long ago—were foreign to her, in comparison. The chain that bound her here was of iron links, and galling[3] to her inmost soul, but could never be broken.

It might be, too—doubtless it was so, although she hid the secret from herself, and grew pale whenever it struggled out of her heart, like a serpent from its hole, —it might be that another feeling kept her within the scene and pathway that had been so fatal. There dwelt, there trode[4] the feet of one with whom she deemed herself connected in a union, that, unrecognised on earth, would bring them together before the bar of final judgment, and make that their marriage-altar, for a joint futurity of endless retribution. Over and over again, the tempter of souls had thrust this idea upon Hester's contemplation, and laughed at the passionate and desperate joy with which she seized, and then strove to cast it from her. She barely looked the idea in the face, and hastened to bar it in its dungeon. What she compelled herself to believe—what, finally, she reasoned upon, as her motive for continuing a resident of New England was half a truth, and half a self-delusion. Here, she said to herself, had been the scene of her guilt, and here should be the scene of her earthly punishment; and so, perchance, the torture of her daily shame would at length purge her soul, and work out another purity than that which she had lost; more saint-like, because the result of martyrdom.

Hester Prynne, therefore, did not flee. On the outskirts of the town, within the verge of the peninsula, but not in close vicinity to any other habitation, there was a small thatched cottage. It had been built by an earlier settler, and abandoned, because the soil about it was too sterile for cultivation, while its comparative remoteness put it out of the sphere of that social activity which already marked the habits of the emigrants. It stood on the shore, looking across a basin of the sea at the forest-covered hills, towards the west. A clump of scrubby trees, such as alone grew on the peninsula, did not so much conceal the cottage from view, as seem to denote that here was some object which would fain have been, or at least ought to be, concealed. In this little, lonesome dwelling, with some slender means that she possessed, and by the license of the magistrates, who still kept an inquisitorial watch over her, Hester established herself, with her infant child. A mystic shadow of suspicion immediately attached itself to the spot. Children, too young to comprehend wherefore this woman should be shut out from the sphere of human charities, would creep nigh enough to behold her plying her needle at the cottage-window, or standing in the doorway, or labouring in her little garden, or coming forth along the pathway that led townward; and, discerning the scarlet letter on her breast, would scamper off with a strange, contagious fear.

Lonely as was Hester's situation, and without a friend on earth who dared to show himself, she, however, incurred no risk of want. She possessed an art that sufficed, even in a land that afforded comparatively little scope for its exercise, to supply food for her thriving infant and herself. It was the art—then, as now, almost the only one within a woman's grasp—of needlework. She bore on her breast, in the curiously embroidered letter, a specimen of her delicate and imaginative skill, of which the dames of a court might gladly have availed themselves, to add the richer and more spiritual adornment of human ingenuity to their fabrics of silk and gold. Here, indeed, in the sable[5] simplicity that generally characterised the Puritanic modes of dress, there might be an infrequent call for the finer productions of her handiwork. Yet the taste of the age, demanding whatever was elaborate in compositions of this kind, did not fail to extend its influence over our stern progenitors, who had cast behind them so many fashions which it might seem harder to dispense with. Public ceremonies, such as ordinations, the installation of magistrates, and all that could give majesty to the forms in which a new government manifested itself to the people, were, as a matter of policy, marked by a stately and well-conducted ceremonial, and a sombre, but yet a studied magnificence. Deep ruffs, painfully wrought bands, and gorgeously embroidered gloves were all deemed necessary to the official state of men assuming the reins of power; and were readily allowed to individuals dignified by rank or wealth, even while sumptuary[6] laws forbade these and similar extravagances to the plebeian order. In the array of funerals, too, —whether for the apparel of the dead body, or to typify, by manifold emblematic-devices of sable cloth and snowy lawn, the sorrow of the survivors, —there was a frequent and characteristic demand for such labour as Hester Prynne could supply. Baby-linen—for babies then wore robes of state—afforded still another possibility of toil and emolument.

By degrees, nor very slowly, her handiwork became what would now be termed the fashion. Whether from commiseration for a woman of so miserable a destiny; or from the morbid curiosity that gives a fictitious value even to common or worthless things; or by whatever other intangible circumstance was then, as now, sufficient to bestow, on some persons, what others might seek in vain; or because Hester really filled a gap which must otherwise have remained vacant; it is certain that she had ready and fairly requited employment for as many hours as she saw fit to occupy with her needle. Vanity, it may be, chose to mortify itself, by putting on, for ceremonials of pomp and state, the garments that had been wrought by her sinful hands. Her needle-work was seen on the ruff of the Governor; military men wore it on their scarfs, and the minister on his hand; it decked the baby's little cap; it was shut up, to be mildewed and moulder away, in the coffins of the dead. But it is not recorded that, in a single instance, her skill was called in aid to embroider the white veil which was to cover the pure blushes of a bride. The exception indicated the ever relentless vigour with which society frowned upon her sin.

Hester sought not to acquire anything beyond a subsistence, of the plainest and most ascetic description, for herself, and a simple abundance for her child. Her own dress was of the coarsest materials and the most sombre hue; with only that one ornament, —the scarlet letter, —which it was her doom to wear. The child's attire, on the other hand, was distinguished by a fanciful, or, we might rather say, a fantastic ingenuity, which served, indeed, to heighten the airy charm that early began to develop itself in the little girl, but which appeared to have also a deeper meaning. We may speak further of it hereafter. Except for that small expenditure in the decoration of her infant, Hester bestowed all her superfluous means in charity, on wretches less miserable than herself, and who not infrequently insulted the hand that fed them. Much of the time, which she might readily have applied to the better efforts of her art, she employed in making coarse garments for the poor. It is probable that there was an idea of penance in this mode of occupation, and that she offered up a real sacrifice of enjoyment, in devoting so many hours to such rude handiwork. She had in her nature a rich, voluptuous, Oriental characteristic—a taste for the gorgeously beautiful, which, save in the exquisite productions of her needle, found nothing else, in all the possibilities of her life, to exercise itself upon. Women derive a pleasure, incomprehensible to the other sex, from the delicate toil of the needle. To Hester Prynne it might have been a mode of expressing, and therefore soothing, the passion of her life. Like all other joys, she rejected it as sin. This morbid meddling of conscience with an immaterial matter betokened, it is to be feared, no genuine and steadfast penitence, but something doubtful, something that might be deeply wrong, beneath.

In this manner, Hester Prynne came to have a part to perform in the world. With her native energy of character, and rare capacity, it could not entirely cast her off, although it had set a mark upon her, more intolerable to a woman's heart than that which branded the brow of Cain. In all her intercourse with society, however, there was nothing that made her feel as if she belonged to it. Every gesture, every word, and even the silence of those with whom she came in contact, implied, and often expressed, that she was banished, and as much alone as if she inhabited another sphere, or communicated with the common nature by other organs and senses than the rest of human kind. She stood apart from moral interests, yet close beside them, like a ghost that revisits the familiar fireside, and can no longer make itself seen or felt; no more smile with the household joy, nor mourn with the kindred sorrow; or, should it succeed in manifesting its forbidden sympathy, awakening only terror and horrible repugnance. These emotions, in fact, and its bitterest scorn besides, seemed to be the sole portion that she retained in the universal heart. It was not an age of delicacy; and her position, although she understood it well, and was in little danger of forgetting it, was often brought before her vivid self-perception, like a new anguish, by the rudest touch upon the tenderest spot. The poor, as we have already said, whom she sought out to be the objects of her bounty, often reviled the hand that was stretched forth to succour them. Dames of elevated rank, likewise, whose doors she entered in the way of her occupation, were accustomed to distil drops of bitterness into her heart; sometimes through that alchemy of quiet malice, by which women can concoct a subtile poison from ordinary trifles; and sometimes, also, by a coarser expression, that fell upon the sufferer's defenceless breast like a rough blow upon an ulcerated[7] wound. Hester had schooled herself long and well; she never responded to these attacks, save by a flush of crimson that rose irrepressibly over her pale cheek, and again subsided into the depths of her bosom. She was patient—a martyr, indeed, —but she forbore[8] to pray for her enemies; lest, in spite of her forgiving aspirations, the words of the blessing should stubbornly twist themselves into a curse.

Continually, and in a thousand other ways, did she feel the innumerable throbs of anguish that had been so cunningly contrived for her by the undying, the ever-active sentence of the Puritan tribunal. Clergymen paused in the street to address words of exhortation[9], that brought a crowd, with its mingled grin and frown, around the poor, sinful woman. If she entered a church, trusting to share the Sabbath smile of the Universal Father, it was often her mishap to find herself the text of the discourse. She grew to have a dread of children; for they had imbibed from their parents a vague idea of something horrible in this dreary woman, gliding silently through the town, with never any companion but one only child. Therefore, first allowing her to pass, they pursued her at a distance with shrill cries, and the utterance of a word that had no distinct purport to their own minds, but was none the less terrible to her, as proceeding from lips that babbled it unconsciously. It seemed to argue so wide a diffusion of her shame, that all nature knew of it; it could have caused her no deeper pang, had the leaves of the trees whispered the dark story among themselves, —had the summer breeze murmured about it, —had the wintry blast shrieked it aloud! Another peculiar torture was felt in the gaze of a new eye. When strangers looked curiously at the scarlet letter, —and none ever failed to do so they branded it afresh into Hester's soul; so that, oftentimes[10], she could scarcely refrain, yet always did refrain, from covering the symbol with her hand. But then, again, an accustomed eye had likewise its own anguish to inflict. Its cool stare of familiarity was intolerable. From first to last, in short, Hester Prynne had always this dreadful agony in feeling a human eye upon the token; the spot never grew callous[11]; it seemed, on the contrary, to grow more sensitive with daily torture.

But sometimes, once in many days, or perchance in many months, she felt an eye—a human eye—upon the ignominious brand, that seemed to give a momentary relief, as if half of her agony were shared. The next instant, back it all rushed again, with still a deeper throb of pain; for, in that brief interval, she had sinned anew. Had

Hester sinned alone?

Her imagination was somewhat affected, and, had she been of a softer moral and intellectual fibre, would have been still more so, by the strange and solitary anguish of her life. Walking to and fro, with those lonely footsteps, in the little world with which she was outwardly connected, it now and then appeared to Hester, — if altogether fancy, it was nevertheless too potent to be resisted, — she felt or fancied, then, that the scarlet letter had endowed her with a new sense. She shuddered to believe, yet could not help believing, that it gave her a sympathetic knowledge of the hidden sin in other hearts. She was terror-stricken by the revelations that were thus made. What were they? Could they be other than the insidious whispers of the bad angel, who would fain[12] have persuaded the struggling woman, as yet only half his victim, that the outward guise of purity was but a lie, and that, if truth were everywhere to be shown, a scarlet letter would blaze forth on many a bosom besides Hester Prynne's? Or, must she receive those intimations—so obscure, yet so distinct—as truth? In all her miserable experience, there was nothing else so awful and so loathsome as this sense. It perplexed, as well as shocked her, by the irreverent inopportuneness[13] of the occasions that brought it into vivid action. Sometimes the red infamy upon her breast would give a sympathetic throb, as she passed near a venerable minister or magistrate, the model of piety and justice, to whom that age of antique reverence looked up, as to a mortal man in fellowship with angels. "What evil thing is at hand?" would Hester say to herself. Lifting her reluctant eyes, there would be nothing human within the scope of view, save the form of this earthly saint! Again, a mystic sisterhood would contumaciously assert itself, as she met the sanctified frown of some matron, who, according to the rumour of all tongues, had kept cold snow within her bosom throughout life. That unsunned snow in the matron's bosom, and the burning shame on Hester Prynne's—what had the two in common? Or, once more, the electric thrill would give her warning, —"Behold, Hester, here is a companion!"—and, looking up, she would detect the eyes of a young maiden glancing at the scarlet letter, shyly and aside, and quickly averted, with a faint, chill crimson in her cheeks; as if her purity were somewhat sullied by that momentary glance. O Fiend, whose talisman was that fatal symbol, wouldst thou leave nothing, whether in youth or age, for this poor sinner to revere?—such loss of faith is ever one of the saddest results of sin. Be it accepted as a proof that all was not corrupt in this poor victim of her own frailty, and man's hard law, that Hester Prynne yet struggled to believe that no fellow-mortal was guilty like herself.

The vulgar, who, in those dreary old times, were always contributing a grotesque horror to what interested their imaginations, had a story about the scarlet letter which we might readily work up into a terrific legend. They averred[14], that the symbol was not mere scarlet cloth, tinged in an earthly dye-pot, but was red-hot with infernal fire, and could be seen glowing all alight, whenever Hester Prynne walked abroad in the night-time. And we must needs say, it seared Hester's bosom so deeply, that perhaps there was more truth in the rumour than our modern incredulity may be inclined to admit.

## Notes

1. Shocking, explicit, sensational.

2. An extremely unpleasant experience, especially one that lasts for a long time.

3. Making you feel annoyed or angry, especially because something is not fair.

4. The past tense of tread: to walk or step on something; to press or crush something into the floor or ground when you walk.

5. The skin and fur of the sable, used for making expensive coats and artists' brushes.

6. Intended to regulate personal behaviour on moral or religious grounds.

7. Covered with an ulcer or ulcers.

8. The past tense of forbear.

9. Appeal / urging.

10. Often.

11. Cold-hearted, insensitive.

12. Willingly or with pleasure.

13. (formal) Being ill-timed /inconvenient.

14. To say something in a very determined way because you believe strongly in it or you are certain it is true.

## Questions

1. What are the symbolic meanings of "Needle Work" in this chapter?

2. Try to illustrate the theme of this part.

### (7) Harriet Beecher Stowe (1811—1896)

Harriet Beecher was born in Litchfield, Connecticut, the seventh child and fourth daughter of Lyman Beecher, an eminent Evangelical Calvinist minister, and Roxana Foote Beecher. Her father was a controversial Calvinist preacher. Her mother died when she was four. When she was 11 years old, she entered Hartford Female Seminary, a school founded by her sister Catherine. At that time Hartford Female Seminary was one of only a handful of schools that took the education of girls seriously. In Hartford, she came into contact with fugitive slaves and learned about life in the south. Later she settled in Maine with her husband, a professor at her father's Theological Seminary.

In 1834, she began her literary career when she won the prize contest of the Western Monthly Magazine. Soon she was a regular contributor of stories and essays. In 1843, her first book, The Mayflower, appeared. In 1852, her best known novel, Uncle Tom's Cabin, was published. She was influenced by many people. The most prominent influences in her life were from her father, her sister, her younger brother, and her husband. When she visited Kentucky, she witnessed the life of slaves, which provided material for her later novels. Again, she was influenced by the strong and anti-slavery sentiment in her father's school. The sentiment became her tone of the novels. It is said that President Lincoln said to her, "So you are the little woman who wrote the book that made this big war."

Her writing career spanned 51 years, and she did this while she was busy raising seven children. She wrote 30 books, including novels, three travel memoirs, and articles, and she was influential in both her writings and her public stances on social issues of the day.

*Uncle Tom's Cabin* was the first American novel translated into Chinese.

*Uncle Tom's Cabin* depicts the harsh life of African Americans during slavery. Incensed by the passage of the Fugitive Slave Act in 1850, which made it criminal for anybody to aid an escaping slave, Stowe began writing Uncle Tom's Cabin, which was serialized during 1851 in Washington, D.C.'s weekly antislavery journal, The National Era. In this setting, the novel was well received, but its audience was limited to adherents to the abolitionist cause. The novel had an entirely different impact when it appeared in book form in 1852. It sold around 3,000 copies the day of publication and more than 350,000 copies by the end of the year. As one reviewer (in the Literary World) put it: "No literary work of any character or merit, whether of poetry or prose, or imagination or observation, fancy or fact, truth or fiction, that has ever been written since there have been writers or readers, has ever commanded so great a popular success." Between 1852 and 1860 it was reprinted in twenty-two languages; and in the United States during the last half of the 19th-century, it was outsold only by the Bible. The book helped push abolitionism from the margins to the mainstream, and thus helped move the nation closer to Civil War—an outcome that, in fact, Stowe had hoped to avert by her depictions of slave suffering. Her aim had been to inspire voluntary emancipation by compellingly demonstrating the evil and Unchristian nature of slavery.

The following text used is that of the first American edition of

*Uncle Tom's Cabin* (1852), which is from *The Norton Anthology of American Literature* (shorter 6th edition).

## Chapter XII SELECT INCIDENT OF LAWFUL TRADE

"In Ramah there was a voice heard,—weeping, and lamentation, and great mourning; Rachel weeping for her children, and would not be comforted."[1] Mr.Haley and Tom jogged onward in their wagon, each, for a time, absorbed in his own reflections. Now, the reflections of two men sitting side by side are a curious thing,—seated on the same seat, having the same eyes, ears, hands and organs of all sorts, and having pass before their eyes the same objects,—it is wonderful what a variety we shall find in these same reflections!

As, for example, Mr.Haley: he thought first of Tom's length, and breadth, and height, and what he would sell for, if he was kept fat and in good case till he got him into market. He thought of how he should make out his gang; he thought of the respective market value of certain supposititious men and women and children who were to compose it, and other kindred topics of the business; then he thought of himself, and how humane he was, that whereas other men chained their "niggers" hand and foot both, he only put fetters on the feet, and left Tom the us e of his hands, as long a s he behaved well; and he sighed to think how ungrateful human nature was, so that there was even room to doubt whether To m appreciated his mercies. He had been taken in so by "niggers" whom he had favored; but still he was astonished to consider how good-natured he yet remained!

As to Tom, he was thinking over some words of an unfashionable old book, which kept running through his head again and again, as follows: "We have here no continuing city, but we seek one to come; wherefore God himself is not ashamed to be called our God; for he hath prepared for us a city." [2] These words of an ancient volume, got up principally by "ignorant and unlearned men," have, through all time, kept up, somehow, a strange sort of power over the minds of poor, simple fellows, like Tom. They stir up the soul from its depths, and rouse, as with trumpet call, courage, energy, and enthusiasm, where before was only the blackness of despair.

Mr.Haley pulled out of his pocket sundry newspapers, and began looking over their advertisements, with absorbed interest. He was not a remarkably fluent reader, and was in the habit of reading in a sort of recitative hal faloud, by way of calling in his ears to verify the deductions of his eyes. In this tone he slowly recited the following paragraph:

"EXECUTOR'S SALE,—NEGROES!—Agreeably to order of court, will be sold, on Tuesday, February 20, before the Court-house door, in the town of Washington, Kentucky, the following negroes: Hagar, aged 60 ; John, aged 30 ; Ben, aged 21 ; Saul, aged 25 ; Albert, aged 14. Sold for the benefit of the creditors and heirs of the estate of Jesse Blutchford, Esq.

SAMUEL MORRIS,

THOMA S FLINT,

Executors."

"This yer I must look at," said he to Tom, for want of somebody else to talk to.

"Ye see, I'm going to get up a prime gang to take down with ye, Tom; it'll make it sociable and pleasant like, —good company will, ye know. We must drive right to Washington[3] first and foremost, and then I'll clap you into jail, while I does the business."

Tom received this agreeable intelligence quite meekly; simply wondering, in his own heart, how many of these doomed men had wives and children, and whether they would feel as he did about leaving them. It is to be confessed, too, that the naive, off-hand information that he was to be thrown into jail by no means produced an agreeable impression on a poor fellow who had always prided himself on a strictly honest and upright course of life. Yes, Tom, we must confess it, was rather proud of his honesty, poor fellow,— not having very much else to be proud of;—if he had belonged to some of the higher walks of society, he, perhaps, would never have been reduced to such straits. However, the day wore on, and the evening saw Haley and To m comfortably accommodate d in Washington,—the one in a tavern, and the other in a jail.

About eleven o'clock the next day, a mixed throng was gathered around the court-house steps,—smoking, chewing, spitting, swearing, and conversing, according to their respective tastes and turns,— waiting for the auction to commence. The men and women to be sold sat in a group apart, talking in a low tone to each other. The woman who had been advertised by the name of Hagar was a regular African in feature and figure. She might have been sixty, but was older than that by hard work and disease, was partially blind, and somewhat crippled with rheumatism. By her side stood her only remaining son, Albert, a bright-looking little fellow of fourteen years. The boy was the only survivor of a large family, who had been successively sold away from her to a southern market. The mother held on to him with both her shaking hands, and eyed with intense trepidation every one who walked up to examine him.

"Don't be feard, Aunt Hagar," said the oldest of the men, "I spoke to Mas'r Thomas about it, and he thought he might manage to sell you in a lot both together.""Dey needn't call me worn out yet," said she, lifting her shaking hands. "I can cook yet, and scrub, and scour,—I'm wuth a buying, if I do come cheap; —tell em dat ar,—you tell em," she added, earnestly.

Haley here forced his way into the group, walked up to the old man, pulled his mouth open and looked in, felt of his teeth, made him stand and straighten himself, bend his back, and perform various evolutions to show his muscles; and then passed on to the next, and put him through the same trial. Walking up last to the boy, he felt of his arms, straightened his hands, and looked at his fingers, and made him jump, to show his agility.

"He an't gwine to be sold widout me!" said the old woman, with passionate eagerness; "he and I goes in a lot together; I's rail strong yet, Mas'r, and can do heaps o' work,—heaps on it, Mas'r."

"On plantation?" said Haley, with a contemptuous glance. "Likely story!" and, as if satisfied with his examination, he walked out and looked, and stood with his hands in his pocket, his cigar in his mouth, and his hat cocked on one side, ready for action.

"What think of em?" said a man who had been following Haley's examination, a s if to make up his own mind from it.

"Wal," said Haley, spitting, "I shall put in, I think, for the youngerly one s and the boy."

"They want to sell the boy and the old woman together," said the man.

"Find it a tight pull;—why, she's an old rack o' bones,—not worth her salt."

"You wouldn't, then?" said the man.

"Anybody'd be a fool't would. She's half blind, crooked with rheumatis, and foolish to boot."

"Some buys up these yer old critturs, and ses there's a sight more wear in 'em than a body'd think," said the man, reflectively.

"No go, 't all," said Haley; "wouldn't take her for a present,—fact,—I've seen, now."

"Wal, 'tis kinder pity, now, not to buy her with her son,—he r heart seems so sot on him,—s'pos e they fling her in cheap."

"Them that's got money to spend that ar way, it's all well enough. I shall bid off on that ar boy for a plantation-hand;—wouldn't be bothered with her, no way,—not if they'd give her to me," said Haley.

"She'll take on desp't," said the man.

"Nat'lly, she will," said the trader, coolly.

The conversation was here interrupted by a busy hu m in the audience; and the auctioneer, a short, bustling, important fellow, elbowed his way into the crowd. The old woman drew in her breath, and caught instinctively at her son.

“Keep close to yer mammy, Albert,—close,—dey’ll put us up togedder,” she said.

“O, mammy, I’m feared they won’t,” said the boy.

“Dey must, child; I can’t live, no ways, if they don’t,” said the old creature, vehemently.

The stentorian tones of the auctioneer, calling out to clear the way, now announced that the sale was about to commence. A place was cleared, and the bidding began. The different men on the list were soon knocked off at prices which showed a pretty brisk demand in the market; two of them fell to Haley.

“Come, now, young un,” said the auctioneer, giving the boy a touch with his hammer, “be up and show your springs, now.”

“Put us two up togedder, togedder,—do please, Mas’r,” said the old woman, holding fast to her boy.

“Be off,” said the man, gruffy, pushing her hands away; “you come last. Now, darkey, spring;” and, with the word, he pushed the boy toward the block, while a deep, heavy groan rose behind him. The boy paused, and looked back; but there was no time to stay, and, dashing the tears from his large, bright eyes, he was up in a moment.

His fine figure, alert limbs, and bright face, raised an instant competition, and half a dozen bids simultaneously met the ear of the auctioneer. Anxious, half-frightened, he looked from side to side, as he heard the clatter of contending bids,—now here, now there,—till the hammer fell. Haley had got him. He was pushed from the block toward his new master, but stopped one moment, and looked back, when his poor old mother, trembling in every limb, held out her shaking hands toward him.

"Buy me too, Mas'r, for de dear Lord's sake!—buy me,—I shall die if you don't!"

"You'll die if I do, that's the kink of it," said Haley,—"no!" And he turned on his heel.

The bidding for the poor old creature was summary. The man who had addressed Haley, and who seemed not destitute of compassion, bought her for a trifle, and the spectators began to disperse.

The poor victims of the sale, who had been brought up in one place together for years, gathered round the despairing old mother, whose agony was pitiful to see.

"Couldn't dey leave me one? Mas'r allers said I should have one,—he did," she repeated over and over, in heartbroken tones.

"Trust in the Lord, Aunt Hagar," said the oldest of the men, sorrowfully.

"What good will it do?" said she, sobbing passionately.

"Mother, mother,—don't! don't!" said the boy. "They say you's got a good master."

"I don't care,—I don't care. O, Albert! oh, my boy! you's my last baby. Lord, how ken I?"

"Come, take her off, can't some of ye?" said Haley, dryly; "don't do no good for her to go on that ar way."

The old men of the company, partly by persuasion and partly by force, loosed the poor creature's last despairing hold, and, as they led her off to her new master's wagon, strove to comfort her.

"Now!" said Haley, pushing his three purchases together, and producing a bundle of handcuffs, which he proceeded to put on their wrists; and fastening each handcuff to a long chain, he drove them before him to the jail.

A few days saw Haley, with his possessions, safely deposited on one of the Ohio boats. It was the commencement of his gang, to be augmented, as the boat moved on, by various other merchandise of the same kind, which he, or his agent, had stored for him in various points along shore.

The La Belle Riviere, as brave and beautiful a boat as ever walked the waters of her namesake river, was floating gayly down the stream, under a brilliant sky, the stripes and stars of free America waving and fluttering over head; the guards crowded with well-dressed ladies and gentlemen walking and enjoying the delightful day. All was full of life, buoyant and rejoicing;— all but Haley's gang, who were stored, with other freight, on the lower deck, and who, somehow, did not seem to appreciate their various privileges, as they sat in a knot, talking to each other in low tones.

"Boys," said Haley, coming up, briskly, "I hope you keep up good heart, and are cheerful. Now, no sulks, ye see; keep stiff upper lip, boys; do well by me, and I'll do well by you."

The boys addressed responded the invariable "Yes, Mas'r," for ages the watchword of poor Africa; but it's to be owned they did not look particularly cheerful; they had their various little prejudices in favor of wives, mothers, sisters, and children, seen for the last time,—and though "they that wasted them required of them mirth," [4] it was not instantly forthcoming.

"I've got a wife," spoke out the article enumerated as "John, aged thirty," and he laid his chained hand on Tom's knee,—"and she don't know a word about this, poor girl!"

"Where does she live?" said Tom.

"In a tavern a piece down here," said John; "I wish, now, I could see her once more in this world," he added.

Poor John! It was rather natural; and the tears that fell, as he spoke, cam e as naturally as if he had been a white man. To m drew a long breath from a sore heart, and tried, in his poor way, to comfort him.

And over head, in the cabin, sat fathers and mothers, husbands and wives; and merry, dancing children moved round among them, like so many little butterflies, and everything was going on quite easy and comfortable.

"O, mamma," said a boy, who had just com e up from below, "there's a negro trader on board, and he's brought four or five slaves down there."

"Poor creatures!" said the mother, in a tone between grief and indignation.

"What's that?" said another lady.

"Some poor slaves below," said the mother.

"And they've got chains on," said the boy.

"What a sham e to our country that such sights are to be seen!" said another lady.

"O, there's a great deal to be said on both sides of the subject," said a genteel woman, who sat at her state-room door sewing, while her little girl and boy were playing round her. "I've been south, and I must say I think the negroes are better off than they would be to be free."

"In some respects, some of them are well off, I grant," said the lady to whose remark she had answered. "The most dreadful part of slavery, to my mind, is its outrages on the feelings and affections,—the separating of families, for example."

"That is a bad thing, certainly," said the other lady, holding up a baby's dress she had just completed, and looking intently on its trimmings; "but then, I fancy, it don't occur often."

"O, it does," said the first lady, eagerly; "I've lived many years in Kentucky and Virginia both, and I've seen enough to make any one's heart sick. Suppose, ma'am, your two children, there, should be taken from you, and sold?"

"We can't reason from our feelings to those of this class of persons," said the other lady, sorting out some worsteds on her lap.

"Indeed, ma'am, you can know nothing of them, if you say so," answered the first lady, warmly. "I was born and brought up among them. I know they do feel, just as keenly,—even more so, perhaps,—as we do."

The lady said "Indeed!" yawned, and looked out the cabin window, and finally repeated, for a finale, the remark with which she had begun,—"After all, I think they are better off than they would be to be free."

"It's undoubtedly the intention of Providence that the African race should be servants,—kept in a low condition," said a grave-looking gentleman in black, a clergyman, seated by the cabin door. " 'Cursed be Canaan; a servant of servants shall he be,' the scripture says."[5]

"I say, stranger, is that ar what that text means?" said a tall man, standing by.

"Undoubtedly. It pleased Providence, for some inscrutable reason, to doom the race to bondage, ages ago; and we must not set up our opinion against that."

"Well, then, we'll all go ahead and buy up niggers," said the man, "if that's the way of Providence,—won't we, Squire?" said he, turning to Haley, who had been standing, with his hands in his pockets, by the stove, and intently listening to the conversation.

"Yes," continued the tall man, "we must all be resigned to the decrees of Providence. Niggers must be sold, and trucked round, and kept under; it's what they's made for. 'Pears like this yer view's quite refreshing, an't it, stranger?" said he to Haley.

"I never thought on't," said Haley. "I couldn't have said as much, myself; I ha'nt no laming. I took up the trade just to make a living; if't an't right, I calculated to 'pent on't in time, ye know." "And now you'll save yerself the trouble, won't ye?" said the tall man. "See what't is, now, to know scripture. If ye'd only studied yer Bible, like this yer good man, ye might have know'd it before, and saved ye a heap o' trouble. Ye could jist have said, 'Cussed be'—what's his name?—'and 't would all have come right.' " And the stranger, who was no other than the honest drover whom we introduced to our readers in the Kentucky tavern[6], sat down, and began smoking, with a curious smile on his long, dry face.

A tall, slender young man, with a face expressive of great feeling and intelligence, here broke in, and repeated the words, " 'All things whatsoever ye would that men should do unto you, do ye even so unto them.' I suppose," he added, "that is scripture, as much as 'Cursed be Canaan.' "

"Wal, it seems quite as plain a text, stranger," said John the drover, "to poor fellows like us, now;" and John smoked on like a volcano.

The young man paused, looked as if he was going to say more, when suddenly the boat stopped, and the company mad e the usual steamboat rush, to see where they were landing.

"Both them ar chaps parsons?" said John to one of the men, as they were going out.

The man nodded.

As the boat stopped, a black woman cam e running wildly up the plank, darted into the crowd, flew up to where the slave gang sat, and threw her arms round that unfortunate piece of merchandise before enumerated— "John, aged thirty," and with sobs and tears bemoaned him as her husband.

But what needs tell the story, told too oft,—every day told,—of heartstrings rent and broken,—the weak broken and torn for the profit and convenience of the strong! It needs not to be told;—every day is telling it,—telling it, too, in the ear of One who is not deaf, though he be long silent.

The young man who had spoken for the cause of humanity and Go d before stood with folded arms, looking on this scene. He turned, and Haley was standing at his side. "My friend," he said, speaking with thick utterance, "how can you, how dare you, carry on a trade like this? Look at those poor creatures! Here I am, rejoicing in my heart that I am going home to my wife and child; and the same bell which is a signal to carry me onward towards them will part this poor man and his wife forever. Depend upon it, God will bring you into judgment for this."

The trader turned away in silence.

"I say, now," said the drover, touching his elbow, "there's differences in parsons, an't there? 'Cussed be Canaan ' don't seem to go down with this 'un, does it?" Haley gave an uneasy growl. "And that ar an't the worse on't," said John; "mabb e it won't go down with the Lord, neither, when ye come to settle with Him, one o' these days, as all on us must, I reckon."

Haley walked reflectively to the other end of the boat. "If I make pretty handsomely on one or two next gangs," he thought, "I reckon I'll stop off this yer; it's really getting dangerous." And he took out his pocket-book, and began adding over his accounts,—a process which many gentlemen besides Mr.Haley have found a specific[7] for an uneasy conscience.

The boat swept proudly away from the shore, and all went on merrily, as before. Men talked, and loafed, and read, and smoked. Women sewed, and children played, and the boat passed on her way.

One day, when she lay to for a while at a small town in Kentucky, Haley went up into the place on a little matter of business.

Tom, whose fetters did not prevent his taking a moderate circuit, had drawn near the side of the boat, and stood listlessly gazing over the railings. After a time, he saw the trader returning, with an alert step, in company with a colored woman, bearing in her arms a young child. She was dressed quite respectably, and a colored man followed her, bringing along a small trunk. The woman came cheerfully onward, talking, as she came, with the man who bore her trunk, and so passed up the plank into the boat. The bell rung, the steamer whizzed, the engine groaned and coughed, and away swept the boat down the river.

The woman walked forward among the boxes and bales of the lower deck, and, sitting down, busied herself with chirruping to her baby.

Haley made a turn or two about the boat, and then, coming up, seated himself near her, and began saying something to her in an indifferent undertone.

Tom soon noticed a heavy cloud passing over the woman's brow; and that she answered rapidly, and with great vehemence.

"I don't believe it, —I won't believe it!" he heard her say. "You're jist a foolin with me."

"If you won't believe it, look here!" said the man, drawing out a paper; "this yer's the bill of sale, and there's your master's name to it; and I paid down good solid cash for it, too, I can tell you,—so, now!"

"I don't believe Mas'r would cheat me so; it can't be true!" said the woman, with increasing agitation.

"You can ask any of these men here, that can read writing. Here!" he said, to a man that was passing by, "jist read this yer, won't you! This yer gal won't believe me, when I tell her what't is."

"Why, it's a bill of sale, signed by John Fosdick," said the man, "making over to you the girl Lucy and her child. It's all straight enough, for aught I see."

The woman's passionate exclamations collected a crowd around her, and the trader briefly explained to them the cause of the agitation.

"He told me that I was going down to Louisville, to hire out as cook to the same tavern where my husband works, —that's what Mas'r told me, his own self; and I can't believe he'd lie to me," said the woman.

"But he has sold you, my poor woman, there's no doubt about it," said a good-natured looking man, who had been examining the papers; "he has done it, and no mistake."

"Then it's no account talking," said the woman, suddenly growing quite calm; and, clasping her child tighter in her arms, she sat down on her box, turned her back round, and gazed listlessly into the river.

"Going to take it easy, after all!" said the trader. "Gal's got grit, I see."

The woman looked calm, as the boat went on; and a beautiful soft summer breeze passed like a compassionate spirit over her head, —the gentle breeze, that never inquires whether the brow is dusky or fair that it fans. And she saw sunshine sparkling on the water, in golden ripples, and heard gay voices, full of ease and pleasure, talking around her everywhere; but her heart lay as if a great stone had fallen on it. Her baby raised himself up against her, and stroked her cheeks with his little hands; and, springing up and down, crowing and chatting, seemed determined to arouse her. She strained him suddenly and tightly in her arms, and slowly one tear after another fell on his wondering, unconscious face; and gradually she seemed, and little by little, to grow calmer, and busied herself with tending and nursing him.

The child, a boy of ten months, was uncommonly large and strong of his age, and very vigorous in his limbs. Never, for a moment, still, he kept his mother constantly busy in holding him, and guarding his springing activity.

"That's a fine chap!" said a man, suddenly stopping opposite to him, with his hands in his pockets. "How old is he?"

"Ten months and a half," said the mother.

The man whistled to the boy, and offered him part of a stick of candy, which he eagerly grabbed at, and very soon had it in a baby's general depository, to wit, his mouth.

"Rum fellow!" said the man. "Knows what's what!" and he whistled, and walked on. When he had got to the other side of the boat, he came across Haley, who was smoking on top of a pile of boxes.

The stranger produced a match, and lighted a cigar, saying, as he did so, "Decentish kind o' wench you've got round there, stranger."

"Why, I reckon she is tol'able fair," said Haley, blowing the smoke out of his mouth.

"Taking her down south?" said the man.

Haley nodded, and smoked on.

"Plantation hand?" said the man.

"Wal," said Haley, "I'm fillin' out an order for a plantation, and I think I shall put her in. They telled me she was a good cook; and they can us e her for that, or set her at the cotton-picking. She's got the right fingers for that; I looked at 'em. Sell well, either way;" and Haley resumed his cigar.

"They won't want the young 'un on a plantation," said the man.

"I shall sell him, first chance I find," said Haley, lighting another cigar.

"S'pose you'd be selling him tol'able cheap," said the stranger, mounting the pile of boxes, and sitting down comfortably.

"Don't know 'bout that," said Haley; "he's a pretty smart young 'un, — straight, fat, strong; flesh as hard as a brick!"

"Very true, but then there's all the bother and expense of raisin'."

"Nonsense!" said Haley; "they is raised as easy as any kind of critter there is going; they an't a bit more trouble than pups. This yer cha p will be running all round, in a month."

"I've got a good place for raisin', and I thought of takin' in a little more stock," said the man. "One cook lost a young 'un last week,—got drownded in a wash-tub, while she was a hangin' out clothes,—and I reckon it would be well enough to set her to raisin' this yer."

Haley and the stranger smoked a while in silence, neither seeming willing to broach the test question of the interview. At last the man resumed: "You wouldn't think of wantin' more than ten dollars for that ar chap, seeing you rawst get him off yer hand, any how?" Haley shook his head, and spit impressively.

"That won't do, no ways," he said, and began his smoking again.

"Well, stranger, what will you take?"

"Well, now," said Haley, "I could raise that ar chap myself, or get him raised; he's oncommon likely and healthy, and he'd fetch a hundred dollars, six months hence; and, in a year or two, he'd bring two hundred, if I had him in the right spot;—so I shan't take a cent less nor fifty for him now."

"O, stranger! that's rediculous, altogether," said the man.

"Fact!" said Haley, with a decisive nod of his head.

"I'll give thirty for him," said the stranger, "but not a cent more."

"Now, I'll tell ye what I will do," said Haley, spitting again, with renewed decision. "I'll split the difference, and say forty-five; and that's the most I will do."

"Well, agreed!" said the man, after an interval.

"Done!" said Haley. "Where do you land?" "At Louisville," said the man.

"Louisville," said Haley. "Very fair, we get there about dusk. Chap will be asleep,—all fair,—get him off quietly, and no screaming,—happens beautiful,—I like to do everything quietly,—I hates all kind of agitation and fluster." And so, after a transfer of certain bills had passed from the man's pocket-book to the trader's, he resumed his cigar.

It was a bright, tranquil evening when the boat stopped at the wharf at Louisville. The woman had been sitting with her baby in her arms, now wrapped in a heavy sleep. When she heard the name of the place called out, she hastily laid the child down in a little cradle formed by the hollow among the boxes, first carefully spreading under it her cloak; and then she sprung to the side of the boat, in hopes that, among the various hotel-waiters who thronged the wharf, she might see her husband. In this hope, she pressed forward to the front rails, and, stretching far over them, strained her eyes intently on the moving heads on the shore, and the crowd pressed in between her and the child.

"Now's your time," said Haley, taking the sleeping child up, and handing him to the stranger. "Don't wake him up, and set him to crying, now; it would make a devil of a fuss with the gal." The man took the bundle carefully, and was soon lost in the crowd that went up the wharf.

When the boat, creaking, and groaning, and puffing, had loosed from the wharf, and was beginning slowly to strain herself along, the woman returned to her old seat. The trader was sitting there,—the child was gone!

"Why, why,—where?" she began, in bewildered surprise.

"Lucy," said the trader, "your child's gone; you may as well know it first as last. You see, I know'd you couldn't take him down south; and I got a chance to sell him to a first-rate family, that'll raise him better than you can."

The trader had arrived at that stage of Christian and political perfection which has been recommended by some preachers and politicians of the north, lately, in which he had completely overcome every humane weakness and prejudice. His heart was exactly where yours, sir, and mine could be brought, with proper effort and cultivation. The wild look of anguish and utter despair that the woman cast on him might have disturbed one less practised; but he was used to it. He had seen that same look hundreds of times. You can get used to such things, too, my friend; and it is the great object of recent efforts to make our whole northern community used to them, for the glory of the Union. So the trader only regarded the mortal anguish which he saw working in those dark features, those clenched hands, and suffocating breathings, as necessary incidents of the trade, and merely calculated whether she was going to scream, and get up a commotion on the boat; for, like other supporters of our peculiar institution, he decidedly disliked agitation.

But the woman did not scream. The shot had passed too straight and direct through the heart, for cry or tear.

Dizzily she sat down. Her slack hands fell lifeless by her side. Her eyes looked straight forward, but she saw nothing. All the noise and hum of the boat, the groaning of the machinery, mingled dreamily to her bewildered ear; and the poor, dumb-stricken heart had neither cry nor tear to show for its utter misery. She was quite calm.

The trader, who, considering his advantages, was almost as humane as some of our politicians, seemed to feel called on to administer such consolation as the case admitted of.

"I know this yer come s kinder hard, at first, Lucy," said he; "but such a smart, sensible gal as you are, won't give way to it. You see it's necessary, and can't be helped!"

"O! don't, Mas'r, don't!" said the woman, with a voice like one that is smothering.

"You're a smart wench, Lucy," he persisted; "I mean to do well by ye, and get ye a nice place down river; and you'll soon get another husband,—such a likely gal as you."

"O! Mas'r, if you only won't talk to me now," said the woman, in a voice of such quick and living anguish that the trader felt that there was something at present in the case beyond his style of operation. He got up, and the woman turned away, and buried her head in her cloak.

The trader walked up and down for a time, and occasionally stopped and looked at her.

"Take s it hard, rather," he soliloquized, "but quiet, tho';—let her sweat a while; she'll com e right, by and by!"

Tom had watched the whole transaction from first to last, and had a perfect understanding of its results. To him, it looked like something unutterably horrible and cruel, because, poor, ignorant black soul! he had not learned to generalize, and to take enlarged views. If he had only been instructed by certain ministers of Christianity, he might have thought better of it, and seen in it an every-day incident of a lawful trade; a trade which is the vital support of an institution which some American divines tell us has no evils but such as are inseparable from any other relations in social and domestic life. But Tom, as we see, being a poor, ignorant fellow, whose reading had been confined entirely to the New Testament, could not comfort and solace himself with views like these. His very soul bled within him for what seemed to him the wrongs of the poor suffering thing that lay like a crushed reed on the boxes; the feeling, living, bleeding, yet immortal thing, which American state law coolly classes with the bundles, and bales, and boxes, among which she is lying.

Tom drew near, and tried to say something; but she only groaned. Honestly, and with tears running down his own cheeks, he spoke of a heart of love in the skies, of a pitying Jesus, and an eternal home; but the ear was deaf with anguish, and the palsied heart could not feel.

Night came on, —night calm, unmoved, and glorious, shining down with her innumerable and solemn angel eyes, twinkling, beautiful, but silent. There was no speech nor language, no pitying voice nor helping hand, from that distant sky. One after another, the voices of business or pleasure died away; all on the boat were sleeping, and the ripples at the prow were plainly heard. To m stretched himself out on a box, and there, as he lay, he heard, ever and anon, a smothered sob or cry from the prostate creature, —"O! what shall I do? O Lord! O good Lord, do help me!" and so, ever and anon, until the murmur died away in silence.

At midnight, Tom waked, with a sudden start. Something black passed quickly by him to the side of the boat, and he heard a splash in the water. No one else saw or heard anything. He raised his head,—the woman's place was vacant! He got up, and sought about him in vain. The poor bleeding heart was still, at last, and the river rippled and dimpled just as brightly as if it had not closed above it.

Patience! patience! ye whose hearts swell indignant at wrongs like these. Not one throb of anguish, not one tear of the oppressed, is forgotten by the Man of Sorrows, the Lord of Glory. In his patient, generous bosom he bears the anguish of a world. Bear thou, like him, in patience, and labor in love; for sure as he is God, "the year of his redeemed shall come."[8]

The trader waked up bright and early, and came out to see to his live stock. It was now his turn to look about in perplexity.

"Where alive is that gal?" he said to Tom.

Tom, who had learned the wisdom of keeping counsel, did not feel called on to state his observations and suspicions, but said he did not know.

"She surely couldn't have got off in the night at any of the landings, for I was awake, and on the look-out, whenever the boat stopped. I never trust these yer things to other folks."

This speech was addressed to Tom quite confidentially, as if it was some-thing that would be specially interesting to him. Tom made no answer.

The trader searched the boat from stem to stern, among boxes, bales and barrels, around the machinery, by the chimneys, in vain.

"Now, I say, Tom, be fair about this yer," he said, when, after a fruitless search, he came where Tom was standing. "You know something about it, now. Don't tell me,—I know you do. I saw the gal stretched out here about ten o'clock, and ag'in at twelve, and ag'in between one and two; and then at four she was gone, and you was sleeping right there all the time. Now, you know something,—you can't help it."

"Well, Mas'r," said Tom, "towards morning something brushed by me, and I kinder half woke; and then I hearn a great splash, and then I clare woke up, and the gal was gone. That's all I know on't."

The trader was not shocked nor amazed; because, as we said before, he was used to a great many things that you are not used to. Even the awful presence of Death struck no solemn chill upon him. He had seen Death many times,—met him in the way of trade, and got acquainted with him,— and he only thought of him as a hard customer, that embarrassed his property operations very unfairly; and so he only swore that the gal was a baggage, and that he was devilish unlucky, and that, if things went on in this way, he should not make a cent on the trip. In short, he seemed to consider himself an ill-used man, decidedly; but there was no help for it, as the woman had escaped into a state which never will give up a fugitive,—not even at the demand of the whole glorious Union. The trader, therefore, sat discontentedly down, with his little account-book, and put down the missing body and soul under the head of losses!

"He's a shocking creature, isn't he,—this trader? so unfeeling! It's dreadful, really!"

"O, but nobody thinks anything of these traders! They are universally despised,—never received into any decent society."

But who, sir, makes the trader? Who is most to blame? The enlightened, cultivated, intelligent man, who supports the system of which the trader is the inevitable result, or the poor trader himself? You make the public sentiment that calls for his trade, that debauches and depraves him, till he feels no shame in it; and in what are you better than he?

Are you educated and he ignorant, you high and he low, you refined and he coarse, you talented and he simple?

In the day of a future Judgment, these very considerations may make it more tolerable for him than for you.

In concluding these little incidents of lawful trade, we must beg the world not to think that American legislators are entirely destitute of humanity, as might, perhaps, be unfairly inferred from the great efforts made in our national body to protect and perpetuate this species of traffic.

Who does not know how our great men are outdoing themselves, in declaiming against the foreign slave-trade. There are a perfect host of Clarksons and Wilberforces[9] risen up among us on that subject, most edifying to hear and behold. Trading negroes from Africa, dear reader, is so horrid! It is not to be thought of! But trading them from Kentucky,—that's quite another thing!

…

## Notes

1. Paraphrase of Jeremiah 31.15.

2. Amalgam of Hebrews 11.16 and Hebrews 13.14.

3. Washington, Louisiana, upriver from New Orleans; the town is certainly chosen for the name' s echoes of George Washington and the nation's capital.

4. Paraphrase of Psalm 137.3.

5. Genesis 9.25, from the story of Noah and his son Ham; a passage cited to justify slavery on the assumption that Africans were Ham' s descendants.

6. Mr.Symmes; seech. VI, "The Mother's Struggle."

7. Healing tonic.

8. Paraphrase of Isaiah 63.4

9. Thomas Clarkson (1760 — 1846) and William Wilberforce (1759 — 1833): English abolitionists, architects of the 1807 act of

Parliament abolishing the slave trade. A similar act was passed by the U.S. Congress the same year; it prohibited importation of slaves from abroad but allowed the trade within the United States.

## Questions

1. How much do you know about Tom in this Chapter? And what are the chief qualities of his character?

2. There are many citations from the Bible. Why, do you think, are the Scriptures cited by Tom as well as the author?

### (8) Ralph Waldo Emerson (1803—1882)

Emerson was born in Boston on May 25, 1803, son of a Unitarian minister and the second of five surviving boys. His father was a famous minister who encouraged young Ralph to pursue philosophy at a young age. He was educated in Boston and, like his father, he graduated from Harvard in 1821. His father passed away when he was eight and Emerson was left to support his four other brothers. Despite the hardships, all the Emerson boys, except one, graduated from Harvard University. In 1825, he began to study at the Harvard Divinity School, and then next year he was licensed to preach by the Middlesex Association of Ministers. His first and only placement was at the important second Unitarian church of Boston, where he became sole pastor in 1830. In 1832, Emerson traveled to Europe where he met poets Samuel Taylor Coleridge and William Wordsworth, who introduced him to the romantic notions of nature and philosophy. Three years after he became the sole Pastor, he had a crisis of faith, finding that he was "not interested in" the rite of communion. Eventually, his controversial views caused his resignation. However, he never ceased to be both teacher and preacher, although without the support of any concrete idea of God. After returning to the United States, he lectured on natural history, biology, and history. In 1835, he married again and settled with his wife at the east end of the village of Concord, Massachusetts, and spent the rest of his life there.

He began a career as a public lecturer, which lasted almost 50 years. Emerson's point of view may shift from one pole of a subject to the other, even within a single work, for his mind moved like that of a dramatist who embodies felt or imagined moods in various characters, but the subject remains Emersonian. He first achieved national fame in 1841, when he published Essays, a collection based on material from his journals and lectures. He went on to publish several more volumes of essays, including *Essays, the Second Volume* (1844), *Representative Men*(1849), and *The Conduct of Life*(1860). His lectures, *The American Scholar*(1837) and *Address at Divinity College*(1838), challenged the Harvard intelligentsia and warned about a lifeless Christian tradition. He was ostracized by Harvard for many years, but his message attracted young disciples, who joined the informal Transcendental Club, organized in 1836 by the Unitarian clergyman F. H. Hedge. He considered himself primarily a poet and published two successful volumes of poetry, *Poems* (1847) and *May-Day and Other Pieces* (1867). Like his essays, Emerson's poems express his beliefs in individuality and in humanity's spiritual connection to nature.

His essays have speech-like characteristics and a prophetic

tone, a sermon-like quality, often linked to his practice as a Unitarian minister. Emerson's aim was not merely to charm his readers, but encourage them to cultivate "self-trust," to become what they ought to be, and to be open to the intuitive world of experience. Much of his spiritual insight comes from his readings in Eastern religion, especially Hinduism, Confucianism, and Islamic Sufism (Islamic mysticism).

Ralph Waldo Emerson was one of the most influential writers and thinkers of the 19th century in the United States. Emerson was also the first major American literary and intellectual figure to widely explore, write seriously about, and seek to broaden the domestic audience for classical Asian and Middle Eastern works. He not only gave countless readers their first exposure to non-Western modes of thinking, metaphysical concepts, and sacred mythologies, but he also shaped the way subsequent generations of American writers and thinkers approached the vast cultural resources of Asia and the Middle East.

The following is from his first book *Nature* (1836), a collection of essays, which sum up his ideas and describe how humans find God within nature. Emerson emphasized individualism and rejected traditional authority. He invited the world to "enjoy an original relation to the universe" and emphasized "the infinitude of the private man." All creation is one, he believed—people should try to live a simple life in harmony with nature and with others. This book is a lengthy essay that became the Transcendental Club's unofficial statement of belief.

## Chapter I

To go into solitude, a man needs to retire as much from his chamber as from society. I am not solitary whilst I read and write, though nobody is with me. But if a man would be alone, let him look at the stars.

The rays that come from those heavenly worlds, will separate between him and vulgar things. One might think the atmosphere was made transparent with this design, to give man, in the heavenly bodies, the perpetual presence of the sublime. Seen in the streets of cities, how great they are! If the stars should appear one night in a thousand years, how would men believe and adore; and preserve for many generations the remembrance of the city of God which had been shown! But every night come out these preachers of beauty, and light the universe with their admonishing smile.

The stars awaken a certain reverence, because though always present, they are always inaccessible; but all natural objects make a kindred impression. When the mind is open to their influence. Nature never wears a mean appearance. Neither does the wisest man extort all her secret, and lose his curiosity by finding out all her perfection. Nature never became a toy to a wise spirit. The flowers, the animals, the mountains, reflected all the wisdom of his best hour, as much as they had delighted the simplicity of his childhood.

When we speak of nature in this manner, we have a distinct but most poetical sense in the mind. We mean the integrity of impression mad e by manifold natural objects. It is this which distinguishes the stick of timber of the wood-cutter, from the tree of the poet. The charming landscape which I saw this morning, is indubitably made up of some twenty or thirty farms. Miller owns this field, Locke that, and Manning the woodland beyond. But none of them owns the landscape. There is a property in the horizon which no man has but he whose eye can integrate all the parts, that is, the poet. This is the best part of these men's farms, yet to this their land-deeds give them no title[4].

To speak truly, few adult persons can see nature. Most persons do not see the sun. At least they have a very superficial seeing. The sun illuminates only the eye of the man, but shines into the eye and the heart of the child. The lover of nature is he whose inward and outward sense s are still truly adjusted to each other; who has retained the spirit of infancy even into the era of manhood[5]. His intercourse with heaven and earth, becomes part of his daily food. In the presence of nature, a wild delight runs through the man, in spite of real sorrows. Nature says, —he is my creature, and maugre[6] all his impertinent griefs, he shall be glad with me. Not the sun or the summer alone, but every hour and season yields its tribute of delight; for every hour and change corresponds to and authorizes a different state of the mind, from breathless noon to grimmest midnight. Nature is a setting that fits equally well a comic or a mourning piece. In good health, the air is a cordial of incredible virtue. Crossing a bare common, in snow puddles, at twilight, under a clouded sky, without having in my thoughts any occurrence of special good fortune, I have enjoyed a perfect exhilaration. Almost I fear to think how glad I am. In the woods too, a man casts off his years, as the snake his slough, and at what period soever of life, is always a child. In the woods, is perpetual youth. Within these plantations of God, a decorum and sanctity reign, a perennial festival is dressed, and the guest sees not how he should tire of them in a thousand years. In the woods, we return to reason and faith. There I feel that nothing can befall me in life, — no disgrace, no calamity, (leaving me my eyes,) which nature cannot repair. Standing on the bare ground, —my head bathed by the blithe air, and uplifted into infinite space, — all mean egotism vanishes. I become a transparent eye-ball[7]. I am nothing. I see all. The currents of the Universal Being circulate through me; I am part or particle of God. The name of the nearest friend sounds then foreign and accidental. To be brothers, to be acquaintances, —master or servant, is then a trifle and a disturbance. I am the lover of uncontained and immortal beauty. In the wilderness, I find something more dear and connate[8] than in streets or villages. In the tranquil landscape, and especially in the distant line of the horizon, man beholds somewhat as beautiful as his own nature.

The greatest delight which the fields and woods minister, is the suggestion of an occult relation between man and the vegetable. Jam not alone and unacknowledged. They nod to me and I to them. The waving of the boughs in the storm, is new to me and old. It takes me by surprise, and yet is not unknown. Its effect is like that of a higher thought or a better emotion coming over me, when 1 deemed I was thinking justly or doing right.

Yet it is certain that the power to produce this delight, does not reside in nature, but in man, or in a harmony of both. It is necessary to us e these pleasures with great temperance. For, nature is not always tricked in holiday attire, but the same scene which yesterday breathed perfume and glittered as for the frolic of the nymphs, is overspread with melancholy today. Nature always wears the colors of the spirit[9]. To a man laboring under calamity, the heat of his own fire hath sadness in it. Then, there is a kind of contempt of the landscape felt by him who has just lost by death a dear friend. The sky is less grand as it shuts down over less worth in the population.

## Notes

1. Emerson found the motto from the Roman philosopher Plotinus (205? — 270?) in his copy of Ralph Cudworth's The True Intellectual System of the Universe (1820).

2. An echo of Ezekiel 37.1-14, especially 37.4, where God tells Ezekiel to "Prophesy upon these bones, and say unto them, O ye dry bones, hear the word of the Lord." Emerson had left the ministry but was still writing as a prophet.

3. Emerson takes "not me" from Thomas Carlyle's Sartor Resartus (1833 — 34), where it appears as a translation of the recent German philosophical term for everything but the self.

4. Cf. the opening paragraphs of "Where I Lived, and What I Lived For," chapter 2 of Thoreau's Walden.

5. An echo of Samuel Taylor Coleridge's Biographia Literaria, ch.4, in which Coleridge defines the character and privilege of genius as the

ability to carry the feelings of childhood into the powers of adulthood.

6. Despite.

7. The most famous phrase in the essay, endlessly ridiculed and explicated. As Sealts says in The Composition of Nature. Emerson is not "merely repeating what he had already said about the implications of the preceding sentence on the bare common". When the speaker leaves the village for the woods, "the level of discourse is significantly shifted along with the setting, and the ensuing episode takes place on what Emerson would later call another 'platform' of experience."

8. Related.

9. See Emerson's maturer broodings on subjectivity in "Experience" (p.556).

## Questions

1. Combined with Emerson's ideas of Oversoul, try to explain "I become a transparent eye-ball. I am nothing. I see all."

2. Try to compare Emerson's ideas with Wang Yangming's ideas.

### (9) Henry David Thoreau (1817—1862)

Thoreau was born in Concord, Massachusetts, in 1817 and died there in 1862, at the age of forty-four. After graduating from Harvard in 1837, he struck up a friendship with fellow Concord resident Ralph Waldo Emerson, whose essay Nature he had first encountered earlier that year. Although the two American thinkers had a turbulent relationship due to serious philosophical and personal differences, they had a profound and lasting effect upon one another. Never marrying, and horrified by the one proposal that he received, his most complex personal relationship outside his family was with his older neighbor, Ralph Waldo Emerson; though, the discrepancies between their rarefied ideals of friendship and the realities of social commerce finally left them frustrated with each other. Although he was never one to affiliate himself with groups, he became known as a reliable abolitionist speaker. Thoreau moved into the political forefront only with his defense of John Brown.

His first book, *A Week on the Concord and Merrimack Rivers* (1849), was still a work in progress. In 1845, he went to live in the woods by Walden Pond for two years and two months (1845—1847). This "experiment" in living on the outskirts of town was an intensive time of examination for Thoreau, as he drew close to nature and contemplated the final ends of his own life, which was otherwise at risk of ending in quiet desperation. Thoreau's experiences during this period provided him with material for his masterpiece *Walden* (1854), condensing his experiences at the Walden Pond into one year. Thoreau used the four seasons as a structural framework for the book. A unique blend of natural observation, social criticism, and philosophical insight, Walden is now generally regarded as the supreme work of Transcendentalist literature. Carefully and deliberately crafted, Thoreau's work reflects the economy for which he drove throughout his life and about which he wrote in Walden. Thoreau always questioned the rules that were presented to him, and his *Civil Disobedience*(1849) was his objection to the Mexican War

(1846—1848) to some extent.

Thoreau has yet to achieve his full recognition as a great prose stylist, a lover of nature, a New England mystic, or as a powerful social philosopher.

The following text is an excerpt of the second chapter of *Waldon*, which is from *The Norton Anthology of American Literature* (shorter 6th edition).

## ChapterII Where I Lived, and What I Lived For

At a certain season of our life we are accustomed to consider every spot as the possible site of a house. I have thus surveyed the country on every side within a dozen miles of where I live. In imagination I have bought all the farms in succession, for all were to be bought and I knew their price. I walked over each farmer's premises, tasted his wild apples, discoursed on husbandry with him, took his farm at his price, at any price, mortgaging it to him in my mind; even put a higher price on it, —took every thing but a deed of it, —took his word for his deed, for I dearly love to talk, —cultivated it, and him too to some extent, I trust, and withdrew when I had enjoyed it long enough, leaving him to carry it on. This experience entitled me to be regarded as a sort of real-estate broker by my friends. Wherever I sat, there I might live, and the landscape radiated from me accordingly. What is a house but a sed.es, a seat? —better if a country seat. I discovered many a site for a house not likely to be soon improved, which some might have thought too far from the village, but to my eyes the village was too far from it. Well, there I might live, I said; and there I did live, for an hour, a summer and a winter life; saw how I could let the years run off, buffet the winter through, and see the spring com e in. The future inhabitants of this region, wherever they may place their houses, may be sure that they have been anticipated. An afternoon sufficed to lay out the land into orchard woodlot and pasture, and to decide what fine oaks or pines should be left to stand before the door, and whence each blasted tree could be seen to the best advantage; and then I let it lie, fallow perchance, for a man is rich in proportion to the number of things which he can afford to let alone.

My imagination carried me so far that I even had the refusal of several farms, —the refusal was all I wanted, —but I never got my fingers burned by actual possession. The nearest that I came to actual possession was when I bought the Hollowell Place, and had begun to sort my seeds, and collected materials with which to make a wheelbarrow to carry it on or off with; but before the owner gave me a deed of it, his wife—every man has such a wife— changed her mind and wished to keep it, and he offered me ten dollars to release him. Now, to speak the truth, I had but ten cents in the world, and it surpassed my arithmetic to tell, if I was that man who had ten cents, or who had a farm, or ten dollars, or all together. However, I let him keep the ten dollars and the farm too, for I had carried it far enough; or rather, to be generous, I sold him the farm for just what I gave for it, and, as he was not a rich man, mad e him a present of ten dollars, and still had my ten cents, and seeds, and materials for a wheelbarrow left. I found thus that I had been a rich man without any damage to my poverty. But I retained the landscape, and I have since annually carried off what it yielded without a wheelbarrow. With respect to landscapes, —

"I am monarch of all I survey,

My right there is none to dispute."[1]

I have frequently seen a poet withdraw, having enjoyed the most valuable part of a farm, while the crusty farmer supposed that he had got a few wild apples only. Why, the owner does not know it for many years when a poet has put his farm in rhyme, the most admirable kind of invisible fence, has fairly impounded it, milked it, skimmed it, and got all the cream, and left the farmer only the skimmed milk.

The real attractions of the Hollowell farm, to me, were; its complete retirement, being about two miles from the village, half a mile from the nearest neighbor, and separated from the highway by a broad field; its bounding on the river, which the owner said protected it by its fogs from frosts in the spring, though that was nothing to me; the gray color and ruinous state of the house and barn, and the dilapidated fences, which put such an interval between me and the last occupant; the hollow and lichencovered apple trees, gnawed by rabbits, showing what kind of neighbors I should have; but above all, the recollection I had of it from my earliest voyages up the river, when the house was concealed behind a dens e grove of red maples, through which I heard the house-dog bark. I was in haste to buy it, before the proprietor finished getting out some rocks, cutting down the hollow apple trees, and grubbing up some young birches which had sprung up in the pasture, or, in short, had made any more of his improvements.

To enjoy these advantages I was ready to carry it on; like Atlas,[9] to take the world on my shoulders, —I never heard what compensation he received for that, —and do all those things which had no other motive or excuse but that I might pay for it and be unmolested in my possession of it; for I knew all the while that it would yield the most abundant crop of the kind I wanted if I could only afford to let it alone. But it turned out as I have said.

All that I could say, then, with respect to farming on a large scale, (I have always cultivated a garden,) was, that I had had my seeds ready. Many think that seeds improve with age. I have no doubt that time discriminates between the good and the bad; and when at last I shall plant, I shall be less likely to be disappointed. But I would say to my fellows, once for all, as long as possible live free and uncommitted. It makes but little difference whether you are committed to a farm or the county jail.

Old Cato, whose "De Re Rustica" is my "Cultivator," says, and the only translation I have seen makes sheer nonsense of the passage, "When you think of getting a farm, turn it thus in your mind, not to buy greedily; nor spare your pains to look at it, and do not think it enough to go round it once. The oftener you go there the more it will please you, if it is good." I think I shall not buy greedily, but go round and round it as long as I live, and be buried in it first, that it may please me the more at last.

…

We must learn to reawaken and keep ourselves awake, not by mechanical aids, but by an infinite expectation of the dawn, which does not forsake us in our soundest sleep. I know of no more encouraging fact than the unquestionable ability of man to elevate his life by a conscious endeavor. It is some thing to be able to paint a particular picture, or to carve a statue, and so to make a few objects beautiful; but it is far more glorious to carve and paint the very atmosphere and medium through which we look, which morally we can do. To affect the quality of the day, that is the highest of arts. Every man is tasked to make his life, even in its details, worthy of the contemplation of his most elevated and critical hour. If we refused, or rather used up, such paltry information as we get, the oracles would distinctly inform us how this might be done.

I went to the woods because I wished to live deliberately, to front only the essential facts of life, and see if I could not learn what it had to teach, and not, when I came to die, discover that I had not lived. I did not wish to live what was not life, living is so dear; nor did I wish to practise resignation, unless it was quite necessary. I wanted to live deep and suck out all the marrow of life, to live so sturdily and Spartan-like as to put to rout all that was not life, to cut a broad swath and shave close, to drive life into a corner, and reduce it to its lowest terms, and, if it proved to be mean, why then to get the whole and genuine meanness of it, and publish its meanness to the world; or if it were sublime, to know it by experience, and be able to give a true account of it in my next excursion. For most men, it appears to me, are in a strange uncertainty about it, whether it is of the devil or of God, and have somewhat hastily concluded that it is the chief end of man here to "glorify Go d and enjoy him forever."[3]

Still we live meanly, like ants; though the fable tells us that we were long ago changed into men;[4] like pygmies we fight with cranes; it is error upon error, and clout upon clout, and our best virtue has for its occasion a superfluous and evitable wretchedness. Our life is frittered away by detail. An honest man has hardly need to count more than his ten fingers, or in extreme case she may add his ten toes, and lump the rest. Simplicity, simplicity, simplicity! I say, let your affairs be as two or three, and not a hundred or a thousand; instead of a million count half a dozen, and keep your accounts on your thumb nail. In the midst of this chopping sea of civilized life, such are the clouds and storms and quicksands and thousand-and-one items to be allowed for, that a man has to live, if he would not founder and go to the bottom and not make his port at all, by dead reckoning, and he must be a great calculator indeed who succeeds. Simplify, simplify. Instead of three meals a day, if it be necessary eat but one; instead of a hundred dishes, five; and reduce other things in proportion. Our life is like a German Confederacy,[5] made up of petty states, with its boundary forever fluctuating, so that even a German cannot tell you how it is bounded at any moment. The nation itself, with all its so called internal improvements, which, by the way, are all external and superficial, is just such an unwieldy and overgrown establishment, cluttered with furniture and tripped up by its own traps, ruined by luxury and heedless expense, by want of calculation and a worthy aim, as the million households in the land; and the only cur e for it as for them is in a rigid economy, a stern and more than Spartan simplicity of life and elevation of purpose. It lives too fast. Men think that it is essential that the Nation have commerce, and export ice, and talk through a telegraph, and ride thirty miles an hour, without a doubt, whether they do or not; but whether we should live like baboons or like men, is a little uncertain. If we do not get out sleepers,[6] and forge rails, and devote days and nights to the work, but go to tinkering upon our lives to improve them, who will build railroads? And if railroads are not built, how shall we get to heaven in season? But if we stay at home and mind our business, who will want railroads? We do not ride on the railroad; it rides upon us. Did you ever think what those sleepers are that underlie the railroad? Each one is a man, an Irish-man, or a Yankee man. The rails are laid on them, and they are covered with sand, and the cars run smoothly over them. They are sound sleepers, I assure you. And every few years a new lot is laid down and run over; so that, if some have the pleasure of riding on a rail, others have the misfortune to be ridden upon. And when they run over a man that is walking in his sleep, a supernumerary sleeper in the wrong position, and wake him up, they suddenly stop the cars, and make a hue and cry about it, as if this were an exception. I am glad to know that it takes a gang of men for every five miles to keep the sleepers down and level in their beds a s it is, for this is a sign that they may sometime get up again.

Why should we live with such hurry and waste of life? We are determined to be starved before we are hungry. Men say that a stitch in time saves nine, and so they take a thousand stitches to-day to save nine to-morrow. As for work, we haven't any of any consequence. We have the Saint Vitus' dance,[7] and cannot possibly keep our heads still.

If I should only give a few pulls at the parish bell-rope, as for a fire, that is, without setting the bell, there is hardly a man on his farm in the outskirts of Concord, notwithstanding that press of engagements which was his excuse so many times this morning, nor a boy, nor a woman, I might almost say, but would forsake all and follow that sound, not mainly to save property from the flames, but, if we will confess the truth, much more to see it burn, since burn it must, and we, be it known, did not set it on fire,—or to see it put out, and have a hand in it, if that is done as handsomely; yes, even if it were the parish church itself. Hardly a man takes a half hour's nap after dinner, but when he wakes he holds up his head and asks, "What's the news?" as if the rest of mankind had stood his sentinels. Some give directions to be waked every half hour, doubtless for no other purpose; and then, to pay for it, they tell what they have dreamed. After a night's sleep the news is as indispensable as the breakfast. "Pray tell me any thing new that has happened to a man any where on this globe", —and he reads it over his coffee and rolls, that a ma n had had his eyes gouged out this morning on the Wachito River; never dreaming the while that he lives in the dark unfathomed mammoth cave of this world, and has but the rudiment of an eye himself.[8]

…

Time is but the stream I go a-fishing in. I drink at it; but while I drink I see the sandy bottom and detect how shallow it is. Its thin current slides away, but eternity remains. I would drink deeper; fish in the sky, whose bottom is pebbly with stars. I cannot count one. I know not the first letter of the alphabet. I have always been regretting that I was not as wise as the day I was born. The intellect is a cleaver; it discerns and rifts its way into the secret of things. I do not wish to be any more busy with my hands than is necessary. My head is hands and feet. I feel all my best faculties concentrated in it. My instinct tells me that my head is an organ for burrowing, as some creatures use their snout and fore-paws, and with it I would mine and burrow my way through these hills. I think that the richest vein is somewhere hereabouts; so by the divining rod and thin rising vapors I judge; and here I will begin to mine.

## Notes

1. William Cowper's "Verses Supposed to Be Written by Alexander Selkirk," with the pun italicized. Selkirk was Daniel Defoe's mode l for Robinson Crusoe.

2. A Titan whom Zeus forced to stand on the earth, supporting the heavens on his head and in his hands as punishment for warring against the Olympian gods.

3. From the Shorter Catechism in the New England Primer.

4. In a Greek fable Aeacus persuaded Zeus to turn ants into men. The Trojans are compared to cranes lighting with pygmies (Iliad, boo k 3).

5. Later in the century Germany was unified under Prince Ottovon Bismarck (1815 — 1898). first chancellor of the German Empire.

6. Wooden railroad ties (another pun).

7. Chorea, a severe nervous disorder characterize d by jerky motions.

8. Sightless fish had been found in Kentucky's Mammoth Cave.

"Wachito": also spelled "Ouachita," a tributary of the Red River. Thoreau refers to a common-enough incident in backwoods brawling.

## Questions

1. As the experiences described in this text, Thoreau believed that people needed to simplify their lives and rekindle their connection with nature. Do you agree or not? Please give your reasons.

2. Try to compare with Taoism.

# Part IV The Age of Realism (1865—1918)

## 1. Historical Background

Between two great wars—the Civil War and the First World War, the United States of America came of age. In a period of less than 50 years, it was transformed from a rural republic to an urban state. The frontier vanished. Great factories and steel mills, transcontinental railroad lines, flourishing cities, and vast agricultural holdings marked the land. With this economic growth and affluence came corresponding problems. Nationwide businesses came to dominate whole industries, either independently or in combination with others. Working conditions were often poor. Cities grew so quickly that they could not properly house or govern their growing populations.

The Civil War brought needs that enormously stimulated manufacturing, efficient and economical processes based on the exploitation of iron, steam, and electric power, as well as the forward march of science and invention. In 1876, Alexander Graham Bell exhibited a telephone instrument and, within half a century, 16 million telephones would quicken the social and economic life of the nation. The growth of business was sped up by the invention of the typewriter in 1867, the calculation machine in 1888, and the cash register in 1897.

Thomas Edison's incandescent lamp eventually lit millions of homes. The Homestead Act of 1862 promised 160 acres of land to anyone who would farm it for five years. This shifted the westward movement into higher gear. Westward expansion was boosted by completion of the first Transcontinental Railroad in 1868. As the national railroads grew, the covered wagon—a symbol of the American pioneer—was replaced by the railroad as the main means of transportation. These and many other applications of science and ingenuity resulted in a new level of productivity in almost every field.

In 1904, more than 5,000 previously independent concerns were consolidated into some 300 industrial trusts. The "cooperation" and the "trust", such as the United States Steel Cooperation and the Standard of Oil Company by John D. Rockefeller, were developed to control both production and the market. These powerful individuals successfully squeezed out their competitors and accumulated vast wealth and power—social and political, as well as economic. Their ostentatious displays of wealth led Mark Twain to dub this period "The Gilded Age," implying a thin veneer of glitter over something of a poor quality.

In this new industry order, the city was the nerve center, bringing to a focus all the nation's dynamic economic forces: vast accumulations of capital, business and financial institutions, spreading railroad yards, coal factories, and armies of the manual and clerical workers. Villages began attracting people from the countryside and from lands across the sea, growing into towns and towns into cities almost overnight. In 1870, the U.S. population was 38.5 million; by

1910, it had grown to 92 million, and by 1920, to 123 million. This increase in population came about almost entirely on account of immigration, as did the population shift from country to city. Around 25 million people, mostly Europeans, entered the United States between the Civil War and World War I.

Despite the great changes in industry, agriculture remained the nation's basic occupation. The revolution in agriculture involved the shift from hand labor to machine farming, and from subsistence to commercial agriculture.

In the 1880s, the South pushed hard to attract industry. Thirty years after the Civil War, the South remained largely poor, overwhelmingly agrarian, and economically dependent. Its society enforced a rigid social segregation of blacks from whites and tolerated recurrent racial violence. As in the East, expansion into the plains and mountains by miners, ranchers, and settlers led to increase in conflicts with the Indians of the west. In 1876, the last serious Sioux war erupted when the Dakota gold rush penetrated the Black Hills, which ended in the death of hundreds of Sioux men, women, and children.

The last decades of the 19th century were a period of imperial expansion for the United States, as it extended its influence, and at times its domain, over widely scattered areas in the Atlantic and Pacific oceans, and into Central America. The United States took a different course than its European rivals, however, because of its own history of struggle against European empires and its unique democratic development.

Indeed, just beneath the nation's prosperity, discontentment grew.

Women, African Americans, and workers agitated for changes in their social, economic, and political status. Women still did not have the right to vote. Most African Americans, despite emancipation, were hardly better off in 1914 than they had been in 1850. Labor reform was desperately needed; bitter struggles erupted between emerging workers' unions and management.

## 2. Literature of the Period

In American literature, the Civil War brought the Romantic period to an end and the age of Realism came into existence. The rapid transcontinental settlement and new urban industrial circumstances were accompanied by the development of a national literature of great abundance and variety. New themes, new forms, new subjects, new regions, new authors, and new audiences all emerged in the literature of this half century. In fiction, industrial workers and the rural poor, ambitious business leaders and vagrants, prostitutes, and unheroic soldiers became familiar figures. Women from many social groups, African Americans, Native Americans, other ethnic minorities, and immigrants all began to write for publications, and a rapidly burgeoning market for printed work helped establish authorship as a possible career.

Generally speaking, the writings of this period are an expression of realistic impulses, which are represented by: realists, such as Mark Twain(1835—1910), Henry James(1843—1916), and William Dean Howells (1837—1920); local colorists, such as Sarah Orne Jewett (1849—1909), Joel Chandler Harris (1848—1908), Kate Chopin (1850—1904), and Bret Hart (1836—1902); naturalists, such as Stephen Crane (1871—1900), Frank Norris (1870—1902), and Jack London (1876—1916); and "muckrakers," such as Upton Sinclair (1878—1968) and Theodore Dreiser (1871—1945).

Broadly speaking, Realism is used to label a movement in English, European, and American literature that gathered force from the 1830s to the end of the century. It was, ultimately, nothing more or less than the attempt to write a literature that recorded life as it was lived rather than life as it ought to be lived or had been lived in times past. As defined by William Dean Howells, realism "is nothing more and nothing less than the truthful treatment of material." and seeks to create the illusion of everyday life being lived by ordinary people in familiar surroundings—life seen through a clear glass window (though partly opened to allow for the full range of sense experience).

William Dean Howells was a prolific writer and wrote volumes of drama, poetry, and novels, in addition to travel critiques and an autobiography. In all his life, he wrote eight critical books, 1,700 book reviews, and 35 novels. *Their Wedding Journey*(1871), *A Foregone Conclusion* (1875), *A Modern Instance* (1882), *The Rise of Silas Lampham*(1885), and *A Hazard of New Fortunes*(1890) played a great role in shaping the public taste for themes of realism. *The Rise of Silas Lampham* was one of the first American novels of the manners, and one of the first novels to look at the American businessman and a self-made millionaire.

As a critic of eminent standing, his theory is mainly shown in his *Criticism and Fiction* (1891). He defined realism as a fidelity to experience in which some ordinary traits of American life is often talked of, the common feelings of commonplace people are revealed, and man is looked upon in his habitual moods rather than his heroic or occasional phases. In Howells' opinion, realism is a concern with psychological conflicts instead of near photographic pictures of externals; truth with morality is the highest beauty and the job of the critic is to describe and interpret instead of arbitrarily evaluating. Writers should describe the "smiling aspects of life," which is opposite to the Transcendentalists.

At the end of the century, from the Realism movement grew Naturalism, which also focused on truthfully portraying the lives of ordinary people. Naturalists, however, believed that a person's fate is determined by the environment, heredity, and chance. As a result, they often depicted characters whose lives were shaped by forces. They could never understand nor control them, but endured with strength and dignity, thereby affirming the significance of their existence. Naturalism is evolved from realism when the author's tone in writing becomes less serious and less sympathetic, but more detached, ironic, and more pessimistic. Bierce, Crane, Dreiser, London, and Norris are usually the figures identified as the leading American naturalists of this period.

Naturalism, like realism, had come from Europe. Under the influence of the Civil War, the social upheaval, and Darwinism, the naturalists emphasized that the world was amoral, that men and women had no free will, that their lives were controlled by heredity and the environment, that religious "truths" were illusory, that the destiny of humanity was misery in life and oblivion in death. Therefore, the pessimistic and deterministic mood are pervaded in their works.

Frank Norris's early writing tended to be romantic, however, being influenced by Emile Zola, the French naturalist, his *McTeague* (1899) and *Vandover and the Brute* (1899, 1914 published) sought to describe with realistic detail the influence of heredity and environment on human life. His "Epic of Wheat" a trilogy on the production, distribution, and consumption of wheat, *The Octopus* (1901), *The Pit* (1903), and *The Wolf* (unwritten), also reveals his deterministic view clearly.

Jack London, pseudonym of John Griffith Chaney, (1876—1916), was one of the most extensively translated of American authors. His best-known works—among them *The Call of the Wild* (1903) and *White Fang* (1906)—depict elemental struggles for survival. In 1894, he became a militant socialist which he remained all his life. In addition to *Martin Eden*, he wrote two other autobiographical novels of considerable interest: *The Road* (1907) and *John Barleycorn* (1913). Other important novels are *The Sea-Wolf* (1904), which features a Nietzschean superman hero, Humphrey Van Weyden, who battles the vicious Wolf Larsen; and *The Iron Heel* (1908), a fantasy of the future that is a terrifying anticipation of fascism. According to critic Earl Labor, "The essential creative tension for London's literary artistry, is the opposition of materialism versus spiritualism—that is, the tension between the logical and the scientific on the one hand and the irrational and mystical on the other."

Moreover, there is another literary trend during this period, that is the Local Colorism literature. Regional writing, also called local color, another expression of the realistic impulse, resulted from the desire to both preserve distinctive ways of life before industrialization dispersed or homogenized them, and to come to terms with the harsh realities that seemed to replace these early and allegedly happier times. Local Color as a trend first made its presence in the late 1860s and early seventies. Local colorists concerned themselves with presenting and interpreting the local character of their regions. They tended to identify and glorify, but they never forgot to keep an eye on the truthful color of local life.

The work of Bret Harte (1836—1902) told us the life of American western miners in *The Luck of Roaring Camp* (1868) which mainly described the frontier character. Hamlin Garland wrote in his collection *Main-Travelled Roads* (1891) about the bleak and exhausting life of farmers of the upper Midwest in which we see local color not as nostalgia but as realism in the service of social protest. Kate Chopin (1850—1904), not unlike Mark Twain, may be thought of as a regional writer interested in preserving the customs, language, and landscapes of a region of the South. Chopin's short stories and her novel *The Awakening* (1899) pick up, almost literally, where Twain's books leave off—in the northern Louisiana countryside and, downriver, in New Orleans. Chopin, in The Awakening, gives us unique access to the interior life a Protestant woman awakening to her oppressions and repressions in the context of a Catholic community. The title *The Awakening* also has served to crystallize many women's issues of the turn of the century, and ever since, is a testimony to the potential for regional realism to expose the lie of attempts to derogate it as a genre.

The years 1902 to 1908 marked the era of greatest reform activity. Both writers and journalists strongly protested practices and principles inherited from the 18th-century rural republic that were proving inadequate for a 20th-century urban state, and they became known as "muckrakers." Years before, in 1873, Mark Twain had exposed American society to critical scrutiny in *The Gilded Age*. In his sensational novel, *The Jungle* (1906), Upton Sinclair (1878—1968) exposed unsanitary conditions in the great Chicago meat-packing houses and the grip of the beer trust on the nation's meat supply. Theodore Dreiser in *The Finance* and *The Titan* made it easy for laymen to understand the machinations of big business. This "literature of exposure" had a vital effect in inspiring thousands of people to action.

During these fifty years a vast body of nonfictional prose was also devoted to the description, analysis, and critique of social, economic, and political institutions, and to the unsolved social problems that were one consequence of the rapid growth and change of the time. Much of this writing had literary ambitions, survives as literature, and continues to have genuine power. Walt Whitman and Emily Dickinson, though, whose roots are in the antebellum period, continued their work into the 1880s. In a half century the great changes and the lives of many Americans were enormously presented in the literature of diversion: nostalgic poetry, sentimental and melodramatic drama, and swashbuckling historical novels despite the ostensible triumph of realism.

## 3. Representative Writers' Work

### (1) Kate Chopin (1850—1904)

Kate Chopin, named Katherine O'Flaherty, was born to a prominent St. Louis family and read widely as a girl. In June, 1870, she married Oscar Chopin, with whom she lived in his native New Orleans, Louisiana, and later on a plantation near Cloutiersville, Louisiana, until his death in 1882. After he died she began to write about the Creole and Cajun people she had observed in the South. Her first novel, *At Fault* (1890), was set in a noisy town inhabited by Creoles, descendants of the original French and Spanish settlers and Cajuns descendants of French Canadian settlers who arrived later. Through vivid descriptions and dialect, Chopin captured the local color of the region. Her stories published in *Bayou Folk* (1894)and *Acadie* (1897), exhibited a deep understanding of the different attitudes of the Louisiana natives. She wrote more than 100 stories. Two of these stories, *Désirée's Baby* and *Madame Celestin's Divorce*, continue to be widely anthologized. In 1899, Chopin published *The Awakening*, a realistic novel about the sexual and artistic awakening of a young wife and mother who abandons her family and eventually commits suicide. This work was roundly condemned in its time because of its sexual frankness and its portrayal of an interracial marriage, going out of print for more than 50 years. When it was rediscovered in the 1950s, critics marveled at the beauty of its writing and its modern sensibilities.

Chopin's work has been categorized within the "local color" genre. Through her stories, Kate Chopin wrote her own autobiography and documented her surroundings; she lived in a time when her surroundings included the abolitionist movements and the emergence of feminism. Many of her stories and sketches were about her life in Louisiana, and the addition of her less than typical portrayals of women as their own individuals with wants and needs. Chopin's seemingly different writing style did in fact emerge from an admiration of Guy de Maupassant but went beyond Maupassant's technique and style.

The following story is published in her collection *A Night in Acadie* in 1897. A widely acclaimed, frequently anthologized story, it is set in antebellum New Orleans and deals with slavery, the Southern social system, Creole culture, and the ambiguity of racial identity. Désirée, an ever adopted child, and her husband, Armand, are happily married. So content is Armand that he has stopped mistreating his slaves. But when Désirée gives birth to a child who is obviously of mixed racial ancestry, Armand forces her and the child into exile and to a tragic end, and then becomes more brutal toward his slaves. When Armand ordered some of his slaves to build a bonfire and fuel it with letters and personal belongings of Desiree, he found a letter which his mother wrote to his father saying that Armand's mother was of the race that he despised. Armand was the parent who was not one hundred percent white, not Desiree.

*Désirée's Baby* focuses on Kate Chopin's experience with the Creoles of Louisiana.The idea of slavery and the atmosphere of plantation life was a reality in Louisiana.The issue of racism that the story brings up was an indispensable truth in the 19th century.

## Desiree's Baby[1]

As the day was pleasant, Madam e Valmonde drove over to L'Abri to see Desiree and the baby.

It made her laugh to think of Desiree with a baby. Why, it seemed but yesterday that Desiree was little more than a baby herself; when Monsieur in riding through the gateway of Valmonde had found her lying asleep in the shadow of the big stone pillar.

The little one awoke in his arms and began to cry for "Dada". That was as much as she could do or say. Some people thought she might have strayed there of her own accord, for she was of the toddling age. The prevailing belief was that she had been purposely left by a party of Texans, whose canvas-covered wagon, late in the day, had crossed the ferry that Coton Mai's kept, just below the plantation. In time Madame Valmonde abandoned every speculation but the one that Desiree had been sent to her by a beneficent Providence to be the child of her affection, seeing that she was without child of the flesh. For the girl grew to be beautiful and gentle, affectionate and sincere,—the idol of Valmonde.

It was no wonder, when she stood one day against the stone pillar in whose shadow she had lain asleep, eighteen years before, that Armand Aubigny riding by and seeing her there, had fallen in love with her. That was the way all the Aubignys fell in love, as if struck by a pistol shot. The wonder was that he had not loved her before; for he had known her since his father brought him home from Paris, a boy of eight, after his mother died there. The passion that awoke in him that day, when he saw her at the gate, swept along like an avalanche, or like a prairie fire, or like anything that drives headlong over all obstacles.

Monsieur Valmonde grew practical and wanted things well

considered: that is, the girl's obscure origin. Armand looked into her eyes and did not care. He was reminded that she was nameless. What did it matter about a name when he could give her one of the oldest and proudest in Louisiana? He ordered the corbeille[2] from Paris, and contained himself with what patience he could until it arrived; then they were married.

Madam e Valmonde had not seen Desiree and the baby for four weeks. When she reached L'Abri she shuddered at the first sight of it, as she always did. It was a sad looking place, which for many years had not known the gentle presence of a mistress, old Monsieur Aubigny having married and buried his wife in France, and she having loved her own land too well ever to leave it. The roof came down steep and black like a cowl, reaching out beyond the wide galleries that encircled the yellow stuccoed house. Big, solemn oaks grew close to it, and their thick-leaved, far-reaching branches shadowed it like a pall. Young Aubigny's rule was a strict one, too, and under it his negroes had forgotten how to be gay, as they had been during the old master's easy-going and indulgent lifetime.

The young mother was recovering slowly, and lay full length, in her soft white muslins and laces, upon a couch. The baby was beside her, upon her arm, where he had fallen asleep, at her breast. The yellow nurse woman sat beside a window fanning herself.

Madame Valmonde bent her portly figure over Desiree and kissed her, holding her an instant tenderly in her arms. Then she turned to the child.

"This is not the baby!" she exclaimed, in startled tones. French was the language spoken at Valmonde in those days.

"I knew you would be astonished," laughed Desiree, "at the way he has grown. The little cochon de lait![3] Look at his legs, mamma, and his hands and fingernails,—real finger-nails. Zandrine had to cut them this morning. Isn't it true, Zandrine?"

The woman bowed her turbaned head majestically, "Maissi, Madame."

"And the way he cries," went on Desiree, "is deafening. Armand heard him the other day as far away as La Blanche's cabin."

Madame Valmonde had never removed her eyes from the child. She lifted it and walked with it over to the window that was lightest. She scanned the baby narrowly, then looked as searchingly at Zandrine, whose face was turned to gaze across the fields.

"Yes, the child has grown, has changed," said Madame Valmonde, slowly, as she replaced it beside its mother. "What does Armand say?"

Desiree's face became suffused with a glow that was happiness itself.

"Oh, Armand is the proudest father in the parish, I believe, chiefly because it is a boy, to bear his name; though he says not,—that he would have loved a girl as well. But I know it isn't true. I know he says that to please me. And mamma," she added, drawing Madame Valmonde's head down to her, and speaking in a whisper, "he hasn't punished one of them—not one of them—since baby is born. Even Negrillon, who pretended to have burnt his leg that he might rest from work—he only laughed, and said Negrillon was a great scamp. Oh, mamma, I'm so happy; it frightens me."

What Desiree said was true. Marriage, and later the birth of his son had softened Armand Aubigny's imperious and exacting nature greatly. This was what made the gentle Desiree so happy, for she loved him desperately. When he frowned she trembled, but loved him. When he smiled, she asked no greater blessing of God. But Armand's dark, handsome face had not often been disfigured by frowns since the day he fell in love with her.

When the baby was about three months old, Desiree awoke one day to the conviction that there was something in the air menacing her peace. It was at first too subtle to grasp. It had only been a disquieting suggestion; an air of mystery among the blacks; unexpected visits from far-off neighbors who could hardly account for their coming. Then a strange, an awful change in her husband's manner, which she dared not ask him to explain. When he spoke to her, it was with averted eyes, from which the old love-light seemed to have gone out. He absented himself from home; and when there, avoided her presence and that of her child, without excuse. And the very spirit of Satan seemed suddenly to take hold of him in his dealings with the slaves. Desiree was miserable enough to die.

She sat in her room, one hot afternoon, in her peignoir,[4] listlessly drawing through her fingers the strands of her long, silky brown hair that hung about her shoulders. The baby, half naked, lay asleep upon her own great mahogany bed, that was like a sumptuous throne, with its satin-lined half-canopy. One of La Blanche's little quadroon[5] boys—half naked too—stood fanning the child slowly with a fan of peacock feathers. Desiree's eyes had been fixed absently and sadly upon the baby, while she was striving to penetrate the threatening mist that she felt closing about her. She looked from her child to the boy who stood beside him, and back again; over and over. "Ah!" It was a cry that she could not help; which she was not conscious of having uttered. The blood turned like ice in her veins, and a clammy moisture gathered upon her face.

She tried to speak to the little quadroon boy; but no sound would come, at first. When he heard his name uttered, he looked up, and his mistress was pointing to the door. He laid aside the great, soft fan, and obediently stole away, over the polished floor, on his bare tiptoes.

She stayed motionless, with gaze riveted upon her child, and her face the picture of fright.

Presently her husband entered the room, and without noticing her, went to a table and began to search among some papers which covered it.

"Armand," she called to him, in a voice which must have stabbed him, if he was human. But he did not notice. "Armand," she said again. Then she rose and tottered towards him. "Armand," she panted once more, clutching his arm, "look at our child. What does it mean? tell me."

He coldly but gently loosened her fingers from about his arm and thrust the hand away from him. "Tell me what it means!" she cried despairingly.

"It means," he answered lightly, "that the child is not white; it means that you are not white."

A quick conception of all that his accusation meant for her nerved her with unwonted courage to deny it. "It is a lie; it is not true, I am white! Look at my hair, it is brown; and my eyes are gray, Armand, you know they are gray. And my skin is fair," seizing his wrist. "Look at my hand; whiter than yours, Armand," she laughed hysterically.

"As white as La Blanche's," [6] he returned cruelly; and went away leaving her alone with their child.

When she could hold a pen in her hand, she sent a despairing letter to Madame Valmonde.

"My mother, they tell me I am not white. Armand has told me I am not white. For God's sake tell them it is not true. You must know it is not true. I shall die. I must die. I cannot be so unhappy, and live."

The answer that came was as brief:

"My own Desiree: Come home to Valmonde; back to your mother who loves you. Come with your child."

When the letter reached Desiree she went with it to her husband's study, and laid it open upon the desk before which she sat. She was like a stone image: silent, white, motionless after she placed it there.

In silence he ran his cold eyes over the written words. He said nothing. "Shall I go, Armand?" she asked in tones sharp with agonized suspense.

"Yes, go."

" Do you want me to go?"

"Yes, I want you to go."

He thought Almighty God had dealt cruelly and unjustly with him; and felt, somehow, that he was paying Him back in kind when he stabbed thus into his wife's soul. Moreover he no longer loved her, because of the unconscious injury she had brought upon his home and his name.

She turned away like one stunned by a blow, and walked slowly towards the door, hoping he would call her back.

"Good-by, Armand," she moaned.

He did not answer her. That was his last blow at fate.

Desiree went in search of her child. Zandrine was pacing the sombre gallery with it. She took the little one from the nurse's arms with no word of explanation, and descending the steps, walked away, under the live-oak branches.

It was an October afternoon; the sun was just sinking. Out in the still fields the negroes were picking cotton.

Desiree had not changed the thin white garment nor the slippers which she wore. Her hair was uncovered and the sun's rays brought a golden gleam from its brown meshes. She did not take the broad, beaten road which led to the far-off plantation of Valmonde. She walked across a deserted field, where the stubble bruised her tender feet, so delicately shod, and tore her thin gown to shreds.

She disappeared among the reeds and willows that grew thick along the banks of the deep, sluggish bayou; and she did not come back again.

Some weeks later there was a curious scene enacted at L'Abri. In the centre of the smoothly swept back yard was a great bonfire. Armand Aubigny sat in the wide hallway that commanded a view of the spectacle; and it was he who dealt out to a half dozen negroes the material which kept this fire ablaze.

A graceful cradle of willow, with all its dainty furbishings, was laid upon the pyre, which had already been fed with the richness of a priceless layette.[7] Then there were silk gowns, and velvet and satin ones added to these; laces, too, and embroideries; bonnets and gloves; for the corbeille had been of rare quality.

The last thing to go was a tiny bundle of letters; innocent little scribblings that Desiree had sent to him during the days of their espousal. There was the remnant of one back in the drawer from which he took them. But it was not Desiree's; it was part of an old letter from his mother to his father. He read it. She was thanking God for the blessing of her husband's love:—

"But, above all," she wrote, "night and day, I thank the good God for having so arranged our lives that our dear Armand will never know that his mother, who adores him, belongs to the race that is cursed with the brand of slavery."

1893

## Notes

1. First published in Vogue, January 14, 1893: first published in book form in Bayou Folk (1894), the source of the present text.

2. Literally, basket (French). In this context, a hope chest filled with fine linens, clothes, and other gifts meant to serve as the material foundation for their married life.

3. Suckling pig (French).

4. Dressing gown (French).

5. A person who is one-quarter African American.

6. The cruelty Involves the double irony: La Blanche (the white) is

black.

7. Clothes, bedding, toilet articles, and other items needed to care for a newborn.

## Questions

1. what's the theme of the story?

2. "A graceful cradle of willow, with all its dainty furbishings, was laid upon the pyre, which had already been fed with the richness of a priceless layette. Then there were silk gowns, and velvet and satin ones added to these; laces, too, and embroideries; bonnets and gloves; for the corbeille had been of rare quality." why did the author describe the belongings which will be burnt in detail?

### （2）Bret Harte (1836—1902)

Francis Bret Harte was born in Albany, New York, on August 25, 1839. In 1854, his mother, a widow, moved him to California. In California Harte worked as a miner, school teacher, express messenger, printer, and journalist. While in San Francisco writing for *The Californian* he worked with Mark Twain, Charles Warren Stoddard, Prentice Mulford, and the editor, Henry Webb. He contributed many poems and prose pieces to the paper. Bret Harte was appointed Secretary of the United States Mint branch in San Francisco. He held that office until 1870.

Harte became the first editor of the *Overland Monthly*. *The Luck of Roaring Camp* published in the *Overland Monthly* brought him instant and wide fame. He was thereafter requested to contribute poems and articles to a number of publications. His stories of the

American West were much in demand in the eastern United States. In 1871, he moved to New York, later moving to Boston. Harte continued to write poetry and prose, and enjoyed wide popularity.

In 1878, Bret Harte was appointed United States Consul in Crefeld, Germany. Harte was transferred to Glasgow, Scotland, in 1880. Thereafter he resided in London. He died in Camberely, England, on May 6, 1902.

The following story tells about a morning on November 23, 1850, some of the town leaders had met secretly and decided to force some people to leave. They thought Poker Flat in the small western town would be a better place to live if those people were gone. Besides Oakhurst, a gambler, two women of no morals were led to the edge of town. They were the "Duchess" as she was called and "Mother Shipton." A man called Uncle Billy was added to the group. He was known to drink too much. Some people thought that he had also stolen some gold, they had no proof. But that did not matter. Uncle Billy was just no good and he had to go. Besides, there was a young couple named Tom Simson and Piney Woods, eloped for love. The "outcasts" were told that if they ever came back, they would be killed. The outcasts were headed for Sandy Bar, a camp not too far away. But it was high up in the cold Sierra Mountains, and the path was anything but smooth. They were tardied and trapped by heavy snow, which formed a prison they could not escape. They lost their horses. The snow continued to fall. the little group of outcasts tried to keep up their spirits. They tried to stay as warm as they could. But the hunger got worse with each passing day. At midnight on the tenth day, Mother Shipton called Oakhurst to her side. She said, "Give this to the young ones." In a bag was all her food. She had not eaten for days. She had saved the food for the others. She turned quietly to the wall of the log house, and died. John Oakhurst gave Tom Simson a pair of snowshoes and asked him to try to walk back to Poker Flat for help. When night came, Oakhurst who went out for help had not returned. The two women, hungry, weak, and cold to even add more wood to the fire, passed the stormy night and had frozen to death when they were found. The rescuers from town said that they had been right to force the outcasts to leave Poker Flat. But they never thought the punishment would end up like this. Justice was one thing, but freezing people to death was not their aim. John Oakhurst was found at last, commit suicide. Under a tall tree a playing card was stuck into the wood by a knife. On the card was written: "Beneath this tree lies the body of John Oakhurst, who had some bad luck starting the twenty-third of November, eighteen fifty. He handed in his cards on the seventh of December, the same year."

## The Outcasts of Poker Flat[1]

As Mr.John Oakhurst, gambler, stepped into the main street of Poker Flat on the morning of the twenty-third of November, 1850, he was conscious of a change in its moral atmosphere from the preceding night. Two or three men, conversing earnestly together, ceased as he approached, and exchanged significant glances. There was a Sabbath lull in the air, which, in a settlement unused to Sabbath influences, looked ominous.

Mr.Oakhurst's calm, handsome face betrayed small concern of these indications. Whether he was conscious of any predisposing cause, was another question. "I reckon they're after somebody," he reflected; "likely it's me." He returned to his pocket the handkerchief with which he had been whipping away the red dust of Poker Flat from his neat boots, and quietly discharged his mind of any further conjecture.

In point of fact, Poker Flat was "after somebody". It had lately suffered the loss of several thousand dollars, two valuable horses, and a prominent citizen. It was experiencing a spasm of virtuous reaction, quite as lawless and ungovernable as any of the acts that had provoked it. A secret committee[2] had determined to rid the town of all improper persons. This was done permanently in regard of two men who were then hanging from the boughs of a sycamore in the gulch, and temporarily in the banishment of certain other objectionable characters. I regret to say that some of these were ladies. It is but due to the sex, however, to state that their impropriety was professional, and it was only in such easily established standards of evil that Poker Flat ventured to sit in judgment.

Mr.Oakhurst was right in supposing that he was included in this category. A few of the committee had urged hanging him as a possible example, and a sure method of reimbursing themselves from his pockets of the sum she had won from them. "It's agin justice," said Jim Wheeler, "to let this yer young man from Roaring Camp—

an entire stranger—carry away our money." But a crude sentiment of equity residing in the breasts of those who had been fortunate enough to win from Mr.Oakhurst, overruled this narrower local prejudice.

Mr.Oakhurst received his sentence with philosophic calmness, none the less coolly, that he was aware of the hesitation of his judges. He was too much of a gambler not to accept Fate. With him life was at best an uncertain game, and he recognized the usual percentage in favor of the dealer.

A body of armed men accompanied the deported wickedness of Poker Flat to the outskirts of the settlement. Besides Mr.Oakhurst, who was known to be a coolly desperate man, and for whose intimidation the armed escort was intended, the expatriated party consisted of a young woman familiarly known as "The Duchess"; another, who had gained the infelicitous title of "Mother Shipton," and "Uncle Billy," a suspected sluices-robber and confirmed drunkard. The cavalcade provoked no comments from the spectators, nor was any word uttered by the escort. Only when the gulch which marked the uttermost limit of Poker Flat was reached, the leader spoke briefly and to the point. The exiles were forbidden to return at the peril of their lives.

As the escort disappeared, their pent-up feelings found vent in a few hysterical tears from "The Duchess," some bad language from Mother Shipton, and a Partheian[4] volley of expletives from Uncle Billy. The philosophic Oakhurst alone remained silent. He listened calmly to Mother Shipton's desire to cut somebody's heart out, to the repeated statements of "The Duchess" that she would die in the road, and to the alarming oaths that seemed to be bumped out of Uncle Billy as he rode forward. With the easy good-humor characteristic of his class, he insisted upon exchanging his own riding-horse, "Five Spot," for the sorry mule which the Duchess rode. But even this act did not draw the party into any closer sympathy. The young woman readjusted her somewhat draggled plumes with a feeble, faded coquetry; Mother Shipton eyed the possessor of "Five Spot" with malevolence, and Uncle Billy included the whole party in one sweeping anathema.

The road to Sandy Bar—a camp that not having as yet experienced the regenerating influences of Poker Flat, consequently seemed to offer some invitation to the emigrants—lay over a steep mountain range. It was distant a day's severe journey. In that advanced season, the party soon passed out of the moist, temperate regions of the foot-hills, into the dry, cold, bracing air of the Sierras. The trail was narrow and difficult. At noon the Duchess, rolling out of her saddle upon the ground, declared her intention of going no further, and the party halted.

The spot was singularly wild and impressive. A wooded amphitheatre, surrounded on three sides by precipitous cliffs of naked granite, sloped gently toward the crest of another precipice that overlooked the valley. It was undoubtedly the most suitable spot for a camp, had camping been advisable. But Mr.Oakhurst knew that scarcely half the journey to Sandy Bar was accomplished, and the party were not equipped or provisioned for delay. This fact he pointed out to his companions curtly, with a philosophic commentary on the folly of "throwing up their hand before the game was played out." But they were furnished with liquor, which in this emergency stood them in place of food, fuel, rest and prescience. In spite of his remonstrances, it was not long before they were more or less under its influence. Uncle Billy passed rapidly from a bellicose state into one of stupor, the Duchess became maudlin, and Mother Shipton snored. Mr.Oakhurst alone remained erect, leaning against a rock, calmly surveying them.

Mr.Oakhurst did not drink. It interfered with a profession which required coolness, impassiveness and presence of mind, and, in his own language, he "couldn't afford it." As he gazed at his recumbent fellow-exiles, the loneliness begotten of his pariah-trade, his habits of life, his very vices, for the first time seriously oppressed him. He bestirred himself in dusting his black clothes, washing his hands and face, and other acts characteristic of his studiously neat habits, and for a moment forgot his annoyance. The thought of deserting his weaker and more pitiable companions never perhaps occurred to him. Yet he could not help feeling the want of that excitement, which singularly enough was most conducive to that calm equanimity for which he was notorious. He looked at the gloomy walls that rose a thousand feet sheer above the circling pines around him; at the sky, ominously clouded; at the valley below, already deepening into shadow. And doing so, suddenly he heard his own name called.

A horseman slowly ascended the trail. In the fresh, open face of the newcomer, Mr.Oakhurst recognized Tom Simson, otherwise known as "The Innocent" of Sandy Bar. He had met him some months before over a "little game," and had, with perfect equanimity, won the entire fortune—amounting to some forty dollars—of that guileless youth. After the game was finished, Mr.Oakhurst drew the youthful speculator behind the door and thus addressed him: "Tommy, you're a good little man, but you can't gamble worth a cent. Don't try it over again." He then handed him his money back, pushed him gently from the room, and so made a devoted slave of Tom Simson.

There was a remembrance of this in his boyish and enthusiastic greeting of Mr.Oakhurst. He had started, he said, to go to Poker Flat to seek his fortune. "Alone?" No, not exactly alone; in fact—a giggle—he had run away with Piney Woods. Didn't Mr.Oakhurst remember Piney? She that used to wait on the table at the Temperance House? They had been engaged a long time, but old Jake Wood s had objected, and so they had run away, and were going to Poker Flat to be married, and here they were. And they were tired out, and how lucky it was they had found a place to camp and company. All this The Innocent delivered rapidly, while Piney—a stout, comely damsel of fifteen—emerged from behind the pine tree, where she had been blushing unseen, and rode to the side of her lover.

Mr.Oakhurst seldom troubled himself with sentiment. Still less with propriety. But he had a vague idea that the situation was not felicitous. He retained, however, his presence of mind sufficiently to kick Uncle Billy, who was about to say something, and Uncle Billy was sober enough to recognize in Mr.Oakhurst's kick a superior power that would not bear trifling. He then endeavored to dissuade Tom Simson from delaying further, but in vain. He even pointed out the fact that there was no provision, nor means of making a camp. But, unluckily, "The Innocent" met this objection by assuring the party that he was provided with an extra mule loaded with provisions, and by the discovery of a rude attempt at a log-house near the trail. "Piney can stay with Mrs.Oakhurst," said The Innocent, pointing to the Duchess, "and I can shift for myself."

Nothing but Mr.Oakhurst's admonishing foot saved Uncle Billy from bursting into a roar of laughter. As it was, he felt compelled to retire up the canyon until he could recover his gravity. There he confided the joke to the tall pine trees, with many slaps of his leg, contortions of his face, and the usual profanity. But when he returned to the party, he found them seated by a fire—for the air had grown strangely chill and the sky overcast—in apparently amicable conversation. Piney was actually talking in an impulsive, girlish fashion to the Duchess, who was listening with an interest and animation she had not shown for many days. The Innocent was holding forth, apparently with equal effect, to Mr.Oakhurst and Mother Shipton, who was actually relaxing into amiability. "Is this yer a d—d picnic?" said Uncle Billy, with inward scorn, as he surveyed the sylvan group, the glancing firelight and the tethered animals in the foreground. Suddenly an idea mingled with the alcoholic fumes that disturbed his brain. It was apparently of a jocular nature, for he felt impelled to slap his leg again and cram his fist into his mouth.

As the shadows crept slowly up the mountain, a slight breeze rocked the tops of the pine trees, and moaned through their long and gloomy aisles. The ruined cabin, patched and covered with pine boughs, was set apart for the ladies. As the lovers parted, they unaffectedly exchanged a parting kiss, so honest and sincere that it might have been heard above the swaying pines. The frail Duchess and the malevolent Mother Shipton were probably too stunned to remark upon this last evidence of simplicity, and so turned without a word to the hut. The fire was replenished, the men lay down before the door, and in a few minutes were asleep.

Mr.Oakhurst was a light sleeper. Toward morning he awoke benumbed and cold. As he stirred the dying fire, the wind, which was now blowing strongly, brought to his cheek that which caused the blood to leave it—snow!

He started to his feet with the intention of awakening the sleepers, for there was no time to lose. But turning to where Uncle Billy had been lying he found him gone. A suspicion leaped to his brain and a curse to his lips. He ran to the spot where the mules had been tethered; they were no longer there. The tracks were already rapidly disappearing in the snow.

The momentary excitement brought Mr.Oakhurst back to the fire with his usual calm. He did not waken the sleepers. The Innocent slumbered peacefully, with a smile on his good-humored, freckled face; the virgin Piney slept beside her frailer sisters as sweetly as though attended by celestial guardians, and Mr.Oakhurst, drawing his blanket over his shoulders, stroked his mustachios and waited for the dawn. It came slowly in a whirling mist of snowflakes, that dazzled and confused the eye. What could be seen of the landscape appeared magically changed. He looked over the valley, and summed up the present and future in two words— "Snowed in!"

A careful inventory of the provisions, which, fortunately for the party, had been stored within the hut, and so escaped the felonious fingers of Uncle Billy, disclosed the fact that with care and prudence they might last ten days longer. “That is,” said Mr.Oakhurst, sotto voce[5] to The Innocent, “if you're willing to board us. If you ain't—and perhaps you'd better not—you can wait till Uncle Billy gets back with provisions.” For some occult reason, Mr.Oakhurst could not bring himself to disclose Uncle Billy's rascality, and so offered the hypothesis that he had wandered from the camp and had accidentally stampeded the animals. He dropped a warning to the Duchess and Mother Shipton, who of course knew the facts of their associate's defection. “They'll find out the truth about us all, when they find out anything,” he added, significantly, “and there's no good frightening them now.”

Tom Simson not only put all his worldly store at the disposal of Mr.Oakhurst, but seemed to enjoy the prospect of their enforced seclusion. “We'll have a good camp for a week, and then the snow'll melt, and we'll all go back together.” The cheerful gayety of the young man and Mr.Oakhurst's calm infected the others. The Innocent, with the aid of pine boughs, extemporized a thatch for the roofless cabin, and the Duchess directed Piney in the rearrangement of the interior with a taste and tact that opened the blue eyes of that provincial maiden to their fullest extent. “I reckon now you're used to fine things at Poker Flat,” said Piney. The Duchess turned away sharply to conceal something that reddened her cheeks through its professional tint, and Mother Shipton requested Piney not to “chatter.” But when Mr.Oakhurst returned from a weary search for the trail, he heard the sound of happy laughter echoed from the rocks. He stopped in some alarm, and his thoughts first naturally reverted to the whiskey—which he had prudently cached. "And yet it don't somehow sound like whiskey," said the gambler. It was not until he caught sight of the blazing fire through the still blinding storm, and the group around it, that he settled to the conviction that it was "square fun".

Whether Mr.Oakhurst had cached his cards with the whiskey as something debarred the free access of the community, I cannot say. It was certain that, in Mother Shipton's words, he "didn't say cards once" during that evening. Haply the time was beguiled by an accordeon, produced somewhat ostentatiously by Tom Simson, from his pack. Notwithstanding some difficulties attending the manipulation of this instrument, Piney Woods managed to pluck several reluctant melodies from its keys, to an accompaniment by The Innocent on a pair of bone castinets. But the crowning festivity of the evening was reached in a rude camp-meeting hymn, which the lovers, joining hands, sang with great earnestness and vociferation. I fear that a certain defiant tone and Covenanter's swing[6] to its chorus, rather than any devotional quality, caused it to speedily infect the others, who at last joined in the refrain:

> "I'm proud to live in the service of the Lord,
> And I'm bound to die in His army."[7]

The pines rocked, the storm eddied and whirled above the miserable group, and the flames of their altar leaped heavenward, as if in token of the vow.

At midnight the storm abated, the rolling clouds parted, and the stars glittered keenly above the sleeping camp. Mr.Oakhurst, whose professional habits had enabled him to live on the smallest possible amount of sleep, in dividing the watch with Tom Simson, somehow managed to take upon himself the greater part of that duty. He excused himself to The Innocent, by saying that he had "often been a week without sleep." "Doing what?" asked Tom. "Poker!" replied Oakhurst, sententiously; "when a man gets a streak of luck—nigger-luck[8]—he don't get tired. The luck gives in first. Luck," continued the gambler, reflectively, "is a mighty queer thing. All you know about it for certain is that it's bound to change. And it's finding out when it's going to change that makes you. We've had a streak of bad luck since we left Poker Flat—you come along and slap you get into it, too. If you can hold your cards right along you're all right. For," added the gambler, with cheerful irrelevance,

"I'm proud to live in the service of the Lord,
And I'm bound to die in His army."

The third day came, and the sun, looking through the white-curtained valley, saw the outcasts divide their slowly decreasing store of provisions for the morning meal. It was one of the peculiarities of that mountain climate that its rays diffused a kindly warmth over the wintry landscape, as if in regretful commiseration of the past. But it revealed drift on drift of snow piled high around the hut; a hopeless, uncharted, trackless sea of white lying below the rocky shores to which the castaways still clung. Through the marvellously clear air, the smoke of the pastoral village of Poker Flat rose miles away. Mother Shipton saw it, and from a remote pinnacle of her rocky fastness, hurled in that direction a final malediction. It was her last vituperative attempt, and perhaps for that reason was invested with a certain degree of sublimity. It did her good, she privately informed the Duchess. "Just you go out there and cuss, and see." She then set herself to the task of amusing "the child," as she and the Duchess were pleased to call Piney. Piney was no chicken, but it was a soothing and ingenious theory of the pair to thus account for the fact that she didn't swear and wasn't improper.

When night crept up again through the gorges, the reedy notes of the accordeon rose and fell in fitful spasms and long-drawn gasp s by the flickering camp-fire. But music failed to fill entirely the aching void left by insufficient food, and a new diversion was proposed by Piney—story-telling. Neither Mr.Oakhurst nor his female companions caring to relate their personal experiences, this plan would have failed, too, but for The Innocent. Some months before he had chanced upon a stray copy of Mr.Pope's[9] ingenious translation of the Iliad. He now proposed to narrate the principal incidents of that poem—having thoroughly mastered the argument and fairly forgotten the words—in the current vernacular of Sandy Bar. And so for the rest of that night the Homeric demi-gods again walked the earth. Trojan bully and wily Greek wrestled in the winds, and the great pines in the canyon seemed to bow to the wrath of the son of Peleus.[10] Mr.Oakhurst listened with quiet satisfaction. Most especially was he interested in the fate of "Ash-heels,"[2] as The Innocent persisted in denominating the "swift-footed Achilles".

So with small food and much of Homer and the accordeon, a week passed over the heads of the outcasts. The sun again forsook them, and again from leaden skies the snow-flakes were sifted over the land. Day by day closer around them drew the snowy circle, until at last they looked from their prison over drifted walls of dazzling white, that towered twenty feet above their heads. It became more and more difficult to replenish their fires, even from the fallen trees beside them, now half-hidden in the drifts. And yet no one complained. The lovers turned from the dreary prospect and looked into each other's eyes, and were happy. Mr.Oakhurst settled himself coolly to the losing game before him. The Duchess, more cheerful than she had been, assumed the care of Piney. Only Mother Shipton—once the strongest of the party—seemed to sicken and fade. At midnight on the tenth day she called Oakhurst to her side. "I'm going," she said, in a voice of querulous weakness, "but don't say anything about it. Don't waken the kids. Take the bundle from under my head and open it." Mr.Oakhurst did so. It contained Mother Shipton's rations for the last week, untouched. "Give 'em to the child," she said, pointing to the sleeping Piney. "You've starved yourself," said the gambler. "That's what they call it," said the woman querulously, as she lay down again, and turning her face to the wall, passed quietly away.

The accordeon and the bones were put aside that day, and Homer was forgotten. When the body of Mother Shipton had been committed to the snow, Mr.Oakhurst took The Innocent aside, and showed him a pair of snow-shoes, which he had fashioned from the old pack-saddle.

"There's one chance in a hundred to save her yet," he said, pointing to Piney; "but it's there," he added, pointing toward Poker Flat. "If you can reach there in two days she's safe." "And you?" asked Tom Simson. "I'll stay here," was the curt reply.

The lovers parted with a long embrace. "You are not going, too," said the Duchess, as she saw Mr.Oakhurst apparently waiting to accompany him. "As far as the canyon." he replied. He turned suddenly, and kissed the Duchess, leaving her pallid face aflame, and her trembling limbs rigid with amazement.

Night came, but not Mr.Oakhurst. It brought the storm again and the whirling snow. Then the Duchess, feeding the fire, found that some one had quietly piled beside the hut enough fuel to last a few days longer. The tears rose to her eyes, but she hid them from Piney.

The women slept but little. In the morning, looking into each other's faces, they read their fate. Neither spoke; but Piney, accepting the position of the stronger, drew near and placed her arm around the Duchess's waist. They kept this attitude for the rest of the day. That night the storm reached its greatest fury, and rending asunder the protecting pines, invaded the very hut.

Toward morning they found themselves unable to feed the fire, which gradually died away. As the embers slowly blackened, the Duchess crept closer to Piney, and broke the silence of many hours: "Piney, can you pray?" "No, dear," said Piney, simply. The Duchess, without knowing exactly why, felt relieved, and putting her head upon Piney's shoulder, spoke no more. And so reclining, the younger and purer pillowing the head of her soiled sister upon her virgin breast, they fell asleep.

The wind lulled as if it feared to waken them. Feathery drifts of snow, shaken from the long pine boughs, flew like white-winged birds, and settled about them as they slept. The moon through the rifted clouds looked down upon what had been the camp. But all human stain, all trace of earthly travail, was hidden beneath the spotless mantle mercifully flung from above.

They slept all that day and the next, nor did they waken when voices and footsteps broke the silence of the camp. And when pitying fingers brushed the snow from their wan faces, you could scarcely have told from the equal peace that dwelt upon them, which was she that had sinned. Even the Law of Poker Flat recognized this, and turned away, leaving them still locked in each other's arms.

But at the head of the gulch, on one of the largest pine trees, they found the deuce of clubs pinned to the bark with a bowie knife. It bore the following, written in pencil, in a firm hand:

BENEATH THIS TREE

LIES THE BODY

OF

JOHN OAKHURST,

WHO STRUCK A STREAK OF BAD LUCK

ON THE 23D OF NOVEMBER, 1850,

AND

HANDED IN HIS CHECKS

ON THE 7TH DECEMBER, 1850

And pulseless and cold, with a Derringer[12] by his side and a bullet in his heart, though still calm as in life, beneath the snow, lay he who was at once the strongest and yet the weakest of the outcasts of Poker Flat.

1869,1870

## Notes

1. First published in Overland Monthly, January 1869, the source of the text printed here, and collected in "The Luck of Roaring Camp" and Other Sketches (1870).

2. I.e., vigilance committee — a group of vigilantes organized to suppress and punish crime summarily when the processes of law appear inadequate.

3. An inclined trough or flume for washing or separating gold from earth. Mother Shipton (1488 — 1560), an English witch who allegedly was carried off by the devil and bore him an imp. Her prophecies were edited by S. Baker in 1797.

4. An ancient people of southwest Asia noted for firing shots while in real or feigned retreat.

5. In an undertone (Latin).

6. Covenanters were Scottish Presbyterians of the 16th and 17th centuries who bound themselves by a series of oaths or covenants to the Presbyterian doctrine and demanded separation from the Church of England. "Covenanter's swing" indicates that the hymn is sung with a vigorous rhythm with a martial beat.

7. Refrain of the early America n spiritual "Service of the Lord".

8. I.e., very good fortune.

9. Alexander Pope (1688 — 1744), English poet who translated Homer's Iliad (and Odyssey) into the heroic couplets for which Pope is famous.

10. Achilles, chief hero on the Greek side of the Trojan War.

11. The mispronunciation emphasizes Achilles' one vulnerable spot, his heel, by which his mother, Thetis, held him when she dipped him in the river Styx to make him invulnerable.

12. Short-barreled pocket pistol, named after its 19th-century' American inventor, Henry Deringer.

## Questions

1. What are the characteristics of the outcasts?

2. There are many descriptions of the environment, what is the function about the description of the snow at the beginning of the story?

### (3) Henry James (1843—1916)

Henry James is generally regarded as the forerunner of the 20th-century "stream of consciousness" novels and the founder of psychological realism. He not only bridged the 19th and 20th centuries, but connected America and Europe. Both his literary creations and novel theories are dominant in the English world. He opened a new era of modern novels, who connected art form with human values. He abandoned traditional ways of telling a story, but developing a new point of view in which one character also serves as narrator of a story. Above all, he focused his attention on the philosophical and psychological meaning of a novel.

Born in a wealthy family, Henry James's father was an imminent philosophy and reformer, and his brother was a famous philosopher and psychologist. Although an American by blood, James's early education was heavily filled with European flavor. He developed a lifelong friendship with William Dean Howells, who became his "moral police." His famous works are *The American*(1877), *Daisy Miller*(1878), *The Portrait of a Lady* (1881), *The Ambassadors* (1903), *The Wings of the Dove* (1902), and *The Golden Bowl* (1904).

He writes about the "international theme", that is, the confrontation itself between American naivety, innocence, purity, and European sophistication, experience, and corruption. In all of his "international" novels, the two different societies and cultures are brought to face each other. He writes about the conflict between life in reality and art as well as the conflict between the material world and the spiritual world. Artists' loneliness is often talked about.

His writing style is an overelaborate style. The language is highly refined, polished, insightful, accurate, and obscure. The construction of story is very complicated and intricate. He emphasizes the inner awareness and inward movement of characters. Thus, he is called the founder of psychological realism, the forerunner of "stream of consciousness" novels. In his *The Art of Fiction*(1884), he points out that the aim of the novel is to present life. Art must be related to life. The artist should write about anything that concerns him, even the ugly and the common place. The only reason for the existence of a novel is that it does "attempt to represent life".

*Daisy Miller* was the first work James published which brought about a greater recognition of his witty writing style and narrator obstructed character development. The novella was the closest to instant success which James enjoyed during his lifetime. William Dean Howells observed that the country was split "between Daisy Millerites and anti-Daisy Millerites." It is a novel related to cultural shock, the innocent American coming with the sophisticated English. This story serves as a psychological description of the mind of a young man and an analysis of the traditional views of society where he is a clear outsider. Henry James uses this story to discuss what he thinks Europeans and Americans believe about each other. And more generally, the prejudice found in any culture. The main theme of the novel is a collision of moral values between America and Europe. The following is from the first chapter.

## Daisy Miller: A Study[1]

At the little town of Vevey, in Switzerland, there is a particularly comfortable hotel. There are, indeed, many hotels; for the entertainment of tourists is the business of the place, which, as many travelers will remember, is seated upon the edge of a remarkably blue lake[2]—a lake that it behoves every tourist to visit. The shore of the lake presents an unbroken array of establishments of this order, of every category, from the "grand hotel" of the newest fashion, with a chalk-white front, a hundred balconies, and a dozen flags flying from its roof, to the little Swiss pension of an elder day, with its name inscribed in German-looking lettering upon a pink or yellow wall, and an awkward summer-house in the angle of the garden. One of the hotels at Vevey, however, is famous, even classical, being distinguished from many of its upstart neighbors by an air both of luxury and of maturity. In this region, in the month of June, American travelers are extremely numerous; it may be said, indeed, that Vevey assumes at this period some of the characteristics of an American watering-place. There are sights and sounds which evoke a vision, an echo, of Newport and Saratoga.[3] There is a flitting hither and thither of "stylish" young girls, a rustling of muslin flounces, a rattle of dance-music in the morning hours, a sound of high-pitched voices at all times. You receive an impression of these things at the excellent inn of the "Trois Couronnes," [4] and are transported in fancy to the Ocean House or to Congress Hall. But at the "Trois Couronnes," it must be added, there are other features that are much at variance with these suggestions: neat German waiters, who look like secretaries of legation; Russian princesses sitting in the garden; little Polish boys walking about, held by the hand, with their governors; a view of the snowy crest of the Dent du Midi[5] and the picturesque towers of the Castle of Chillon.

I hardly know whether it was the analogies or the differences that were uppermost in the mind of a young American, who, two or three years ago, sat in the garden of the "Trois Couronnes," looking about him, rather idly, at some of the graceful objects I have mentioned. It was a beautiful summer morning, and in whatever fashion the young American looked at things, they must have seemed to him charming. He had come from Geneva the day before, by the little steamer, to see his aunt, who was staying at the hotel— Geneva having been for a long time his place of residence. But his aunt had a headache—his aunt had almost always a headache—and now she was shut up in her room, smelling camphor, so that he was at liberty to wander about. He was some seven-and-twenty years of age; when his friends spoke of him, they usually said that he was at Geneva, "studying". When his enemies spoke of him they said—but, after all, he had no enemies; he was an extremely amiable fellow, and universally liked. What I should say is, simply, that when certain persons spoke of him they affirmed that the reason of his spending so much time at Geneva was that he was extremely devoted to a lady who lived there—a foreign lady—a person older than himself. Very few Americans—indeed I think none—had ever seen this lady, about whom there were some singular stories. But Winterbourne had an old attachment for the little metropolis of Calvinism;[6] he had been put to school there as a boy, and he had afterwards gone to college there—circumstances which had led to his forming a great many youthful friendships. Many of these he had kept, and they were a source of great satisfaction to him.

After knocking at his aunt's door and learning that she was indisposed, he had taken a walk about the town, and then he had come in to his breakfast. He had now finished his breakfast, but he was drinking a small cup of coffee, which had been served to him on a little table in the garden by one of the waiters who looked like an attache.[7] At last he finished his coffee and lit a cigarette. Presently a small boy came walking along the path—an urchin of nine or ten. The child, who was diminutive for his years, had an aged expression of countenance, a pale complexion, and sharp little features. He was dressed in knickerbockers, with red stockings, which displayed his poor little spindleshanks; he also wore a brilliant red cravat. He carried in his hand a long alpenstock, the sharp point of which he thrust into everything that he approached—the flower-beds, the garden-benches, the trains of the ladies' dresses. In front of Winterbourne he paused, looking at him with a pair of bright, penetrating little eyes.

"Will you give me a lump of sugar?" he asked, in a sharp, hard little voice— a voice immature, and yet, somehow, not young.

Winterbourne glanced at the small table near him, on which his coffee service rested, and saw that several morsels of sugar remained. "Yes, you may take one," he answered; "but I don't think sugar is good for little boys."

This little boy stepped forward and carefully selected three of the coveted fragments, two of which he buried in the pocket to his knickerbockers, depositing the other as promptly in another place. He poked his alpenstock, lance-fashion, into Winterbourne's bench, and tried to crack the lump of sugar with his teeth.

"Oh, blazes; it's har-r-d!" he exclaimed, pronouncing the adjective in a peculiar manner.

Winterbourne had immediately perceived that he might have the honor of claiming him as a fellow-countryman. "Take care you don't hurt your teeth," he said, paternally.

"I haven't got any teeth to hurt. They have all come out. I have only got seven teeth. My mother counted them last night, and one came out right afterwards. She said she'd slap me if any more came out. I can't help it. It's this old Europe. It's the climate that makes them come out. In America they didn't come out. It's these hotels."

Winterbourne was much amused. "If you eat three lumps of sugar, your mother will certainly slap you," he said.

"She's got to give me some candy, then," rejoined his young interlocutor. "I can't get any candy here—any American candy. American candy's the best candy."

"And are American little boys the best little boys?" asked Winterbourne.

"I don't know. I'm an American boy," said the child.

"I see you are one of the best!" laughed Winterbourne.

"Are you an American man?" pursued this vivacious infant. And then, on Winterbourne's affirmative reply— "American men are the best," he declared.

His companion thanked him for the compliment; and the child, who had now got astride of his alpenstock, stood looking about him, while he attacked a second lump of sugar. Winterbourne wondered if he himself had been like this in his infancy, for he had been brought to Europe at about this age.

"Here comes my sister!" cried the child, in a moment. "She's an American girl."

Winterbourne looked along the path and saw a beautiful young lady advancing. "American girls are the best girls," he said, cheerfully, to his young companion.

"My sister ain't the best!" the child declared. "She's always blowing at me."

"I imagine that is your fault, not hers," said Winterbourne. The young lady meanwhile had drawn near. She was dressed in white muslin, with a hundred frills and flounces, and knots of pale-colored ribbon. She was bare-headed; but she balanced in her hand a large parasol, with a deep border of embroidery; and she was strikingly, admirably pretty. "How pretty they are!" thought Winterbourne, straightening himself in his seat, as if he were prepared to rise.

The young lady paused in front of his bench, near the parapet of the garden, which overlooked the lake. The little boy had now converted his alpenstock into a vaulting pole, by the aid of which he was springing about in the gravel, and kicking it up not a little.

"Randolph," said the young lady, "what are you doing?"

"I'm going up the Alps," replied Randolph. "This is the way!" And he gave another little jump, scattering the pebbles about Winterbourne's ears.

"That's the way they come down," said Winterbourne.

"He's an American man!" cried Randolph, in his little hard voice.

The young lady gave no heed to this announcement, but looked straight at her brother. "Well, I guess you had better be quiet," she simply observed.

It seemed to Winterbourne that he had been in a manner presented. He got up and stepped slowly towards the young girl, throwing away his cigarette. "This little boy and I have made acquaintance," he said, with great civility. In Geneva, as he had been perfectly aware, a young man was not at liberty to speak to a young unmarried lady except under certain rarely-occurring conditions; but here at Vevey, what conditions could be better than these? — a pretty American girl coming and standing in front of you in a garden. This pretty American girl, however, on hearing Winterbourne's observation, simply glanced at him; she then turned her head and looked over the parapet, at the lake and the opposite mountains. He wondered whether he had gone too far; but he decided that he must advance farther, rather than retreat. While he was thinking of something else to say, the young lady turned to the little boy again.

"I should like to know where you got that pole," she said.

"I bought it!" responded Randolph.

"You don't mean to say you're going to take it to Italy!"

"Yes, I am going to take it to Italy!" the child declared.

The young girl glanced over the front of her dress, and smoothed out a knot or two of ribbon. Then she rested her eyes upon the prospect again. "Well, I guess you had better leave it somewhere," she said, after a moment.

"Are you going to Italy?" Winterbourne inquired, in a tone of great respect.

The young lady glanced at him again. "Yes, sir," she replied. And she said nothing more.

"Are you—a—going over the Simplon?"[8] Winterbourne pursued, a little embarrassed.

"I don't know," she said, "I suppose it's some mountain.

Randolph, what mountain are we going over?"

"Going where?" the child demanded.

"To Italy," Winterbourne explained.

"I don't know," said Randolph. "I don't want to go to Italy. I want to go to America."

"Oh, Italy is a beautiful place!" rejoined the young man.

"Can you get candy there?" Randolph loudly inquired.

"I hope not," said his sister. "I guess you have had enough candy, and mother thinks so too."

"I haven't had any forever so long—for a hundred weeks!" cried the boy, still jumping about.

The young lady inspected her flounces and smoothed her ribbons again; and Winterbourne presently risked an observation upon the beauty of the view. He was ceasing to be embarrassed, for he had begun to perceive that she was not in the least embarrassed herself. There had not been the slightest alteration in her charming complexion; she was evidently neither offended nor fluttered. If she looked another way when he spoke to her, and seemed not particularly to hear him, this was simply her habit, her manner. Yet, as he talked a little more, and pointed out some of the objects of interest in the view, with which she appeared quite unacquainted, she gradually gave him more of the benefit of her glance; and then he saw that this glance was perfectly direct and unshrinking. It was not, however, what would have been called an immodest glance, for the young girl's eyes were singularly honest and fresh. They were wonderfully pretty eyes; and, indeed, Winterbourne had not seen for a long time anything prettier than his fair countrywoman's various features—her complexion, her nose, her ears, her teeth. He had a great relish for feminine beauty; he was addicted to observing and analyzing it; and as regards this young lady's face he made several observations. It was not at all insipid, but it was not exactly expressive; and though it was eminently delicate, Winterbourne mentally accused it—very forgivingly—of a want of finish. He thought it very possible that Master Randolph's sister was a coquette; he was sure she had a spirit of her own; but in her bright, sweet, superficial little visage there was no mockery, no irony. Before long it became obvious that she was much disposed towards conversation. She told him that they were going to Rome for the winter—she and her mother and Randolph. She asked him if he was a "real American"; she wouldn't have taken him for one; he seemed more like a German—this was said after a little hesitation, especially when he spoke. Winterbourne, laughing, answered that he had met Germans who spoke like Americans; but that he had not, so far as he remembered, met an American who spoke like a German. Then he asked her if she would not be more comfortable in sitting upon the bench which he had just quitted. She answered that she liked standing up and walking about; but she presently sat down. She told him she was from New York State— "if you know where that is." Winterbourne learned more about her by catching hold of her small, slippery brother and making him stand a few minutes by his side.

"Tell me your name, my boy," he said.

"Randolph C. Miller," said the boy, sharply. "And I'll tell you her name"; and he leveled his alpenstock at his sister.

"You had better wait till you are asked!" said this young lady, calmly.

"I should like very much to know your name," said Winterbourne.

"Her name is Daisy Miller!" cried the child. "But that isn't her real name; that isn't her name on her cards."

"It's a pity you haven't got one of my cards!" said Miss Miller.

"Her real name is Annie P. Miller," the boy went on.

"Ask him his name," said his sister, indicating Winterbourne.

But on this point Randolph seemed perfectly indifferent; he continued to supply information with regard to his own family. "My father's name is Ezra B. Miller," he announced. "My father ain't in Europe; my father's in a better place than Europe."

Winterbourne imagined for a moment that this was the manner in which the child had been taught to intimate that Mr.Miller had been removed to the sphere of celestial rewards. But Randolph immediately added, "My father's in Schenectady. He's got a big business. My father's rich, you bet."

"Well!" ejaculated Miss Miller, lowering her parasol and looking at the embroidered border. Winterbourne presently released the child, who departed, dragging his alpenstock along the path. "He doesn't like Europe," said the young girl. "He wants to go back."

"To Schenectady, you mean?"

"Yes; he wants to go right home. He hasn't got any boys here. There is one boy here, but he always goes round with a teacher; they won't let him play."

"And your brother hasn't any teacher?" Winterbourne inquired.

"Mother thought of getting him one, to travel round with us. There was a lady told her of a very good teacher; an American lady—perhaps you know her—Mrs.Sanders. I think she came from Boston. She told her of this teacher, and we thought of getting him to travel round with us. But Randolph said he didn't want a teacher traveling round with us. He said he wouldn't have lessons when he was in the cars.[9] And we are in the cars about half the time. There was an English lady we met in the cars—I think her name was Miss Featherstone; perhaps you know her. She wanted to know why I didn't give Randolph lessons—give him 'instruction', she called it. I guess he could give me more instruction than I could give him. He's very smart."

"Yes," said Winterbourne; "he seems very smart."

"Mother's going to get a teacher for him as soon as we get to Italy. Can you get good teachers in Italy?"

"Very good, I should think," said Winterbourne.

"Or else she's going to find some school. He ought to learn some more. He's only nine. He's going to college." And in this way Miss Miller continued to converse upon the affairs of her family, and upon other topics. She sat there with her extremely pretty hands, ornamented with very brilliant rings, folded in her lap, and with her pretty eyes now resting upon those of Winterbourne, now wandering over the garden, the people who passed by, and the beautiful view. She talked to Winterbourne as if she had known him a long time. He found it very pleasant. It was many years since he heard a young girl talk so much. It might have been said of this unknown young lady, who had come and sat down beside him upon a bench, that she chattered. She was very quiet, she sat in a charming tranquil attitude; but her lips and her eyes were constantly moving. She had a soft, slender, agreeable voice, and her tone was decidedly sociable. She gave Winterbourne a history of her movements and intentions, and those of her mother and brother, in Europe, and enumerated, in particular, the various hotels at which they had stopped. "That English lady in the cars," she said— "Miss Featherstone—asked me if we didn't all live in hotels in America. I told her I had never been in so many hotels in my life as since I came to Europe. I have never seen so many—it's nothing but hotels." But Miss Miller did not make this remark with a querulous accent; she appeared to be in the best humor with everything. She declared that the hotels were very good, when once you got used to their ways, and that Europe was perfectly sweet. She was not disappointed—not a bit. Perhaps it was because she had heard so much about it before. She had ever so many intimate friends that had been there ever so many times. And then she had had ever so many dresses and things from Paris. Whenever she put on a Paris dress she felt as if she were in Europe.

"It was a kind of wishing-cap," said Winterbourne.

"Yes," said Miss Miller, without examining this analogy; "it always made me wish I was here. But I needn't have done that for dresses. I am sure they send all the pretty ones to America; you see the most frightful things here. The only thing I don't like," she proceeded, "is the society. There isn't any society; or, if there is, I don't know where it keeps itself. Do you? I suppose there is some society somewhere, but I haven't seen anything of it. I'm very fond of society, and I have always had a great deal of it. I don't mean only in Schenectady, but in New York. I used to go to New York every winter. In New York I had lots of society. Last winter I had seventeen dinners given me; and three of them were by gentlemen," added Daisy Miller. "I have more friends in New York than in Schenectady—more gentlemen friends; and more young lady friends too," she resumed in a moment. She paused again for an instant; she was looking at Winterbourne with all her prettiness in her lively eyes and in her light, slightly monotonous smile. "I have always had," she said, "a great deal of gentlemen's society."

Poor Winterbourne was amused, perplexed, and decidedly charmed. He had never yet heard a young girl express herself in just this fashion; never, at least, save in cases where to say such things seemed a kind of demonstrative evidence of a certain laxity of deportment. And yet was he to accuse Miss Daisy Miller of actual or potential inconduite,[10] as they said at Geneva? He felt that he had lived at Geneva so long that he had lost a good deal; he had become dishabituated to the American tone. Never, indeed, since he had grown old enough to appreciate things, had he encountered a young American girl of so pronounced a type as this. Certainly she was very charming; but how deucedly sociable! Was she simply a pretty girl from New York State—were they all like that, the pretty girls who had a good deal of gentlemen's society? Or was she also a designing, an audacious, an unscrupulous young person? Winterbourne had lost his instinct in this matter, and his reason could not help him. Miss Daisy Miller looked extremely innocent. Some people had told him that, after all, American girls were exceedingly innocent; and others had told him that, after all, they were not. He was inclined to think Miss Daisy Miller was a flirt—a pretty American flirt. He had never, as yet, had any relations with young ladies of this category. He had known, here in Europe, two or three women—persons older than Miss Daisy Miller, and provided, for respectability's sake, with husbands—who were great coquettes—dangerous, terrible women, with whom one's relations were liable to take a serious turn. But this young girl was not a coquette in that sense; she was very unsophisticated; she was only a pretty American flirt. Winterbourne was almost grateful for having found the formula that applied to Miss Daisy Miller. He leaned back in his seat; he remarked to himself that she had the most charming nose he had ever seen; he wondered what were the regular conditions and limitations of one's intercourse with a pretty American flirt. It presently became apparent that he was on the way to learn.

"Have you been to that old castle?" asked the young girl, pointing with her parasol to the far-gleaming walls of the Chateau de Chillon.

"Yes, formerly, more than once," said Winterbourne. "You too, I suppose, have seen it?"

"No, we haven't been there. I want to go there dreadfully. Of course I mean to go there. I wouldn't go away from here without having seen that old castle."

"It's a very pretty excursion," said Winterbourne, "and very easy to make. You can drive, you know, or you can go by the little steamer."

"You can go in the cars," said Miss Miller.

"Yes; you can go in the cars," Winterbourne assented. "Our

courier[11] says they take you right up to the castle," the young girl continued. "We were going last week; but my mother gave out. She suffers dreadfully from dyspepsia. She said she couldn't go. Randolph wouldn't go either; he says he doesn't think much of old castles. But I guess we'll go this week, if we can get Randolph."

"Your brother is not interested in ancient monuments?" Winterbourne inquired, smiling.

"He says he don't care much about old castles. He's only nine. He wants to stay at the hotel. Mother's afraid to leave him alone, and the courier won't stay with him; so we haven't been to many places. But it will be too bad if we don't go up there." And Miss Miller pointed again at the Chateau de Chillon.

"I should think it might be arranged," said Winterbourne.

"Couldn't you get some one to stay—for the afternoon—with Randolph?" Miss Miller looked at him a moment; and then, very placidly— "I wish you would stay with him!" she said.

Winterbourne hesitated a moment. "I would much rather go to Chillon with you."

"With me?" asked the young girl, with the same placidity.

She didn't rise, blushing, as a young girl at Geneva would have done; and yet Winterbourne, conscious that he had been very bold, thought it possible she was offended. "With your mother," he answered very respectfully.

But it seemed that both his audacity and his respect were lost upon Miss Daisy Miller. "I guess my mother won't go, after all," she said. "She don't like to ride round in the afternoon. But did you really mean what you said just now; that you would like to go up there?"

"Most earnestly," Winterbourne declared.

"Then we may arrange it. If mother will stay with Randolph, I guess Eugenio will."

"Eugenio?" the young man inquired.

"Eugenio's our courier. He doesn't like to stay with Randolph; he's the most fastidious man I ever saw. But he's a splendid courier. I guess he'll stay at home with Randolph if mother does, and then we can go to the castle."

Winterbourne reflected for an instant as lucidly as possible— "we" could only mean Miss Daisy Miller and himself. This programme seemed almost too agreeable for credence; he felt as if he ought to kiss the young lady's hand. Possibly he would have done so and quite spoiled the project; but at this moment another person—presumably Eugenio—appeared. A tall, handsome man, with superb whiskers, wearing a velvet morning-coat and a brilliant watch-chain, approached Miss Miller, looking sharply at her companion. "Oh, Eugenio!" said Miss Miller, with the friendliest accent.

Eugenio had looked at Winterbourne from head to foot; he now bowed gravely to the young lady. "I have the honor to inform mademoiselle that luncheon is upon the table."

Miss Miller slowly rose. "See here, Eugenio," she said. "I'm going to that old castle, any way."

"To the Chateau de Chillon, mademoiselle?" the courier inquired. "Mademoiselle had made arrangements?" he added, in a tone which struck Winterbourne as very impertinent.

Eugenio's tone apparently threw, even to Miss Miller's own apprehension, a slightly ironical light upon the young girl's situation. She turned to Winterbourne, blushing a little—a very little. "You won't back out?" she said.

"I shall not be happy till we go!" he protested.

"And you are staying in this hotel?" she went on. "And you are really an American?"

The courier stood looking at Winterbourne, offensively. The young man, at least, thought his manner of looking an offence to Miss Miller; it conveyed an imputation that she "picked up" acquaintances. "I shall have the honor of presenting to you a person who will tell you all about me," he said smiling, and referring to his aunt.

"Oh well, we'll go some day," said Miss Miller. And she gave him a smile and turned away. She put up her parasol and walked back to the inn beside Eugenio. Winterbourne stood looking after her; and as she moved away, drawing her muslin furbelows over the gravel, said to himself that she had the tournure of a princess.

## Notes

1. First published in the Cornhill Magazine 37 (June — July 1878). The text reprinted here follows the first British book edition, published by Macmillan in 1879. Punctuation and spelling have been Americanized.

2. Lac Leman, or Lake of Geneva.

3. Newport. Rhode Island, and Saratoga, New York, resort areas for the rich, where the Ocean House and Congress Hall (below) are located.

4. Three Crowns (French).

5. The highest peak in the Dents du Midi, a mountain group in the Alps in southwest Switzerland.

6. Geneva, where John Calvin (1509 — 1564) centered his Protestant regime.

7. I.e., like a member of the diplomatic corps.

8. A pass in the Alps between Switzerland and Italy.

9. Railway cars.

10. Misconduct (French).

11. Social guide.

## Questions

1. "He thought it very possible that Master Randolph's sister was a coquette; he was sure she had a spirit of her own; but in her bright, sweet, superficial little visage there was no mockery, no irony." On what basis did Winterbourne say Daisy was a coquette? And why?

2. Try to analyze the plot of this passage.

### (4) Mark Twain (1835—1910)

Mark Twain, pseudonym of Samuel Langhorne Clemens, a humorist, journalist, lecturer, and novelist who acquired international fame for his travel narratives, especially *The Innocents Abroad* (1869), *Roughing It* (1872), and *Life on the Mississippi* (1883), and for his adventure stories of boyhood, especially *The Adventures of Tom Sawyer* (1876) and *Adventures of Huckleberry Finn* (1885). His social satire is The Gilded Age, written in collaboration with Charles Dudley War-ner. The novel explored the scrupulous individualism in a world of fantastic speculation and unstable values, and gave its name to the get-rich-quick years of the post-Civil war era. By the turn of the century, with the publication of *The Man that Corrupted Hadleyburg* (1900) and *The Mysterious Stranger* (1916), the change in Mark Twain from an optimist to an almost despairing pessimist could be felt, and his cynicism and disillusionment with what Twain referred to regularly as the "damned human race" became obvious.

A gifted raconteur, distinctive humorist, and irascible moralis, he transcended the apparent limitations of his origins to become a popular public figure and one of America's best and most beloved writers, whom H. L. Mencken considered "the true father of our national literature." and William Faulkner called Twain "the father of American literature".

Twain grew up in Hannibal, Missouri, which provided the setting for Huckleberry Finn and Tom Sawyer. In 1865, his humorous story, The Celebrated Jumping Frog of Calaveras County was published, which was based on a story he heard at the Angels Hotel in Angels Camp, California, where he had spent some time as a miner. The short story brought international attention, even being translated to classic Greek. His wit andsatire, in prose and in speech, earned praise from critics and peers, and he was a friend to presidents, artists, industrialists, and European royalty.

Twain is known as a local colorist who preferred to present social life through portraits of the local characters of his readings, including people living in that area, the landscape, and other peculiarities like the customs, dialects, costumes, and so on. Unlike Henry James and Howells, Mark Twain wrote about the lower class people because they were the people he knew so well and their life was the one he himself had visited.

Another fact that made Twain unique is his magic power with language, his use of vernacular. His words are clear, concrete, and direct, in effect, and his sentence structures are simple, even ungrammatical. And Twain carefully used the colloquialisms to cast his protagonists in their everyday life. What's more, his characters confined to a particular region and to a particular historical moment speak with a strong accent, which is true to his local color reasoning. In this approach, different characters from different literary or cultural backgrounds talk differently, as is the case with Huck, Tom, and Jim. His style of language was later taken up by his descendants, Sherwood Anderson and Hemingway, and influenced generations of authors.

His humor is remarkable, too. It is fun to return to, for most of his works tend to be funny, containing some practical jokes, comical details, or witty remarks, and some of them are actually tall tales. However, his humor is not only of witty remarks or mocking small things of farcical elements, making people laugh at life, but a kind of artistic style used to criticize the social injustices and satirizes the decayed romanticism.

*Huckleberry Finn* is Twain's finest book and an outstanding American novel which marks the climax of Twain's literary creativity. Hemingway once described the novel as the one book from which "all modern American literature comes."

Its narrator is Huck, son of the village drunkard, is uneducated, superstitious, and sometimes credulous; but he also has a native shrewdness, a cheerfulness that is hard to put down, compassionate tolerance, and an instinctive tendency to reach the right decisions about important matters. He runs away from his persecuting father and, with his companion, the runaway slave Jim, makes a long and frequently interrupted voyage floating down the Mississippi River on a raft. During the journey Huck meets and comes to know members of greatly varied groups, so that the book memorably portrays almost every class living on or along the river. Huck overcomes his initial prejudices and learns to respect and love Jim. A thread that runs through adventure after adventure is the theme of man's inhumanity to man—of human cruelty.

The following is the first chapter which opens with Huck telling his story. Briefly, he describes what he has experienced since, The Adventure of Tom Sawyer, which proceeded this novel.

## Adventures of Huckleberry Finn[1]

(Tom Sawyer's Comrade)

Scene: The Mississippi Valley

Time: Forty to Fifty Years Ago[2]

NOTICE

Persons attempting to find a motive in this narrative will be prosecuted; persons attempting to find a moral in it will be banished; persons attempting to find a plot in it will be shot.

BY ORDER OF THE AUTHOR

PER G.G., CHIEF OF ORDNANCE .

Explanatory

In this book a number of dialects are used, to wit: the Missouri negro dialect; the extremest form of the backwoods South-Western dialect; the ordinary "Pike-County"[3] dialect; and four modified varieties of this last. The shadings have not been done in a hap-hazard fashion, or by guess-work; but pains takingly, and with the trustworthy guidance and support of personal familiarity with these several forms of speech.

I make this explanation for the reason that without it many readers would suppose that all these characters were trying to talk alike and not succeeding.

THE AUTHOR

## Chapter I

You don't know about me, without you have read a book by the name of "The Adventures of Tom Sawyer,"[4] but that ain't no matter. That book was made by Mr.Mark Twain, and he told the truth, mainly. There was things which he stretched, but mainly he told the truth. That is nothing. I never seen anybody but lied, one time or another, without it was Aunt Polly, or the widow, or maybe Mary. Aunt Polly—Tom's Aunt Polly, she is—and Mary, and the Widow Douglas, is all told about in that book—which is mostly a true book; with some stretchers, as I said before.

Now the way that the book winds up, is this: Tom and me found the money that the robbers hid in the cave, and it made us rich. We got six thousand dollars apiece—all gold. It was an awful sight of money when it was piled up. Well, Judge Thatcher, he took it and put it out at interest, and it fetched us a dollar a day apiece, all the year round—more than a body could tell what to do with. The Widow Douglas, she took me for her son, and allowed she would sivilize me; but it was rough living in the house all the time, considering how dismal regular and decent the widow was in all her ways; and so when I couldn't stand it no longer, I lit out. I got into my old rags, and my sugarhogshead[5] again, and was free and satisfied. But Tom Sawyer, he hunted me up and said he was going to start a band of robbers, and I might join if I would go back to the widow and be respectable. So I went back.

The widow she cried over me, and called me a poor lost Iamb, and she called me a lot of other names, too, but she never meant no harm by it. She put me in them new clothes again, and I couldn't do nothing but sweat and sweat, and feel all cramped up. Well, then, the old thing commenced again. The widow rung a bell for supper, and you had to come to time. When you got to the table you couldn't go right to eating, but you had to wait for the widow to tuck down her head and grumble a little over the victuals, though there warn't really anything the matter with them. That is, nothing only everything was cooked by itself. In a barrel of odds and ends it is different; things get mixed up, and the juice kind of swaps around, and the things go better.

After supper she got out her book and learned me about Moses and the Bulrushers;[6] and I was in a sweat to find out all about him; but by-and-by she let it out that Moses had been dead a considerable long time; so then I didn't care no more about him; because I don't take no stock in dead people.

Pretty soon I wanted to smoke, and asked the widow to let me. But she wouldn't. She said it was a mean practice and wasn't clean, and I must try to not do it any more. That is just the way with some people. They get down on a thing when they don't know nothing about it. Here she was a bothering about Moses, which was no kin to her, and no use to anybody, being gone, you see, yet finding a power of fault with me for doing a thing that had some good in it. And she took snuff too; of course that was all right, because she done it herself.

Her sister, Miss Watson, a tolerable slim old maid, with goggles on, had just come to live with her, and took a set at me now, with a spelling-book. She worked me middling hard for about an hour, and then the widow made her ease up. I couldn't stood it much longer. Then for an hour it was deadly dull, and I was fidgety. Miss Watson would say, "Don't put your feet up there, Huckleberry"; and "don't scrunch up like that, Huckleberry—set up straight"; and pretty soon she would say, "Don't gap and stretch like that, Huckleberry—why don't you try to behave?" Then she told me all about the bad place, and I said

I wished I was there. She got mad, then, but I didn't mean no harm. All I wanted was to go somewheres; all I wanted was a change, I warn't particular. She said it was wicked to say what I said; said she wouldn't say it for the whole world; she was going to live so as to go to the good place. Well, I couldn't see no advantage in going where she was going, so I made up my mind I wouldn't try for it. But I never said so, because it would only make trouble, and wouldn't do no good.

Now she had got a start, and she went on and told me all about the good place. She said all a body would have to do there was to go around all day long with a harp and sing, forever and ever.[7] So I didn't think much of it. But I never said so. I asked her if she reckoned Tom Sawyer would go there, and, she said, not by a considerable sight. I was glad about that, because I wanted him and me to be together.

Miss Watson she kept pecking at me, and it got tiresome and lonesome. By-and-by they fetched the niggers[8] in and had prayers, and then everybody was off to bed. I went up to my room with a piece of candle and put it on the table. Then I set down in a chair by the window and tried to think of something cheerful, but it warn't no use. I felt so lonesome 1 most wished I was dead. The stars was shining, and the leaves rustled in the woods ever so mournful; and I heard an owl, away off, who-whooing about somebody that was dead, and a whippowill and a dog crying about somebody that was going to die; and the wind was trying to whisper something to me and I couldn't make out what it was, and so it made the cold shivers run over me. Then away out in the woods I heard that kind of a sound that a ghost makes when it wants to tell about something that's on its mind and can't make itself understood, and so can't rest easy in its grave and has to go about that way every night grieving. I got so down-hearted and scared, I did wish 1 had some company. Pretty soon a spider went crawling up my shoulder, and I flipped it off and it lit in the candle; and before I could budge it was all shriveled up. I didn't need anybody to tell me that that was an awful bad sign and would fetch me some bad luck, so I was scared and most shook the clothes off of me. I got up and turned around in my tracks three times and crossed my breast every time; and then I tied up a little lock of my hair with a thread to keep witches away. But I hadn't no confidence. You do that when you've lost a horse-shoe that you've found, instead of nailing it up over the door, but I hadn't ever heard anybody say it was any way to keep off bad luck when you'd killed a spider.

I set down again, a shaking all over, and got out my pipe for a smoke; for the house was all as still as death, now, and so the widow wouldn't know. Well, after a long time I heard the clock away off in the town go boom— boom—boom—twelve licks—and all still again—stiller than ever. Pretty soon I heard a twig snap, down in the dark amongst the trees—something was a stirring. I set still and listened. Directly I could just barely hear a "me-yow! me-yowl" down there. That was good! Says I, "me-yow! me-yow!" as soft as I could, and then I put out the light and scrambled out of the window onto the shed. Then I slipped down to the ground and crawled in amongst the trees, and sure enough there was Tom Sawyer waiting for me.

## Notes

1. Adventures of Huckleberry Finn was first published in England in December 1884. The text printed here is a corrected version of the first American edition of 1885.

2. I.e., in 1835 or 1845 — well before the Civil War.

3. Pike County, Missouri.

4. Published in 1876.

5. A large barrel.

6. Pharaoh's daughter discovered the infant Moses floating in the Nile in a basket woven from bulrushes (Exodus 2). She adopted him into the royal family just as the widow has adopted Huck.

7. Conventional conceptions of the Christian heaven were satirized early and late in Twain's writings.

8. Huck appropriately speaks the colloquial word used in the South to describe black slaves; it is not used derisively or contemptuously by him, though for much of the narrative Huck expresses the racial prejudices of his time and place.

## Questions

1. List some examples to interpret Twain's humor.

2. If this story were written from the point of the third person, what would be the effect?

### （5）Theodore Dreiser (1871—1945)

As a novelist who was the outstanding American practitioner

of naturalism, Dreiser was the leading figure in a national literary movement that replaced the observance of Victorian notions of propriety with the unflinching presentation of real-life subject matter. Among other themes, his novels explore the new social problems that had arisen in a rapidly industrializing America.

Dreiser was the ninth of ten surviving children in a family whose perennial poverty forced frequent moves between small Indiana towns and Chicago in search of a lower cost of living. Dreiser's own harsh experience of poverty as a youth and his early yearnings for wealth and success would become dominant themes in his novels, and the misadventures of his brothers and sisters in early adult life gave him additional material on which to base his characters. Dreiser received a sporadic education, and he began a career as a newspaper reporter in Chicago in 1892 and worked his way to the East Coast. While writing for a Pittsburgh newspaper in 1894, he read works by the scientists T. H. Huxley and John Tyndall, and adopted the speculations of the philosopher Herbert Spencer. Through these readings and his own experience, Dreiser came to believe that human beings are helpless in the grip of instincts and social forces beyond their control, and he judged human society as an unequal contest between the strong and the weak.

Dreiser began writing his first novel, *Sister Carrie*, in 1899. The story line of which involves a young kept woman whose "immorality" goes unpunished, led the publisher to limit the book's advertising, and consequently, it sold fewer than 500 copies. In the next nine years he achieved notable financial success as an editor-in-chief of several women's magazines. Somewhat encouraged by the earlier response to *Sister Carrie* in England and the novel's republication in America, Dreiser returned to writing fiction. The reception accorded to his second novel, *Jennie Gerhardt* (1911), the story of a woman who submits sexually to rich and powerful men to help her poverty-stricken family, lent him further encouragement. The first two volumes of a projected trilogy of novels based on the life of the American transportation magnate Charles T. Yerkes, *The Financier* (1912) and *The Titan* (1914), followed. In his next major novel, *The 'Genius'* (1915), he transformed his own life and numerous love affairs into a sprawling semi-autobiographical chronicle that was censured by the New York Society for the Suppression of Vice. In 1925, Dreiser's first novel in a decade, *An American Tragedy*, based on a celebrated murder case, was published. This book brought Dreiser a degree of critical and commercial success he had never before attained and would not thereafter equal. The book's highly critical view of the American legal system also made him the adopted champion of social reformers. A visit to the Soviet Union in 1927 produced a skeptical critique of that communist society entitled *Dreiser Looks at Russia* (1928). His only other significant publications in the late 1920s were collections of stories and sketches written earlier. The Great Depression of the 1930s ended Dreiser's prosperity and intensified his commitment to social causes. In the middle and late 1930s, his growing social consciousness and his interest in science converged to produce a vaguely mystical philosophy.

In 1938, Dreiser moved from New York to Los Angeles with Helen Richardson, who had been his mistress since 1920. Both *The*

*Bulwark* and *The Stoic* were published posthumously (1946 and 1947, respectively). A collection of Dreiser's philosophical speculations, Notes on Life, appeared in 1974.

As a naturalistic writer, Dreiser stressed determinism in his novels. His characters can't assert their will against natural and economic forces. He held that people are not entirely to blame for what they are and what they did. Again, he developed the capacity for photographic and relentless observation, thereby truthfully reflecting the society and people of his time and making his novels very believable and convincing. Almost all of his main characters are based on real people. Environment settings and social backgrounds are vividly described. His novels are full of tragedy, serious subjects, and the miserable side of society. He broke through the genteel tradition, revealed the life of the lower class people, and dared to expose the vulgar and ugly side of society. His powerful frankness widens the social and sexual range possible for literature in America.

His languages is very awkward, and his tone is very serious, which is a kind of natural narrative method. Free from an article's limitations, his narratives include a larger quantity of material and detailed descriptions. His great theme was the tremendous tensions that can arise among ambition, desire, and social morality. The new social problems that had arisen in the rapid industrialized America are also explored.

The following text is the first chapter of *Sister Carrie* (1899), in which is the story of a woman who flees the country life for Chicago, Illinois, and falls into a wayward life of sin.

Dissatisfied with her rural Wisconsin home, 18-year-old Caroline Meeber, referred to as Sister Carrie, takes a train to Chicago, where her older sister Minnie and her husband, Sven Hanson, have agreed to take her in. She encounters Drouet, a salesman, on the train, which gives her a first impression of rich people. In this chapter, many environments and their settings are vividly described, which shows Dreiser's view of environmental determinism.

## Chapter I

### THE MAGNET ATTRACTING: A WAIF AMID FORCES

When Caroline Meeber boarded the afternoon train for Chicago, her total outfit consisted of a small trunk, a cheap imitation alligator-skin satchel, a small lunch in a paper box, and a yellow leather snap purse, containing her ticket, a scrap of paper with her sister's address in Van Buren Street[1], and four dollars in money. It was in August, 1889. She was eighteen years of age, bright, timid, and full of the illusions of ignorance and youth. Whatever touch of regret at parting characterised her thoughts, it was certainly not for advantages now being given up. A gush of tears at her mother's farewell kiss, a touch in her throat when the cars clacked by the flour mill where her father worked by the day, a pathetic sigh as the familiar green environs of the village passed in review, and the threads which bound her so lightly to girlhood and home were irretrievably broken.

To be sure there was always the next station, where one might descend and return. There was the great city, bound more closely by these very trains which came up daily. Columbia City was not so very far away, even once she was in Chicago. What, pray, is a few hours--a few hundred miles? She looked at the little slip bearing her sister's address and wondered. She gazed at the green landscape, now passing in swift review, until her swifter thoughts replaced its impression with vague conjectures of what Chicago might be.

When a girl leaves her home at eighteen, she does one of two things. Either she falls into saving hands and becomes better, or she rapidly assumes the cosmopolitan standard of virtue and becomes worse. Of an intermediate balance, under the circumstances, there is no possibility. The city has its cunning wiles, no less than the infinitely smaller and more human tempter. There are large forces which allure with all the soulfulness of expression possible in the most cultured human. The gleam of a thousand lights is often as effective as the persuasive light in a wooing and fascinating eye. Half the undoing of the unsophisticated and natural mind is accomplished by forces wholly superhuman. A blare of sound, a roar of life, a vast array of human hives, appeal to the astonished senses in equivocal terms. Without a counsellor at hand to whisper cautious interpretations, what falsehoods may not these things breathe into the unguarded ear! Unrecognised for what they are, their beauty, like music, too often relaxes, then weakens, then perverts the simpler human perceptions.

Caroline, or Sister Carrie, as she had been half affectionately termed by the family, was possessed of a mind rudimentary in its power of observation and analysis. Self-interest with her was high, but not strong. It was, nevertheless, her guiding characteristic. Warm with the fancies of youth, pretty with the insipid prettiness of the formative period, possessed of a figure promising eventual shapeliness and an eye alight with certain native intelligence, she was a fair example of the middle American class—two generations removed from the emigrant. Books were beyond her interest—knowledge a sealed book. In the intuitive graces she was still crude. She could scarcely toss her head gracefully. Her hands were almost ineffectual. The feet, though small, were set flatly. And yet she was interested in her charms, quick to understand the keener pleasures of life, ambitious to gain in material things. A half-equipped little knight she was, venturing to reconnoitre the mysterious city and dreaming wild dreams of some vague, far-off supremacy, which should make it prey and subject—the proper penitent, groveling at a woman's slipper.

"That," said a voice in her ear, "is one of the prettiest little resorts in Wisconsin."

"Is it?" she answered nervously.

The train was just pulling out of Waukesha[2]. For some time she had been conscious of a man behind. She felt him observing her mass of hair. He had been fidgetting, and with natural intuition she felt a certain interest growing in that quarter. Her maidenly reserve, and a certain sense of what was conventional under the circumstances, called her to forestall and deny this familiarity, but the daring and magnetism of the individual, born of past experiences and triumphs, prevailed. She answered.

He leaned forward to put his elbows upon the back of her seat and proceeded to make himself volubly agreeable.

"Yes, that is a great resort for Chicago people. The hotels are swell. You are not familiar with this part of the country, are you?"

"Oh, yes, I am," answered Carrie. "That is, I live at Columbia City. I have never been through here, though."

"And so this is your first visit to Chicago," he observed.

All the time she was conscious of certain features out of the side of her eye. Flush, colourful cheeks, a light moustache, a grey fedora hat. She now turned and looked upon him in full, the instincts of self-protection and coquetry mingling confusedly in her brain.

"I didn't say that," she said.

"Oh," he answered, in a very pleasing way and with an assumed air of mistake, "I thought you did."

Here was a type of the travelling canvasser for a manufacturing house—a class which at that time was first being dubbed by the slang of the day "drummers."[3] He came within the meaning of a still newer term, which had sprung into general use among Americans in 1880, and which concisely expressed the thought of one whose dress or manners are calculated to elicit the admiration of susceptible young women—a "masher". His suit was of a striped and crossed pattern of brown wool, new at that time, but since become familiar as a business suit. The low crotch of the vest revealed a stiff shirt bosom of white and pink stripes. From his coat sleeves protruded a pair of linen cuffs of the same pattern, fastened with large, gold plate buttons, set with the common yellow agates known as "cat's-eyes". His fingers bore several rings—one, the ever-enduring heavy seal—and from his vest dangled a neat gold watch chain, from which was suspended the secret insignia of the Order of Elks[4]. The whole suit was rather tight-fitting, and was finished off with heavy-soled tan shoes, highly polished, and the grey fedora hat. He was, for the order of intellect represented, attractive, and whatever he had to recommend him, you may be sure was not lost upon Carrie, in this, her first glance.

Lest this order of individual should permanently pass, let me put down some of the most striking characteristics of his most successful manner and method. Good clothes, of course, were the first essential, the things without which he was nothing. A strong physical nature, actuated by a keen desire for the feminine, was the next. A mind free of any consideration of the problems or forces of the world and actuated not by greed, but an insatiable love of variable pleasure. His method was always simple. Its principal element was daring, backed, of course, by an intense desire and admiration for the sex. Let him meet with a young woman once and he would approach her with an air of kindly familiarity, not unmixed with pleading, which would result in most cases in a tolerant acceptance. If she showed any tendency to coquetry he would be apt to straighten her tie, or if she "took up" with him at all, to call her by her first name. If he visited a department store it was to lounge familiarly over the counter and ask some leading Questions: In more exclusive circles, on the train or in waiting stations, he went slower. If some seemingly vulnerable object appeared he was all attention—to pass the compliments of the day, to lead the way to the parlor car, carrying her grip, or, failing that, to take a seat next her with the hope of being able to court her to her destination.

Pillows, books, a footstool, the shade lowered; all these figured in the things which he could do. If, when she reached her destination he did not alight and attend her baggage for her, it was because, in his own estimation, he had signally failed.

A woman should some day write the complete philosophy of clothes. No matter how young, it is one of the things she wholly comprehends. There is an indescribably faint line in the matter of man's apparel which somehow divides for her those who are worth glancing at and those who are not. Once an individual has passed this faint line on the way downward he will get no glance from her. There is another line at which the dress of a man will cause her to study her own. This line the individual at her elbow now marked for Carrie. She became conscious of an inequality. Her own plain blue dress, with its black cotton tape trimmings, now seemed to her shabby. She felt the worn state of her shoes.

"Let's see," he went on, "I know quite a number of people in your town. Morgenroth the clothier and Gibson the dry goods man."

"Oh, do you?" she interrupted, aroused by memories of longings their show windows had cost her.

At last he had a clew to her interest, and followed it deftly. In a few minutes he had come about into her seat. He talked of sales of clothing, his travels, Chicago, and the amusements of that city.

"If you are going there, you will enjoy it immensely. Have you relatives?"

"I am going to visit my sister," she explained.

"You want to see Lincoln Park," he said, "and Michigan Avenue[5].

They are putting up great buildings there. It's a second New York—great. So much to see—theatres, crowds, fine houses—oh, you'll like that."

There was a little ache in her fancy of all he described. Her insignificance in the presence of so much magnificence faintly affected her. She realised that hers was not to be a round of pleasure, and yet there was something promising in all the material prospect he set forth. There was something satisfactory in the attention of this individual with his good clothes. She could not help smiling as he told her of some popular actress of whom she reminded him. She was not silly, and yet attention of this sort had its weight.

"You will be in Chicago some little time, won't you?" he observed at one turn of the now easy conversation.

"I don't know," said Carrie vaguely—a flash vision of the possibility of her not securing employment rising in her mind.

"Several weeks, anyhow," he said, looking steadily into her eyes.

There was much more passing now than the mere words indicated. He recognised the indescribable thing that made up for fascination and beauty in her. She realised that she was of interest to him from the one standpoint which a woman both delights in and fears. Her manner was simple, though for the very reason that she had not yet learned the many little affectations with which women conceal their true feelings. Some things she did appeared bold. A clever companion—had she ever had one—would have warned her never to look a man in the eyes so steadily.

"Why do you ask?" she said.

"Well, I'm going to be there several weeks. I'm going to study stock at our place and get new samples. I might show you 'round."

"I don't know whether you can or not. I mean I don't know whether I can. I shall be living with my sister, and—" "Well, if she minds, we'll fix that." He took out his pencil and a little pocket note-book as if it were all settled. "What is your address there?"

She fumbled her purse which contained the address slip.

He reached down in his hip pocket and took out a fat purse. It was filled with slips of paper, some mileage books, a roll of greenbacks. It impressed her deeply. Such a purse had never been carried by any one attentive to her. Indeed, an experienced traveller, a brisk man of the world, had never come within such close range before. The purse, the shiny tan shoes, the smart new suit, and the air with which he did things, built up for her a dim world of fortune, of which he was the centre. It disposed her pleasantly toward all he might do.

He took out a neat business card, on which was engraved Bartlett, Caryoe & Company, and down in the left-hand corner, Chas. H. Drouet.

"That's me," he said, putting the card in her hand and touching his name. "It's pronounced Drew-eh. Our family was French, on my father's side."

She looked at it while he put up his purse. Then he got out a letter from a bunch in his coat pocket. "This is the house I travel for," he went on, pointing to a picture on it, "corner of State and Lake." There was pride in his voice. He felt that it was something to be connected with such a place, and he made her feel that way.

"What is your address?" he began again, fixing his pencil to write.

She looked at his hand.

"Carrie Meeber," she said slowly. "Three hundred and fifty-four West Van Buren Street, care S. C. Hanson."

He wrote it carefully down and got out the purse again. "You'll be at home if I come around Monday night?" he said.

"I think so," she answered.

How true it is that words are but the vague shadows of the volumes we mean. Little audible links, they are, chaining together great inaudible feelings and purposes. Here were these two, bandying little phrases, drawing purses, looking at cards, and both unconscious of how inarticulate all their real feelings were. Neither was wise enough to be sure of the working of the mind of the other. He could not tell how his luring succeeded.

She could not realise that she was drifting, until he secured her address. Now she felt that she had yielded something--he, that he had gained a victory. Already they felt that they were somehow associated. Already he took control in directing the conversation. His words were easy. Her manner was relaxed.

They were nearing Chicago. Signs were everywhere numerous. Trains flashed by them. Across wide stretches of flat, open prairie they could see lines of telegraph poles stalking across the fields toward the great city. Far away were indications of suburban towns, some big smokestacks towering high in the air.

Frequently there were two-story frame houses standing out in the open fields, without fence or trees, lone outposts of the approaching army of homes.

To the child, the genius with imagination, or the wholly untravelled, the approach to a great city for the first time is a wonderful thing. Particularly if it be evening—that mystic period between the glare and gloom of the world when life is changing from one sphere or condition to another. Ah, the promise of the night. What does it not hold for the weary! What old illusion of hope is not here forever repeated! Says the soul of the toiler to itself, "I shall soon be free. I shall be in the ways and the hosts of the merry. The streets, the lamps, the lighted chamber set for dining, are for me. The theatre, the halls, the parties, the ways of rest and the paths of song-these are mine in the night." Though all humanity be still enclosed in the shops, the thrill runs abroad. It is in the air. The dullest feel something which they may not always express or describe. It is the lifting of the burden of toil.

Sister Carrie gazed out of the window. Her companion, affected by her wonder, so contagious are all things, felt anew some interest in the city and pointed out its marvels. Already vast net-works of tracks the sign and insignia of Chicago—stretched on either hand. There were thousands of cars and a clangor of engine bells. At the sides of this traffic stream stood dingy houses, smoky mills, tall elevators.[6] Through the interstices, evidences of the stretching city could be seen. Street cars waited at crossings for the train to go by. Gatemen toiled at wooden arms which closed the streets. Bells clanged, the rails clacked, whistles sounded afar off.

"This is Northwest Chicago," said Drouet. "This is the Chicago River," and he pointed to a little muddy creek, crowded with the huge masted wanderers from far-off waters nosing the black-posted banks. With a puff, a clang, and a clatter of rails it was gone. "Chicago is getting to be a great town," he went on. "It's a wonder. You'll find lots to see here."

She did not hear this very well. Her heart was troubled by a kind of terror. The fact that she was alone, away from home, rushing into a great sea of life and endeavour, began to tell. She could not help but feel a little choked for breath—a little sick as her heart beat so fast. She half closed her eyes and tried to think it was nothing, that Columbia City was only a little way off.

"Chicago! Chicago!" called the brakeman, slamming open the door. They were rushing into a more crowded yard, alive with the clatter and clang of life. She began to gather up her poor little grip and closed her hand firmly upon her purse. Drouet arose, kicked his legs to straighten his trousers, and seized his clean yellow grip.

"I suppose your people will be here to meet you?" he said. "Let me carry your grip."

"Oh, no," she said. "I'd rather you wouldn't. I'd rather you wouldn't be with me when I meet my sister."

"All right," he said in all kindness. "I'll be near, though, in case she isn't here, and take you out there safely."

"You're so kind," said Carrie, feeling the goodness of such attention in her strange situation.

"Chicago!" called the brakeman, drawing the word out long.

They were under a great shadowy train shed, where the lamps were already beginning to shine out, with passenger cars all about and the train moving at a snail's pace. The people in the car were all up and crowding about the door.

"Well, here we are," said Drouet, leading the way to the door. "Good-bye, till I see you Monday."

"Good-bye," she answered, taking his proffered hand.

"Remember, I'll be looking till you find your sister."

She smiled into his eyes.

They filed out, and he affected to take no notice of her. A lean-faced, rather commonplace woman recognised Carrie on the platform and hurried forward.

"Why, Sister Carrie!" she began, and there was embrace of welcome.

Carrie realised the change of affectional atmosphere at once. Amid all the maze, uproar, and novelty she felt cold reality taking her by the hand. No world of light and merriment. No round of amusement. Her sister carried with her most of the grimness of shift and toil.

"Why, how are all the folks at home?" she began; "how is father, and mother?"

Carrie answered, but was looking away. Down the aisle, toward the gate leading into the waiting-room and the street, stood Drouet. He was looking back. When he saw that she saw him and was safe with her sister he turned to go, sending back the shadow of a smile. Only Carrie saw it. She felt something lost to her when he moved away.

When he disappeared she felt his absence thoroughly. With her sister she was much alone, a lone figure in a tossing, thoughtless sea.

## Notes

1. East-west Chicago street that, roughly, divides the city in half.

2. A city in Wisconsin about 100 miles north of Chicago on Lake Michigan.

3. "Canvassers" and "drummers" are salesmen.

4. A fraternal organization.

5. A fashionable street of stores, office buildings, and the Art Institute. "Lincoln Park": a large lakefront park, home to a zoo and other attractions.

6. Grain elevators.

## Questions

1. What does "the magnet attracting" mean? Who is a waif? What are the forces?

2. "When he saw that she saw him and was safe with her sister he turned to go, sending back the shadow of a smile. Only Carrie saw it. She felt something lost to her when he moved away. When he disappeared she felt his absence thoroughly." What did Carrie lose?

### (6) Stephen Crane (1871—1900)

During his tragically brief life, Stephen Crane established himself as both a leader of the Naturalist movement and one of the greatest writers of his time. Born in Newark, New Jersey, Crane was the youngest in a family of 14 children. His desire to write was inspired by his family: his father, a Methodist minister, and his mother, a devout woman dedicated to social concerns, were both writers of religious articles; and two of his brothers were journalists. Early in his career, Crane worked as a newspaper writer in New York City. His experiences there inspired his first novel *Maggie: A Girl of the Streets* (1893). Its grimly realistic portrayal of life in the city's slums was so frank and shocking that Crane was unable to find a publisher, so he printed the book at his own expense.

Influenced by the Darwinism of the times, Crane viewed individuals as victims of purposeless forces and believed that they encountered only hostility in their relationships with other individuals, with society, with nature, and with God. Crane's second novel, *The Red Badge of Courage* (1895), is a classic of American literature that realistically depicts the psychological complexities of fear and courage on the battlefield. Influenced by William Dean Howells's theory of realism, Crane utilized his keen observations, as well as personal experiences, to achieve a narrative vividness and sense of immediacy matched by few American writers before him. This work won him international fame. Often compared to Impressionist paintings, *The Red Badge of Courage* is a series of vivid episodes in which a young soldier, Henry Fleming, confronts a gamut of emotions—fear, courage, pride, and humility—in his attempt to understand his battlefield experiences; in this respect, Fleming represents the "everyman" of war.

His often-anthologized short stories *The Open Boat*(1897—1898),

*The Blue Hotel*(1898), and *The Bride Comes to Yellow Sky*(1898) are among the most skillfully crafted stories in American literature. Crane also authored a single collection of poetry, *The Black Riders, and Other Lines* (1895). Although not widely known, this volume of free verse foreshadowed the work of the Imagist poets with its concise, vivid images.

In 1897, after marrying Cora Taylor, the proprietor of the dubiously named Hotel de Dream—a combination hotel, nightclub, and brothel—they moved to England, where Crane formed literary friendships with Joseph Conrad, H. G. Wells, and Henry James.

The story here is mainly about a lieutenant getting injured while dividing coffee on the battlefield and goes all the way to the hospital, only to lose his arm there. The battlefield is filled with chaos and described with irony. All characters are described as if reaching into the depths of their hearts.

## An Episode of War [1]

The lieutenant's rubber blanket lay on the ground, and upon it he had poured the company's supply of coffee. Corporals and other representatives of the grimy and hot-throated men who lined the breastwork had come for each squad's portion.

The lieutenant was frowning and serious at this task of division. His lips pursed as he drew with his sword various crevices in the heap until brown squares of coffee, astoundingly equal in size, appeared on the blanket. He was on the verge of a great triumph in mathematics and the corporals were thronging forward, each to reap a little square, when suddenly the lieutenant cried out and looked quickly at a man near him as if he suspected it was a case of personal assault. The others cried out also when they saw blood upon the lieutenant's sleeve.

He had winced like a man stung, swayed dangerously, and then straightened. The sound of his hoarse breathing was plainly audible. He looked sadly, mystically, over the breastwork at the green face of a wood where now were many little puffs of white smoke. During this moment, the men about him gazed statue-like and silent, astonished and awed by this catastrophe which had happened when catastrophes were not expected—when they had leisure to observe it.

As the lieutenant stared at the wood, they too swung their heads so that for another moment all hands, still silent, contemplated the distant forest as if their minds were fixed upon the mystery of a bullet's journey.

The officer had, of course, been compelled to take his sword at once into his left hand. He did not hold it by the hilt. He gripped it at the middle of the blade, awkwardly. Turning his eyes from the hostile wood, he looked at the sword as he held it there, and seemed puzzled as to what to do with it, where to put it. In short this weapon had of a sudden become a strange thing to him. He looked at it in a kind of stupefaction, as if he had been miraculously endowed with a trident, a sceptre, or a spade.

Finally, he tried to sheath it. To sheath a sword held by the left hand, at the middle of the blade, in a scabbard hung at the left hip, is a feat worthy of a sawdust ring. This wounded officer engaged in a desperate struggle with the sword and the wobbling scabbard, and during the time of it, he breathed like a wrestler.

But at this instant the men, the spectators, awoke from their stone-like poses and crowded forward sympathetically. The orderly-sergeant took the sword and tenderly placed it in the scabbard. At the time, he leaned nervously backward, and did not allow even his finger to brush the body of the lieutenant. A wound gives strange dignity to him who bears it. Well men shy from this new and terrible majesty. It is as if the wounded man's hand is upon the curtain which hangs before the revelations of all existence, the meaning of ants, potentates, wars, cities, sunshine, snow, a feather dropped from a bird's wing, and the power of it sheds radiance upon a bloody form, and makes the other men understand sometimes that they are little. His comrades look at him with large eyes thoughtfully. Moreover, they fear vaguely that the weight of a finger upon him might send him headlong, precipitate the tragedy, hurl him at once into the dim grey unknown. And so the orderly-sergeant while sheathing the sword leaned nervously backward.

There were others who proffered assistance. One timidly presented his shoulder and asked the lieutenant if he cared to lean upon it, but the latter waved them away mournfully. He wore the look of one who knows he is the victim of a terrible disease and understands his helplessness. He again stared over the breastwork at the forest, and then turning went slowly rearward. He held his right wrist tenderly in his left hand, as if the wounded arm was made of very brittle glass.

And the men in silence stared at the wood, then at the departing lieutenant—then at the wood, then at the lieutenant.

As the wounded officer passed from the line of battle, he was enabled to see many things which as a participant in the fight were unknown to him. He saw a general on a black horse gazing over the lines of blue infantry at the green woods which veiled his problems. An aide galloped furiously, dragged his horse suddenly to a halt, saluted, and presented a paper. It was, for a wonder, precisely like an historical painting.

To the rear of the general and his staff, a group, composed of a bugler, two or three orderlies, and the bearer of the corps standard, all upon maniacal horses, were working like slaves to hold their ground, preserve their respectful interval, while the shells bloomed in the air about them, and caused their chargers to make furious quivering leaps.

A battery, a tumultuous and shining mass, was swirling toward the right. The wild thud of hoofs, the cries of the riders shouting blame and praise, menace and encouragement, and, last, the roar of the wheels, the slant of the glistening guns, brought the lieutenant to an intent pause. The battery swept in curves that stirred the heart; it made halts as dramatic as the crash of a wave on the rocks, and when it fled onward, this aggregation of wheels, levers, motors, had a beautiful unity, as if it were a missile. The sound of it was a war-chorus that reached into the depths of man's emotion.

The lieutenant, still holding his arm as if it were of glass, stood watching this battery until all detail of it was lost, save the figures of the riders, which rose and fell and waved lashes over the black mass.

Later he turned his eyes toward the battle where the shooting sometimes crackled like bush-fires, sometimes sputtered with exasperating irregularity, and sometimes reverberated like the thunder. He saw the smoke rolling upward and saw crowds of men who ran and cheered, or stood and blazed away at the inscrutable distance.

He came upon some stragglers and they told him how to find the field hospital. They described its exact location. In fact these men, no longer having part in the battle, knew more of it than others. They told the performance of every corps, every division, the opinion of every general. The lieutenant, carrying his wounded arm rearward, looked upon them with wonder.

At the roadside a brigade was making coffee and buzzing with talk like a girls' boarding-school. Several officers came out to him and inquired concerning things of which he knew nothing. One, seeing his arm, began to scold. "Why, man, that's no way to do. You want to fix that thing." He appropriated the lieutenant and the lieutenant's wound. He cut the sleeve and laid bare the arm, every nerve of which softly fluttered under his touch. He bound his handkerchief over the wound, scolding away in the meantime. His tone allowed one to think that he was in the habit of being wounded every day. The lieutenant hung his head, feeling, in this presence, that he did not know how to be correctly wounded.

The low white tents of the hospital were grouped around an old schoolhouse. There was here a singular commotion. In the foreground two ambulances interlocked wheels in the deep mud. The drivers were tossing the blame of it back and forth, gesticulating and berating, while from the ambulances, both crammed with wounded, there came an occasional groan. An interminable crowd of bandaged men were coming and going. Great numbers sat under the trees nursing heads or arms or legs. There was a dispute of some kind raging on the steps of the school-house. Sitting with his back against a tree a man with a face as grey as a new army blanket was serenely smoking a corn-cob pipe. The lieutenant wished to rush forward and inform him that he was dying.

A busy surgeon was passing near the lieutenant. "Good morning," he said with a friendly smile. Then he caught sight of the lieutenant's arm and his face at once changed. "Well, let's have a look at it." He seemed possessed suddenly of a great contempt for the lieutenant. This wound evidently placed the latter on a very low social plane. The doctor cried out impatiently. What mutton-head had tied it up that way anyhow. The lieutenant answered: "Oh, a man."

When the wound was disclosed the doctor fingered it disdainfully. "Humph," he said. "You come along with me and I'll 'tend to you." His voice contained the same scorn as if he were saying: "You will have to go to jail."

The lieutenant had been very meek but now his face flushed, and he looked into the doctor's eyes. "I guess I won't have it amputated," he said.

"Nonsense, man! nonsense! nonsense!" cried the doctor. "Come along, now. I won't amputate it. Come along. Don't be a baby."

"Let go of me," said the lieutenant, holding back wrathfully. His glance fixed upon the door of the old school-house, as sinister to him as the portals of death.

And this is the story of how the lieutenant lost his arm. When he reached home his sisters, his mother, his wife, sobbed for a long time at the sight of the flat sleeve. "Oh, well," he said, standing shamefaced amid these tears. "I don't suppose it matters so much as all that."

1899

## Notes

1. First published in the English magazine *The Gentlewoman* (December 1899). The source of the text printed here is Vol. 6 of the University of Virginia edition of *The Works of Stephen Crane*.

## Questions

1. According to Naturalists, human beings are weak and feeble while confronting the power of determinism. Try to find some examples to illustrate it in the text.

2. "And the men in silence stared at the wood, then at the departing lieutenant — then at the wood, then at the lieutenant." Try to find the symbolic meaning of the "Wood".

# Part V The Age of Modernism (1918—1945)

## 1. Historical Background

There are three great events in this period: the end of the First World War, the Great Depression, and the Second World War.

### (1) The End of the First World War

American president Wilson signed the armistice with Germany in November, 1918, which marked the end of the First World War in America. The First World War contributed to an economic boom and made the United States the strongest capitalist country. Rapid industrialization and urbanization brought fierce competition in America. The sound of production could be heard everywhere. The economic boom of the United States created an abundant supply of goods, such as cars, household appliances, and other daily consumer goods. Entertainment, tourism, leisure, and other urban lifestyles, as well as advertising and media, contributed to the rise of consumerism in the United States. But the First World War had a great impact on the American mind and spirit. People began to doubt democracy and freedom in the United States. They were "lost" and despaired for their own fate. Instead of hoping for a better future, they preferred the views of "seize the day" and "carpe diem".

Harding was elected as American president in 1921. He abolished Wilson's wartime measures, encouraged investment, gave capitalists more freedom, and adopted protectionism in international trade, which led to "industrial prosperity" of the 1920s. From 1923 to 1929, the world's capitalism entered a relatively stable period. In the United States, due to the update to fixed capital, the rise of construction, the expansion of the automobile and steel industry, and the surge in the export of goods and capital, it saw a new rise in American industry and commerce in 1923. At the same time, the monopolies spread across the banking and industrial sectors—especially water, electricity, and gas utilities—and even into the retail commercial sector. The rule of Coolidge witnessed an economic boom in the United States. Private monopoly capital greatly expanded. However, due to the deformed development and overproduction of infant industries, sectors of the national economy were seriously unbalanced, and its agriculture was in a prolonged and slow crisis. In October, 1929, the economic crisis firstly occurred in the United States.

### （2）The Great Depression

The Great Depression was an economic slump in North America, Europe, and other industrialized areas of the world that began in 1929 and lasted until about 1939. It was the longest and most severe depression ever experienced by the industrialized western world. The Great Depression may be said to have begun with a catastrophic collapse of stock-market prices on the New York Stock Exchange in October 1929. The market crash marked the beginning of a decade of high unemployment, poverty, low profits, deflation, plunging farm incomes, and lost opportunities for economic growth and personal advancement. The Great Depression had important consequences in the political sphere. It led to the election of the Democrat Franklin D. Roosevelt to the presidency in late 1932. Roosevelt introduced a number of major changes in the structure of the American economy, using increased government regulation and massive public-works projects to promote a recovery. But despite this active intervention, mass unemployment and economic stagnation continued, though on a somewhat reduced scale, with about 15 percent of the work force still unemployed in 1939 at the outbreak of World War II. After that, unemployment dropped rapidly as American factories were flooded with orders from overseas for armaments and munitions. The depression ended completely soon after the United States' entry into World War II in 1941.

### (3) The Second World War

The Second World War broke out in September, 1939, when Germany invaded Poland, and England together with France, declared war on Germany. During the first years of the War, most Americans, who still felt bitter about the result of the First World War, favored America's neutrality. Japanese planes, on the morning of December 7, 1941, suddenly showered bombs on the American fleet and military installations in Pearl Harbor, Hawaii. About 3,000 Americans were killed or wounded with the loss of 247 planes and 18 ships. A few minutes later, Japan declared war on America and the U.S. government responded by declaring war against Japan the following day. This formally brought America into the Second World War against fascism.

After the Pacific War broke out, the Unites States gradually increased its aid to China. War materials, including military equipment, munitions, and food were shipped to China in support of the war against Japan. Nearly two thousand American airmen sacrificed their lives while flying war materials to China over the Himalaya Mountains. America's war efforts were mainly concentrated in Europe which was far more important in the eyes of Americans. Several million American soldiers and large amounts of war materials were transported to the battlefields in Europe.

Soldiers fought overseas while Americans at home also sacrificed. Many women entered the workforce to help make munitions and implements of war. These women were represented through the iconic "Rosie the Riveter." On the 6th and 9th of August in 1945, American aircraft dropped two atom bombs in Japan, killing nearly 200,000 people. On August 15, 1945, Japan surrendered unconditionally and the Second World War ended. Soon after the surrender, American troops occupied Japan.

After the Second World War, America became the strongest power in the capitalist world. The three Axis powers were destroyed while other capitalist countries were greatly weakened. Many countries were deep in debt to America. European countries had not recovered from war destruction and the capitalist world market was wide open to American goods. The demobilization of more than 10 million American soldiers who soon returned to civil life resulted in the baby-boom, which in turn increased consumption. America's large productivity enabled the country to produce enough goods for the market, resulting in economic prosperity.

## 2. Literature of the Period

From the beginning of the 20th century, American literature entered the period of modernism. Modernism is a cultural movement that generally includes the progressive art of architecture, design, literature, music, dance, painting, and other visual arts which emerged at the beginning of the 20th century, particularly in the years following World War I. It was a movement of artists and designers who rebelled against late 19th-century academic and historic tradition, and embraced the new economic, social, and political aspects of the emerging modern world. The distinctive feature of literary modernism was its strong and conscious break with traditional forms, perceptions, and techniques of expression, and its great concern with language and all aspects of medium. It was persistently experimental.

### (1) The Achievements of Poetry

The poets of the time can be roughly divided into three groups: Chicago poets, expatriate poets, and New England Poets.

① Chicago poets: In the early 20th century, Chicago became the center of poetry revolution, where poets expressed their attitude against traditional techniques, writing purposes, and themes of poetry. Their main publication is called Poetry. Chicago poets adhered to the tradition of Whitman, both in poetry form and theme to reflect the thoughts and feelings of the common people through poetry. The representative poets include Vachel Lindsay (1879—1931), Edgar Lee

Masters (1869—1950), Carl Sandburg (1878—1967), and Hart Crane (1899—1932).

② Expatriate poets: The leading figures are Ezra Pound (1885—1972) and T.S. Eliot (1888—1965). When Pound first arrived in London in 1908, he created imagism with the British poet Hulme. The imagism poetry is characterized as having a specific theme, clear image, plain language, no unrelated image, and free form. American imagism poets who accepted his ideas included Amy Lowell (1874—1925), Hilda Doolittle (1886—1961), and William Carlos Williams (1883—1963). Eliot was a leading figure in the new poetry movement. His *The Waste Land* (1922) expresses the spiritual disillusionment of the western people with the use of many European literary allusions, myths, historical events, and imagination. *The Waste Land* is regarded as an epoch-making work in western modern literature.

③ New England Poets: Robert Frost (1874—1963) and Edward Arlington Robinson (1869—1935) belong to this third group of poets. They were influenced by the new poetry movement but did not fully accept its principles and proposals. The major works of Frost include *A Boy's Will, West-Running Brook*, and *A Further Range*. The best known work of Robinson is *The Children of the Night*.

### （2）The Achievements of Drama

Because of Puritanism's opposition to drama, American drama developed slowly. At the end of the 19th century, European drama witnessed its heyday. The playwrights of this era tried to abandon the conventions of the old plays and experimented boldly with different techniques, even using two different techniques in one play, such as the combination of realism and romanticism or symbolism. This style, integrating fantasy with reality, accelerated the development of the Theatre of the Absurd since the Second World War. The dramas of this period focused on social problems and exposing the dark side of society through criticism of purpose, for example, *The Adding Machine* (1923) by Elmer Rice (1892—1962), and *Waiting for Lefty* (1935) by Clifford Odets (1906—1963), etc.

Among them, the most famous playwright was Eugene O'Neill (1888—1953). He followed the traditional writing form and conducted some innovations as well. He fully absorbed the advantages of naturalism, symbolism, and expressionism. His major works include *Beyond the Horizon* (1918), *Emperor Jones* (1920), *The Hairy Ape* (1921), *The Great God Brown* (1925), and *Strange Interlude* (1927). O'Neill created a unique style, which made American drama reach unprecedented prosperity in the 1920s and 1930s, and truly became an important part of American literature. He is a very important figure in the history of American drama.

### (3) The Achievements of Novels

The country witnessed the prosperity of novel between the two World Wars. Many novelists showed their talent in novel writing.

Gertrude Stein (1874—1946), who lived overseas, had the greatest influence on American writers in the 1920s. She made a bold reform on traditional novel techniques in her masterpiece *The Lives of Three Women* (1903). She absorbed the technique of film to express emotion in pictures. She advocated simple diction in writing. Her creative ideas and practices had a great influence on Anderson and other young writers who emerged after the First World War.

Other notable female writers around World War I include Edith Wharton (1862—1937), Ellen Glasgow (1874—1945), and Willa Gather (1873—1947). They were local writers who followed the realistic tradition and were concerned about the influence of wealth and materialism on traditional morality.

With the rise of big industry and big cities, some American writers began to expose the people's spirit trapped to the idea of an ungated life in small towns, and the narrow and vulgar traditional ideas. Sinclair Lewis (1885—1951) and Sherwood Anderson (1876—1941) are the two representative writers. In 1930, Lewis became the first American writer to win the Nobel Prize for Literature.

Many young writers who published their works in the 1920s are often called the "Lost Generation". The main representative writers are John Dos Passes (1896—1970), F. Scott Fitzgerald (1896—1940), and Ernest Hemingway (1899—1961). John Dos Passes is one of the earliest writers to show young people's resistance to society. F. Scott Fitzgerald's first novel, *This Side of Paradise* (1920), and more than 100 short stories by him, truly reflect the abundant material and barren spirituality of the people in the Jazz Age, and vividly reproduce the desperation of the American youth in the 1920s. Ernest Hemingway is another leading figure of the "Lost Generation." His masterpieces include *The Sun Also Rises* (1926), *A Farewell to Arms* (1929), *For Whom the Bell Tolls* (1940), and *The Old Man and the Sea* (1952).

John Steinbeck (1902—1968) was a very important novelist in the 1930s. His masterpiece *The Grapes of Wrath* (1939), reflected

The Great Depression of the 1930s. The novel deeply revealed the serious social problems in the United States through the story of the Joad family, a sharecropper in Oklahoma, who is forced to leave their hometown to make a living in the west.

During this period, some southern writers stepped onto the literature stage. The most important one is William Faulkner (1897—1962). In all, he wrote 19 novels and more than 70 short stories, most of which were set in a fictional place called Yoknapatawpha in Mississippi. His major works include *The Sound and The Fury* (1929), *Light in August* (1932), *Absalom, Absalom*! (1936), and *Go Down, Moses* (1942).

### (4) Literary Criticism

Literary criticism began to play a leading role in American literature between the two World Wars. The most influential literary theory is the "new criticism." The new criticism accepted Eliot's theory, opposed to the criticizing method that introduces the background of the work, the life of the author, and the writing process of the work. New criticism considered literary works as art and focused on the detailed analysis of the work itself. Although the new criticism often ignores the social significance of works and separates the relationship between works and history, it proposes a series of theoretical principles, which have played a great role in promoting the development of American literary theory. The leading figures include R. P. Blackmur (1904—1965), John Crowe Ransom (1888—1974), Kenneth Burke (1897—1993), and Cleanth Brooks (1906—1994).

### (5) Harlem Renaissance

From the late 1920s to the early 1930s, the black writers living in the slums of Harlem, New York, created a large number of works to depict the miserable life of African Americans, which was called the "Harlem Renaissance." The leading figures are Claude McKay (1890—1948), Countee Cullen (1903—1946), Jean Toomer (1894—1967), and Langston Hughes (1902—1967). The economic crisis of the 1930s slowed the development of the Harlem Renaissance. However, a group of black writers led by Richard Wright (1908—1960) still published a lot of works. *Wright's Native Son* (1940) won a similar reputation to Dreiser's *An American Tragedy* (1925). Wright's novels are famous for well-knitted plots, concise language, and rich passion.

## 3. Representative Writers' Works

### (1) Ernest Hemingway (1899—1961)

Ernest Hemingway (1899—1961) was born into a doctor's family. After graduating from high school, he worked as a journalist. The requirements of the journalist profession for writing had a great impact on the content and style of his later works. During the first World War, Hemingway joined a volunteer ambulance team and was wounded by shrapnel on the Italian front. Such experiences provided indispensable material for his famous book *A Farewell to Arms* (1929) and many other short stories. After the war, he went to Paris to work as a journalist and met several American writers, including Stein and Pound, who were living in Europe. He received their help in writing.

In 1925, he published a collection of short stories, *In Our Time*, which attracted people's attention. *The Sun Also Rises* (1926), the first full-length novel, describes the American youth who lived in Paris after the First World War, were lost and empty, and sought spiritual comfort by drinking alcohol and the stimulation of love. It established Hemingway's position in the literary field and made him the representative of the "Lost Generation". The novel *A Farewell to Arms*, describes the irreparable psychological trauma and the collapse of traditional beliefs brought about by the war through the story of Henry, the hero, who was injured and lost his lover and child in World War I. Similarly, *For Whom the Bell Tolls* (1940) uses the Spanish Civil War as the setting to depict the protagonist fighting for beliefs and ideals, and bravely facing death in a cruel battle. His last book, *The Old Man and the Sea* (1952), which embodies his life values and code of conduct, won him the Nobel Prize for literature in 1954. In 1961, he committed suicide under the torture of illness.

Hemingway is a very important writer of the 20th century. He not only describes the disasters and emptiness faced by mankind, but also shows the courage and dignity of people in adversity. His protagonists may be confused and desperate, but in the face of pain, they will talk and laugh with determination and never give up their humanity. Hemingway's style of writing inherits the tradition of Mark Twain's colloquial style. His writing is simple and plain, but its connotation is very rich. As his metaphor goes: the dignity of an iceberg's movement is that only one-eighth of it emerges from the water.

The following text is the third chapter of *The Sun Also Rises*.

## The Sun Also Rises[1]

### Chapter III

[It was a warm spring night]

It was a warm spring night and I sat at a table on the terrace of the Napolitain after Robert[2] had gone, watching it get dark and the electric signs come on, and the red and green stop-and-go traffic-signal, and the crowd going by, and the horse-cabs clippety-clopping along at the edge of the solid taxi traffic, and the poules[3]going by, singly and in pairs, looking for the evening meal. I watched a good-looking girl walk past the table and watched her go up the street and lost sight of her, and watched another, and then saw the first one coming back again. She went by once more and I caught her eye, and she came over and sat down at the table. The waiter came up.

"Well, what will you drink?" I asked.

"Pernod."

"That's not good for little girls."

"Little girl yourself. Dites garçon, un pernod."[4]

"A pernod for me, too."

"What's the matter?" she asked. "Going on a party?"

"Sure. Aren't you?"

"I don't know. You never know in this town."

"Don't you like Paris?"

"No."

"Why don't you go somewhere else?"

"Isn't anywhere else."

"You're happy, all right."

"Happy, hell!"

Pernod is greenish imitation absinthe.[5] When you add water it turns milky. It tastes like licorice and it has a good uplift, but it drops you just as far. We sat and drank it, and the girl looked sullen.

"Well," I said, "are you going to buy me a dinner?"

She grinned and I saw why she made a point of not laughing. With her mouth closed she was a rather pretty girl. I paid for the saucers and we walked out to the street. I hailed a horse-cab and the driver pulled up at the curb. Settled back in the slow,smoothly rolling fiacre we moved up the Avenue de l'Opéra,[6] passed the locked doors of the shops, their windows lighted, the Avenue broad and shiny and almost deserted. The cab passed the New York Herald bureau with the window full of clocks.

"What are all the clocks for?" she asked.

"They show the hour all over America."

"Don't kid me."

We turned off the Avenue up the Rue des Pyramides, through the traffic of the Rue de Rivoli, and through a dark gate into the Tuileries.[7] She cuddled against me and I put my arm around her. She looked up to be kissed. She touched me with one hand and I put her hand away.

"Never mind."

"What's the matter? You sick?"

"Yes."

"Everybody's sick. I'm sick, too."

We came out of the Tuileries into the light and crossed the Seine and then turned up the Rue des Saints Pères.[8]

"You oughtn't to drink pernod if you're sick."

"You neither."

"It doesn't make any difference with me. It doesn't make any difference with a woman."

"What are you called?"

"Georgette. How are you called?"

"Jacob."

"That's a Flemish name."

"American too."

"You're not Flamand?"

"No, American."

"Good, I detest Flamands."

By this time we were at the restaurant. I called to the cocher[9] to stop. We got out and Georgette did not like the looks of the place.

"This is no great thing of a restaurant."

"No," I said. "Maybe you would rather go to Foyot's.[10] Why don't you keep the cab and go on?"

I had picked her up because of a vague sentimental idea that it would be nice to eat with some one. It was a long time since I had dined with a poule, and I had forgotten how dull it could be. We went into the restaurant, passed Madame Lavigne at the desk and into a little room. Georgette cheered up a little under the food.

"It isn't bad here," she said. "It isn't chic, but the food is all right."

"Better than you eat in Liège."

"Brussels,[11] you mean."

We had another bottle of wine and Georgette made a joke. She smiled and showed all her bad teeth, and we touched glasses.

"You're not a bad type," she said. "It's a shame you're sick. We get on well. What's the matter with you, anyway?"

"I got hurt in the war," I said.

"Oh, that dirty war."

We would probably have gone on and discussed the war and agreed that it was in reality a calamity for civilization, and perhaps would have been better avoided. I was bored enough. Just then from the other room someone called: "Barnes! I say, Barnes! Jacob Barnes!"

"It's a friend calling me," I explained, and went out.

There was Braddocks at a big table with a party: Cohn, Frances Clyne,[12] Mrs.Braddocks, several people I did not know.

"You're coming to the dance, aren't you?" Braddocks asked.

"What dance?"

"Why, the dancings. Don't you know we've revived them?" Mrs. Braddocks put in.

"You must come, Jake. We're all going," Frances said from the end of the table. She was tall and had a smile.

"Of course, he's coming," Braddocks said. "Come in and have coffee with us, Barnes."

"Right."

"And bring your friend," said Mrs.Braddocks laughing. She was a Canadian and had all their easy social graces.

"Thanks, we'll be in," I said. I went back to the small room.

"Who are your friends?" Georgette asked.

"Writers and artists."

"There are lots of those on this side of the river."

"Too many."

"I think so. Still, some of them make money."

"Oh, yes."

We finished the meal and the wine. "Come on," I said. "We're going to have coffee with the others."

Georgette opened her bag, made a few passes at her face as she looked in the little mirror, re-defined her lips with the lipstick, and straightened her hat.

"Good," she said.

We went into the room full of people and Braddocks and the men at his table stood up.

"I wish to present my fiancée, Mademoiselle Georgette Leblanc," I said.

Georgette smiled that wonderful smile, and we shook hands all round.

"Are you related to Georgette Leblanc,[13] the singer?" Mrs. Braddocks asked.

"Connaispas,"[14] Georgette answered.

"But you have the same name," Mrs.Braddocks insisted cordially.

"No," said Georgette. "Not at all. My name is Hobin."

"But Mr.Barnes introduced you as Mademoiselle Georgette

Leblanc. Surely he did," insisted Mrs.Braddocks, who in the excitement of talking French was liable to have no idea what she was saying.

"He's a fool," Georgette said.

"Oh, it was a joke, then," Mrs.Braddocks said.

"Yes," said Georgette. "To laugh at."

"Did you hear that, Henry?" Mrs.Braddocks called down the table to Braddocks. "Mr.Barnes introduced his fiancée as Mademoiselle Leblanc, and her name is actually Hobin."

"Of course, darling. Mademoiselle Hobin, I've known her for a very long time."

"Oh, Mademoiselle Hobin," Frances Clyne called, speaking French very rapidly and not seeming so proud and astonished as Mrs. Braddocks at its coming out really French. "Have you been in Paris long? Do you like it here? You love Paris, do you not?"

"Who's she?" Georgette turned to me. "Do I have to talk to her?"

She turned to Frances, sitting smiling, her hands folded, her head poised on her long neck, her lips pursed ready to start talking again.

"No, I don't like Paris. It's expensive and dirty."

"Really? I find it so extraordinarily clean. One of the cleanest cities in all Europe."

"I find it dirty."

"How strange! But perhaps you have not been here very long."

"I've been here long enough."

"But it does have nice people in it. One must grant that."

Georgette turned to me. "You have nice friends."

Frances was a little drunk and would have liked to have kept it up but the coffee came, and Lavigne with the liqueurs, and after that we all went out and started for Braddocks's dancing-club.

The dancing-club was a bal musette in the Rue de la Montagne Sainte Geneviève.[15] Five nights a week the working people of the Pantheon quarter[16] danced there. One night a week it was the dancing-club. On Monday nights it was closed. When we arrived it was quite empty, except for a policeman sitting near the door, the wife of the proprietor back of the zinc bar, and the proprietor himself. The daughter of the house came down-stairs as we went in. There were long benches, and tables ran across the room, and at the far end a dancing-floor.

"I wish people would come earlier," Braddocks said. The daughter came up and wanted to know what we would drink. The proprietor got up on a high stool beside the dancing-floor and began to play the accordion. He had a string of bells around one of his ankles and beat time with his foot as he played. Every one danced. It was hot and we came off the floor perspiring.

"My God," Georgette said. "What a box to sweat in!"

"It's hot."

"Hot, my God!"

"Take off your hat."

"That's a good idea."

Some one asked Georgette to dance, and I went over to the bar. It was really very hot and the accordion music was pleasant in the hot night. I drank a beer, standing in the doorway and getting the cool breath of wind from the street. Two taxis were coming down the steep street. They both stopped in front of the Bal.[17] A crowd of young men, some in jerseys and some in their shirtsleeves, got out. I could see their hands and newly washed, wavy hair in the light from the door. The policeman standing by the door looked at me and smiled. They came in. As they went in, under the light I saw white hands, wavy hair, white faces, grimacing, gesturing, talking. With them was Brett. She looked very lovely and she was very much with them.

One of them saw Georgette and said: "I do declare. There is an actual harlot. I'm going to dance with her, Lett. You watch me."

The tall dark one, called Lett, said: "Don't you be rash."

The wavy blond one answered: "Don't you worry, dear." And with them was Brett.

I was very angry. Somehow they always made me angry. I know they are supposed to be amusing, and you should be tolerant, but I wanted to swing on one, anyone, anything to shatter that superior, simpering composure. Instead, I walked down the street and had a beer at the bar at the next Bal. The beer was not good and I had a worse cognac to take the taste out of my mouth. When I came back to the Bal there was a crowd on the floor and Georgette was dancing with the tall blond youth, who danced big-hippily, carrying his head on one side, his eyes lifted as he danced. As soon as the music stopped another one of them asked her to dance. She had been taken up by them. I knew then that they would all dance with her. They are like that.

I sat down at a table. Cohn was sitting there. Frances was dancing. Mrs.Braddocks brought up somebody and introduced him as

Robert Prentiss. He was from New York by way of Chicago, and was a rising new novelist. He had some sort of an English accent. I asked him to have a drink.

"Thanks so much," he said, "I've just had one."

"Have another."

"Thanks, I will then."

We got the daughter of the house over and each had a fine à l'eau.[18]

"You're from Kansas City, they tell me," he said.

"Yes."

"Do you find Paris amusing?"

"Yes."

"Really?"

I was a little drunk. Not drunk in any positive sense but just enough to be careless.

"For God's sake," I said, "yes. Don't you?"

"Oh, how charmingly you get angry," he said. "I wish I had that faculty."

I got up and walked over toward the dancing-floor. Mrs. Braddocks followed me. "Don't be cross with Robert," she said. "He's still only a child, you know."

"I wasn't cross," I said. "I just thought perhaps I was going to throw up."

"Your fiancée is having a great success," Mrs.Braddocks looked out on the floor where Georgette was dancing in the arms of the tall, dark one, called Lett.

"Isn't she?" I said.

"Rather," said Mrs.Braddocks.

Cohn came up. "Come on, Jake," he said, "have a drink." We walked over to the bar. "What's the matter with you? You seem all worked up over something?"

"Nothing. This whole show makes me sick is all."

Brett came up to the bar.

"Hello, you chaps."

"Hello, Brett," I said. "Why aren't you tight?"

"Never going to get tight any more. I say, give a chap a brandy and soda."

She stood holding the glass and I saw Robert Cohn looking at her. He looked a great deal as his compatriot must have looked when he saw the promised land.[19] Cohn, of course, was much younger. But he had that look of eager, deserving expectation.

Brett was damned good-looking. She wore a slipover jersey sweater and a tweed skirt, and her hair was brushed back like a boy's. She started all that. She was built with curves like the hull of a racing yacht, and you missed none of it with that wool jersey.

"It's a fine crowd you're with, Brett," I said.

"Aren't they lovely? And you, my dear. Where did you get it?"

"At the Napolitain."

"And have you had a lovely evening?"

"Oh, priceless," I said.

Brett laughed. "It's wrong of you, Jake. It's an insult to all of us. Look at Frances there, and Jo."

This for Cohn's benefit.

"It's in restraint of trade," Brett said. She laughed again.

"You're wonderfully sober," I said.

"Yes. Aren't I? And when one's with the crowd I'm with, one can drink in such safety, too."

The music started and Robert Cohn said: "Will you dance this with me, Lady Brett?"

Brett smiled at him. "I've promised to dance this with Jacob," she laughed.

"You've a hell of a biblical name, Jake."

"How about the next?" asked Cohn.

"We're going," Brett said. "We've a date up at Montmartre."[20]

Dancing, I looked over Brett's shoulder, and saw Cohn, standing at the bar, still watching her.

"You've made a new one there," I said to her.

"Don't talk about it. Poor chap. I never knew it till just now."

"Oh, well," I said. "I suppose you like to add them up."

"Don't talk like a fool."

"You do."

"Oh, well. What if I do?"

"Nothing," I said. We were dancing to the accordion and some one was playing the banjo. It was hot and I felt happy. We passed close to Georgette dancing with another one of them.

"What possessed you to bring her?"

"I don't know, I just brought her."

"You're getting damned romantic."

"No, bored."

"Now?"

"No, not now."

"Let's get out of here. She's well taken care of."

"Do you want to?"

"Would I ask you if I didn't want to?"

We left the floor and I took my coat off a hanger on the wall and put it on. Brett stood by the bar. Cohn was talking to her. I stopped at the bar and asked them for an envelope. The patronne found one. I took a fifty-franc note from my pocket, put it in the envelope, sealed it, and handed it to the patronne[21]

"If the girl I came with asks for me, will you give her this?" I said. "If she goes out with one of those gentlemen, will you save this for me?"

"C'est entendu, Monsieur,"[22] the patronne said. "You go now? So early?"

"Yes," I said.

We started out the door. Cohn was still talking to Brett. She said good night and took my arm. "Good night, Cohn," I said. Outside in the street we looked for a taxi.

"You're going to lose your fifty francs," Brett said.

"Oh, yes."

"No taxis."

"We could walk up to the Pantheon and get one."

"Come on and we'll get a drink in the pub next door and send for one."

"You wouldn't walk across the street."

"Not if I could help it."

We went into the next bar and I sent a waiter for a taxi.

"Well," I said, "we're out away from them."

We stood against the tall zinc bar and did not talk and looked at each other. The waiter came and said the taxi was outside. Brett pressed my hand hard. I gave the waiter a franc and we went out. "Where should I tell him?" I asked.

"Oh, tell him to drive around."

I told the driver to go to the Parc Montsouris,[23] and got in, and slammed the door. Brett was leaning back in the corner, her eyes closed. I sat beside her. The cab started with a jerk.

"Oh, darling, I've been so miserable," Brett said.

## Notes

1. The text is that of the Xrst edition (1926), published by Charles Scribner's Sons. Hemingway's two epigraphs to the novel cite a remark by Gertrude Stein — "You are all a lost generation" — and Ecclesiastes 1.4–7: "One generation passeth away, and another generation cometh: but the earth abideth for ever. ... The sun also ariseth, and the sun goeth down, and hasteth to his place where he arose. ... The wind goeth toward the south, and turneth about unto the north; it whirleth about continually, and the wind returneth again according to his circuits. ... All the rivers run into the sea; yet the sea is not full; unto the place from whence the rivers come, thither they return again."

2. Robert Cohn, an American expatriate writer with whom the

narrator, Jake Barnes, has a barbed, competitive friendship. Barnes like Cohn is an aspiring author, but Cohn has just had his first novel accepted for publication. Cohn also has family money backing his literary career, while Barnes supports himself as a journalist. Cohn has recently become romantically interested in Lady Brett Ashley, a British divorcée whom Barnes met during World War I at a military hospital where she was a volunteer. Although Jake and Brett are intensely attracted to one another, his war wound has left him unable to consummate a sexual relationship. As the chapterbegins, Barnes and Cohn have just had a drink together following the end of Barnes's working day, much of which Cohn spent loitering in Barnes's office.

3. Hens (French, literal trans.); slang for prostitutes.

4. Tell the waiter, a pernod (French).

5. An anise- and herb-U avored, highly alcoholic spirit.

6. Major Parisian thoroughfare running from the Louvre to the Palais Garnier, Paris's central opera house. "Fiacre": a small horse carriage.

7. The large formal garden in the center of Paris. The streets are also in central Paris.

8. St. Peter's Street, on the Left Bank. The Seine divides Paris into the Right Bank, associated with business, wealth, and the state, and the Left Bank, traditionally the neighborhood of artists and students.

9. Coachman.

10. A famous, luxurious restaurant on the Right Bank, frequented by politicians and businessmen.

11. Belgian cities. Liège is historically French speaking; Brussels

historically Dutch speaking.

12. Cohn's possessive partner in a fading romantic relationship. Henry Braddocks is another writer in Barnes and Cohn's circle.

13. A noted French opera singer (1869 — 1941).

14. I don't know (French).

15. Street in the Latin Quarter of the Left Bank, known for its universities and nightlife. "Bal musette": a dance hall with an accordion band.

16. The Left Bank neighborhood surrounding the Pantheon. Designed in 1755 as a church, the building was later converted into a secular memorial and burial place for notable French citizens.

17. I.e., the bal musette.

18. Cognac and water.

19. I.e., like Moses, who was allowed to see but not to enter the promised land (Deuteronomy 34.4). Barnes here and elsewhere in the novel mocks Cohn's Jewish identity.

20. Parisian neighborhood associated with avant garde artists.

21. Landlady, barkeeper (French). In 1925, 50 francs was equivalent to about $2.50 in U.S. dollars, roughly $30.00 in today's money.

22. Understood, sir (French).

23. Large public park on the Left Bank.

## Questions

1. Do you think Jacob Barnes is an anti-hero character created by Hemingway? Why?

2. How does the novel reflect the spirit of "Lost Generation"?

### (2) F. Scott Fitzgerald (1896—1940)

F. Scott Fitzgerald (1896—1940) was born in run-down gentleman's family. With the financial aid of his mother's family, he went to Princeton University to study. When the United States declared war on Germany in 1917, he dropped out of school to join the army. When he was accepting training in the south, he fell in love with Zelda Sayre, a wealthy daughter, who soon broke off her engagement with him because of his underdeveloped career.

In 1920, he published his first novel, *This Side of Paradise*, which won him reputation and fortune, and won Zelda back. After they got married, they lived in luxury and became the representatives of America's postwar thrill-seeking and hedonistic trend. His second novel, *The Beautiful and the Damned* (1922), and two collections of short stories, *Flappers and Philosophers* (1920) and *Tales of the Jazz Age* (1922), were published in the early 1920s. They are the true reflections of the "Jazz Age". In 1924, they went to Paris and became acquainted with Stein, Pound, Hemingway, and other American writers traveling in Europe, where he completed *The Great Gatsby* (1925). This novel depicts the pursuit of money and pleasure in the so-called "Roaring Twenties" and "Jazz Age" after the First World War in the United States, and details the spiritual crisis and the disillusionment of the American dream, showing the social reality under the surface of vanity with a calm and critical tone. A few years later, Zelda was hospitalized for mental breakdowns. Fitzgerald's financial situation became worse and worse. Another major novel, *Tender Is the Night*, was published in 1934, but it was unsuccessful. He had to write film scripts for Hollywood to make ends meet. In 1940, he died of a heart attack. His friend and great critic, Edmund Wilson, published a collection of his essays under the title *The Crack-Up* in 1945.

The following text is the third chapter of *The Great Gatsby*.

## The Great Gatsby
## Chapter III

There was music from my neighbor's house through the summer nights. In his blue gardens men and girls came and went like moths among the whisperings and the champagne and the stars. At high tide in the afternoon I watched his guests diving from the tower of his raft or taking the sun on the hot sand of his beach while his two motor-boats slit the waters of the Sound, drawing aquaplanes over cataracts of foam. On week-ends his Rolls-Royce became an omnibus, bearing parties to and from the city, between nine in the morning and long past midnight, while his station wagon scampered like a brisk yellow bug to meet all trains. And on Mondays eight servants including an extra gardener toiled all day with mops and scrubbing-brushes and hammers and garden-shears, repairing the ravages of the night before.

Every Friday five crates of oranges and lemons arrived from a fruiterer in New York—every Monday these same oranges and lemons left his back door in a pyramid of pulpless halves. There was a machine in the kitchen which could extract the juice of two hundred oranges in half an hour, if a little button was pressed two hundred times by a butler's thumb.

At least once a fortnight a corps of caterers came down with several hundred feet of canvas and enough colored lights to make a Christmas tree of Gatsby's enormous garden. On buffet tables, garnished with glistening hors-d'oeuvre, spiced baked hams crowded against salads of harlequin designs and pastry pigs and turkeys bewitched to a dark gold. In the main hall a bar with a real brass rail was set up, and stocked with gins and liquors and with cordials so long forgotten that most of his female guests were too young to know one from another.

By seven o'clock the orchestra has arrived—no thin five-piece affair but a whole pitful of oboes and trombones and saxophones and viols and cornets and piccolos and low and high drums. The last swimmers have come in from the beach now and are dressing upstairs; the cars from New York are parked five deep in the drive, and already the halls and salons and verandas are gaudy with primary colors and hair shorn in strange new ways and shawls beyond the dreams of Castile. The bar is in full swing and floating rounds of cocktails permeate the garden outside until the air is alive with chatter and laughter and casual innuendo and introductions forgotten on the spot and enthusiastic meetings between women who never knew each other's names.

The lights grow brighter as the earth lurches away from the sun and now the orchestra is playing yellow cocktail music and the opera of voices pitches a key higher. Laughter is easier, minute by minute, spilled with prodigality, tipped out at a cheerful word. The groups change more swiftly, swell with new arrivals, dissolve and form in the same breath—already there are wanderers, confident girls who weave here and there among the stouter and more stable, become for a sharp, joyous moment the center of a group and then excited with triumph glide on through the sea-change of faces and voices and color under the constantly changing light.

Suddenly one of these gypsies in trembling opal, seizes a cocktail out of the air, dumps it down for courage and moving her hands like Frisco dances out alone on the canvas platform. A momentary hush; the orchestra leader varies his rhythm obligingly for her and there is a burst of chatter as the erroneous news goes around that she is Gilda Gray's understudy from the "Follies." The party has begun.

I believe that on the first night I went to Gatsby's house I was one of the few guests who had actually been invited. People were not invited—they went there. They got into automobiles which bore them out to Long Island and somehow they ended up at Gatsby's door. Once there they were introduced by somebody who knew Gatsby and after that they conducted themselves according to the rules of behavior associated with amusement parks. Sometimes they came and went without having met Gatsby at all, came for the party with a simplicity of heart that was its own ticket of admission.

I had been actually invited. A chauffeur in a uniform of robin's egg blue crossed my lawn early that Saturday morning with a surprisingly formal note from his employer—the honor would be entirely Gatsby's, it said, if I would attend his "little party" that night. He had seen me several times and had intended to call on me long before but a peculiar combination of circumstances had prevented it—signed Jay Gatsby in a majestic hand.

Dressed up in white flannels I went over to his lawn a little after seven and wandered around rather ill-at-ease among swirls and eddies of people I didn't know—though here and there was a face I had noticed on the commuting train. I was immediately struck by the number of young Englishmen dotted about; all well dressed, all looking a little hungry and all talking in low earnest voices to solid and prosperous Americans. I was sure that they were selling something: bonds or insurance or automobiles. They were, at least, agonizingly aware of the easy money in the vicinity and convinced that it was theirs for a few words in the right key.

As soon as I arrived I made an attempt to find my host but the two or three people of whom I asked his whereabouts stared at me in such an amazed way and denied so vehemently any knowledge of his movements that I slunk off in the direction of the cocktail table—the only place in the garden where a single man could linger without looking purposeless and alone.

I was on my way to get roaring drunk from sheer embarrassment when Jordan Baker came out of the house and stood at the head of the marble steps, leaning a little backward and looking with contemptuous interest down into the garden.

Welcome or not, I found it necessary to attach myself to someone before I should begin to address cordial remarks to the passers-by.

"Hello!" I roared, advancing toward her. My voice seemed unnaturally loud across the garden.

"I thought you might be here," she responded absently as I came up. "I remembered you lived next door to— —"

She held my hand impersonally, as a promise that she'd take care of me in a minute, and gave ear to two girls in twin yellow dresses who stopped at the foot of the steps.

"Hello!" they cried together. "Sorry you didn't win."

That was for the golf tournament. She had lost in the finals the week before.

"You don't know who we are," said one of the girls in yellow, "but we met you here about a month ago."

"You've dyed your hair since then," remarked Jordan, and I started but the girls had moved casually on and her remark was addressed to the premature moon, produced like the supper, no doubt, out of a caterer's basket. With Jordan's slender golden arm resting in mine we descended the steps and sauntered about the garden. A tray of cocktails floated at us through the twilight and we sat down at a table with the two girls in yellow and three men, each one introduced to us as Mr.Mumble.

"Do you come to these parties often?" inquired Jordan of the girl beside her.

"The last one was the one I met you at," answered the girl, in an alert, confident voice. She turned to her companion: "Wasn't it for you, Lucille?"

It was for Lucille, too.

"I like to come," Lucille said. "I never care what I do, so I always have a good time. When I was here last I tore my gown on a chair, and he asked me my name and address—inside of a week I got a package from Croirier's with a new evening gown in it."

"Did you keep it?" asked Jordan.

"Sure I did. I was going to wear it tonight, but it was too big in the bust and had to be altered. It was gas blue with lavender beads. Two hundred and sixty-five dollars."

"There's something funny about a fellow that'll do a thing like that," said the other girl eagerly. "He doesn't want any trouble with anybody."

"Who doesn't?" I inquired.

"Gatsby. Somebody told me— —"

The two girls and Jordan leaned together confidentially.

"Somebody told me they thought he killed a man once."

A thrill passed over all of us. The three Mr.Mumbles bent forward and listened eagerly.

"I don't think it's so much that," argued Lucille skeptically; "it's more that he was a German spy during the war."

One of the men nodded in confirmation.

"I heard that from a man who knew all about him, grew up with him in Germany," he assured us positively.

"Oh, no," said the first girl, "it couldn't be that, because he was in the American army during the war." As our credulity switched back to her she leaned forward with enthusiasm. "You look at him sometimes when he thinks nobody's looking at him. I'll bet he killed a man."

She narrowed her eyes and shivered. Lucille shivered. We all turned and looked around for Gatsby. It was testimony to the romantic speculation he inspired that there were whispers about him from those who found little that it was necessary to whisper about in this world.

The first supper—there would be another one after midnight—was now being served, and Jordan invited me to join her own party who were spread around a table on the other side of the garden. There were three married couples and Jordan's escort, a persistent undergraduate given to violent innuendo and obviously under the impression that sooner or later Jordan was going to yield him up her person to a greater or lesser degree. Instead of rambling this party had preserved a dignified homogeneity, and assumed to itself the function of representing the staid nobility of the countryside—East Egg condescending to West Egg, and carefully on guard against its spectroscopic gayety.

"Let's get out," whispered Jordan, after a somehow wasteful and inappropriate half hour. "This is much too polite for me."

We got up, and she explained that we were going to find the host—I had never met him, she said, and it was making me uneasy. The undergraduate nodded in a cynical, melancholy way.

The bar, where we glanced first, was crowded but Gatsby was not there. She couldn't find him from the top of the steps, and he wasn't on the veranda. On a chance we tried an important-looking door, and walked into a high Gothic library, panelled with carved English oak, and probably transported complete from some ruin overseas.

A stout[3], middle-aged man with enormous owl-eyed spectacles was sitting somewhat drunk on the edge of a great table, staring with unsteady concentration at the shelves of books. As we entered he wheeled excitedly around and examined Jordan from head to foot.

"What do you think?" he demanded impetuously.

"About what?"

He waved his hand toward the book-shelves.

"About that. As a matter of fact you needn't bother to ascertain. I ascertained. They're real."

"The books?"

He nodded.

"Absolutely real—have pages and everything. I thought they'd be a nice durable cardboard. Matter of fact, they're absolutely real. Pages and—Here! Lemme show you."

Taking our skepticism for granted, he rushed to the bookcases and returned with Volume One of the "Stoddard Lectures."

"See!" he cried triumphantly. "It's a bona fide piece of printed matter. It fooled me. This fella's a regular Belasco. It's a triumph. What thoroughness! What realism! Knew when to stop too—didn't cut the pages. But what do you want? What do you expect?"

He snatched the book from me and replaced it hastily on its shelf muttering that if one brick was removed the whole library was liable to collapse.

"Who brought you?" he demanded. "Or did you just come? I was brought. Most people were brought."

Jordan looked at him alertly, cheerfully without answering.

"I was brought by a woman named Roosevelt," he continued. "Mrs.Claud Roosevelt. Do you know her? I met her somewhere last night. I've been drunk for about a week now, and I thought it might sober me up to sit in a library."

"Has it?"

"A little bit, I think. I can't tell yet. I've only been here an hour. Did I tell you about the books? They're real. They're—"

"You told us."

We shook hands with him gravely and went back outdoors.

There was dancing now on the canvas in the garden, old men pushing young girls backward in eternal graceless circles, superior couples holding each other tortuously, fashionably and keeping in the corners—and a great number of single girls dancing individualistically or relieving the orchestra for a moment of the burden of the banjo or the traps. By midnight the hilarity had increased. A celebrated tenor had sung in Italian and a notorious contralto had sung in jazz and between the numbers people were doing "stunts" all over the garden, while happy vacuous bursts of laughter rose toward the summer sky. A pair of stage "twins"—who turned out to be the girls in yellow—did a baby act in costume and champagne was served in glasses bigger than finger bowls. The moon had risen higher, and floating in the Sound was a triangle of silver scales, trembling a little to the stiff, tinny drip of the banjoes on the lawn.

I was still with Jordan Baker. We were sitting at a table with a man of about my age and a rowdy little girl who gave way upon the slightest provocation to uncontrollable laughter. I was enjoying myself now. I had taken two finger bowls of champagne and the scene had changed before my eyes into something significant, elemental and profound.

At a lull in the entertainment the man looked at me and smiled.

"Your face is familiar," he said, politely. "Weren't you in the Third Division during the war?"

"Why, yes. I was in the Ninth Machine-Gun Battalion."

"I was in the Seventh Infantry until June nineteen-eighteen. I knew I'd seen you somewhere before."

We talked for a moment about some wet, grey little villages in France. Evidently he lived in this vicinity for he told me that he had just bought a hydroplane and was going to try it out in the morning.

"Want to go with me, old sport? Just near the shore along the Sound."

"What time?"

"Any time that suits you best."

It was on the tip of my tongue to ask his name when Jordan looked around and smiled.

"Having a gay time now?" she inquired.

"Much better." I turned again to my new acquaintance. "This is an unusual party for me. I haven't even seen the host. I live over there—" I waved my hand at the invisible hedge in the distance, "and this man Gatsby sent over his chauffeur with an invitation."

For a moment he looked at me as if he failed to understand.

"I'm Gatsby," he said suddenly.

"What!" I exclaimed. "Oh, I beg your pardon."

"I thought you knew, old sport. I'm afraid I'm not a very good host."

He smiled understandingly—much more than understandingly.

It was one of those rare smiles with a quality of eternal reassurance in it, that you may come across four or five times in life. It faced—or seemed to face—the whole external world for an instant, and then concentrated on you with an irresistible prejudice in your favor. It understood you just so far as you wanted to be understood, believed in you as you would like to believe in yourself and assured you that it had precisely the impression of you that, at your best, you hoped to convey. Precisely at that point it vanished—and I was looking at an elegant young rough-neck, a year or two over thirty, whose elaborate formality of speech just missed being absurd. Some time before he introduced himself I'd got a strong impression that he was picking his words with care.

Almost at the moment when Mr.Gatsby identified himself a butler hurried toward him with the information that Chicago was calling him on the wire. He excused himself with a small bow that included each of us in turn.

"If you want anything just ask for it, old sport," he urged me. "Excuse me. I will rejoin you later."

When he was gone I turned immediately to Jordan—constrained to assure her of my surprise. I had expected that Mr.Gatsby would be a florid and corpulent person in his middle years.

"Who is he?" I demanded. "Do you know?"

"He's just a man named Gatsby."

"Where is he from, I mean? And what does he do?"

"Now you're started on the subject," she answered with a wan smile. "Well, —he told me once he was an Oxford man."

A dim background started to take shape behind him but at her next remark it faded away.

"However, I don't believe it."

"Why not?"

"I don't know," she insisted, "I just don't think he went there."

Something in her tone reminded me of the other girl's "I think he killed a man," and had the effect of stimulating my curiosity. I would have accepted without question the information that Gatsby sprang from the swamps of Louisiana or from the lower East Side of New York. That was comprehensible. But young men didn't—at least in my provincial inexperience I believed they didn't—drift coolly out of nowhere and buy a palace on Long Island Sound.

"Anyhow he gives large parties," said Jordan, changing the subject with an urbane distaste for the concrete. "And I like large parties. They're so intimate. At small parties there isn't any privacy."

There was the boom of a bass drum, and the voice of the orchestra leader rang out suddenly above the echolalia of the garden.

"Ladies and gentlemen," he cried. "At the request of Mr.Gatsby we are going to play for you Mr.Vladimir Tostoff's latest work which attracted so much attention at Carnegie Hall last May. If you read the papers you know there was a big sensation." He smiled with jovial condescension and added "Some sensation!" whereupon everybody laughed.

"The piece is known," he concluded lustily, "as 'Vladimir Tostoff's Jazz History of the World.' "

The nature of Mr.Tostoff's composition eluded me, because

just as it began my eyes fell on Gatsby, standing alone on the marble steps and looking from one group to another with approving eyes. His tanned skin was drawn attractively tight on his face and his short hair looked as though it were trimmed every day. I could see nothing sinister about him. I wondered if the fact that he was not drinking helped to set him off from his guests, for it seemed to me that he grew more correct as the fraternal hilarity increased. When the "Jazz History of the World" was over girls were putting their heads on men's shoulders in a puppyish, convivial way, girls were swooning backward playfully into men's arms, even into groups knowing that some one would arrest their falls—but no one swooned backward on Gatsby and no French bob touched Gatsby's shoulder and no singing quartets were formed with Gatsby's head for one link.

"I beg your pardon."

Gatsby's butler was suddenly standing beside us.

"Miss Baker?" he inquired. "I beg your pardon but Mr.Gatsby would like to speak to you alone."

"With me?" she exclaimed in surprise.

"Yes, madame."

She got up slowly, raising her eyebrows at me in astonishment, and followed the butler toward the house. I noticed that she wore her evening dress, all her dresses, like sports clothes—there was a jauntiness about her movements as if she had first learned to walk upon golf courses on clean, crisp mornings.

I was alone and it was almost two. For some time confused and intriguing sounds had issued from a long many-windowed room which overhung the terrace. Eluding Jordan's undergraduate who was now engaged in an obstetrical conversation with two chorus girls, and who implored me to join him, I went inside.

The large room was full of people. One of the girls in yellow was playing the piano and beside her stood a tall, red haired young lady from a famous chorus, engaged in song. She had drunk a quantity of champagne and during the course of her song she had decided ineptly that everything was very very sad—she was not only singing, she was weeping too. Whenever there was a pause in the song she filled it with gasping broken sobs and then took up the lyric again in a quavering soprano. The tears coursed down her cheeks—not freely, however, for when they came into contact with her heavily beaded eyelashes they assumed an inky color, and pursued the rest of their way in slow black rivulets. A humorous suggestion was made that she sing the notes on her face whereupon she threw up her hands, sank into a chair and went off into a deep vinous sleep.

"She had a fight with a man who says he's her husband," explained a girl at my elbow.

I looked around. Most of the remaining women were now having fights with men said to be their husbands. Even Jordan's party, the quartet from East Egg, were rent asunder by dissension[5]. One of the men was talking with curious intensity to a young actress, and his wife after attempting to laugh at the situation in a dignified and indifferent way broke down entirely and resorted to flank attacks—at intervals she appeared suddenly at his side like an angry diamond, and hissed "You promised!" into his ear.

The reluctance to go home was not confined to wayward men. The hall was at present occupied by two deplorably sober men and their highly indignant wives. The wives were sympathizing with each other in slightly raised voices.

"Whenever he sees I'm having a good time he wants to go home."

"Never heard anything so selfish in my life."

"We're always the first ones to leave."

"So are we."

"Well, we're almost the last tonight," said one of the men sheepishly. "The orchestra left half an hour ago."

In spite of the wives' agreement that such malevolence was beyond credibility, the dispute ended in a short struggle, and both wives were lifted kicking into the night.

As I waited for my hat in the hall the door of the library opened and Jordan Baker and Gatsby came out together. He was saying some last word to her but the eagerness in his manner tightened abruptly into formality as several people approached him to say goodbye.

Jordan's party were calling impatiently to her from the porch but she lingered for a moment to shake hands.

"I've just heard the most amazing thing," she whispered. "How long were we in there?"

"Why,—about an hour."

"It was—simply amazing," she repeated abstractedly. "But I swore I wouldn't tell it and here I am tantalizing[4] you." She yawned gracefully in my face. "Please come and see me.... Phone book....

Under the name of Mrs.Sigourney Howard....My aunt...." She was hurrying off as she talked—her brown hand waved a jaunty salute as she melted into her party at the door.

Rather ashamed that on my first appearance I had stayed so late, I joined the last of Gatsby's guests who were clustered around him. I wanted to explain that I'd hunted for him early in the evening and to apologize for not having known him in the garden.

"Don't mention it," he enjoined me eagerly. "Don't give it another thought, old sport." The familiar expression held no more familiarity than the hand which reassuringly brushed my shoulder. "And don't forget we're going up in the hydroplane tomorrow morning at nine o'clock."

Then the butler, behind his shoulder:

"Philadelphia wants you on the phone, sir."

"All right, in a minute. Tell them I'll be right there....good night."

"Good night."

"Good night." He smiled—and suddenly there seemed to be a pleasant significance in having been among the last to go, as if he had desired it all the time. "Good night, old sport....Good night."

But as I walked down the steps I saw that the evening was not quite over. Fifty feet from the door a dozen headlights illuminated a bizarre and tumultuous scene. In the ditch beside the road, right side up but violently shorn of one wheel, rested a new coupé which had left Gatsby's drive not two minutes before. The sharp jut of a wall accounted for the detachment of the wheel which was now getting considerable attention from half a dozen curious chauffeurs. However, as they had left their cars blocking the road a harsh discordant din from those in the rear had been audible for some time and added to the already violent confusion of the scene.

A man in a long duster had dismounted from the wreck and now stood in the middle of the road, looking from the car to the tire and from the tire to the observers in a pleasant, puzzled way.

“See!” he explained. “It went in the ditch.”

The fact was infinitely astonishing to him—and I recognized first the unusual quality of wonder and then the man—it was the late patron of Gatsby’s library.

“How’d it happen?”

He shrugged his shoulders.

“I know nothing whatever about mechanics,” he said decisively.

“But how did it happen? Did you run into the wall?”

“Don’t ask me,” said Owl Eyes, washing his hands of the whole matter. “I know very little about driving—next to nothing. It happened, and that’s all I know.”

“Well, if you’re a poor driver you oughtn’t to try driving at night.”

“But I wasn’t even trying,” he explained indignantly, “I wasn’t even trying.”

An awed hush fell upon the bystanders.

“Do you want to commit suicide?”

“You’re lucky it was just a wheel! A bad driver and not even trying!”

“You don’t understand,” explained the criminal. “I wasn’t driving.

There's another man in the car."

The shock that followed this declaration found voice in a sustained "Ah-h-h!" as the door of the coupé swung slowly open. The crowd—it was now a crowd—stepped back involuntarily and when the door had opened wide there was a ghostly pause. Then, very gradually, part by part, a pale dangling individual stepped out of the wreck, pawing tentatively at the ground with a large uncertain dancing shoe.

Blinded by the glare of the headlights and confused by the incessant groaning of the horns the apparition stood swaying for a moment before he perceived the man in the duster.

"Wha's matter?" he inquired calmly. "Did we run outa gas?"

"Look!"

Half a dozen fingers pointed at the amputated wheel—he stared at it for a moment and then looked upward as though he suspected that it had dropped from the sky.

"It came off," some one explained.

He nodded.

"At first I din' notice we'd stopped."

A pause. Then, taking a long breath and straightening his shoulders he remarked in a determined voice:

"Wonder'ff tell me where there's a gas'line station?"

At least a dozen men, some of them little better off than he was, explained to him that wheel and car were no longer joined by any physical bond.

"Back out," he suggested after a moment. "Put her in reverse."

"But the wheel's off!"

He hesitated.

"No harm in trying," he said.

The caterwauling horns had reached a crescendo and I turned away and cut across the lawn toward home. I glanced back once. A wafer of a moon was shining over Gatsby's house, making the night fine as before and surviving the laughter and the sound of his still glowing garden. A sudden emptiness seemed to flow now from the windows and the great doors, endowing with complete isolation the figure of the host who stood on the porch, his hand up in a formal gesture of farewell.

Reading over what I have written so far I see I have given the impression that the events of three nights several weeks apart were all that absorbed me. On the contrary they were merely casual events in a crowded summer and, until much later, they absorbed me infinitely less than my personal affairs.

Most of the time I worked. In the early morning the sun threw my shadow westward as I hurried down the white chasms of lower New York to the Probity Trust. I knew the other clerks and young bond-salesmen by their first names and lunched with them in dark crowded restaurants on little pig sausages and mashed potatoes and coffee. I even had a short affair with a girl who lived in Jersey City and worked in the accounting department, but her brother began throwing mean looks in my direction so when she went on her vacation in July I let it blow quietly away.

I took dinner usually at the Yale Club—for some reason it was the gloomiest event of my day—and then I went upstairs to the library and studied investments and securities for a conscientious hour. There were generally a few rioters around but they never came into the library so it was a good place to work. After that, if the night was mellow I strolled down Madison Avenue past the old Murray Hill Hotel and over Thirty-third Street to the Pennsylvania Station.

I began to like New York, the racy, adventurous feel of it at night and the satisfaction that the constant flicker of men and women and machines gives to the restless eye. I liked to walk up Fifth Avenue and pick out romantic women from the crowd and imagine that in a few minutes I was going to enter into their lives, and no one would ever know or disapprove. Sometimes, in my mind, I followed them to their apartments on the corners of hidden streets, and they turned and smiled back at me before they faded through a door into warm darkness. At the enchanted metropolitan twilight I felt a haunting loneliness sometimes, and felt it in others—poor young clerks who loitered in front of windows waiting until it was time for a solitary restaurant dinner—young clerks in the dusk, wasting the most poignant moments of night and life.

Again at eight o'clock, when the dark lanes of the Forties were five deep with throbbing taxi cabs, bound for the theatre district, I felt a sinking in my heart. Forms leaned together in the taxis as they waited, and voices sang, and there was laughter from unheard jokes, and lighted cigarettes outlined unintelligible gestures inside. Imagining that I, too, was hurrying toward gayety[6] and sharing their intimate excitement, I wished them well.

For a while I lost sight of Jordan Baker, and then in midsummer I found her again. At first I was flattered to go places with her because she was a golf champion and every one knew her name. Then it was something more. I wasn't actually in love, but I felt a sort of tender curiosity. The bored haughty face that she turned to the world concealed something—most affectations conceal something eventually, even though they don't in the beginning—and one day I found what it was. When we were on a house-party together up in Warwick, she left a borrowed car out in the rain with the top down, and then lied about it—and suddenly I remembered the story about her that had eluded me that night at Daisy's. At her first big golf tournament there was a row that nearly reached the newspapers—a suggestion that she had moved her ball from a bad lie in the semi-final round. The thing approached the proportions of a scandal—then died away. A caddy retracted his statement and the only other witness admitted that he might have been mistaken. The incident and the name had remained together in my mind.

Jordan Baker instinctively avoided clever, shrewd men, and now I saw that this was because she felt safer on a plane where any divergence from a code would be thought impossible. She was incurably dishonest. She wasn't able to endure being at a disadvantage, and given this unwillingness, I suppose she had begun dealing in subterfuges when she was very young in order to keep that cool, insolent smile turned to the world and yet satisfy the demands of her hard jaunty body.

It made no difference to me. Dishonesty in a woman is a thing you never blame deeply—I was casually sorry, and then I forgot. It was on that same house party that we had a curious conversation about driving a car. It started because she passed so close to some workmen that our fender flicked a button on one man's coat.

"You're a rotten driver," I protested. "Either you ought to be more careful or you oughtn't to drive at all."

"I am careful."

"No, you're not."

"Well, other people are," she said lightly.

"What's that got to do with it?"

"They'll keep out of my way," she insisted. "It takes two to make an accident."

"Suppose you met somebody just as careless as yourself."

"I hope I never will," she answered. "I hate careless people. That's why I like you."

Her grey, sun-strained eyes stared straight ahead, but she had deliberately shifted our relations, and for a moment I thought I loved her. But I am slow-thinking and full of interior rules that act as brakes on my desires, and I knew that first I had to get myself definitely out of that tangle back home. I'd been writing letters once a week and signing them: "Love, Nick," and all I could think of was how, when that certain girl played tennis, a faint mustache of perspiration appeared on her upper lip. Nevertheless there was a vague understanding that had to be tactfully broken off before I was free.

Every one suspects himself of at least one of the cardinal[7] virtues, and this is mine: I am one of the few honest people that I have ever known.

## Notes

1. A region of Spain, once an independent kingdom renowned for its lace and embroidered shawls.

2. It refers to the Ziegfeld Follies, a musical theatrical revue produced by Florenz Ziegfeld, very popular in the 1920s. Gilda Gray was one of its famous stars.

3. Rather fat.

4. Disagreement between people or within a group.

5. To make a person or an animal want sth that they cannot have or do.

6. Happiness.

7. Most important; having other things based on it.

## Questions

1. What kind of person is Gatsby?

2. Please analyze the theme of this novel.

### （3）Willa Cather (1873—1947)

Willa Cather (1873—1947), a female writer, was born in Virginia, America. She moved to Nebraska in western America with her family and then settled in a railway town. In the process of growing up, she met and made friends with a large number of immigrants. The immigrants from Europe and their tough life became an important resource for her works.

In 1890, she went to university and published her novels and drama reviews during her sophomore year. After graduation, she acted as a magazine editor and created some short stories to fill the pages' layouts. In 1908, she met a famous female writer living in Maine, New England, named Sarah Orne Jewett, who suggested her to write the immigrant's life into her novels. In 1912, she quit the job of editing, devoting herself to writing. Her major works include *O Pioneers*! (1913), *The Song of the Lark* (1915), *My Antonia* (1918), *One of Ours* (1922), *A Lost Lady* (1923), and *The Professor's House* (1925). In her later life, Cather became more and more indifferent towards real life. Her nostalgia was growing and preferred to solve problems of the real world with traditional methods.

Cather does not like use ingenious plot, exaggerated language, or over-descriptive details of environments and characters in writing. The sceneries, characters, and emotions are mixed together harmoniously in her works, which allows for her readers to enjoy the reading much more.

The following text is excerpted from *The Norton Anthology of American Literature* (shorter 6th edition).

## The Sculptor's Funeral

A group of the townspeople stood on the station siding of a little Kansas town, awaiting the coming of the night train, which was already twenty minutes overdue. The snow had fallen thick over everything; in the pale starlight the line of bluffs across the wide, white meadows south of the town made soft, smoke-coloured curves against the clear sky. The men on the siding stood first on one foot and then on the other, their hands thrust deep into their trousers pockets, their overcoats open, their shoulders screwed up with the cold; and they glanced from time to time toward the southeast,where the railroad track wound along the river shore. They conversed in low tones and moved about restlessly, seeming uncertain as to what was expected of them. There was but one of the company who looked as if he knew exactly why he was there, and he kept conspicuously apart; walking to the far end of the platform, returning to the station door, then pacing up the track again,his chin sunk in the high collar of his overcoat, his burly shoulders dropping forward, his gait heavy and dogged. Presently he was approached by a tall,pare, grizzled man clad in a faded Grand Army[1] suit, who shuffled out from the group and advanced with a certain deference, craning his neck forward until his back made the angle of a jack-knife three-quarters open.

"I reckon she's a-goin' to be pretty late agin tonight, Jim," he remarked in a squeaky falsetto. "S'pose it's the snow?"

"I don't know," responded the other man with a shade of annoyance, speaking from out an astonishing cataract of red beard that grew fiercely and thickly in all directions.

The spare man shifted the quill toothpick he was chewing to the other side of his mouth. "It ain't likely that anybody from the East will come with the corpse, I s'pose," he went on reflectively.

"I don't know," responded the other, more curtly than before.

It's too bad he didn't belong to some lodge or other. I like an order funeral[2] myself. They seem more appropriate for people of some repytation, the spare man continued, with an ingratiating concession in his shrill voice, as he carefully placed his toothpick in his vest pocket. He always carried the flag at the G. A. R. funerals in the town.

The heavy man turned on his heel, without replying, and walked up the siding. The spare man rejoined the uneasy group. "Jim's ez full ez a tick, ez ushel," he commented commiseratingly.

Just then a distant whistle sounded, and there was a shuffling of feet on the platform. A number of lanky boys, of all ages, appeared as suddenly and slimily as eels wakened by the crack of thunder; some came from the waiting-room, where they had been warming themselves by the red stove, or half asleep on the slat benches; others uncoiled themselves from baggage trucks or slid out of express wagons. Two clambered down from the driver's seat of a hearse that stood backed up against the siding. They straightened their stooping shoulders and lifted their heads, and a flash of momentary animation kindled their dull eyes at that cold, vibrant scream, the worldwide call for men. It stirred them like the note of a trumpet; just as it had often stirred the man who was coming home tonight, in his boyhood.

The night express shot, red as a rocket, from out the eastward marsh lands and wound along the river shore under the long lines of shivering poplars that sentinelled the meadows, the escaping steam hanging in grey masses against the pale sky and blotting out the Milky Way. In a moment the red glare from the headlight streamed up the snow-covered track before the siding and glittered on the wet, black rails. The burly man with the dishevelled red beard walked swiftly up the platform toward the approaching train,uncovering his head as he went. The group of men behind him hesitated,glanced questioningly at one another, and awkwardly followed his example. The train stopped, and the crowd shuffled up to the express car just as the door was thrown open, the man in the G. A. R. suit thrusting his head forward with curiosity. The express messenger appeared in the doorway,accompanied by a young man in a long ulster and travelling cap.

"Are Mr.Merrick's friends here?" inquired the young man.

The group on the platform swayed uneasily. Philip Phelps, the banker, responded with dignity: "We have come to take charge of the body. Mr.Merrick's father is very feeble and can't be about."

"Send the agent out here," growled the express messenger, "and tell the operator to lend a hand."

The coffin was got out of its rough-box and down on the snowy platform.The townspeople drew back enough to make room for it and then formed a close semicircle about it, looking curiously at the palm leaf which lay across the black cover. No one said anything. The baggage man stood by his truck,waiting to get at the trunks. The engine panted heavily, and the fireman dodged in and out among the wheels with his yellow torch and long oil-can,snapping the spindle boxes. The young Bostonian, one of the dead sculptor's pupils who had come with the body, looked about him helplessly. He turned to the banker, the only one of that black, uneasy, stoop-shouldered group who seemed enough of an individual to be addressed.

"None of Mr.Merrick's brothers are here?" he asked uncertainly.

The man with the red beard for the first time stepped up and joined the others. "No, they have not come yet;[3] the family is scattered. The body will be taken directly to the house." He stooped and took hold of one of the handles of the coffin.

"Take the long hill road up, Thompson, it will be easier on the horses," called the liveryman-' as the undertaker snapped the door of the hearse and prepared to mount to the driver's seat.

Laird, the red-bearded lawyer, turned again to the stranger: "We didn't know whether there would be any one with him or not," he explained. "It's a long walk, so you'd better go up in the hack." He pointed to a single battered conveyance, but the young man replied stiffly: "Thank you, but I think I will go up with the hearse. If you don't object," turning to the undertaker, "I'll ride with you."

They clambered up over the wheels and drove off in the starlight up the long, white hill toward the town. The lamps in the still village were shining from under the low, snow-burdened roofs; and beyond, on every side, the plains reached out into emptiness, peaceful and wide as the soft sky itself, and wrapped in a tangible, white silence.

When the hearse backed up to a wooden sidewalk before a naked, weather beaten frame house, the same composite, ill-defined group that had stood upon the station siding was huddled about the gate. The front yard was an icy swamp, and a couple of warped planks, extending from the sidewalk to the door, made a sort of rickety footbridge. The gate hung on one hinge, and was opened wide with difficulty. Steavens, the young stranger, noticed that something black was tied to the knob of the front door.

The grating sound made by the casket, as it was drawn from the hearse, was answered by a scream from the house; the front door was wrenched open, and a tall, corpulent woman rushed out bareheaded into the snow and flung herself upon the coffin, shrieking: "My boy, my boy! And this is how you've come home to me!"

As Steavens turned away and closed his eyes with a shudder of unutterable repulsion, another woman, also tall, but flat and angular, dressed entirely in black, darted out of the house and caught Mrs. Merrick by the shoulders, crying sharply: "Come, come, mother; you mustn't go on like this!" Her tone changed to one of obsequious solemnity as she turned to the banker: "The parlour is ready, Mr.Phelps."

The bearers carried the coffin along the narrow boards, while the under-taker ran ahead with the coffin-rests. They bore it into a large, unheated room that smelled of dampness and disuse and furniture polish, and set it down under a hanging lamp ornamented with jingling glass prisms and before a "Rogers group" of John Alden and Priscilla, wreathed with smilax. Henry Steavens stared about him with the sickening conviction that there had been a mistake, and that he had somehow arrived at the wrong destination. He looked at the clover-green Brussels,[4] the fat plush upholstery, among the hand-painted china placques and panels and vases, for some mark of identification,—for something that might once conceivably have belonged to Harvey Merrick. It was not until he recognized his friend in the crayon portrait of a little boy in kilts and curls, hanging above the piano, that he felt willing to let any of these people approach the coffin.

"Take the lid off, Mr.Thompson; let me see my boy's face,"

wailed the elder woman between her sobs. This time Steavens looked fearfully, almost beseechingly into her face, red and swollen under its masses of strong, black,shiny hair. He flushed, dropped his eyes, and then, almost incredulously,looked again. There was a kind of power about her face—a kind of brutal handsomeness, even; but it was scarred and furrowed by violence, and so coloured and coarsened by fiercer passions that grief seemed never to have laid a gentle finger there. The long nose was distended and knob bed at the end, and there were deep lines on either side of it; her heavy, black brows almost met across her forehead, her teeth were large and square, and set far apart—teeth that could tear. She filled the room; the men were obliterated,seemed tossed about like twigs in an angry water, and even Steavens felt himself being drawn into the whirlpool.

The daughter—the tall, raw-boned woman in crepe, with a mourning comb in her hair which curiously lengthened her long face—sat stiffly upon the sofa, her hands, conspicuous for their large knuckles, folded in her lap, her mouth and eyes drawn down, solemnly awaiting the opening of the coffin. Near the door stood a mulatto woman, evidently a servant in the house, with a timid bearing and an emaciated face pitifully sad and gentle. She was weeping silently, the corner of her calico apron lifted to her eyes, occasionally suppressing a long, quivering sob. Steavens walked over and stood beside her.

Feeble steps were heard on the stairs, and an old man, tall and frail, odorous of pipe smoke, with shaggy, unkept grey hair and a dingy beard, tobacco stained about the mouth, entered uncertainly. He went slowly up to the coffin and stood rolling a blue cotton handkerchief between his hands, seeming so pained and embarrassed by his wife's orgy of grief that he had no consciousness of anything else.

"There, there, Annie, dear, don't take on so," he quavered timidly, putting out a shaking hand and awkwardly patting her elbow. She turned and sank upon his shoulder with such violence that he tottered a little. He did not even glance toward the coffin, but continued to look at her with a dull, frightened, appealing expression, as a spaniel looks at the whip. His sunken cheeks slowly reddened and burned with miserable shame. When his wife rushed from the room, her daughter strode after her with set lips. The servant stole up to the coffin, bent over it for a moment, and then slipped away to the kitchen, leaving Steavens, the lawyer, and the father to themselves. The old man stood looking down at his dead son's face. The sculptor's splendid head seemed even more noble in its rigid stillness than in life. The dark hair had crept down upon the wide forehead; the face seemed strangely long, but in it there was not that repose we expect to find in the faces of the dead. The brows were so drawn that there were two deep lines above the beaked nose, and the chin was thrust forward defiantly. It was as though the strain of life had been so sharp and bitter that death could not at once relax the tension and smooth the countenance into perfect peace—as though he were still guarding something precious, which might even yet be wrested from him.

The old man's lips were working under his stained beard. He turned to the lawyer with timid deference: "Phelps and the rest are comin' back to set up with Harve, ain't they?" he asked. "Thank 'ee, Jim, thank ee." He brushed the hair back gently from his son's forehead. "He was a good boy, Jim; always a good boy. He was ez gentle ez a child and the kindest of 'em all—only we didn't none of us ever onderstand him." The tears trickled slowly down his beard and dropped upon the sculptor's coat.

"Martin, Martin! Oh, Martin! come here," his wife wailed from the top of the stairs. The old man started timorously: "Yes, Annie, I'm coming." He turned away, hesitated, stood for a moment in miserable indecision; then reached back and patted the dead man's hair softly, and stumbled from the room.

"Poor old man, I didn't think he had any tears left. Seems as if his eyes would have gone dry long ago. At his age nothing cuts very deep," remarked the lawyer.

Something in his tone made Steavens glance up. While the mother had been in the room, the young man had scarcely seen any one else; but now, from the moment he first glanced into Jim Laird's florid face and blood-shot eyes, he knew that he had found what he had been heartsick at not finding before—the feeling, the understanding, that must exist in some one, even here.

The man was red as his beard, with features swollen and blurred by dissipation, and a hot, blazing blue eye. His face was strained—that of a man who is controlling himself with difficulty—and he kept plucking at his beard with a sort of fierce resentment. Steavens, sitting by the window, watched him turn down the glaring lamp, still its jangling pendants with an angry gesture, and then stand with his hands locked behind him, staring down into the master's face. He could not help wondering what link there had been between the porcelain vessel and so sooty a lump of potter's clay.

From the kitchen an uproar was sounding; when the dining-room door opened, the import of it was clear. The mother was abusing the maid for having forgotten to make the dressing for the chicken salad which had been prepared for the watchers. Steavens had never heard anything in the least like it; it was injured, emotional, dramatic abuse, unique and masterly in its excruciating cruelty, as violent and unrestrained as had been her grief of twenty minutes before. With a shudder of disgust the lawyer went into the dining-room and closed the door into the kitchen.

"Poor Roxy's getting it now," he remarked when he came back. "The Merricks took her out of the poor-house years ago; and if her loyalty would let her, I guess the poor old thing could tell tales that would curdle your blood. She's the mulatto woman who was standing in here a while ago, with her apron to her eyes. The old woman is a fury; there never was anybody like her. She made Harvey's life a hell for him when he lived at home; he was so sick ashamed of it. I never could see how he kept himself sweet."

"He was wonderful," said Steavens slowly, "wonderful; but until tonight I have never known how wonderful."

"That is the eternal wonder of it, anyway; that it can come even from such a dung heap as this," the lawyer cried, with a sweeping gesture which seemed to indicate much more than the four walls within which they stood.

"I think I'll see whether I can get a little air. The room is so close I am beginning to feel rather faint," murmured Steavens, struggling with one of the windows. The sash was stuck, however, and would not yield, so he sat down dejectedly and began pulling at his collar. The lawyer came over, loosened the sash with one blow of his red fist and sent the window up a few inches. Steavens thanked him, but the nausea which had been gradually climbing into his throat for the last half hour left him with but one desire—a desperate feeling that he must get away from this place with what was left of Harvey Merrick. Oh, he comprehended well enough now the quiet bitterness of the smile that he had seen so often on his master's lips!

Once when Merrick returned from a visit home, he brought with him a singularly feeling and suggestive bas-relief of a thin, faded old woman, sitting and sewing something pinned to her knee; while a full-lipped, full-blooded little urchin, his trousers held up by a single gallows, [5] stood beside her,impatiently twitching her gown to call her attention to a butterfly he had caught. Steavens, impressed by the tender and delicate modelling of the thin, tired face, had asked him if it were his mother. He remembered the dull flush that had burned up in the sculptor's face.

The lawyer was sitting in a rocking-chair beside the coffin, his head thrown back and his eyes closed. Steavens looked at him earnestly, puzzled at the line of the chin, and wondering why a man should conceal a feature of such distinction under that disfiguring shock of beard. Suddenly, as though he felt the young sculptor's keen glance, Jim Laird opened his eyes.

Was he always a good deal of an oyster? [6] he asked abruptly. "He was terribly shy as a boy."

"Yes, he was an oyster, since you put it so," rejoined Steavens. "Although he could be very fond of people, he always gave one the impression of being detached. He disliked violent emotion; he was reflective, and rather distrustful of himself—except, of course, as regarded his work. He was sure enough there. He distrusted men pretty thoroughly and women even more, yet some- how without believing ill of them. He was determined, indeed, to believe the best; but he seemed afraid to investigate."

"A burnt dog dreads the fire," said the lawyer grimly, and closed his eyes.

Steavens went on and on, reconstructing that whole miserable boyhood. All this raw, biting ugliness had been the portion of the man whose mind was to become an exhaustless gallery of beautiful impressions—so sensitive that the mere shadow of a poplar leaf flickering against a sunny wall would be etched and held there for ever. Surely, if ever a man had the magic word in his finger tips, it was Merrick. Whatever he touched, he revealed its holiest secret; liberated it from enchantment and restored it to its pristine loveliness. Upon whatever he had come in contact with, he had left a beautiful record of the experience—a sort of ethereal signature; a scent, a sound, a colour that was his own.

Steavens understood now the real tragedy of his master's life; neither love nor wine, as many had conjectured; but a blow which had fallen earlier and cut deeper than anything else could have done—a shame not his, and yet so unescapably his, to hide in his heart from his very boyhood. And without— the frontier warfare; the yearning of a boy, cast ashore upon a desert of newness and ugliness and sordidness, for all that is chastened and old, and noble with traditions.

At eleven o'clock the tall, flat woman in black announced that the watchers were arriving, and asked them to "step into the dining-room."

As Steavens rose, the lawyer said dryly; "You go on—it'll be a good experience for you. I'm not equal to that crowd tonight; I've had twenty years of them." As Steavens closed the door after him he glanced back at the lawyer, sitting by the coffin in the dim light, with his chin resting on his hand.

The same misty group that had stood before the door of the express car shuffled into the dining-room. In the light of the kerosene lamp they sepa- rated and became individuals. The minister, a pale, feeble-looking man with white hair and blond chin-whiskers, took his seat beside a small side table and placed his Bible upon it. The Grand Army man sat down behind the stove and tilted his chair back comfortably against the wall, fishing his quill toothpick from his waistcoat pocket. The two bankers, Phelps and Elder, sat off in a corner behind the dinner-table, where they could finish their discussion of the new usury law and its effect on chattel security loans. The real estate agent, an old man with a smiling, hypocritical face, soon joined them. The coal and lumber dealer and the cattle shipper sat on opposite sides of the hard coal-burner, their feet on the nickel-work. Steavens took a book from his pocket and began to read. The talk around him ranged through various topics of local interest while the house was quieting down. When it was clear that the members of the family were in bed, the Grand Army man hitched his shoulders and, untangling his long legs, caught his heels on the rounds of his chair.

"S'pose there'll be a will, Phelps?" he queried in his weak falsetto.

The banker laughed disagreeably, and began trimming his nails with a pearl-handled pocket-knife.

"There'll scarcely be any need for one, will there?" he queried in his turn.

The restless Grand Army man shifted his position again, getting his knees still nearer his chin. "Why, the ole man says Harve's done right well lately," he chirped.

The other banker spoke up. "I reckon he means by that Harve ain't asked him to mortgage any more farms lately, so as he could go on with his education."

"Seems like my mind don't reach back to a time when Harve wasn't bein' edycated," tittered the Grand Army man.

There was a general chuckle. The minister took out his handkerchief and blew his nose sonorously. Banker Phelps closed his knife with a snap. "It's too bad the old man's sons didn't turn out better," he remarked with reflective authority. "They never hung together. He spent money enough on Harve to stock a dozen cattle-farms, and he might as well have poured it into Sand Creek. If Harve had stayed at home and helped nurse what little they had, and gone into stock on the old man's bottom farm, they might all have been well fixed. But the old man had to trust everything to tenants and was cheated right and left."

"Harve never could have handled stock none," interposed the

cattleman. "He hadn't it in him to be sharp. Do you remember when he bought Sander's mules for eight-year olds, when everybody in town knew that Sander's father- in-law give 'em to his wife for a wedding present eighteen years before, an' they was full-grown mules then?"

The company laughed discreetly, and the Grand Army man rubbed his knees with a spasm of childish delight.

"Harve never was much account for anything practical, and he shore was never fond of work," began the coal and lumber dealer. "I mind the last time he was home; the day he left, when the old man was out to the barn helpin' his hand hitch up to take Harve to the train, and Cal Moots was patchin' up the fence; Harve, he come out on the step and sings out, in his ladylike voice: Cal Moots, Cal Moots! please come cord my trunk.' "

"That's Harve for you," approved the Grand Army man. "I kin hear him howlin' yet, when he was a big feller in long pants and his mother used to whale him with a rawhide in the barn for lettin' the cows git foundered in the cornfield when he was drivin' 'em home from pasture. He killed a cow of mine that-a-way onct—a pure Jersey and the best milker I had, an' the ole man had to put up for her. Harve, he was watchin' the sun set acrost the marshes when the anamile got away."

"Where the old man made his mistake was in sending the boy East to school," said Phelps, stroking his goatee and speaking in a deliberate, judicial tone. "There was where he got his head full of nonsense. What Harve needed, of all people, was a course in some first-class Kansas City business college."

The letters were swimming before Steavens's eyes. Was it

possible that these men did not understand, that the palm on the coffin meant nothing to them? The very name of their town would have remained for ever buried in the postal guide had it not been now and again mentioned in the world in connection with Harvey Merrick's. He remembered what his master had said to him on the day of his death, after the congestion of both lungs had shut off any probability of recovery, and the sculptor had asked his pupil to send his body home. "It's not a pleasant place to be lying while the world is moving and doing and bettering," he had said with a feeble smile, "but it rather seems as though we ought to go back to the place we came from, in the end. The townspeople will come in for a look at me; and after they have had their say, I shan't have much to fear from the judgment of God!"

The cattleman took up the comment. "Forty's young for a Merrick to cash in; they usually hang on pretty well. Probably he helped it along with whisky."

"His mother's people were not long lived, and Harvey never had a robust constitution," said the minister mildly. He would have liked to say more. He had been the boy's Sunday-school teacher, and had been fond of him; but he felt that he was not in a position to speak. His own sons had turned out badly, and it was not a year since one of them had made his last trip home in the express car, shot in a gambling-house in the Black Hills.

"Nevertheless, there is no disputin' that Harve frequently looked upon the wine when it was red, also variegated, and it shore made an oncommon fool of him," moralized the cattleman.

Just then the door leading into the parlour rattled loudly and every one started involuntarily, looking relieved when only Jim Laird came out. The Grand Army man ducked his head when he saw the spark in his blue, blood- shot eye. They were all afraid of Jim; he was a drunkard, but he could twist the law to suit his client's needs as no other man in all western Kansas could do, and there were many who tried. The lawyer closed the door behind him, leaned back against it and folded his arms, cocking his head a little to one side. When he assumed this attitude in the court-room, ears were always pricked up, as it usually foretold a flood of withering sarcasm.

"I've been with you gentlemen before," he began in a dry, even tone, "when you've sat by the coffins of boys born and raised in this town; and, if I remember rightly, you were never any too well satisfied when you checked them up. What's the matter, anyhow? Why is it that reputable young men are as scarce as millionaires in Sand City? It might almost seem to a stranger that there was some way something the matter with your progressive town. Why did Ruben Sayer, the brightest young lawyer you ever turned out, after he had come home from the university as straight as a die, take to drinking and forge a check and shoot himself? Why did Bill Merrit's son die of the shakes in a saloon in Omaha? Why was Mr.Thomas's son, here, shot in a gambling- house? Why did young Adams burn his mill to beat the insurance companies and go to the pen?"

The lawyer paused and unfolded his arms, laying one clenched fist quietly on the table. "I'll tell you why. Because you drummed nothing but money and knavery into their ears from the time they wore knickerbockers; because you carped away at them as you've been carping here tonight, holding our friends Phelps and Elder up to them for their models, as our grandfathers held up George Washington and John Adams. But the boys were young, and raw at the business you put them to, and how could they match coppers with such artists as Phelps and Elder? You wanted them to be successful rascals; they were only unsuccessful ones—that's all the difference. There was only one boy ever raised in this borderland between ruffianism and civilization who didn't come to grief, and you hated Harvey Merrick more for winning out than you hated all the other boys who got under the wheels. Lord, Lord, how you did hate him! Phelps, here, is fond of saying that he could buy and sell us all out any time he's a mind to; but he knew Harve wouldn't have given a tinker's damn for his bank and all his cattlefarms put together; and a lack of appreciation, that way, goes hard with Phelps.

Old Nimrod thinks Harve drank too much; and this from such as Nimrod and me!

"Brother Elder says Harve was too free with the old man's money—fell short in filial consideration, maybe. Well, we can all remember the very tone in which brother Elder swore his own father was a liar, in the county court; and we all know that the old man came out of that partnership with his son as bare as a sheared lamb. But maybe I'm getting personal, and I'd better be driving ahead at what I want to say."

The lawyer paused a moment, squared his heavy shoulders, and went on: "Harvey Merrick and I went to school together, back East. We were dead in earnest, and we wanted you all to be proud of us some day. We meant to be great men. Even I, and I haven't lost my sense of humour, gentlemen, I meant to be a great man. I came back here to practise, and I found you didn't in the least want me to be a great man. You wanted me to be a shrewd lawyer— oh, yes! Our veteran here wanted me to get him an increase of pension, because he had dyspepsia; Phelps wanted a new county survey that would put the widow Wilson's little bottom farm inside his south line; Elder wanted to lend money at 5 per cent, a month, and get it collected; and Stark here wanted to wheedle old women up in Vermont into investing their annuities in real-estate mortgages that are not worth the paper they are written on. Oh, you needed me hard enough, and you'll go on needing me! "

"Well, I came back here and became the damned shyster you wanted me to be. You pretend to have some sort of respect for me; and yet you'll stand up and throw mud at Harvey Merrick, whose soul you couldn't dirty and whose hands you couldn't tie. Oh, you're a discriminating lot of Christians! There have been times when the sight of Harvey's name in some Eastern paper has made me hang my head like a whipped dog; and, again, times when I liked to think of him off there in the world, away from all this hog- wallow, climbing the big, clean up-grade he'd set for himself. "

"And we? Now that we've fought and lied and sweated and stolen, and hated as only the disappointed strugglers in a bitter, dead little Western town know how to do, what have we got to show for it? Harvey Merrick wouldn't have given one sunset over your marshes for all you've got put together, and you know it. It's not for me to say why, in the inscrutable wisdom of God, a genius should ever have been called from this place of hatred and bitter waters; but I want this Boston man to know that the drivel he's been hearing here tonight is the only tribute any truly great man could have from such a lot of sick, side-tracked, burnt-dog, land-poor sharks as the here-present financiers of Sand City—upon which town may God have mercy!"

The lawyer thrust out his hand to Steavens as he passed him, caught up his overcoat in the hall, and had left the house before the Grand Army man had had time to lift his ducked head and crane his long neck about at his fellows.

Next day Jim Laird was drunk and unable to attend the funeral services. Steavens called twice at his office, but was compelled to start East without seeing him. He had a presentiment that he would hear from him again, and left his address on the lawyer's table; but if Laird found it, he never acknowledged it. The thing in him that Harvey Merrick had loved must have gone under ground with Harvey Merrick's coffin; for it never spoke again, and Jim got the cold he died of driving across the Colorado mountains to defend one of Phelps's sons who had got into trouble out there by cutting government timber.

## Notes

1. I.e.,Grand Army of the Republic (G.A.R.),or the Union Army, which fought for the  the Civil War. This story. originally published in 1905, is set in present time. when Civil War veterans would have been in their sixties.

2. Lodgers("orders") — e.g.the Mason and Elks used a portion of club dues to cover members' funeral expenses.

3. Keeper of a vehicle-rental service.

4. Inexpensive factory-made carpet of a type developed in Brussels Belgium composed of colored wool strand looped through a linen foundation.

5. Suspender.

6. A self-contained person (slang).

## Questions

1. Please analyze the character Harvey Merrick in this work.
2. Do you think this short story is a feminism work? Why?

### (4) John Steinbeck (1902—1968)

John Ernst Steinbeck (1902—1968) was one of the greatest novelists in America. His mother, Olive Hamilton, was a former school teacher, who exerted a strong influence on Steinbeck. He was fond of a distinctive way of thinking. He formed a family and lived in a small rural town, where he made acquaintances with farmers and workers of the lower classes. Steinbeck had the experiences of working as a farm laborer, fruit-picker, and bricklayer, among others things, which made him fully aware of the miseries found in the life of migrants and the hideous nature of society. It provided rich material and sources for him to go and write such novels as *In Dubious Battle* (1936), *Of Mice and Men* (1937), and *The Grapes of Wrath* (1939).

John Steinbeck wrote a total of 27 books, including 16 novels, six non-fiction books, and five collections of short stories. At first, he received no recognition and reputation. Few critics paid attention to him and his works until the publication of *Tortilla Flat* in 1935. Then he stepped on his way to success with the popularity of his later works one by one. Steinbeck reached the peak of his writing career by the time of his universally-acknowledged greatest novel, *The Grapes of Wrath*, which won him the Favorite Fiction Book of 1939, the National Book Award and the Pulitzer Prize in 1940, and most especially, the Nobel Prize for Literature in 1962.

Steinbeck had a thorough understanding of the lives of people at the bottom of society. Many of his works laid emphasis on the simplicity and goodness of the downtrodden, which he studied many times over. In his speech at Stockholm in 1962, Steinbeck said that the writer was delegated to declare and to celebrate man's proven capacity for greatness of heart and spirit for gallantry in defeat, for courage, compassion and love. He had been considered as a social-protest writer, a realist, and a humanist as well. He obtained universal recognition for his vivid descriptions and sharp criticism of the human condition.

The following text is the 12th chapter of *The Grapes of Wrath* excerpted from *The Norton Anthology of American Literature* (shorter 6th edition).

## The Grapes of Wrath
## Chapter 12

Highway 66 is the main migrant road. 66—the long concrete path across the country, waving gently up and down on the map, from the Mississippi to Bakersfield—over the red lands and the gray lands, twisting up into the mountains, crossing the Divide and down into the bright and terrible desert, and across the desert to the mountains again, and into the rich California valleys.

66 is the path of a people in flight, refugees from dust and shrinking land,from the thunder of tractors and shrinking ownership, from the desert's slow northward invasion, from the twisting winds that howl up out of Texas, from the floods that bring no richness to the land and steal what little richness is there. From all of these the people are in flight, and they come into 66 from the tributary side roads, from the wagon tracks and the rutted country roads. 66 is the mother road, the road of flight.

Clarksville and Ozark and Van Buren and Fort Smith on 64, and there's an end of Arkansas. And all the roads into Oklahoma City, 66 down from Tulsa, 270 up from McAlester. 81 from Wichita Falls south, from Enid north. Edmond, McLoud, Purcell. 66 out of Oklahoma City; El Reno and Clinton, going west on 66. Hydro, Elk City, and Texola; and there's an end to Oklahoma. 66 across the Panhandle of Texas. Shamrock and McLean, Conway and Amarillo, the yellow. Wildorado and Vega and Boise, and there's an end of Texas. Tucumcari and Santa Rosa and into the New Mexican mountains to Albuquerque, where the road comes down from Santa Fe. Then down the gorged Rio Grande to Los Lunas and west again on 66 to Gallup, and there's the border of New Mexico.

And now the high mountains. Holbrook and Winslow and Flagstaff in the high mountains of Arizona. Then the great plateau[1] rolling like a ground swell. Ashfork and Kingman and stone mountains again, where water must be hauled and sold. Then out of the broken sun-rotted mountains of Arizona to the Colorado, with green reeds on its banks, and that's the end of Arizona. There's California just over the river, and a pretty town to start it. Needles, on the river. But the river is a stranger in this place. Up from Needles and over a burned range, and there's the desert. And 66 goes on over the terrible desert, where the distance shimmers and the black center mountains hang unbearably in the distance. At last there's Barstow, and more desert until at last the mountains rise up again, the good mountains, and 66 winds through them. Then suddenly a pass, and below the beautiful valley, below orchards[2] and vineyards[3] and little houses, and in the distance a city. And, oh, my God, it's over.

The people in flight streamed out on 66, sometimes a single car, sometimes a little caravan. All day they rolled slowly along the road, and at night they stopped near water. In the day ancient leaky radiators sent up columns of steam, loose connecting rods hammered and pounded. And the men driving the trucks and the overloaded cars listened apprehensively. How far between towns? It is a terror between towns. If something breaks—well, if something breaks we camp right here while Jim walks to town and gets a part and walks back and—how much food we got?

Listen to the motor. Listen to the wheels. Listen with your ears and with your hands on the steering wheel; listen with the palm of your hand on the gear-shift lever; listen with your feet on the floor boards. Listen to the pound- ing old jalopy with all your senses; for a change of tone, a variation of rhythm may mean—a week here? That rattle—that's tappets. Don't hurt a bit. Tap- pets can rattle till Jesus comes again without no harm. But that thudding as the car moves along—can't hear that—just kind of feel it. Maybe oil isn't gettin' someplace. Maybe a bearing's startin' to go. Jesus, if it's a bearing, what'll we do? Money's goin' fast.

And why's the son-of-a-bitch heat up so hot today? This ain't no climb. Le's look. God Almighty, the fan belt's gone! Here, make a belt outa this little piece a rope. Le's see how long—there. I'll splice the ends. Now take her slow—slow, till we can get to a town. That rope belt won't last long.

'F we can on'y get to California where the oranges grow before this here of jug blows up. 'F we on'y can.

And the tires two layers of fabric worn through. On'y a four-ply tire. Might get a hundred miles more outa her if we don't hit a rock an' blow her. Which'H we take—a hundred, maybe, miles, or maybe spoil the tube? Which? A hundred miles. Well, that's somepin you got to think about. We got tube patches. Maybe when she goes she'll only spring a leak. How about makin' a boot? Might get five hundred more miles. Le's go on till she blows.

We got to get a tire, but, Jesus, they want a lot for a of tire. They look a fella over. They know he got to go on. They know he can't wait. And the price goes up.

Take it or leave it. I ain't in business for my health. I'm here-a-sellin' tires. I ain't givin' 'em away. I can't help what happens to you. I got to think what happens to me.

How far's the nex' town?

I seen forty-two cars a you fellas go by yesterday. Where you all come from? Where all of you goin'?

Well, California's a big State.

Well, California's a big State.

It ain't that big. The whole United States ain't that big. It ain't that big. It ain't big enough. There ain't room enough for you an' me, for your kind an' my kind, for rich and poor together all in one country, for thieves and honest men. For hunger and fat. Whyn't you go back where you come from?

This is a free country. Fella can go where he wants.

That's what you think! Ever hear of the border patrol on the California line? Police from Los Angeles—stopped you bastards, turned you back. Says, if you can't buy no real estate we don't want you. Says, got a driver's license? Le's see it. Tore it up. Says you can't come in without no driver's license.

It's a free country.

Well, try to get some freedom to do. Fella says you're jus' as free as you got jack to pay for it.

In California they got high wages. I got a han'bill here tells about it.

Baloney! I seen folks comin' back. Somebody's kiddin' you. You want that tire or don't ya?

Got to take it, but, Jesus, mister, it cuts into our money! We ain't got much left.

Well, I ain't no charity. Take her along.

Got to, I guess. Let's look her over. Open her up, look a' the casing—you son-of-a-bitch, you said the casing was good. She's broke damn near through.

The hell she is. Well—by George! How come I didn't see that?

You did see it, you son-of-a-bitch. You wanta charge us four bucks for a busted casing. I'd like to take a sock at you.

Now keep your shirt on. I didn't see it, I tell you. Here—tell ya what I'll do. I'll give ya this one for three-fifty.

You'll take a flying jump at the moon! We'll try to make the nex' town.

Think we can make it on that tire?

Got to. I'll go on the rim before I'd give that son-of-a-bitch a dime.

What do ya think a guy in business is? Like he says, he ain't in it for his health. That's what business is. What'd you think it was? Fella's got— See that sign 'longside the road there? Service Club. Luncheon Tuesday, Colmado Hotel? Welcome, brother. That's a Service Club. Fella had a story. Went to one of them meetings an' told the story to all them business men. Says, when I was a kid my ol' man give me a haltered heifer an' says take her down an' git her serviced. An' the fella says, I done it, an' ever' time since then when I hear a business man talkin' about service, I wonder who's gettin' screwed. Fella in business got to lie an' cheat, but he calls it somepin else. That's what's important. You go steal that tire an' you're a thief, but he tried to steal your four dollars for a busted tire. They call that sound business.

Danny in the back seat wants a cup a water.

Have to wait. Got no water here.

Listen—that the rear end?

Can't tell.

Sound telegraphs through the frame.

There goes a gasket. Got to go on. Listen to her whistle. Find a nice place to camp an' I'll jerk the head off. But, God Almighty, the food's gettin' low, the money's gettin' low. When we can't buy no more gas—what then?

Danny in the back seat wants a cup a water. Little fella's thirsty.

Listen to that gasket whistle.

Chee-rist! There she went. Blowed tube an' casing all to hell. Have to fix her. Save that casing to make boots; cut' em out an' stick'em inside a weak place.

Cars pulled up beside the road, engine heads off, tires mended. Cars limping along 66 like wounded things, panting and struggling. Too hot, loose connections, loose bearings, rattling bodies.

Danny wants a cup of water.

People in flight along 66. And the concrete road shone like a mirror under the sun, and in the distance the heat made it seem that there were pools of water in the road.

Danny wants a cup a water.

He'll have to wait, poor little fella. He's hot. Nex' service station. Service station, like the fella says.

Two hundred and fifty thousand people over the road. Fifty thousand old cars—wounded, steaming. Wrecks along the road, abandoned. Well, what happened to them? What happened to the folks in that car? Did they walk? Where are they? Where does the courage come from? Where does the terrible faith come from?

And here's a story you can hardly believe, but it's true, and it's funny and it's beautiful. There was a family of twelve and they were forced off the land. They had no car. They built a trailer out of junk and loaded it with their possessions. They pulled it to the side of 66 and waited. And pretty soon a sedan picked them up. Five of them rode in the sedan and seven on the trailer, and a dog on the trailer. They got to California in two jumps. The man who pulled them fed them. And that's true. But how can such courage be, and such faith in their own species? Very few things would teach such faith.

The people in flight from the terror behind—strange things happen to them, some bitterly cruel and some so beautiful that the faith is refired forever.

## Notes

1. An area of flat land that is higher than the land around it.
2. An area of land on which fruit trees are grown.
3. An area of land where grape vines are grown in order to produce wine.

## Questions

1. What is highway 66 to the immigrants in this novel?
2. Please make a comparison between The Grapes of Wrath and Chuang Guandong written by Gao Mantang, a Chinese writer.

### (5) Robert Frost (1874—1963)

Robert Frost (1874—1963) was called the "Poet of New England" because nine generations of his ancestors had lived there. Therefore, his poetry had a strong and plain New England color. He was born in San Francisco. When he was 11, his father, a newspaper editor, died and his mother took him home to Ponrens, Massachusetts. He once studied at Dartmouth College, worked as a laborer, and taught at a school. After marrying Eleanor White in 1897, he went to Harvard. Two years later he moved to a farm near Derry, New Hampshire, which was given by his grandfather. He farmed the land for eleven years and taught for four years. At the same time, he continued to write poems for publication, and by 1911 had earned nearly $200. He devoted several years to writing poetry to test whether he could make a living on writing poetry. Hearing of the low cost of living in England, he sold his farm and moved his whole family to Gloucestershire in 1912.

His first poetry anthology, *A Boy's Will*, was published in Britain in 1913, followed by *North of Boston* (1914). Both works were well received in Britain and were soon republished in the United States. When Frost returned to the United States in 1915, he found himself famous. He was appointed as a professor of English at Amherst College, and in 1916 was elected as an academician of the American National Academy of Arts and Letters. Four of his poems that were later published won Pulitzer Prizes: *New Hamphshire* (1923), *Collected Poems* (1930), *A Further Range* (1936), and *A Witness Tree* (1942).

Frost's poetry is popular partly because of his use of traditional poetic forms and iambic pentameter lines. He often uses simple words in his poetry to show his deep thinking towards life. It can be said that his poetry is so finely crafted that not a word is superfluous

The following poems are excerpted from *The Norton Anthology of American Literature* (shorter 6th edition).

### The Pasture

I'm going out to clean the pasture spring;
I'll only stop to rake the leaves away
(And wait to watch the water clear, I may):
I shan't be gone long.—You come too.

I'm going out to fetch the little calf
That's standing by the mother. It's so young
It totters when she licks it with her tongue.
I shan't be gone long.—You come too.

## Questions

1. What kind of scene is described in this short poem?
2. What is the function of "You come too" in this poem?

### Mending Wall

Something there is that doesn't love a wall,
That sends the frozen-ground-swell under it,
And spills the upper boulders in the sun,

And makes gaps even two can pass abreast.
The work of hunters is another thing;
I have come after them and made repair
Where they have left not one stone on a stone,
But they would have the rabbit out of hiding,
To please the yelping dogs. The gaps I mean,
No one has seen them made or heard them made,
But at spring mending-time we find them there.
I let my neighbor know beyond the hill;
And on a day we meet to walk the line
And set the wall between us once again.
We keep the wall between us as we go.
To each the boulders that have fallen to each.
And some are loaves and some so nearly balls
We have to use a spell to make them balance:
"Stay where you are until our backs are turned!"
We wear our fingers rough with handling them.
Oh, just another kind of outdoor game,
One on a side. It comes to little more:
There where it is we do not need the wall:
He is all pine and I am apple orchard.
My apple trees will never get across
And eat the cones under his pines, I tell him.
He only says, "Good fences make good neighbors."
Spring is the mischief in me, and I wonder
If I could put a notion in his head:

"Why do they make good neighbors? Isn't it
Where there are cows? But here there are no cows.
Before I built a wall I'd ask to know
What I was walling in or walling out,
And to whom I was like to give offense.
Something there is that doesn't love a wall,
That wants it down." I could say "Elves" to him,
But it's not elves exactly, and I'd rather
He said it for himself. I see him there
Bringing a stone grasped firmly by the top
In each hand, like an old-stone savage armed.
He moves in darkness as it seems to me,
Not of woods only and the shade of trees.
He will not go behind his father's saying,
And he likes having thought of it so well
He says again, "Good fences make good neighbors."

## Questions

1. What is the function of this wall in this poem?

2. How do you understand this sentence "Good fences make good neighbors"?

## The Road Not Taken

Two roads diverged in a yellow wood,
And sorry I could not travel both
And be one traveler, long I stood
And looked down one as far as I could
To where it bent in the undergrowth;

Then took the other, as just as fair,
And having perhaps the better claim,
Because it was grassy and wanted wear;
Though as for that, the passing there
Had worn them really about the same,

And both that morning equally lay
In leaves no step had trodden black.
Oh, I kept the first for another day!
Yet knowing how way leads on to way,
I doubted if I should ever come back.

I shall be telling this with a sigh
Somewhere ages and ages hence:
Two roads diverged in a wood, and I—
I took the one less traveled by,

And that has made all the difference.

## Questions

1. What is the theme of this poem?

2. Please make a comparison between this poem with "Yu Wo Suo Yu Ye" (《鱼我所欲也》) written by Mencius?

### (6) Ezra Pound (1885—1972)

Ezra Pound, born in Idaho and raised in Pennsylvania, was a great poet in 20th-century American literature. He was also a pioneer of American literature, persistently giving guidance and help to young writers, including Robert Frost and T. S. Eliot. In 1908, he came to Europe to escape from the narrow-minded and suffocating American socicty and culture, in his view, devoting himself to the imagist movement. As a foreign correspondent of *Poetry* in Chicago, he made great contributions to the prosperity of American poetry. He created two collections of poems, *Exultations* and *Personoe*, published in London in 1909, a poetry translation *Cathay* published in 1915, and a monumental work called by himself *Cantos* (1925—1970), which contains 109 poems and 8 unfinished drafts involving all aspects of world literature and history. Pound's poetry laid the foundation for the development of modern poetry. *Des Imahistes* (1914), edited by him, was significant in the rise of modern poetry.

The following poems are excerpted from *The Norton Anthology of American Literature* (shorter 6th edition).

## In a Station of the Metro[1]

The apparition of these faces in the crowd;
Petals on a wet, black bough.

### Notes

1. Paris subway.

### Questions

1. What do "petals" and "bough" stand for in this poem?

2. What is the logic relationship between the first line and the second line?

## The River-Merchant's Wife: A Letter[1]

While my hair was still cut straight across my forehead
I played about the front gate, pulling flowers.
You came by on bamboo stilts, playing horse,
You walked about my seat, playing with blue plums.
And we went on living in the village of Chokan:
Two small people, without dislike or suspicion.

At fourteen I married My Lord you.

I never laughed, being bashful.
Lowering my head, I looked at the wall.
Called to, a thousand times, I never looked back.

At fifteen I stopped scowling,
I desired my dust to be mingled with yours
Forever and forever and forever.
Why should I climb the look out?

At sixteen you departed,
You went into far Ku-to-en, by the river of swirling eddies,
And you have been gone five months.
The monkeys make sorrowful noise overhead.

You dragged your feet when you went out.
By the gate now, the moss is grown, the different mosses,
Too deep to clear them away!
The leaves fall early this autumn, in wind.
The paired butterflies are already yellow with August
Over the grass in the West garden;
They hurt me. I grow older.
If you are coming down through the narrows of the river Kiang,
Please let me know beforehand,
And I will come out to meet you
As far as Cho-fu-Sa.

By Rihaku

## Notes

1. Adaptation from the Chinese of Li Po (701-762), named Rihaku in Japanese, from the papers of Ernest Fenollosa, an American scholar whose widow gave his papers on Japan and China to Pound.

## Questions

1. Is there any mistake or misunderstanding in this translated version by Pound compared with the original poem "Chang Ge Xing" created by Li Po?

2. What is Pound's contribution to English poetry?

### （7）William Carlos Williams (1883—1963)

Born in Rutherford, New Jersey, William Carlos Williams was one of the most famous American poets in the 20th century. After he received a medical degree at the University of Pennsylvania, he went on to further study at the University of Leipzig in Germany. In 1910, he returned to his hometown and began his medical career. Although he was busy at his job as a doctor, he still insisted on writing prose and poetry. Williams was particularly good at seeking beauty, interest, and significance in the trifles of daily life. His poems were often about the daily life that are too normal to be noticed, like spring, plums, and wheelbarrows. Because of his career as a doctor, he had the opportunity to meet people living in various conditions and at different periods in their life, from birth to death. Such meticulous observations gave his poems and short stories deep insight and content. His classmate at the

University of Pennsylvania, Ezra Pound, and other Imagists, had a great influence on his poetry. At the same time, he also imitated the style of Whitman and actively developed the form of free verse. Due to his insistence of writing in the Native American language, his poetry has a strong rural feature. His lyrical poems are mainly collated in *Collected Later Poems* (1950) and *Collected Early Poems* (1951).

The following poem is excerpted from *The Norton Anthology of American Literature* (shorter 6th edition).

## The Red Wheelbarrow[1]

so much depends
upon

a red wheel
barrow

glazed with rain
water

beside the white
chickens

### Notes

1. Numbered XXII in Spring and All.

## Questions

1. What are the images described in this poem?
2. Why every word in this poem is not capitalized?

### （8）T. S. Eliot (1888—1965)

T. S. Eliot (1888—1965) is a great British and American modernist poet, dramatist, and literary critic of the 20th century. As a poet, Eliot integrated the unique thinking of modernism into symbols, images, and metaphors, and formed his own unique poetic skills; as a critic, he put forward a series of incisive and unique insights, such as "objective correlative," "impersonalization," and "traditional view." Eliot was awarded the Nobel Prize for literature in 1948 for his masterpiece *Four Quartets* (1943). His arrival changed the existing order of English literature. Eliot's poetry and literary criticism changed the taste of an entire generation and created a whole new set of standards for literary appreciation.

Eliot was born in America on September 26, 1888. At the age of six, Eliot first studied at Mrs.Lockwood's School. Four years later, he was enrolled in the Smith Academy. Eliot spent a happy seven-year period in learning Latin and Greek, together with Greek and Roman history, English and American history, elementary mathematics, and French and German languages. Strict family influences and an excellent school education paved a golden way for Eliot's eventual arrival at Harvard University in 1906. After being awarded a bachelor's degree in 1910 and a master's degree in

1911, T.S. Eliot embarked to Europe and set foot into philosophy. In 1914, T. S. Eliot entered a crucial turning point in his life; he was introduced to Ezra Pound, who created a door for him to achieve literary greatness several years later. T. S. Eliot's first book, *Prufrock and Other Observations* (1917), came out and was enormously appreciated and eulogized among critics. Almost at the same time, T. S. Eliot issued the literary journal *Criterion*, in which his masterpiece *The Wasteland* was published in 1922.

Throughout his life, T.S. Eliot did not only create excellent poems and dramas, but also cultivated insightful observations and thoughts as a critical critic. For example, he published various critical works, such as *Tradition and Individual Talents* (1919), *The Sacred Wood* (1920), *Tradition and Experimentation in Present-Day Literature* (1929), *Essays Ancient and Modern* (1936), and *Notes toward the Definition of Culture* (1940).

The following poem is excerpted from *The Norton Anthology of American Literature* (shorter 6th edition).

## The Love Song of J. Alfred Prufrock

S'io credessi che mia risposta fosse
a persona che mat tornasse al mondo,
qiiesta fiamma staria senza piu scosse.
Ma per cid che giammai di questo fondo
non tornd vivo alcun, s'i'odo il vero,

senza tenia d'infamia ti rispondo.[1]

Let us go then, you and I,
When the evening is spread out against the sky
Like a patient etherised upon a table;
Let us go, through certain half-deserted streets,
The muttering retreats
Of restless nights in one-night cheap hotels
And sawdust restaurants with oyster-shells:
Streets that follow like a tedious argument
Of insidious intent
To lead you to an overwhelming question
Oh, do not ask, 'What is it?'
Let us BO and make our visit.

In the room the women come and go
Talking of Michelangelo.
The yellow fog that rubs its back upon the window-panes,

The yellow smoke that rubs its muzzle on the window-panes,
Licked its tongue into the corners of the evening,

Lingered upon the pools that stand in drains,
Let fall upon its back the soot that falls from chimneys,
Slipped by the terrace, made a sudden leap,
And seeing that it was a soft October night,

Curled once about the house, and fell asleep.

And indeed there will be time [2]
For the yellow smoke that slides along the street
Rubbing its back upon the window-panes;
There will be time, there will be time
To prepare a face to meet the faces that you meet;
There will be time to murder and create,
And time for all the works and days[3] of hands
That lift and drop a question on your plate;
Time for you and time for me,
And time yet for a hundred indecisions,
And for a hundred visions and revisions,
Before the taking of a toast and tea.

In the room the women come and go
Talking of Michelangelo.

And indeed there will be time
To wonder, 'Do I dare?'and, 'Do I dare?'
Time to turn back and descend the stair,
With a bald spot in the middle of my hair—
(They will say: 'How his hair is growing thin!')
My morning coat, my collar mounting firmly to the chin,
My necktie rich and modest, but asserted by a simple pin—
(They will say: 'But how his arms and legs are thin!')

Do I dare
Disturb the universe?
In a minute there is time
For decisions and revisions which a minute will reverse.
For I have known them all already, known them all—
Have known the evenings, mornings, afternoons,
I have measured out my life with coffee spoons;
I know the voices dying with a dying fall [4]
Beneath the music from a farther room.
So how should I presume?

And I have known the eyes already, known them all—
The eyes that fix you in a formulated phrase,
And when I am formulated, sprawling on a pin,
When I am pinned and wriggling on the wall,
Then how should I begin
To spit out all the butt-ends of my days and ways?
And how should I presume?
And I have known the arms already, known them all—
Arms that are braceleted and white and bare
(But in the lamplight, downed with light brown hair!)
Is it perfume from a dress
That makes me so digress?
Arms that lie along a table, or wrap about a shawl.
And should I then presume?
And how should I begin?

Shall I say, I have gone at dusk through narrow streets
And watched the smoke that rises from the pipes
Of lonely men in shirt-sleeves, leaning out of windows?...
I should have been a pair of ragged claws
Scuttling across the floors of silent seas.

And the afternoon, the evening, sleeps so peacefully!
Smoothed by long fingers,
Asleep...tired...or it malingers,
Stretched on the floor, here beside you and me.
Should I, after tea and cakes and ices,
Have the strength to force the moment to its crisis?
But though I have wept and fasted, wept and prayed,
Though I have seen my head (grown slightly bald) brought in upon a platter,[5]
I am no prophet—and here's no great matter;
I have seen the moment of my greatness flicker,
And I have seen the eternal Footman hold my coat, and snicker,
And in short, I was afraid.

And would it have been worth it, after all,
After the cups, the marmalade, the tea,
Among the porcelain, among some talk of you and me,
Would it have been worth while,
To have bitten off the matter with a smile,

To have squeezed the universe into a ball
To roll it towards some overwhelming question,
To say: 'I am Lazarus, [6] come from the dead,
Come back to tell you all, I shall tell you all'—
If one, settling a pillow by her head,
Should say: 'That is not what I meant at all.
That is not it, at all.'

And would it have been worth it, after all,
Would it have been worth while,
After the sunsets and the dooryards and the sprinkled streets,
After the novels, after the teacups, after the skirts that trail along the floor—
And this, and so much more?—
It is impossible to say just what I mean!
But as if a magic lantern threw the nerves in patterns on a screen:
Would it have been worth while
If one, settling a pillow or throwing off a shawl,
And turning toward the window, should say:
'That is not it at all,
That is not what I meant, at all.'

No! I am not Prince Hamlet, nor was meant to be;
Am an attendant lord, one that will do
To swell a progress, [7] start a scene or two,

Advise the prince; no doubt, an easy tool,
Deferential, glad to be of use,

Politic, cautious, and meticulous;
Full of high sentence,[8] but a bit obtuse;
At times, indeed, almost ridiculous—
Almost, at times, the Fool.

I grow old…I grow old…
I shall wear the bottoms of my trousers rolled.

Shall I part my hair behind? Do I dare to eat a peach?
I shall wear white flannel trousers, and walk upon the beach.
I have heard the mermaids singing, each to each.

I do not think that they will sing to me.
I have seen them riding seaward on the waves
Combing the white hair of the waves blown back
When the wind blows the water white and black.
We have lingered in the chambers of the sea
By sea-girls wreathed with seaweed red and brown
Till human voices wake us, and we drown.

## Notes

1. If I thought that my reply would be to one who would ever return to the world, this flame would stay without further movement;

but since none has ever returned alive from this depth, if what I hear is true, I answer you without fear of infamy (Italian; *Dante's Inferno* 27.61 — 66). The speaker, Guido da Montefeltro, consumed in flame as punishment for giving false counsel, confesses his shame without fear of its being reported since he believes Dante cannot return to earth.

2. An echo of Andrew Marvell, "*To His Coy Misress*" (1681): "Had we but world enough and time."

3. Works and Days is a didactic poem about farming by the Greek poet Hesiod (8th century B.C.E.).

4. Echo of Duke Orsino's invocation of music in Shakespeare's Twelfth Night 1.1 A: "If music be the food of love, play on…That strain again! It had a dying fall."

5. The head of the prophet John the Baptist, who was killed at the behest of Princess Salome, was brought to her on a platter (see Mark 6.17 — 20, Matthew 14.3-11).

6. The resurrection of Lazarus is recounted in John 11.1 — 44.

7. A journey or procession made by royal courts and often portrayed on Elizabethan stages.

8. Opinions, sententiousness.

## Questions

1. Is this poem a "love song"? Why?

2. What is the theme of this poem?

### (9) Eugene O'Neill (1888—1953)

Eugene Glastone O'Neill (1888—1953) is one of the most important American playwrights and the winner of the 1936 Nobel Prize for Literature. O'Neill wrote more than 30 plays, starting from his earliest one-act play, in 1916, until he stopped writing, in 1943, because of an illness and family misfortune. O'Neill devoted himself to creating serious plays, experimenting with various artistic techniques, and exploring psychological and social problems with a realistic attitude, which helped the American dramas get rid of the previous modes of sad comedies and tragic plot, and really matured.

O'Neill spent his childhood touring with his father, a Catholic of Irish descent. O'Neill studied at Princeton University in 1906 but was expelled the following year. He once panned for gold in Honduras, worked as a sailor in South America and South Africa, and roamed around the shores of the seaports. Unfortunately, he also suffered from tuberculosis. He went to Harvard University in 1914 to study drama writing with George Pierce Baker and joined the Provincetown Theater Company in 1916. In the same year, *Bound East for Cardiff* (1916) became O'Neill's first play performed on stage.

O'Neill's early plays were realistic, based mainly on his youth experience at sea. In addition to *Bound East for Cardiff*, some of the best plays of this period include *In the Zone* (1917), *The Long Voyage Home* (1917), and *The Moon of the Caribbees* (1918). O'Neill created a series of experiments in the middle of his writing career: *Emperor Jones* (1920) and *The Hairy Ape* (1922), two expressionist plays. *In The Great God Brown* (1926), characters wore masks to show or hide their inner natures. *Strange Interlude* (1928) used the stream of consciousness to allow characters to express their inner thoughts through asides. *Desire Under the Elms* (1924) and *Mourning Becomes Electra* (1931) transplanted the elements of the ancient Greek tragedy into the American setting. O'Neill created plays with realism in his old age and fulfilled his dream to write his autobiographical plays, representing the highest level of his written plays. Plays in this period include *The Iceman Cometh* (1939), *A Touch of The Poet* (1935—1942), *Long Day's Journey Into Night* (1939—1941), *The Moon for The Misbegotten* (1943), *Hughie* (1941), and *More Stately Mansions* (unfinished, 1935—1941).

The following text is the first act of *Long Day's Journey into Night* excerpted from T*he Norton Anthology of American Literature* (shorter 6th edition).

**Long Day's Journey into Night**

CHARACTERS

JAMES TYRONE

MARY CAVAN TYRONE, his wife

JAMES TYRONE, JR., their elder son

EDMUND TYRONE, their younger son

CATHLEEN, second girl[1]

SCENES

ACT 1 Living room of the Tyrones' summer home 8:30 A.M. of a day in August, 1912

ACT 2 SCENE 1 The same, around 12:45

SCENE 2 The same, about a half hour later

ACT 3 The same, around 6:30 that evening

ACT 4 The same, around midnight

## Act 1

SCENE—Living room of JAMES TYRONE'S summer home on a morning in August, 1912.

At rear are two double doorways with portieres. The one at right leads into a front parlor with the formally arranged, set appearance of a room rarely occupied. The other opens on a dark, windowless back parlor, never used except as a passage from living room to dining room. Against the wall between the doorways is a small bookcase, with a picture of Shakespeare above it, containing novels by Balzac, Zola, Stendhal, philosophical and sociological works by Schopenhauer, Nietzsche, Marx, Engels, Kropotkin, Max Sterner, plays by Ibsen, Shaw, Strindberg, poetry by Swinburne, Rossetti, Wilde, Ernest Dowson, Kipling, etc. [2]

In the right wall, rear, is a screen door leading out on the porch which extends halfway around the house. Farther forward, a series of three windows looks over the front lawn to the harbor and the avenue that runs along the water front. A small wicker table and an ordinary oak desk are against the wall, flanking the windows.

In the left wall, a similar series of windows looks out on the grounds in back of the house. Beneath them is a wicker couch with cushions, its head toward rear. Farther back is a large, glassed-in bookcase with sets of Dumas, Victor Hugo, Charles Lever, three sets of Shakespeare, The World's Best Literature in fifty large volumes, Hume's History of England, Thiers' History of the Consulate and Empire, Smollett's History of England, Gibbon's Roman Empire and miscellaneous volumes of old plays, poetry, and several histories of Ireland. The astonishing thing about these sets is that all the volumes have the look of having been read and reread.

The hardwood floor is nearly covered by a rug, inoffensive in design and color. At center is a round table with a green shaded reading lamp, the cord plugged in one of the four sockets in the chandelier above. Around the table within reading-light range are four chairs, three of them wicker armchairs, the fourth (at right front of table) a varnished oak rocker with leather bottom.

It is around 8:30. Sunshine comes through the windows at right.

As the curtain rises, the family have fust finished breakfast, MARY TYRONE and her husband enter together from the back parlor, coming from the dining room.

MARY is fifty-four, about medium height. She still has a young, graceful figure, a trifle plump, but showing little evidence of middle-aged waist and hips, although she is not tightly corseted. Her face is distinctly Irish in type. It must once have been extremely pretty, and is still striking. It does not match her healthy figure but is thin and pale with the bone structure prominent. Her nose is long and straight, her mouth wide with full, sensitive lips. She uses no rouge or any sort of make-up. Her high forehead is framed by thick, pure white hair. Accentuated by her pallor and white hair, her dark brown eyes appear black. They are unusually large and beautiful, with black brows and long curling lashes.

What strikes one immediately is her extreme nervousness. Her hands are never still. They were once beautiful hands, with long, tapering fingers, but rheumatism has knotted the joints and warped the fingers, so that now they have an ugly crippled look. One avoids looking at them, the more so because one is conscious she is sensitive about their appearance and humiliated by her inability to control the nervousness which draws attention to them.

She is dressed simply but with a sure sense of what becomes her. Her hair is arranged with fastidious care. Her voice is soft and attractive. When she is merry,there is a touch of Irish lilt in it.

Her most appealing quality is the simple, unaffected charm of a shy convent-girl youthfulness she has never lost—an innate unworldly innocence.

JAMES TYRONE is sixty-five but looks ten years younger. About five feet eight, broad-shouldered and deep-chested, he seems taller and slenderer because of his bearing, which has a soldierly quality of head up, chest out, stomach in, shoulders squared. His face has begun to break down but he is still remarkably good looking—a big, finely shaped head, a handsome profile, deep-set light-brown eyes. His grey hair is thin with a bald spot like a monk's tonsure.

The stamp of his profession is unmistakably on him. Not that he indulges in any of the deliberate temperamental posturings of the stage star. He is by nature and preference a simple, unpretentious man, whose inclinations are still close to his humble beginnings and his Irish farmer forebears. But the actor shows in all his unconscious habits of speech, movement and gesture. These have the quality of belonging to a studied technique. His voice is remarkably fine, resonant and flexible, and he takes great pride in it.

His clothes, assuredly, do not costume any romantic part. He wears a thread- bare, ready-made, grey sack suit and shineless black shoes, a collar-less shirt with a thick white handkerchief knotted loosely around his throat. There is nothing picturesquely careless about this get-up. It is commonplace shabby. He believes in wearing his clothes to the limit of usefulness, is dressed now for gardening, and doesn't give a damn how he looks.

He has never been really sick a day in his life. He has no nerves. There is a lot of stolid, earthy peasant in him, mixed with streaks of sentimental melancholy and rare flashes of intuitive sensibility.

TYRONE'S arm is around his wife's waist as they appear from the back parlor.

Entering the living room he gives her a playful hug.

YRONE You're a fine armful now, Mary, with those twenty pounds you've gained.

MARY [smiles affectionately] I've gotten too fat, you mean, dear. I really ought to reduce.

TYRONE None of that, my lady! You're just right. We'll have no talk of reducing. Is that why you ate so little breakfast?

MARY So little? I thought I ate a lot.

TYRONE You didn't. Not as much as I'd like to see, anyway.

MARY [teasingly] Oh you! You expect everyone to eat the enormous breakfast you do. No one else in the world could without dying of indigestion.

[She comes forward to stand by the right of table.]

TYRONE [following her] I hope I'm not as big a glutton as that sounds.

[with hearty satisfaction] But thank God, I've kept my appetite and I've the digestion of a young man of twenty, if I am sixty-five.

MARY You surely have, James. No one could deny that.

[She laughs and sits in the wicker armchair at right rear of table. He comes around in back of her and selects a cigar from a box on the table and cuts off the end with a little clipper. From the dining room JAMIE S and EDMUND'S voices are heard. Mary turns her head that way.] Why did the boys stay in the dining room, I wonder? Cathleen must be waiting to clear the table.

YRONE [jokingly but with an undercurrent of resentment] It's a secret confab they don't want me to hear, I suppose. I'll bet they're cooking up some new scheme to touch the Old Man.

[She is silent on this, keeping her head turned toward their voices. Her hands appear on the table top, moving restlessly. He lights his cigar and sits down in the rocker at right of table, which is his chair, and puffs contentedly. ]

There's nothing like the first after-breakfast cigar, if it's a good one, and this new lot have the right mellow flavor. They're a great bargain, too. I got them dead cheap. It was McGuire put me on to them.

MARY [a trifle acidly] I hope he didn't put you on to any new piece of property at the same time. His real estate bargains don't work out so well.

TYRONE [defensively] I wouldn't say that, Mary. After all, he was the one who advised me to buy that place on Chestnut Street and I made a quick turnover on it for a fine profit.

MARY [smiles now with teasing affection] I know. The famous one stroke of good luck. I'm sure McGuire never dreamed—[Then she pats his hand.] Never mind, James. I know it's a waste ofbreath trying to convince you you're not a cunning real estate speculator.

TYRONE [huffily] I've no such idea. But land is land, and it's safer than the stocks and bonds of Wall Street swindlers, [then placatingly] But let's not argue about business this early in the morning. [A pause. The boys' voices are again heard and one of them has a fit of coughing, MARY listens worriedly. Her fingers play nervously on the table top.]

MARY James, it's Edmund you ought to scold for not eating enough. He hardly touched anything except coffee. He needs to eat to keep up his strength. I keep telling him that but he says he simply has no appetite. Of course, there's nothing takes away your appetite like a bad summer cold.

TYRONE Yes, it's only natural. So don't let yourself get worried—

MARY [quickly] Oh, I'm not. I know he'll be all right in a few days if he takes care of himself, [as if she wanted to dismiss the subject but can't] But it does seem a shame he should have to be sick right now.

TYRONE Yes, it is bad luck. [He gives her a quick, worried look.] But you mustn't let it upset you, Mary. Remember, you've got to take care of yourself, too.

MARY [quickly] I'm not upset. There's nothing to be upset about. What makes youthink I'm upset?

TYRONE Why, nothing, except you've seemed a bit high-strung the past few days. MARY [forcing a smile] I have? Nonsense, dear. It's your imagination, [with sudden tenseness] You really must not watch me all the time, James. I mean, it makes me self-conscious.

TYRONE [putting a hand over one of her nervously playing ones] Now, now, Mary. That's your imagination. If I've watched you it was to admire how fat and beautiful you looked. [His voice is suddenly moved by deep feeling. ] I can't tell you the deep happiness it gives me, darling, to see you as you've been since you came back to us, your dear old self again. [He leans over and kisses her cheek impulsively—then turning back adds with a con- strained air] So keep up the good work, Mary.

MARY [has turned her head away] I will, dear. [She gets up restlessly and goes to the windows at right.] Thank heavens, the fog is gone. [She turns back.] I do feel out of sorts this morning. I wasn't able to get much sleep with that awful foghorn going all night long.

TYRONE Yes, it's like having a sick whale in the back yard. It kept me awake, too.

MARY [affectionately amused] Did it? You had a strange way

of showing your restlessness. You were snoring so hard I couldn't tell which was the foghorn! [She comes to him, laughing, and pats his cheek playfully.] Ten foghorns couldn't disturb you. You haven't a nerve in you. You've never had.

TYRONE [his vanity piqued—testily] Nonsense. You always exaggerate about my snoring.

MARY I couldn't. If you could only hear yourself once— [A burst of laughter comes from the dining room. She turns her head, smiling.] What's the joke, I wonder?

TYRONE [grumpily] It's on me. I'll bet that much. It's always on the Old Man.

MARY [teasingly] Yes, it's terrible the way we all pick on you, isn't it? You're so abused! [She laughs—then with a pleased, relieved air] Well, no matter what the joke is about, it's a relief to hear Edmund laugh. He's been so down in the mouth lately. TYRONE [ignoring this—resentfully] Some joke of Jamie's, I'll wager. He's forever making sneering fun of somebody, that one.

MARY Now don't start in on poor Jamie, dear, [without conviction] He'll turn out all right in the end, you wait and see.

TYRONE He'd better start soon, then. He's nearly thirty-four.

MARY [ignoring this] Good heavens, are they going to stay in the dining room all day? [She goes to the back parlor doorway and calls] Jamie! Edmund! Come in the living room and give Cathleen a chance to clear the table. [EDMUND calls back, "We're coming, Mama." She goes back to the table.]

TYRONE [grumbling] You'd find excuses for him no matter what he did.

MARY [sitting down beside him, pats his hand] Shush.

Their sons JAMES, JR., and EDMUND enter together from the back parlor.They are both grinning, still chuckling over what had caused their laughter, and as they come forward they glance at their father and their grins grow broader.

JAMIE, the elder, is thirty-three. He has his father's broad-shouldered, deep- chested physique, is an inch taller and weighs less, but appears shorter and stouter because he lacks TYRONE'S bearing and graceful carriage. He also lacks his father's vitality. The signs of premature disintegration are on him. His face is still good looking, despite marks of dissipation, but it has never been handsome like TYRONE'S, although JAMIE resembles him rather than his mother. He has fine brown eyes, their color midway between his father's lighter and his mother's darker ones. His hair is thinning and already there is indication of a bald spot like TYRONE'S. His nose is unlike that of any other member of the family, pronouncedly aquiline. Combined with his habitual expression of cynicism it gives his countenance a Mephistophelian cast. But on the rare occasions when he smiles with- out sneering, his personality possesses the remnant of a humorous, romantic, irresponsible Irish charm—that of the beguiling ne'er-do-well, with a strain of the sentimentally poetic, attractive to women and popular with men.

He is dressed in an old sack suit, not as shabby as TYRONE'S, and wears a collar and tie. His fair skin is sunburned a reddish, freckled tan.

EDMUND is ten years younger than his brother, a couple of inches taller, thin and wiry. Where JAMIE takes after his father, with little resemblance to his mother, EDMUND looks like both his parents, but is more like his mother. Her big, dark eyes are the dominant feature in his long, narrow Irish face. His mouth has the same quality of hypersensitiveness hers possesses. His high fore-head is hers accentuated, with dark brown hair, sunble ached to red at the ends, brushed straight back from it. But his nose is his father's and his face in profile recalls TYRONE'S. EDMUND'S hands are noticeably like his mother's, with the same exceptionally long fingers. They even have to a minor degree the same nervousness. It is in the quality of extreme nervous sensibility that the likeness of EDMUND to his mother is most marked.

He is plainly in bad health. Much thinner than he should be, his eyes appear feverish and his cheeks are sunken. His skin, in spite of being sunburned a deep brown, has a parched sallowness. He wears a shirt, collar and tie, no coat, old flannel trousers, brown sneakers.

MARY [turns smilingly to them, in a merry tone that is a bit forced] I've been teasing your father about his snoring, [to TYRONE] I'll leave it to the boys, James. They must have heard you. No, not you, Jamie. I could hear you down the hall almost as bad as your father. You're like him. As soon as your head touches the pillow you're off and ten foghorns couldn't wake you. [She stops abruptly, catching JAMIE'S eyes regarding her with an uneasy, probing look.

Her smile vanishes and her manner becomes self- conscious.] Why are you staring, Jamie? [Her hands flutter up to her hair.] Is my hair coming down? It's hard for me to do it up properly now. My eyes are getting so bad and I never can find my glasses.

JAMIE [looks away guiltily] Your hair's all right, Mama. I was only thinking how well you look. TYRONE [heartily] Just what I've been telling her, Jamie. She's so fat and sassy, there'll soon be no holding her. EDMUND Yes, you certainly look grand, Mama. [She is reassured and smiles at him lovingly. He winks with a kidding grin.] I'll back you up about Papa's snoring. Gosh, what a racket! JAMIE I heard him, too. [He quotes, putting on a ham-actor manner] "The Moor, I know his trumpet."[3] [His mother and brother laugh. ]

TYRONE [scathingly] If it takes my snoring to make you remember Shake speare instead of the dope sheet on the ponies, I hope I'll keep on with it. MARY Now, James! You mustn't be so touchy. [JAMIE shrugs his shoulders and sits down in the chair on her right.]

EDMUND [irritably] Yes, for Pete's sake, Papa! The first thing after break- fast! Give it a rest, can't you? [He slumps down in the chair at left of table next to his brother. His father ignores him.]

MARY [reprovingly] Your father wasn't finding fault with you. You don't have to always take Jamie's part. You'd think you were the one ten years older. JAMIE [boredly] What's all the fuss about? Let's forget it.

TYRONE [contemptuously] Yes, forget! Forget everything and face nothing! It's a convenient philosophy if you've no ambition in life except to— MARY James, do be quiet. [She puts an arm around his shoulder—coaxingly] You must have gotten out of the wrong side of the bed this morning, [to the boys, changing the subject] What were you two grinning about like Cheshire cats when you came in? What was the joke?

TYRONE [with a painful effort to be a good sport] Yes, let us in on it, lads. I told your mother I knew damned well it would be one on me, but never mind that, I'm used to it.

JAMIE[dryly] Don't look at me. This is the Kid's story.

EDMUND [grins] I meant to tell you last night, Papa, and forgot it. Yester- day when I went for a walk I dropped in at the Inn—

MARY[worriedly] You shouldn't drink now, Edmund.

EDMUND [ignoring this] And who do you think I met there, with a beautiful bun on, [4] but Shaughnessy, the tenant on that farm of yours.

MARY[smiling] That dreadful man! But he is funny.

TYRONE[scowling] He's not so funny when you're his landlord. He's a wily Shanty Mick, that one. He could hide behind a corkscrew. What's he complaining about now, Edmund—for I'm damned sure he's complain- ing. I suppose he wants his rent lowered. I let him have the place for almost nothing, just to keep someone on it, and he never pays that till I threaten to evict him.

EDMUND No, he didn't beef about anything. He was so pleased with life he even bought a drink, and that's practically unheard of. He was delighted because he'd had a fight with your friend, Harker, the Standard Oil millionaire, and won a glorious victory.

MARY [with amused dismay] Oh, Lord! James, you'll really have to do something—

TYRONE Bad luck to Shaughnessy, anyway!

JAMIE[maliciously] I'll bet the next time you see Harker at the Club and give him the old respectful bow, he won't see you.

EDMUND Yes. Harker will think you're no gentleman for harboring a ten- ant who isn't humble in the presence of a king of America.

TYRONE Never mind the Socialist gabble. I don't care to listen—

MARY [tactfully] Go on with your story, Edmund.

EDMUND [grins at his father provocatively] Well, you remember, Papa, the ice pond on Harker's estate is right next to the farm, and you remember Shaughnessy keeps pigs. Well, it seems there's a break in the fence and the pigs have been bathing in the millionaire's ice pond, and Harker's foreman told him he was sure Shaughnessy had broken the fence on purpose to give his pigs a free wallow. MARY[shocked and amused] Good heavens!

TYRONE[sourly, hut with a trace of admiration] I'm sure he did, too, the dirty scallywag. It's like him.

EDMUND So Harker came in person to rebuke Shaughnessy. [He chuck- les.] A very bonehead play! If I needed any further proof that our ruling plutocrats, especially the ones who inherited their boodle, are not mental giants, that would clinch it.

TYRONE[with appreciation, before he thinks] Yes, he'd be no match for Shaughnessy. [then he growls] Keep your damned anarchist remarks to yourself. I won't have them in my house. [But he is full of eager antici- pation.] What happened?

EDMUND Harker had as much chance as I would with Jack Johnson.[5] Shaughnessy got a few drinks under his belt and was waiting at the gate to welcome him. He told me he never gave Harker a chance to open his mouth. He began by shouting that he was no slave Standard Oil could trample on. He was a King of Ireland, if he had his rights, and scum was scum to him, no matter how much money it had stolen from the poor.

MARY Oh, Lord! [But she can't help laughing.]

EDMUND Then he accused Harker of making his foreman break down the fence to entice the pigs into the ice pond in order to destroy them. The poor pigs, Shaughnessy yelled, had caught their death of cold. Many of them were dying of pneumonia, and several others had been taken down with cholera from drinking the poisoned water. He told Harker he was hiring a lawyer to sue him for damages. And he wound up by saying that he had to put up with poison ivy, ticks, potato bugs, snakes and skunks on his farm, but he was an honest man who drew the line somewhere, and he'd be damned if he'd stand for a Standard Oil thief trespassing. So would Harker kindly remove his dirty feet from the premises before he sicked the dog on him. And Harker did! [He and JAMIE laugh.]

MARY [shocked but giggling] Heavens, what a terrible tongue that man has!

TYRONE[admiringly before he thinks] The damned old scoundrel! By God, you can't beat him! [He laughs—then stops abruptly and scowls.] The dirty blackguard! He'll get me in serious trouble yet. I hope you told him I'd be mad as hell—

EDMUND I told him you'd be tickled to death over the great Irish victory, and so you are. Stop faking, Papa.

TYRONE Well, I'm not tickled to death. MARY [teasingly] You are, too, James. You're simply delighted!

TYRONE No, Mary, a joke is a joke, but—

EDMUND I told Shaughnessy he should have reminded Harker that a Standard Oil millionaire ought to welcome the flavor of hog in his ice water as an appropriate touch.

TYRONE The devil you did! [frowning] Keep your damned Socialist anarchist sentiments out of my affairs!

EDMUND Shaughnessy almost wept because he hadn't thought of that one, but he said he'd include it in a letter he's writing to Harker, along with a few other insults he'd overlooked. [He and JAMIE laugh.]

TYRONE What are you laughing at? There's nothing funny—A fine son you are to help that blackguard get me into a lawsuit! MARY Now, James, don't lose your temper.

TYRONE[turns on JAMIE] And you're worse than he is, encouraging him. I suppose you're regretting you weren't there to prompt Shaughnessy with a few nastier insults. You've a fine talent for that, if for nothing else.

MARY James! There's no reason to scold Jamie.

[JAMIE is about to make some sneering remark to his father, but he shrugs his shoulders. ]

EDMUND [with sudden nervous exasperation] Oh, for God's sake, Papa! If you're starting that stuff again, I'll beat it. [He jumps up.] I left my book upstairs, anyway. [He goes to the front parlor, saying disgustedly] God, Papa, I should think you'd get sick of hearing yourself— [He disappears. TYRONE looks after him angrily.]

MARY You musn't mind Edmund, James. Remember he isn't well. [EDMUND can be heard coughing as he goes upstairs. She adds nervously] A summer cold makes anyone irritable.

JAMIE[genuinely concerned] It's not just a cold he's got. The Kid is damned sick. [His father gives hint a sharp warning look hut he doesn't see it]

MARY [turns on him resentfully] Why do you say that? It is just a cold! Anyone can tell that! You always imagine things!

TYRONE[with another warning glance at JAMIE—easily] All Jamie meant was Edmund might have a touch of something else, too, which makes his cold worse. JAMIESure, Mama. That's all I meant.

TYRONEDoctor Hardy thinks it might be a bit of malarial fever he caught when he was in the tropics. If it is, quinine will soon cure it.

MARY [a look of contemptuous hostility flashes across her face] Doctor Hardy! I wouldn't believe a thing he said, if he swore on a stack of Bibles! I know what doctors are. They're all alike. Anything, they don't care what, to keep you coming to them. [She stops short, overcome by a fit of acute self-consciousness as she catches their eyes fixed on her. Her hands jerk nervously to her hair. She forces a smile.] What is it? What are you looking at? Is my hair—?

TYRONE[puts his arm around her—with guilty heartiness, giving her a playful hug] There's nothing wrong with your hair. The healthier and fatter you get, the vainer you become. You'll soon spend half the day primping before the mirror.

MARY [half reassured] I really should have new glasses. My eyes are so bad now.

TYRONE [with Irish blarney] Your eyes are beautiful, and well you know it. [He gives her a kiss. Her face lights up with a charming, shy embarrassment. Suddenly and startlingly one sees in her face the girl she had once been, not a ghost of the dead, but still a living part of her. ]

MARY You mustn't be so silly, James. Right in front of Jamie!

TYRONE Oh, he's on to you, too. He knows this fuss about eyes and hair is only fishing for compliments. Eh, Jamie?

JAMIE[his face has cleared, too, and there is an old boyish charm in his loving smile at his mother] Yes, You can't kid us, Mama. MARY [laughs and an Irish lilt comes into her voice] Go along with both of you! [then she speaks with a girlish gravity] But I did truly have beautiful hair once, didn't I, James?

TYRONE The most beautiful in the world! MARY It was a rare shade of reddish brown and so long it came down below my knees. You ought to remember it, too, Jamie. It wasn't until after Edmund was born that I had a single grey hair. Then it began to turn white. [The girlishness fades from her face.]

TYRONE[quickly] And that made it prettier than ever.

MARY [again embarrassed and pleased] Will you listen to your father, Jamie—after thirty-five years of marriage! He isn't a great actor for nothing, is he? What's come over you, James? Are you pouring coals of fire on my head for teasing you about snoring? Well, then, I take it all back. It must have been only the foghorn I heard. [She laughs, and they laugh with her. Then she changes to a brisk businesslike air.] But I can't stay with you any longer, even to hear compliments. I must see the cook about dinner and the day's marketing. [She gets up and sighs with humorous exaggeration.] Bridget is so lazy. And so sly. She begins telling me about her relatives so I can't get a word in edgeways and scold her. Well, I might as well get it over. [She goes to the hack-parlor doorway, then turns, her face worried again.] You mustn't make Edmund work on the grounds with you, James, remember, [again with the strange obstinate set to her face] Not that he isn't strong enough, but he'd perspire and he might catch more cold. [She disappears through the back parlor.TYRONE turns on JAMIE condemningly.]

TYRONE You're a fine lunkhead! Haven't you any sense? The one thing to avoid is saying anything that would get her more upset over Edmund.

JAMIE[shrugging his shoulders] All right. Have it your way. I think it's the wrong idea to let Mama go on kidding yourself. It will only make the shock worse when she has to face it. Anyway, you can see she's deliberately fooling herself with that summer cold talk. She knows better.

TYRONE Knows? Nobody knows yet.

JAMIE Well, I do. I was with Edmund when he went to Doc Hardy on Monday. I heard him pull that touch of malaria stuff. He was stalling. That isn't what he thinks any more. You know it as well as I do. You talked to him when you went uptown yesterday, didn't you?

TYRONE He couldn't say anything for sure yet. He's to phone

me today before Edmund goes to him.

JAMIE[slowly] He thinks it's consumption[6] doesn't he, Papa?

TYRONE[reluctantly] He said it might be.

JAMIE[moved, his love for his brother coming out] Poor kid! God damn it! [He turns on his father accusingly.] It might never have happened if you'd sent him to a real doctor when he first got sick.

TYRONE What's the matter with Hardy? He's always been our doctor up here.

JAMIE Everything's the matter with him! Even in this hick burg he's rated third class! He's a cheap old quack!

TYRONE That's right! Run him down! Run down everybody! Everyone is a fake to you! JAMIE[contemptuously] Hardy only charges a dollar. That's what makes you think he's a fine doctor!

TYRONE[stung] That's enough! You're not drunk now! There's no excuse— [He controls himself—a bit defensively] If you mean I can't afford one of the fine society doctors who prey on the rich summer people—

JAMIE Can't afford? You're one of the biggest property owners around here.

TYRONE That doesn't mean I'm rich. It's all mortgaged—

JAMIE Because you always buy more instead of paying off mortgages. If Edmund was a lousy acre of land you wanted, the sky would be the limit!

TYRONE That's a lie! And your sneers against Doctor Hardy are lies! He doesn't put on frills, or have an office in a fashionable location, or drive around in an expensive automobile. That's what you pay for with those other five-dollars-to-look-at-your-tongue fellows, not their skill.

JAMIE[with a scornful shrug of his shoulders] Oh, all right. I'm a fool to argue. You can't change the leopard's spots.

TYRONE[with rising anger] No, you can't. You've taught me that lesson only too well. I've lost all hope you will ever change yours. You dare tell me what I can afford? You've never known the value of a dollar and never will! You've never saved a dollar in your life! At the end of each season you're penniless! You've thrown your salary away every week on whores and whiskey!

JAMIE My salary! Christ!

TYRONE It's more than you're worth, and you couldn't get that if it wasn't for me. If you weren't my son, there isn't a manager in the business who would give you a part, your reputation stinks so. As it is, I have to humble my pride and beg for you, saying you've turned over a new leaf, although I know it's a lie!

JAMIE I never wanted to be an actor. You forced me on the stage.

TYRONE That's a lie! You made no effort to find anything else to do. You left it to me to get you a job and I have no influence except in the theater. Forced you! You never wanted to do anything except loaf in barrooms! You'd have been content to sit back like a lazy lunk and sponge on me for the rest of your life! After all the money I'd wasted on your education, and all you did was get fired in disgrace from every college you went to!

JAMIE Oh, for God's sake, don't drag up that ancient history!

TYRONE It's not ancient history that you have to come home

every summer to live on me.

JAMIE I earn my board and lodging working on the grounds. It saves you hiring a man.

TYRONE Bah! You have to be driven to do even that much! [His anger ebbs into a weary complaint.] I wouldn't give a damn if you ever displayed the slightest sign of gratitude. The only thanks is to have you sneer at me for a dirty miser, sneer at my profession, sneer at every damned thing in the world—except yourself.

JAMIE[wryly] That's not true, Papa. You can't hear me talking to myself, that's all.

TYRONE[stares at him puzzledly, then quotes mechanically] "Ingratitude, the vilest weed that grows"! [7]

JAMIE I could see that line coming! God, how many thousand times ! [He stops, bored with their quarrel, and shrugs his shoulders.] All right, Papa. I'm a bum. Anything you like, so long as it stops the argument.

TYRONE[with indignant appeal now] If you'd get ambition in your head instead of folly! You're young yet. You could still make your mark. You had the talent to become a fine actor! You have it still. You're my son—!

JAMIE[boredly] Let's forget me. I'm not interested in the subject. Neither are you.[TYRONE gives up. JAMIE goes on casually.]

What started us on this? Oh, Doc Hardy. When is he going to call you up about Edmund?

TYRONE Around lunch time. [He pauses—then defensively] I couldn't have sent Edmund to a better doctor. Hardy's treated him whenever he was sick up here, since he was knee high. He knows his constitution as no other doctor could. It's not a question of my being miserly, as you'd like to make out. [bitterly] And what could the finest specialist in America do for Edmund, after he's deliberately ruined his health by the mad life he's led ever since he was fired from college? Even before that when he was in prep school, he began dissipating and playing the Broadway sport to imitate you, when he's never had your constitution to stand it. You're a healthy hulk like me—or you were at his age—but he's always been a bundle of nerves like his mother. I've warned him for years his body couldn't stand it, but he wouldn't heed me, and now it's too late.

JAMIE[sharply] What do you mean, too late? You talk as if you thought—

TYRONE[guiltily explosive] Don't be a damned fool! I meant nothing but what's plain to anyone! His health has broken down and he may be an invalid for a long time.

JAMIE[stares at his father, ignoring his explanation] I know it's an Irish peasant idea consumption is fatal. It probably is when you live in a hovel on a bog, but over here, with modern treatment—

TYRONE Don't I know that! What are you gabbing about, anyway? And keep your dirty tongue off Ireland, with your sneers about peasants and bogs and hovels! [accusingly] The less you say about Edmund's sickness, the better for your conscience! You're more responsible than anyone!

JAMIE[stung] That's a lie! I won't stand for that, Papa!

TYRONE It's the truth! You've been the worst influence for him.

He grew up admiring you as a hero! A fine example you set him! If you ever gave him advice except in the ways of rottenness, I've never heard of it! You made him old before his time, pumping him full of what you consider worldly wisdom, when he was too young to see that your mind was so poisoned by your own failure in life, you wanted to believe every man was a knave with his soul for sale, and every woman who wasn't a whore was a fool!

JAMIE[with a defensive air of weary indifference again] All right. I did put Edmund wise to things, but not until I saw he'd started to raise hell, and knew he'd laugh at me if I tried the good advice, older brother stuff. All I did was make a pal of him and be absolutely frank so he'd learn from my mistakes that—[He shrugs his shoulders—cynically] Well, that if you can't be good you can at least be careful. [His father snorts contemptuously. Suddenly

JAMIE [becomes really moved. ] That's a rotten accusation, Papa. You know how much the Kid means to me, and how close we've always been—not like the usual brothers! I'd do anything for him.

TYRONE[impressed—modifyingly] I know you may have thought it was for the best, Jamie. I didn't say you did it deliberately to harm him.

JAMIE Besides it's damned rot! I'd like to see anyone influence Edmund more than he wants to be. His quietness fools people into thinking they can do what they like with him. But he's stubborn as hell inside and what he does is what he wants to do, and to hell with anyone else! What had I to do with all the crazy stunts he's pulled in the last few years—working his way all over the map as a sailor and all that stuff. I thought that was a damned fool idea, and I told him so. You can't imagine me getting fun out of being on the beach in South America, or living in filthy dives, drinking rotgut, can you? No, thanks! I'll stick to Broadway, and a room with a bath, and bars that serve bonded Bourbon.

TYRONE You and Broadway! It's made you what you are! [with a touch of pride] Whatever Edmund's done, he's had the guts to go off on his own, where he couldn't come whining to me the minute he was broke.

JAMIE[stung into sneering jealousy] He's always come home broke finally, hasn't he? And what did his going away get him? Look at him now! [He is suddenly shamefaced.] Christ! That's a lousy thing to say. I don't mean that.

TYRONE[decides to ignore this] He's been doing well on the paper. I was hoping he'd found the work he wants to do at last.

JAMIE[sneering jealously again] A hick town rag! Whatever bull they hand you, they tell me he's a pretty bum reporter. If he weren't your son— [ashamed again] No, that's not true! They're glad to have him, but it's the special stuff that gets him by. Some of the poems and parodies he's written are damned good, [grudgingly again] Not that they'd ever get him anywhere on the big time, [hastily] But he's certainly made a damned good start.

TYRONE Yes. He's made a start. You used to talk about wanting to become a newspaper man but you were never willing to start at the bottom. You expected—

JAMIE Oh, for Christ's sake, Papa! Can't you lay off me!

TYRONE[stares at him—then looks away—after a pause] It's damnable luck Edmund should be sick right now. It couldn't have come at a worse time for him. [He adds, unable to conceal an almost furtive uneasiness] Or for your mother. It's damnable she should have this to upset her, just when she needs peace and freedom from worry. She's been so well in the two months since she came home. [His voice grows husky and trembles a little.] It's been heaven to me. This home has been a home again. But I needn't tell you, Jamie. [His son looks at him, for the first time with an understanding sympathy. It is as if suddenly a deep bond of common feeling existed between them in which their antagonisms could be forgotten.]

JAMIE[almost gently] I've felt the same way, Papa.

TYRONE Yes, this time you can see how strong and sure of herself she is. She's a different woman entirely from the other times. She has control of her nerves—or she had until Edmund got sick. Now you can feel her growing tense and frightened underneath. I wish to God we could keep the truth from her, but we can't if he has to be sent to a sanatorium. What makes it worse is her father died of consumption. She worshiped him and she's never forgotten. Yes, it will be hard for her. But she can do it! She has the will power now! We must help her, Jamie, in every way we can!

JAMIE[moved] Of course, Papa, [hesitantly] Outside of nerves, she seems perfectly all right this morning.

TYRONE[with hearty confidence now] Never better. She's full of fun and mischief. [Suddenly he frowns at JAMIE suspiciously.] Why do you say, seems? Why shouldn't she be all right? What the hell do you mean?

JAMIE Don't start jumping down my throat! God, Papa, this ought to be one thing we can talk over frankly without a battle.

TYRONE I'm sorry, Jamie, [tensely] But go on and tell me —

JAMIE There's nothing to tell. I was all wrong. It's just that last night— Well, you know how it is, I can't forget the past. I can't help being sus-picious. Any more than you can. [bitterly] That's the hell of it. And it makes it hell for Mama! She watches us watching her—

TYRONE[sadly] I know, [tensely] Well, what was it! Can't you speak out!

JAMIE Nothing, I tell you. Just my damned foolishness. Around three o'clock this morning, I woke up and heard her moving around in the spare room. Then she went to the bathroom. I pretended to be asleep. She stopped in the hall to listen, as if she wanted to make sure I was.

TYRONE[with forced scorn] For God's sake, is that all? She told me herself the foghorn kept her awake all night, and every night since Edmund's been sick she's been up and down, going to his room to see how he was.

JAMIE[eagerly] Yes, that's right, she did stop to listen outside his room. [hesitantly again] It was her being in the spare room that scared me. I couldn't help remembering that when she starts sleeping alone in there, it has always been a sign—

TYRONE It isn't this time! It's easily explained. Where else could she go last night to get away from my snoring? [He gives way to a burst of resentful anger.] By God, how you can live with a mind that sees nothing but the worst motives behind everything is beyond me!

JAMIE[stung] Don't pull that! I've just said I was all wrong. Don't you suppose I'm as glad of that as you are!

TYRONE[mollifyingly] I'm sure you are, Jamie. [A pause. His expression becomes somber. He speaks slowly with a superstitious dread.] It would be like a curse she can't escape if worry over Edmund—It was her long sickness after bringing him into the world that she first—

JAMIE She didn't have anything to do with it!

TYRONE I'm not blaming her.

JAMIE[bitingly] Then who are you blaming? Edmund, for being born?

TYRONE You damned fool! No one was to blame.

JAMIE The bastard of a doctor was! From what Mama's said, he was another cheap quack like Hardy! You wouldn't pay for a first-rate—

TYRONE That's a lie! [furiously] So I'm to blame! That's what you're driving at, is it? You evil-minded loafer!

JAMIE [warningly as he hears his mother in the dining room] Ssh!

[TYRONE gets hastily to his feet and goes to look out the windows at right. JAMIE speaks with a complete change of tone.]

Well, if we're going to cut the front hedge today, we'd better go to work.

[MARY comes in from the back parlor. She gives a quick, suspicious glance from one to the other, her manner nervously self-conscious.]

TYRONE[turns from the window—with an actor's heartiness] Yes, it's too fine a morning to waste indoors arguing. Take a look out the window, Mary. There's no fog in the harbor. I'm sure the spell of it we've had is over now.

MARY [going to him] I hope so, dear, [to JAMIE, forcing a smile] Did I actually hear you suggesting work on the front hedge, Jamie? Wonders will never cease! You must want pocket money badly.

JAMIE[kiddingly] When don't I? [He winks at her, with a derisive glance at his father.] I expect a salary of at least one large iron man[8] at the end of the week—to carouse on! MARY [does not respond to his humor—her hands fluttering over the front of her dress] What were you two arguing about?

JAMIE[shrugs his shoulders] The same old stuff.

MARY I heard you say something about a doctor, and your father accusing you of being evil-minded.

JAMIE[quickly] Oh, that. I was saying again Doc Hardy isn't my idea of the world's greatest physician.

MARY[knows he is lying—vaguely] Oh. No, I wouldn't say he was either. [changing the subject—forcing a smile] That Bridget! I thought I'd never get away. She told me about her second cousin on the police force in St. Louis, [then with nervous irritation] Well, if you're going to work on the hedge why don't you go? [hastily] I mean, take advantage of the sunshine before the fog comes back, [strangely, as if talking aloud to herself] Because I know it will. [Suddenly she is self-consciously aware that they are both staring fixedly at her—

flurriedly, raising her hands] Or I should say, the rheumatism in my hands knows. It's a better weather prophet than you are, James. [She stares at her hands with fascinated repulsion.] Ugh! How ugly they are! Who'd ever believe they were once beautiful? [The} 1 stare at her with a growing dread.]

TYRONE[takes her hands and gently pushes them down] Now, now, Mary. None of that foolishness. They're the sweetest hands in the world. [She smiles, her face lighting up, and kisses him gratefully. He turns to his son.] Come on Jamie. Your mother's right to scold us. The way to start work is to start work. The hot sun will sweat some of that booze fat off your middle. [He opens the screen door and goes out on the porch and disappears down a flight of steps leading to the ground, JAMIE [rises from his chair and, taking off his coat, goes to the door. At the door he turns back but avoids looking at her, and she docs not look at him. ]

JAMIE[with an awkward, uneasy tenderness] We're all so proud of you, Mama, so darned happy. [She stiffens and stares at him with a frightened defiance. He flounders on.] But you've still got to be careful. You mustn't worry so much about Edmund. He'll be all right.

MARY [with a stubborn, bitterly resentful look] Of course, he'll be all right. And I don't know what you mean, warning me to be careful.

JAMIE[rebuffed and hurt, shrugs his shoulders] All right, Mama. I'm sorry I spoke. [He goes out on the porch. She waits rigidly until he disappears down the steps. Then she sinks down in the chair he had occupied, her face betraying a frightened, furtive desperation, her hands roving over the table top, aimlessly moving objects around. She hears EDMUND descending the stairs in the front hall. As he nears the bottom he has a fit of coughing. She springs to her feet, as if she wanted to run away from the sound, and goes quickly to the windows at right. She is looking out, apparently calm, as he enters from the front parlor, a book in one hand. She turns to him, her lips set in a welcoming, motherly smile.]

MARY Here you are. I was just going upstairs to look for you.

EDMUND I waited until they went out. I don't want to mix up in any arguments. I feel too rotten.

MARY [almost resentfully] Oh, I'm sure you don't feel half as badly as you make out. You're such a baby. You like to get us worried so we'll make a fuss over you. [hastily] I'm only teasing, dear. I know how miserably uncomfortable you must be. But you feel better today, don't you? [worriedly, taking his arm] All the same, you've grown much too thin. You need to rest all you can. Sit down and I'll make you comfortable. [He sits down in the rocking chair and she puts a pillow behind his back.] There, How's that?

EDMUND Grand. Thanks, Mama.

MARY [kisses him—tenderly] All you need is your mother to nurse you. Big as you are, you're still the baby of the family to me, you know.

EDMUND [takes her hand—with deep seriousness] Never mind me. You take care of yourself. That's all that counts.

MARY [evading his eyes] But I am, dear, [forcing a laugh] Heavens, don't you see how fat I've grown! I'll have to have all my dresses let out. [She turns away and goes to the windows at right. She attempts a light, amused tone.] They've started clipping the hedge. Poor Jamie! How he hates working in front where everyone passing can see him. There go the Chat- fields in their new Mercedes. It's a beautiful car, isn't it? Not like our secondhand Packard. Poor Jamie! He bent almost under the hedge so they wouldn't notice him. They bowed to your father and he bowed back as if he were taking a curtain call. In that filthy old suit I've tried to make him throw away. [Her voice has grown bitter. ] Really, he ought to have more pride than to make such a show of himself.

EDMUND He's right not to give a damn what anyone thinks. Jamie's a fool to care about the Chatfields. For Pete's sake, who ever heard of them outside this hick burg?

MARY[with satisfaction] No one. You're quite right, Edmund. Big frogs in a small puddle. It is stupid of Jamie. [She pauses, looking out the window—then with an undercurrent of lonely yearning] Still, the Chatfields and people like them stand for something. I mean they have decent, presentable homes they don't have to be ashamed of. They have friends who entertain them and whom they entertain. They're not cut off from everyone. [She turns back from the window.] Not that I want anything to do with them. I've always hated this town and everyone in it. You know that. I never wanted to live here in the first place, but your father liked it and insisted on building this house, and I've had to come here every summer.

EDMUND Well, it's better than spending the summer in a New York hotel, isn't it? And this town's not so bad. I like it well enough. I suppose because it's the only home we've had.

MARY I've never felt it was my home. It was wrong from the start. Everything was done in the cheapest way. Your father would never spend the money to make it right. It's just as well we haven't any friends here. I'd be ashamed to have them step in the door. But he's never wanted family friends. He hates calling on people, or receiving them. All he likes is to hobnob with men at the Club or in a barroom. Jamie and you are the same way, but you're not to blame. You've never had a chance to meet decent people here. I know you both would have been so different if you'd been able to associate with nice girls instead of—You'd never have disgraced yourselves as you have, so that now no respectable parents will let their daughters be seen with you.

EDMUND [irritably] Oh, Mama, forget it! Who cares? Jamie and I would be bored stiff. And about the Old Man, what's the use of talking? You can't change him. MARY [mechanically rebuking] Don't call your father the Old Man. You should have more respect, [then dully] I know it's useless to talk. But sometimes I feel so lonely. [Her lips quiver and she keeps her head turned away. ]

EDMUND Anyway, you've got to be fair, Mama. It may have been all his fault in the beginning, but you know that later on, even if he'd wanted to, we couldn't have had people here—[He flounders guiltily.] I mean, you wouldn't have wanted them.

MARY [wincing—her lips quivering pitifully] Don't. I can't bear having you remind me.

EDMUND Don't take it that way! Please, Mama! I'm trying to

help. Because it's bad for you to forget. The right way is to remember. So you'll always be on your guard. You know what's happened before, [miserably] God, Mama, you know I hate to remind you. I'm doing it because it's been so wonderful having you home the way you've been, and it would be terrible—

MARY [strickenly] Please, dear. I know you mean it for the best, but—[A defensive uneasiness comes into her voice again.] I don't understand why you should suddenly say such things. What put it in your mind this morning?

EDMUND [evasively] Nothing. Just because I feel rotten and blue, I suppose.

MARY Tell me the truth. Why are you so suspicious all of a sudden?

EDMUND I'm not!

MARY Oh, yes you are. I can feel it. Your father and Jamie, too—particularly Jamie.

EDMUND Now don't start imagining things, Mama.

MARY [her hands fluttering] It makes it so much harder, living in this atmosphere of constant suspicion, knowing everyone is spying on me, and none of you believe in me, or trust me.

EDMUND That's crazy, Mama. We do trust you.

MARY If there was only some place I could go to get away for a day, or even an afternoon, some woman friend I could talk to—not about anything serious, simply laugh and gossip and forget for a while—someone besides the servants—that stupid Cathleen!

EDMUND [gets up worriedly and puts his arm around her] Stop

it, Mama. You're getting yourself worked up over nothing.

MARY Your father goes out. He meets his friends in barrooms or at the Club. You and Jamie have the boys you know. You go out. But I am alone. I've always been alone.

EDMUND [soothingly] Come now! You know that's a fib. One of us always stays around to keep you company, or goes with you in the automobile when you take a drive.

MARY [bitterly] Because you're afraid to trust me alone! [She turns on him—sharply.] I insist you tell me why you act so differently this morning—why you felt you had to remind me —

EDMUND [hesitates—then blurts out guiltily] It's stupid. It's just that I wasn't asleep when you came in my room last night. You didn't go back to your and Papa's room. You went in the spare room for the rest of the night.

MARY Because your father's snoring was driving me crazy! For heaven's sake, haven't I often used the spare room as my bedroom? [bitterly] But I see what you thought. That was when—

EDMUND [too vehemently] I didn't think anything!

MARY So you pretended to be asleep in order to spy on me!

EDMUND No! I did it because I knew if you found out I was feverish and couldn't sleep, it would upset you.

MARY Jamie was pretending to be asleep, too, I'm sure, and I suppose your father—

EDMUND Stop it, Mama!

MARY Oh, I can't bear it, Edmund, when even you—! [Her hands flutter up to pat her hair in their aimless, distracted way.

Suddenly a strange undercurrent of revengefulness comes into her voice.] It would serve all of you right if it was true!

EDMUND Mama! Don't say that! That's the way you talk when—

MARY Stop suspecting me! Please, dear! You hurt me! I couldn't sleep because I was thinking about you. That's the real reason! I've been so worried ever since you've been sick. [She puts her arms around him and hugs him with a frightened, protective tenderness.]

EDMUND [soothingly] That's foolishness. You know it's only a bad cold.

MARY Yes, of course, I know that!

EDMUND But listen, Mama. I want you to promise me that even if it should turn out to be something worse, you'll know I'll soon be all right again, anyway, and you won't worry yourself sick, and you'll keep on taking care of yourself—

MARY [frightenedly] I won't listen when you're so silly! There's absolutely no reason to talk as if you expected something dreadful! Of course, I promise you. I give you my sacred word of honor! [then with a sad bitterness] But I suppose you're remembering I've promised before on my word of honor.

EDMUND No!

MARY[her bitterness receding into a resigned helplessness] I'm not blaming you, dear. How can you help it? How can any one of us forget? [strangely] That's what makes it so hard—for all of us. We can't forget.

EDMUND [grabs her shoulder] Mama! Stop it!

MARY [forcing a smile] All right, dear. I didn't mean to be so gloomy. Don't mind me. Here. Let me feel your head. Why, it's nice and cool. You certainly haven't any fever now.

EDMUND Forget! It's you—

MARY But I'm quite all right, dear, [with a quick, strange, calculating, almost sly glance at him] Except I naturally feel tired and nervous this morning, after such a bad night. I really ought to go upstairs and lie down until lunch time and take a nap. [He gives her an instinctive look of suspicion—then, ashamed of himself, looks quickly away. She hurries on nervously.] What are you going to do? Read here? It would be much better for you to go out in the fresh air and sunshine. But don't get overheated, remember. Be sure and wear a hat. [She stops, looking straight at him now. He avoids her eyes. There is a tense pause. Then she speaks jeeringly.] Or are you afraid to trust me alone?

EDMUND [tormentedly] No! Can't you stop talking like that! I think you ought to take a nap. [He goes to the screen door—forcing a joking tone] I'll go down and help Jamie bear up. I love to lie in the shade and watch him work.

[He forces a laugh in which she makes herself join. Then he goes out on the porch and disappears down the steps. Her first reaction is one of relief. She appears to relax. She sinks down in one of the wicker armchairs at rear of table and leans her head back, closing her eyes. But suddenly she grows terribly tense again. Her eyes open and she strains forward, seized by a fit of nervous panic. She begins a desperate battle with herself. Her long fingers, warped and knotted by rheumatism, drum on the arms of the chair, driven by an insistent life of their own, without her consent.]

CURTAIN

## Notes

1. A servant.

2. A variety of 19th-century (especially late-19th-century) authors are cited. Nobody in the audience would be able to read the titles and authors on these books — an example of O'Neill's novelistic approach to theatrical detail, also seen in the minute physical descriptions he provides of the characters' appearance and behavior throughout.

3. Shakespeare's *Othello* 2.1.180.

4. I.e., drunk.

5. Famous prizefighter.

6. Tuberculosis.

7. Shakespeare's *King Lear* 1.4.

8. Slang for "dollar."

## Questions

1. What is the plot of this act?

2. What kind of person is Tyrone in this text?

### (10) Tennessee Williams (1911—1983)

Tennessee Williams (1911—1983) was one of the most important playwrights in America, who had a great influence on American drama and even American culture in the 20th century. He not only wrote dramas, but also cooperated with Hollywood to adapt his dramas into movies. His dramatic works gave up the moral, social, and political criticism of previous realistic works, and paid more attention to "psychological realism". He focused on marginalized and psychologically traumatized individuals, and put their inner animalistic sensibilities on the stage with poetic language and lyrical style.

Williams worked in a shoe factory in his early years and studied off and on at the University of Missouri and the University of Washington. He majored in drama writing at the University of Iowa, where he received his bachelor's degree in 1938. A group of his one-act plays won an award in 1939, which won him reputation. But he did all sorts of jobs, including a theater attendant and a Hollywood screenwriter, before his play *The Glass Menagerie* appeared on Broadway in 1945. Williams wrote about 70 plays altogether (both rewritten and unpublished), 9 of which were adapted to film. His major works include *The Glass Menagerie*, *A Streetcar Named Desire*, and *Cat on a Hot Tin Roof*. These three dramas are set in the southern region of America, describing the decline and decadence of the south, the frustration and nostalgia of the characters, and the suffering and disappearance of desire. His other important dramas include *Summer and Smoke*, *The Rose Tattoo*, *Camino Real*, *Orpheus Descending*, *Sudden Last Summer*, *The Sweet Bird of Youth*, and *The Night of The Iguana*.

After his partner Frank Merlo died, Williams entered a physical and mental breakdown, which led to the overuse of narcotics and alcohol in his old age. Choking to death on a bottle cap, he died in 1983.

The following text is the first scene of *A Streetcar Named Desire* excerpted from *The Norton Anthology of American Literature* (shorter 6th edition).

## A Streetcar Named Desire

And so it was I entered the broken world
To trace the visionary company of love, its voice
An instant in the wind (I know not whither hurled)
But not for long to hold each desperate choice.

—"The Broken Tower" by Hart Crane [1]

THE CHARACTERS

BLANCHE PABLO

STELLA A NEGRO WOMAN

STANLEY A DOCTOR

MITCH A NURSE

EUNICE A YOUNG COLLECTOR

STEVE A MEXICAN WOMAN

### Scene One

The exterior of a two-story corner building on a street in New Orleans which is named Elysian Fields and runs between the L &• N tracks and the river. [2] The section is poor but, unlike corresponding sections in other American cities, it has a raffish charm. The houses are mostly white frame, weathered grey, with rickety outside stairs and galleries and quaintly ornamented gables. This building contains two flats, upstairs and down. Faded white stairs ascend to the entrances of both.

It is first dark of an evening early in May. The sky that shows around the dim white building is a peculiarly tender blue, almost a turquoise, which invests the scene with a kind of lyricism and gracefully attenuates the atmosphere of decay. You can almost feel the warm breath of the brown river beyond the river warehouses with their faint redolences of bananas and coffee. A cor-responding air is evoked by the music of Negro entertainers at a barroom around the corner. In this part of New Orleans you are practically always just around the corner, or a few doors down the street, from a tinny piano being played with the infatuated fluency of brown fingers. This "Blue Piano" expresses the spirit of the life which goes on here.

Two women, one white and one colored, are taking the air on the steps of the building. The white woman is EUNICE, who occupies the upstairs flat; the colored woman a neighbor, for New Orleans is a cosmopolitan city where there is a relatively warm and easy intermingling of races in the old part of town.

Above the music of the "Blue Piano" the voices of people on the street can be heard overlapping.

[Two men come around the corner, STANLEY KOWALSKI and MITCH. They are about twenty-eight or thirty years old, roughly dressed in blue denim work, clothes. STANLEY carries his bowling jacket and a red-stained package from a butcher's. They stop at the foot of the steps.]

STANLEY [bellowing] Hey there! Stella, baby!

[STELLA comes out on the first floor landing, a gentle young woman, about twenty-five, and of a background obviously quite different from her husband's.]

STELLA [mildly] Don't holler at me like that. Hi, Mitch.

STANLEY Catch!

STELLA What?

STANLEY Meat!

[He heaves the package at her. She cries out in protest but manages to catch it: then she laughs breathlessly. Her husband and his companion have already started back around the corner.]

STELLA [calling after him] Stanley! Where are you going?

STANLEY Bowling!

STELLA Can I come watch?

STANLEY Come on. [He goes out.]

STELLA Be over soon, [to the white woman] Hello, Eunice. How are you?

EUNICE I'm all right. Tell Steve to get him a poor boy's sandwich 'cause nothing's left here.

[They all laugh; the colored woman does not stop, STELLA goes out.]

COLORED WOMAN What was that package he th'ew at 'er? [She rises from steps, laughing louder.]

EUNICE You hush, now!

NEGRO WOMAN Catch what!

[She continues to laugh, BLANCHE comes around the corner, carrying a valise. She looks at a slip of paper, then at the building, then again at the slip and again at the building. Her expression is one of shocked disbelief. Her appearance is incongruous to this setting. She is daintily dressed in a white suit with a fluffy bodice, necklace and earrings of pearl,white gloves and hat, looking as if she were arriving at a summer tea or cocktail party in the garden district. She is about five years older than STELLA. Her delicate beauty must avoid a strong light. There is something about her uncertain manner, as well as her white clothes, that suggests a moth.]

EUNICE [finally] What's the matter, honey? Are you lost?

BLANCHE [with faintly hysterical humor] They told me to take a streetcar named Desire, and then transfer to one called Cemeteries[3] and ride six blocks and get off at—Elysian Fields!

EUNICE That's where you are now.

BLANCHE At Elysian Fields?

EUNICE This here is Elysian Fields.

BLANCHE They mustn't have—understood—what number I wanted…

EUNICE What number you lookin' for?

[BLANCHE wearily refers to the slip of paver.]

BLANCHE Six thirty-two.

EUNICE You don't have to look no further.

BLANCHE [uncomprehendingly] I'm looking for my sister, Stella DuBois, I mean—Mrs.Stanley Kowalski.

EUNICE That's the party.—You just did miss her, though.

BLANCHE This—can this be—her home?

EUNICE She's got the downstairs here and I got the up.

BLANCHE Oh. She's—out?

EUNICE You noticed that bowling alley around the corner?

BLANCHE I'm—not sure I did.

EUNICE Well, that's where she's at, watchin' her husband bowl. [There is a pause.] You want to leave your suitcase here an' go find her?

BLANCHE No.

NEGRO WOMAN I'll go tell her you come.

BLANCHE Thanks.

NEGRO WOMAN YOU welcome. [She goes out.]

EUNICE She wasn't expecting you?

BLANCHE No. No, not tonight.

EUNICE Well, why don't you just go in and make yourself at home till they get back.

BLANCHE How could I —do that?

EUNICE We own this place so I can let you in.

[She gets up and opens the downstairs door. A light goes on behind the blind, turning it light blue, BLANCHE slowly follows her into the down-stairs flat. The surrounding areas dim out as the interior is lighted. Two rooms can be seen, not too clearly defined. The one first entered is primarily a kitchen but contains a folding bed to be used by BLANCHE. The room beyond this is a bedroom. Off this room is a narrow door to a bathroom. ]

EUNICE [defensively, noticing BLANCHES look] It's sort of messed up right now but when it's clean it's real sweet.

BLANCHE Is it?

EUNICE Uh-huh, I think so. So you're Stella's sister?

BLANCHE Yes. [wanting to get rid of her] Thanks for letting me in.

EUNICE Por nada, [4] as the Mexicans say, por nadal Stella spoke of you.

BLANCHE Yes?

EUNICE I think she said you taught school.

BLANCHE Yes.

EUNICE And you're from Mississippi, huh?

BLANCHE Yes.

EUNICE She showed me a picture of your home-place, the plantation.

BLANCHE Belle Reve? [5]

EUNICE A great big place with white columns.

BLANCHE Yes...

EUNICE A place like that must be awful hard to keep up.

BLANCHE If you will excuse me, I'm just about to drop.

EUNICE Sure, honey. Why don't you set down?

BLANCHE What I meant was I'd like to be left alone.

EUNICE [offended] Aw. I'll make myself scarce, in that case.

BLANCHE I didn't meant to be rude, but—

EUNICE I'll drop by the bowling alley an' hustle her up. [She goes out the door.]

[BLANCHE sits in a chair very stiffly with her shoulders slightly hunched and her legs pressed close together and her hands tightly clutching her purse as if she were quite cold. After a while the blind look goes out of her eyes and she begins to look slowly around. A cat screeches. She catches her breath with a startled gesture. Suddenly she notices some-thing in a half opened closet. She springs up and crosses to it, and removes a whiskey bottle. She pours a half tumbler of whiskey and tosse sit down. She carefully replaces the bottle and washes out the tumbler at the sink. Then she resumes her seat in front of the table.]

BLANCHE [faintly to herself] I've got to keep hold of myself! [STELLA comes quickly around the corner of the building and runs to the door of the downstairs flat.]

STELLA [calling out joyfully] Blanche!

[For a moment they stare at each other. Then BLANCHE springs up and runs to her with a wild cry. ]

BLANCHE Stella, oh, Stella, Stella! Stella for Star!

[She begins to speak with feverish vivacity as if she feared for either of them to stop and think. They catch each other in a spasmodic embrace.]

BLANCHE Now, then, let me look at you. But don't you look at me, Stella, no, no, no, not till later, not till I've bathed and rested! And turn that over-light off! Turn that off! I won't be looked at in this merciles glare!

[STELLA laughs and complies.] Come back here now! Oh, my baby! Stella! Stella for Star! [She embraces her again. ] I thought you would never come back to this horrible place! What am I saying? I didn't mean to say that. I meant to be nice about it and say—Oh, what a convenient location and such—Ha-a-ha! Precious lamb! You haven't said a word to me.

STELLA You haven't given me a chance to, honey! [She laughs, but her glance at BLANCHE is a little anxious.]

BLANCHE Well, now you talk. Open your pretty mouth and talk while I look around for some liquor! I know you must have some liquor on the place! Where could it be, I wonder? Oh, I spy, I spy!

[She rushes to the closet and removes the bottle; she is shaking all over and panting for breath as she tries to laugh. The bottle nearly slips from her grasp.]

STELLA [noticing] Blanche, you sit down and let me pour the drinks. I don't know what we've got to mix with. Maybe a coke's in the icebox. Look'n see, honey, while I'm—

BLANCHE No coke, honey, not with my nerves tonight! Where—where—where is—?

STELLA Stanley? Bowling! He loves it. They're having a—found some soda!—tournament…

BLANCHE Just water, baby, to chase it! Now don't get worried, your sister hasn't turned into a drunkard, she's just all shaken up and hot and tired and dirty! You sit down, now, and explain this place to me! What are you doing in a place like this?

STELLA Now, Blanche—

BLANCHE Oh, I'm not going to be hypocritical, I'm going to be honestly critical about it! Never, never, never in my worst dreams could I picture—Only Poe! Only Mr.Edgar Allan Poe!—could do it justice! Out there I suppose is the ghoul-haunted woodland of Weir! [6] [She laughs.]

STELLA No, honey, those are the L & N tracks.

BLANCHE No, now seriously, putting joking aside. Why didn't you tell me,why didn't you write me, honey, why didn't you let me know?

STELLA [carefully, pouring herself a drink] Tell you what, Blanche?

BLANCHE Why, that you had to live in these conditions!

STELLA Aren't you being a little intense about it? It's not that bad at all! New Orleans isn't like other cities.

BLANCHE This has got nothing to do with New Orleans. You might as well say—forgive me, blessed baby! [She suddenly stops short.] The subject is closed!

STELLA [a little drily] Thanks.

[During the pause, BLANCHE stares at her. She smiles at BLANCHE.]

BLANCHE [looking down at her glass, which shakes in her hand] You're all I've got in the world, and you're not glad to see me!

STELLA [sincerely] Why, Blanche, you know that's not true.

BLANCHE NO?—I'd forgotten how quiet you were.

STELLA You never did give me a chance to say much, Blanche. So I just got in the habit of being quiet around you.

BLANCHE [vaguely] A good habit to get into…[then, abruptly] You haven't asked me how I happened to get away from the school before the spring term ended.

STELLA Well, I thought you'd volunteer that information—if you wanted to tell me.

BLANCHE You thought I'd been fired?

STELLA No, I—thought you might have—resigned…

BLANCHE I was so exhausted by all I'd been through my—

nerves broke.

[nervously tamping cigarette] I was on the verge of—lunacy, almost! So Mr.Graves—Mr.Graves is the high school superintendent—he suggested I take a leave of absence. I couldn't put all of those details into the wire...[She drinks quickly.] Oh, this buzzes right through me and feels so good!

STELLA Won't you have another?

BLANCHE No, one's my limit.

STELLA Sure?

BLANCHE You haven't said a word about my appearance.

STELLA You look just fine.

BLANCHE God love you for a liar! Daylight never exposed so total a ruin! But you—you've put on some weight, yes, you're just as plump as a little partridge! And it's so becoming to you!

STELLA Now, Blanche—

BLANCHE Yes, it is, it is or I wouldn't say it! You just have to watch around the hips a little. Stand up.

STELLA Not now.

BLANCHE You hear me? I said stand up! [STELLA complies reluctantly.] You messy child, you, you've spilt something on that pretty white lace collar! About your hair—you ought to have it cut in a feather bob with your dainty features. Stella, you have a maid, don't you?

STELLA No. With only two rooms it's—

BLANCHE What? Two rooms, did you say?

STELLA This one and—[She is embarrassed.]

BLANCHE The other one? [She laughs sharply. There is an

embarrassed silence.]

BLANCHE I am going to take just one little tiny nip more, sort of to put the stopper on, so to speak....Then put the bottle away so I won't be tempted. [She rises.] I want you to look at my figure! [She turns around.] You know I haven't put on one ounce in ten years, Stella? I weigh what I weighed the summer you left Belle Reve. The summer Dad died and you left us...

STELLA [a little wearily] It's just incredible, Blanche, how well you're looking.

BLANCHE [They both laugh uncomfortably.] But, Stella, there's only two rooms, I don't see where you're going to put me!

STELLA We're going to put you in here.

BLANCHE What kind of bed's this—one of those collapsible things?

[She sits on it.]

STELLA Does it feel all right?

BLANCHE [dubiously] Wonderful, honey. I don't like a bed that gives much. But there's no door between the two rooms, and Stanley—will it be decent?

STELLA Stanley is Polish, you know.

BLANCHE Oh, yes. They're something like Irish, aren't they?

STELLA Well—

BLANCHE Only not so—highbrow? [They both laugh again in the same way.] I brought some nice clothes to meet all your lovely friends in.

STELLA I'm afraid you won't think they are lovely.

BLANCHE What are they like?

STELLA They're Stanley's friends.

BLANCHE Polacks?

STELLA They're a mixed lot, Blanche.

BLANCHE Heterogeneous—types?

STELLA Oh, yes. Yes, types is right!

BLANCHE Well—anyhow—I brought nice clothes and I'll wear them. I guess you're hoping I'll say I'll put up at a hotel, but I'm not going to put up at a hotel. I want to be near you, got to be with somebody, I can't be alone! Because—as you must have noticed—I'm—not very well.…[Her voice drops and her look is frightened. ]

STELLA You seem a little bit nervous or overwrought or something.

BLANCHE Will Stanley like me, or will I be just a visiting in-law, Stella? I couldn't stand that.

STELLA You'll get along fine together, if you'll just try not to—well—compare him with men that we went out with at home.

BLANCHE Is he so—different?

STELLA Yes. A different species.

BLANCHE In what way; what's he like?

STELLA Oh, you can't describe someone you're in love with! Here's a picture of him! [She hands a photograph to BLANCHE.]

BLANCHE An officer?

STELLA A Master Sergeant in the Engineers' Corps. Those are decorations!

BLANCHE He had those on when you met him?

STELLA I assure you I wasn't just blinded by all the brass.

BLANCHE That's not what I—

STELLA But of course there were things to adjust myself to later on.

BLANCHE Such as his civilian background! [STELLA laughs uncertainly.] How did he take it when you said I was coming?

STELLA Oh, Stanley doesn't know yet.

BLANCHE [frightened] You—haven't told him?

STELLA He's on the road a good deal.

BLANCHE Oh. Travels?

STELLA Yes.

BLANCHE Good. I mean—isn't it?

STELLA [half to herself] I can hardly stand it when he is away for a night...

BLANCHE Why, Stella!

STELLA When he's away for a week I nearly go wild!

BLANCHE Gracious!

STELLA And when he comes back I cry on his lap like a baby... [She smiles to herself. ]

BLANCHE I guess that is what is meant by being in love... [STELLA looks up with a radiant smile. ] Stella—

STELLA What?

BLANCHE [in an uneasy rush] I haven't asked you the things you probably thought I was going to ask. And so I'll expect you to be understanding about what / have to tell you.

STELLA What, Blanche? [Her face turns anxious.]

BLANCHE Well, Stella—you're going to reproach me, I know

that you're bound to reproach me—but before you do—take into consideration—you left! I stayed and struggled! You came to New Orleans and looked out for yourself! I stayed at Belle Reve and tried to hold it together! I'm not meaning this in any reproachful way, but all the burden descended on my shoulders.

STELLA The best I could do was make my own living, Blanche.

[BLANCHE begins to shake again with intensity.]

BLANCHE I know, I know. But you are the one that abandoned Belle Reve, not I! I stayed and fought for it, bled for it, almost died for it!

STELLA Stop this hysterical outburst and tell me what's happened? What do you mean fought and bled? What kind of—

BLANCHE I knew you would, Stella. I knew you would take this attitude about it!

STELLA About—what?—please!

BLANCHE [slowly] The loss—the loss…

STELLA Belle Reve? Lost, is it? No!

BLANCHE Yes, Stella.

[They stare at each other across the yellow-checked linoleum of the table. BLANCHE slowly nods her head and STELLA looks slowly down at her hands folded on the table. The music of the "Blue Piano" grows louder, BLANCHE touches her handkerchief to her forehead.]

STELLA But how did it go? What happened?

BLANCHE [springing up] You're a fine one to ask me how it went!

STELLA Blanche!

BLANCHE You're a fine one to sit there accusing me of it!

STELLA Blanche!

BLANCHE I, I, I took the blows in my face and my body! All of those deaths!The long parade to the graveyard! Father, mother! Margaret, that dreadful way! So big with it, it couldn't be put in a coffin! But had to be burned like rubbish! You just came home in time for the funerals, Stella. And funerals are pretty compared to deaths. Funerals are quiet, but deaths—not always. Sometimes their breathing is hoarse, and sometimes it rattles, and sometimes they even cry out to you, "Don't let me go!" Eventhe old, sometimes, say, "Don't let me go." As if you were able to stop them! But funerals are quiet, with pretty flowers. And, oh, what gorgeous boxes they pack them away in! Unless you were there at the bed when they cried out, "Hold me!" you'd never suspect there was the struggle for breath and bleeding. You didn't dream, but I saw! Saw! Saw! And now you sit there telling me with your eyes that I let the place go! How in hell do you think all that sickness and dying was paid for? Death is expensive, Miss Stella! And old Cousin Jessie's right after Margaret's, hers!Why, the Grim Reaper had put up his tent on our doorstep!...Stella.Belle Reve was his headquarters! Honey—that's how it slipped through my fingers! Which of them left us a fortune? Which of them left a cent of insurance even? Only poor Jessie—one hundred to pay for her coffin. That was all, Stella! And I with my pitiful salary at the school. Yes, accuse me! Sit there and stare at me, thinking I let the place go! I let the place go? Where were you! In bed with your—Polack!

STELLA [springing] Blanche! You be still! That's enough! [She starts out.]

BLANCHE Where are you going?

STELLA I'm going into the bathroom to wash my face.

BLANCHE Oh, Stella, Stella, you're crying!

STELLA Does that surprise you?

BLANCHE Forgive me—I didn't mean to—

[The sound of men's voices is heard, STELLA goes into the bathroom,closing the door behind her. When the men appear, and BLANCHE realizes it must be STANLEY returning, she moves uncertainly from the bathroom door to the dressing table, looking apprehensively toward the front door. STANLEY enters, followed by STEVE and MITCH. STANLEY pauses near his door, STEVE by the foot of the spiral stair, and MITCH is slightly above and to the right of them, about to go out. As the men enter, we hear some of the following dialogue. ]

STANLEY Is that how he got it?

STEVE Sure that's how he got it. He hit the old weather-bird for 300 bucks on a six-number-ticket.

MITCH Don't tell him those things; he'll believe it. [Mitch starts out.]

STANLEY [restraining Mitch] Hey, Mitch—come back here. [BLANCHE, at the sound of voices, retires in the bedroom. She picks up STANLEY'S photo from dressing table, looks at it, puts it down. When STANLEY enters the apartment, she darts and hides behind the screen at the head of bed.]

STEVE [to STANLEY and MITCH] Hey, are we playin' poker tomorrow?

STANLEY Sure—at Mitch's.

MITCH [hearing this, returns quickly to the stair rail] No—not at my place. My mother's still stick!

STANLEY Okay, at my place…[MITCH starts out again.] But you bring the beer!

[MITCH pretends not to hear—calls out "Good night, all," and goes out, singing. EUNICE'S voice is heard, above.]

Break it up down there! I made the spaghetti dish and ate it myself.

STEVE [going upstairs] I told you and phoned you we was playing, [to the men] Jax[7] beer!

EUNICE You never phoned me once.

STEVE I told you at breakfast—and phoned you at lunch…

EUNICE Well, never mind about that. You just get yourself home here once in a while.

STEVE You want it in the papers?

[More laughter and shouts of parting come from the men. STANLEY throws the screen door of the kitchen open and comes in. He is of medium height, about five feet eight or nine, and strongly, compactly built. Animal joy in his being is implicit in all his movements and attitudes. Since earliest manhood the center of his life has been pleasure with women,the giving and taking of it, not with weak indulgence, dependently, but with the power and pride of a richly feathered male bird among hens.Branching out from this complete and satisfying center are all the auxiliary channels of his life, such as his heartiness with men, his appreciation of rough humor, his love of good drink and food and games, his car, his radio, everything that is his, that bears his emblem of the gaudy seed bearer. He sizes women up at a glance, with sexual classifications,crude images flashing into his mind and determining the way he smiles at them.]

BLANCHE [drawing involuntarily back from his stare] You must be Stanley. I'm Blanche.

STANLEY Stella's sister?

BLANCHE Yes.

STANLEY H'lo. Where's the little woman?

BLANCHE In the bathroom.

STANLEY Oh. Didn't know you were coming in town.

BLANCHE I—uh—

STANLEY Where you from, Blanche?

BLANCHE Why, I—live in Laurel.

[He has crossed to the closet and removed the whiskey bottle.]

STANLEY In Laurel, huh? Oh, yeah. Yeah, in Laurel, that's right. Not in my territory. Liquor goes fast in hot weather. [He holds the bottle to the light to observe its depletion.] Have a shot?

BLANCHE No, I—rarely touch it.

STANLEY Some people rarely touch it, but it touches them often.

BLANCHE [faintly] Ha-ha.

STANLEY My clothes're stickin' to me. Do you mind if I make myself comfortable? [He starts to remove his shirt.]

BLANCHE Please, please do.

STANLEY Be comfortable is my motto.

BLANCHE It's mine, too. It's hard to stay looking fresh. I

haven't washed or even powdered my face and—here you are!

STANLEY You know you can catch cold sitting around in damp things, especially when you been exercising hard like bowling is. You're a teacher, aren't you?

BLANCHE Yes.

STANLEY What do you teach, Blanche?

BLANCHE English.

STANLEY I never was a very good English student. How long you here for, Blanche?

BLANCHE I—don't know yet.

STANLEY You going to shack up here?

BLANCHE I thought I would if it's not inconvenient for you all.

STANLEY Good.

BLANCHE Traveling wears me out.

STANLEY Well, take it easy.

[A cat screeches near the window, BLANCHE springs up.]

BLANCHE What's that?

STANLEY Cats…Hey, Stella!

STELLA [faintly, from the bathroom] Yes, Stanley.

STANLEY Haven't fallen in, have you? [He grins at BLANCHE. She tries unsuccessfully to smile back. There is a silence.] I'm afraid I'll strike you as being the unrefined type. Stella's spoke of you a good deal. You were married once, weren't you?

[The music of the polka rises up, faint in the distance.]

BLANCHE Yes. When I was quite young.

STANLEY What happened?

BLANCHE The boy—the boy died. [She sinks back down.] I'm afraid I'm—going to be sick! [Her head falls on her arms.]

## Notes

1. American poet (1899 — 1932).

2. Elysian Fields is in fact a New Orleans street at the northern tip of the French Quarter, between the Louisville & Nashville railroad tracks and the Mississippi River. In Greek mythology, the Elysian Fields are the abode of the blessed in the afterlife.

3. The end of a streetcar line that stopped at a cemetery. Desire is a street in New Orleans.

4. It's nothing (Spanish).

5. Beautiful Dream (French).

6. From the refrain of Poe's gothic ballad "Ulalume" (1847).

7. A local brand of beer.

## Questions

1. Please make an analysis on the character Blanche.

2. How do you understand the conflict between the south and north of America in this work?

### （11）Langston Hughes (1902—1967)

Langston Hughes (1902—1967), born in Joplin, Missouri, began writing poetry when he was in high school. A year after he attended Columbia University in 1921, he dropped out. Driven by his eagerness to travel around the world, he became a sailor on an ocean-going freighter and travelled to Africa and Europe. He once worked in Paris as a cook in a restaurant and gatekeeper at a nightclub. In 1925, once he came back to America, he began working as a waiter at a hotel in Washington, D.C. While working there, he met Vachel Lindsay, a poet holding a reading tour at the hotel at that time, and who recognizes Hughes' poetic talents. Since then, Langston Hughes began to rise to prominence in the literary field and eventually became a leader of the Harlem Renaissance movement and one of the most famous poets in America.

After the publication of his first poem anthology, *The Weary Blues* (1926), he began traveling within the United States and holding public poetry readings. In 1929, Langston Hughes returned to school and obtained his master's degree at Lincoln University after three year of effort. In 1932, he visited the Soviet Union, which he had long admired. And then he came to China and was said that he met Lu Xun there. Langston Hughes also reported on the Spanish Civil War as a journalist and attended the Second International Writers' Congress in Paris. His work of this period truly reflects the labor movement and sharply exposes the hypocritical characteristics of a capitalistic society.

He is best known for his poetry, though he used to write within many genres of literature. His major poems include *Fine Clothes to the Jew* (1927), *The Dream Keeper and Other Poems* (1932), and *Shakespeare in Harlem* (1942).

The following poems are excerpted from *The Norton Anthology of American Literature* (shorter 6th edition).

## The Negro Speaks of Rivers

I've known rivers:
I've known rivers ancient as the world and older than the
  flow of human blood in human veins.

My soul has grown deep like the rivers.

I bathed in the Euphrates when dawns were young.
I built my hut near the Congo and it lulled me to sleep.

I looked upon the Nile and raised the pyramids above it.
I heard the singing of the Mississippi when Abe Lincoln
  went down to New Orleans, and I've seen its
  muddy bosom turn all golden in the sunset

I've known rivers:
Ancient, dusky rivers.

My soul has grown deep like the rivers.

### Questions

1. What is the symbolic meaning of rivers in this poem?
2. Changjiang River, as the mother river of Chinese, is often

praised in Chinese literary works, for example Nian Nu Jiao Chi Bi Huai Gu《念奴娇·赤壁怀古》by Sushi. Please compare these two poems.

## Song for a Dark Girl

Way Down South in Dixie [1]
(Break the heart of me)
They hung my black young lover
To a cross roads tree.

Way Down South in Dixie
(Bruised body high in air)
I asked the white Lord Jesus
What was the use of prayer.

Way Down South in Dixie
(Break the heart of me)
Love is a naked shadow
On a gnarled and naked tree.

### Notes

1. Last line of "Dixie," the popular minstrel song, probably composed by Daniel D.Emmett (1815 — 1904).

## Questions

1. "Way Down South in Dixie" appears for thrice in this poem. What is the function of this sentence?

2. What's the theme of this poem?

### （12）Richard Wright (1908—1960)

Richard Wright (1908—1960), an African American novelist, has created many classic works during his life, among which Native Son (1940) is a masterpiece. It is considered as a milestone in the history of African American literature. Its appearance shocked both American society and the American literature community. It also became an immediate best-seller at that time and established Wright as a pioneer for the "protesting novel", a spokesman for African American issues, and the "father of Black American literature".

Richard Wright was born in a plantation in Mississippi. His grandfather was a slave, his father was an illiterate sharecropper, and his mother was an elementary school teacher. His father abandoned the family, so Wright spent almost of his childhood in an orphanage. Wright finished his junior high school in the local black school. He went to Memphis, Tennessee, and made a living as a postman. Wright moved to Chicago in 1927, where he was employed as a postal clerk. When his job at the post office was eliminated by Hoover's policies during the Great Depression, he was forced to go on financial benefits in 1931. In 1932, he began attending meetings of the John Reed Club. As the club was dominated by the Communist Party,

Wright established a relationship with a number of party members. Especially interested in the literary contacts made at the meetings, Wright formally joined the Communist Party in late 1933. In 1937, Richard Wright moved to New York, where he forged new ties with Communist Party members there after getting established. He broke apart from it in 1944 due to increasing anti-communist sentiments. He worked on the WPA Writers' Project guidebook to the city, *New York Panorama* (1938), and wrote the book's essay on Harlem. Wright became the Harlem editor of the *Daily Worker.* After the appearance of *Uncle Tom's Children* (1938) and *Native Son* (1940), Wright became the most prestigious black novelist, being one of the first African Americans to gain fame and fortune as a professional writer. Afterwards, however, his creative works declined gradually. Wright suffered a lot from poor health and financial difficulties during his last years. He died of a sudden heart attack on November 28, 1960.

As a black writer, Wright grew and lived at the lowest level of the society, full of class oppression and racial discrimination. He has had a strong sense of revolt and rebellion since his childhood, which was full of poverty and hunger. He was the outcast of his family and the black boy abused in society as well. He was filled with hatred and fear toward the world, with such deep-rooted psychological effects fully reflected in his later works. His literary creation fully depended on self-study. It was said that he once wrote a short story for a local black newspaper successfully, which is what likely first aroused his interest in pursuing literary career.

The following text is excerpted from *The Norton Anthology of*

*American Literature* (shorter 6th edition).

## The Man Who Was Almost a Man

Dave struck out across the fields, looking homeward through paling light.What's the use talkin wid em niggers in the field? Anyhow, his mother was putting supper on the table. Them niggers can't understand nothing. One of these days he was going to get a gun and practice shooting, then they couldn't talk to him as though he were a little boy. He slowed, looking at the ground.Shucks, Ahma scareda them even ef they are biggern me! Aw, Ah know what Ahma do. Ahm going by ol Joe's sto n git that Sears Roebuck catlog nlook at them guns. Mebbe Ma will lemme buy one when she gits mah pay from oi man Hawkins. Ahma beg her t gimme some money. Ahm ol ernough to hava gun. Ahm seventeen. Almost a man. He strode, feeling his long loose-jointed limbs. Shucks, a man oughta hava little gun aftah he done worked hard all day.

He came in sight of Joe's store. A yellow lantern glowed on the front porch.He mounted steps and went through the screen door, hearing it bang behind him. There was a strong smell of coal oil and mackerel fish. He felt very confident until he saw fat Joe walk in through the rear door, then his courage began to ooze.

"Howdy, Dave! Whutcha want?"

"How yuh, Mistah Joe? Aw, Ah don wanna buy nothing. Ah jus wanted t see ef yuhd lemme look at tha catlog erwhile."

"Sure! You wanna see it here?"

"Nawsuh. Ah wans t take it home wid me. Ah'll bring it back tomorrow when Ah come in from the fiels."

"You plannin on buying something?"

"Yessuh."

"Your ma lettin you have your own money now?"

"Shucks. Mistah Joe, Ahm gittin t be a man like anybody else!" Joe laughed and wiped his greasy white face with a red bandanna.

"Whut you plannin on buyin?"

Dave looked at the floor, scratched his head, scratched his thigh, and smiled. Then he looked up shyly.

"Ah'll tell yuh, Mistah Joe, ef yuh promise yuh won't tell."

"I promise."

"Waal, Ahma buy a gun."

"A gun? What you want with a gun?"

"Ah wanna keep it."

"You ain't nothing but a boy. You don't need a gun."

"Aw, lemme have the catlog, Mistah Joe. Ah'll bring it back."

Joe walked through the rear door. Dave was elated. He looked around at barrels of sugar and flour. He heard Joe coming back. He craned his neck to see if he were bringing the book. Yeah, he's got it. Gawddog, he's got it!

"Here, but be sure you bring it back. It's the only one I got."

"Sho, Mistah Joe."

"Say, if you wanna buy a gun, why don't you buy one from me? I gotta gun to sell."

"Will it shoot?"

"Sure it'll shoot."

"I'll let you have it for two dollars."

"Just two dollahs? Shucks, Ah could buy tha when Ah git mah pay."

"I'll have it here when you want it."

"Awright, suh. Ah be in fer it."

He went through the door, hearing it slam again behind him. Ahma git some money from Ma n buy me a gun! Only two dollahs! He tucked the thick catalogue under his arm and hurried.

"Where yuh been, boy?" His mother held a steaming dish of black-eyed peas.

"Aw, Ma, Ah just stopped down the road t talk wid the boys."

"Yuh know bettah t keep suppah waitin."

He sat down, resting the catalogue on the edge of the table.

"Yuh git up from there and git to the well n wash yosef! Ah ain feedin no hogs in mah house!"

She grabbed his shoulder and pushed him. He stumbled out of the room, then came back to get the catalogue.

"Whut this?"

"Aw, Ma, it's jusa catlog."

"Who yuh git it from?"

"From Joe, down at the sto."

"Waal, thas good. We kin use it in the outhouse."

"Naw, Ma." He grabbed for it. "Gimme ma catlog, Ma."

She held onto it and glared at him.

"Quit hollerin at me! Whut's wrong wid yuh? Yuh crazy?"

"But Ma, please. It ain mine! It's Joe's! He tol me t bring it back t im termorrow."

She gave up the book. He stumbled down the back steps, hugging the thick book under his arm. When he had splashed water on his face and hands, he groped back to the kitchen and fumbled[1] in a corner for the towel.He bumped into a chair; it clattered to the floor. The catalogue sprawled at his feet. When he had dried his eyes he snatched up the book and held it again under his arm. His mother stood watching him.

"Now, ef yuh gonna act a fool over that ol book, Ah'II take it n burn it up."

"Naw, Ma, please."

"Waal, set down n be still!"

He sat down and drew the oil lamp close. He thumbed page after page, unaware of the food his mother set on the table. His father came in. Then his small brother.

"Whutcha got there, Dave?" his father asked.

"Jusa catlog," he answered, not looking up.

"Yeah, here they is!" His eyes glowed at blue-and-black revolvers. He glanced up, feeling sudden guilt. His father was watching him. He eased the book under the table and rested it on his knees. After the blessing was asked,he ate. He scooped up peas and swallowed fat meat without chewing. Buttermilk helped to wash it down. He did not want to mention money before his father. He would do much better by cornering his mother when she was alone. He looked at his father uneasily out of the edge of his eye.

"Boy, how come yuh don quit foolin wid tha book n eat yo suppah?"

"Yessuh."

"How you n ol man Hawkins gitten erlong?"

"Suh?"

"Can't yuh hear? Why don yuh lissen? Ah ast yu how wuz yuh n ol man Hawkins gittin erlong?"

"Oh, swell, Pa. Ah plows mo lan than anybody over there."

"Waal, yuh oughta keep yo mind on whut yuh doin."

"Yessuh."

He poured his plate full of molasses and sopped it up slowly with a chunk of cornbread. When his father and brother had left the kitchen, he still satand looked again at the guns in the catalogue, longing to muster courage enough to present his case to his mother. Lawd, ef Ah only had tha pretty one! He could almost feel the slickness of the weapon with his fingers. If he had a gun like that he would polish it and keep it shining so it would never rust. N Ah'd keep it loaded, by Gawd!

"Ma?" His voice was hesitant.

"Hunh?"

"Ol man Hawkins give yuh mah money yit?"

"Yeah, but ain no usa yuh thinking bout throwin nona it erway. Ahm keep in tha money sos yuh kin have cloes t go to school this winter."

He rose and went to her side with the open catalogue in his

palms. She was washing dishes, her head bent low over a pan. Shyly he raised the book. When he spoke, his voice was husky, faint.

"Ma, Gawd knows Ah wans one of these."

"One of whut?" she asked, not raising her eyes.

"One of these," he said again, not daring even to point. She glanced up at the page, then at him with wide eyes.

"Nigger, is yuh gone plumb crazy?"

"Aw, Ma."

"Git outta here! Don yuh talk t me bout no gun! Yuh a fool!"

"Ma, Ah kin buy one fer two dollahs."

"Not ef Ah knows it, yuh ain!"

"But yuh promised me one."

"Ah don care whut Ah promised! Yuh ain nothing but a boy yit!"

"Ma, ef yuh lemme buy one Ah'll never ast yuh fer nothing no mo."

"Ah tol yuh t git outta here! Yuh ain gonna toucha penny of tha money fer no gun! Thas how come Ah has Mistah Hawkins t pay yo wages t me, cause Ah knows yuh ain got no sense."

"But, Ma, we needa gun. Pa ain got no gun. We needa gun in the house.

Yuh kin never tell whut might happen."

"Now don yuh try to maka fool outta me, boy! Ef we did hava gun, yuh wouldn't have it!"

He laid the catalogue down and slipped his arm around her waist.

"Aw, Ma, Ah done worked hard alia summer n ain ast yuh fer nothin, is Ah, now?"

"Thas whut yuh spose t do!"

"But Ma, Ah wans a gun. Yuh kin lemme have two dollahs outta mah money. Please, Ma. I kin give it to Pa…Please, Ma! Ah loves yuh, Ma." When she spoke her voice came soft and low.

"What yuh wan wida gun, Dave? Yuh don need no gun. Yuh'll git in trouble. N ef yo pa jus thought Ah let yuh have money t buy a gun he'd hava fit."

"Ah'll hide it, Ma. It ain but two dollahs."

"Lawd, chil, whut's wrong wid yuh?"

"Ain nothing wrong, Ma. Ahm almos a man now. Ah wans a gun."

"Who gonna sell yuh a gun?"

"Ol Joe at the sto."

"N it don cos but two dollahs?"

"Thas all, Ma. Just two dollahs. Please, Ma."

She was stacking the plates away; her hands moved slowly, reflectively. Dave kept an anxious silence. Finally, she turned to him.

"Ah'll let yuh git tha gun ef yuh promise me one thing."

"Whut's tha, Ma?"

"Yuh bring it straight back t me, yuh hear? It be fer Pa."

"Yessum! Lemme go now, Ma."

She stooped, turned slightly to one side, raised the hem of her dress, rolled down the top of her stocking, and came up with a slender wad of bills.

"Here," she said. "Lawd knows yuh don need no gun. But yer pa does. Yuh bring it right back t me, yuh hear? Ahma put it up. Now ef yuh don, Ahma have yuh pa pick yuh so hard yuh won fergit it."

"Yessum."

He took the money, ran down the steps, and across the yard.

"Dave! Yuuuuuh Daaaaave!"

He heard, but he was not going to stop now. "Naw, Lawd!"

The first movement he made the following morning was to reach under his pillow for the gun. In the gray light of dawn he held it loosely, feeling a sense of power. Could kill a man with a gun like this. Kill anybody, black or white. And if he were holding his gun in his hand, nobody could run over him; they would have to respect him. It was a big gun, with a long barrel and a heavy handle. He raised and lowered it in his hand, marveling at its weight.

He had not come straight home with it as his mother had asked; instead he had stayed out in the fields, holding the weapon in his hand, aiming it now and then at some imaginary foe. But he had not fired it; he had been afraid that his father might hear. Also he was not sure he knew how to fire it.

To avoid surrendering the pistol he had not come into the house until he knew that they were all asleep. When his mother had tiptoed to his bedside late that night and demanded the gun, he had first played possum; then he had told her that the gun was hidden outdoors, that he would bring it to her in the morning. Now he lay turning it slowly in his hands. He broke it, took out the cartridges[2], felt them, and then put them back.

He slid out of bed, got a long strip of old flannel from a trunk, wrapped the gun in it, and tied it to his naked thigh while it was still loaded. He did not go in to breakfast. Even though it was not yet daylight, he started for Jim Hawkins' plantation. Just as the sun was rising he reached the barns where the mules and plows were kept.

"Hey! That you, Dave?"

He turned. Jim Hawkins stood eying him suspiciously.

"What're yuh doing here so early?"

"Ah didn't know Ah wuz gittin up so early, Mistah Hawkins. Ah wuz fixint hitch up ol Jenny n take her t the fiels."

"Good. Since you're so early, how about plowing that stretch down by the woods?"

"Suits me, Mistah Hawkins."

"O.K. Go to it!"

He hitched Jenny to a plow and started across the fields. Hot dog! This was just what he wanted. If he could get down by the woods, he could shoot his gun and nobody would hear. He walked behind the plow, hearing the traces creaking, feeling the gun tied tight to his thigh. When he reached the woods, he plowed two whole rows before he decided to take out the gun. Finally, he stopped, looked in all directions, then untied the gun and held it in his hand. He turned to the mule and smiled.

"Know whut this is, Jenny? Naw, yuh wouldn know! Yuhs jusa ol mule! Anyhow, this is a gun, n it kin shoot, by Gawd!"

He held the gun at arm's length. Whut t hell, Ahma shoot this thing! He looked at Jenny again.

"Lissen here, Jenny! When Ah pull this ol trigger, Ah don wan yuh t run n acka fool now!"

Jenny stood with head down, her short ears pricked straight. Dave walked off about twenty feet, held the gun far out from him at arm's length, and turned his head. Hell, he told himself, Ah ain afraid. The gun felt loose in his fingers; he waved it wildly for a moment. Then he shut his eyes and tightened his forefinger. Bloom! A report half deafened him and he though this right hand was torn from his arm. He heard Jenny whinnying and gal-loping over the field, and he found himself on his knees, squeezing his fingers hard between his legs. His hand was numb; he jammed it into his mouth,trying to warm it, trying to stop the pain. The gun lay at his feet. He did not quite know what had happened. He stood up and stared at the gun as thoughit were a living thing. He gritted his teeth and kicked the gun. Yuh almos broke mah arm! He turned to look for Jenny; she was far over the fields,tossing her head and kicking wildly.

"Hol on there, ol mule!"

When he caught up with her she stood trembling, walling her big white eyes at him. The plow was far away; the traces had broken. Then Dave stopped short, looking, not believing. Jenny was bleeding. Her left side was red and wet with blood. He went closer. Lawd, have mercy! Wondah did Ah shoot this mule? He grabbed for Jenny's mane. She flinched, snorted,whirled, tossing her head.

"Hol on now! Hol on."

Then he saw the hole in Jenny's side, right between the ribs. It was round,wet, red. A crimson[3] stream streaked down the front leg, flowing fast. Good Gawd! Ah wuzn't shootin at tha mule. He felt panic. He knew he had to stopt hat blood, or Jenny would bleed to death. He had never seen so much blood in all his life. He chased the mule for a half a mile, trying to catch her.

Finally she stopped, breathing hard, stumpy tail half arched. He caught her mane and led her back to where the plow and gun lay. Then he stooped and grabbed handfuls of damp black earth and tried to plug the bullet hole. Jenny shuddered, whinnied, and broke from him.

"Hol on! Hol on now!"

He tried to plug it again, but blood came anyhow. His fingers were hot and sticky. He rubbed dirt into his palms, trying to dry them. Then again heat tempted to plug the bullet hole, but Jenny shied away, kicking her heels high. He stood helpless. He had to do something. He ran at Jenny; she dodged him. He watched a red stream of blood flow down Jenny's leg and form a bright pool at her feet.

"Jenny…Jenny," he called weakly.

His lips trembled. She's bleeding t death! He looked in the direction of home, wanting to go back, wanting to get help. But he saw the pistol lying in the damp black clay. He had a queer feeling that if he only did something,this would not be; Jenny would not be there bleeding to death.When he went to her this time, she did not move. She stood with sleepy,dreamy eyes; and when he touched her she gave a low-pitched whinny and knelt to the ground, her front knees slopping in blood.

"Jenny…Jenny…" he whispered.

For a long time she held her neck erect; then her head sank, slowly. Her ribs swelled with a mighty heave and she went over.

Dave's stomach felt empty, very empty. He picked up the gun and held it gingerly between his thumb and forefinger. He buried it at the foot of a tree.He took a stick and tried to cover the pool of blood with dirt—but what was the use? There was Jenny lying with her mouth open and her eyes walled and glassy. He could not tell Jim Hawkins he had shot his mule. But he had to tell something. Yeah, Ah'll tell em Jenny started gittin wil n fell on the joint of the plow…But that would hardly happen to a mule. He walked across the field slowly, head down.

It was sunset. Two of Jim Hawkins' men were over near the edge of the woods digging a hole in which to bury Jenny. Dave was surrounded by a knot of people, all of whom were looking down at the dead mule.

"I don't see how in the world it happened," said Jim Hawkins for the tenth time.

The crowd parted and Dave's mother, father, and small brother pushed into the center.

"Where Dave?" his mother called.

"There he is," said Jim Hawkins.

His mother grabbed him.

"Whut happened, Dave? Whut yuh done?"

"Nothin."

" C mon, boy, talk," his father said.

Dave took a deep breath and told the story he knew nobody believed.

"Waal," he drawled. "Ah brung ol Jenny down here sos Ah could do mah plowin. Ah plowed bout two rows, just like yuh see." He stopped and pointed at the long rows of upturned earth. "Then somethin musta been wrong wid ol Jenny. She wouldn ack right a-tall. She started snortin n kickin her heels. Ah tried t hoi her, but she pulled erway, rearin n goin in. Then when the point of the plow was stickin up in the air, she swung erroun n twisted herself back on it…She stuck herself n started t bleed. N fo Ah could do anything, she wuz dead."

"Did you ever hear of anything like that in all your life?" asked Jim Hawkins.

There were white and black standing in the crowd. Thev murmured. Dave's mother came close to him and looked hard into his face. "Tell the truth, Dave," she said.

"Looks like a bullet hole to me," said one man.

"Dave, whut yuh do wid the gun?" his mother asked.

The crowd surged in, looking at him. He jammed his hands into his pockets, shook his head slowly from left to right, and backed away. His eyes were wide and painful.

"Did he hava gun?" asked Jim Hawkins.

"By Gawd, Ah tol yuh tha wu a gun wound," said a man, slapping his thigh.

His father caught his shoulders and shook him till his teeth rattled.

"Tell whut happened, yuh rascal! Tell whut…"

Dave looked at Jenny's stiff legs and began to cry.

"Whut yuh do wid tha gun?" his mother asked.

"Whut wuz he doin wida gun?" his father asked.

"Come on and tell the truth," said Hawkins. "Ain't nobody going to hurt you..."

His mother crowded close to him.

"Did yuh shoot tha mule, Dave?"

Dave cried, seeing blurred white and black faces.

"Ahh ddinn gggo tt sshooot hher...Ah ssswear ffo Gawd Ahh ddin...Ah wuz a-tryin t sssee ef the old gggun would sshoot."

"Where yuh git the gun from?" his father asked.

"Ah got it from Joe, at the sto."

"Where yuh git the money?"

"Ma give it t me."

"He kept worryin me, Bob. Ah had t. Ah tol im t bring the gun right back to me...It was fer yuh, the gun."

"But how yuh happen to shoot that mule?" asked Jim Hawkins.

"Ah wuzn shootin at the mule, Mistah Hawkins. The gun jumped when

Ah pulled the trigger...N fo Ah knowed anythin Jenny was there ableedin."

Somebody in the crowd laughed. Jim Hawkins walked close to Dave and looked into his face.

"Well, looks like you have bought you a mule, Dave."

"Ah swear fo Gawd, Ah didn go t kill the mule, Mistah Hawkins!"

"But you killed her!"

All the crowd was laughing now. They stood on tiptoe and poked heads over one another's shoulders.

"Well, boy, looks like yuh done bought a dead mule! Hahaha!"

"Ain tha ershame."

"Hohohohoho."

Dave stood, head down, twisting his feet in the dirt.

"Well, you needn't worry about it, Bob," said Jim Hawkins to Dave's father.

"Just let the boy keep on working and pay me two dollars a month."

"Whut yuh wan fer yo mule, Mistah Hawkins?"

Jim Hawkins screwed up his eyes.

"Fifty dollars."

"Whut yuh do wid tha gun?" Dave's father demanded.

Dave said nothing.

"Yuh wan me t take a tree n beat yuh till yuh talk!"

"Nawsuh!"

"Whut yuh do wid it?"

"Ah throwed it erway."

"Where?"

"Ah…Ah throwed it in the creek."

"Waal, c mon home. N firs thing in the mawnin git to tha creek n fin tha gun."

"Yessuh."

"Whut yuh pay fer it?"

"Two dollahs."

"Take tha gun n git yo money back n carry it t Mistah Hawkins, yuh near? N don fergit Ahma lam you black bottom good fer this! Now march yosef on home, suh!"

Dave turned and walked slowly. He heard people laughing. Dave glared, his eyes welling with tears. Hot anger bubbled in him. Then he swallowed and stumbled on.

That night Dave did not sleep. He was glad that he had gotten out of killing the mule so easily, but he was hurt. Something hot seemed to turnover inside him each time he remembered how they had laughed. He tossed on his bed, feeling his hard pillow. N Pa says he's gonna beat me...He remembered other beatings, and his back quivered. Naw, naw, Ah sho donwan im t beat me tha way no mo. Dam em all! Nobody ever gave him any-thing. All he did was work. They treat me like a mule, n then they beat me.He gritted his teeth. N Ma had t tell on me.

Well, if he had to, he would take old man Hawkins that two dollars. But that meant selling the gun. And he wanted to keep that gun. Fifty dollars for a dead mule.

He turned over, thinking how he had fired the gun. He had an itch to fireit again. Ef other men kin shoota gun, by Gawd, Ah kin! He was still, listening. Mebbe they all sleepin now. The house was still. He heard the soft breathing of his brother. Yes, now! He would go down and get that gun and see if he could fire it! He eased out of bed and slipped into overalls.

The moon was bright. He ran almost all the way to the edge of the woods.He stumbled over the ground, looking for the spot where he had buried the gun. Yeah, here it is. Like a hungry dog scratching for a bone, he pawed it up. He puffed his black cheeks and blew dirt from the trigger and barrel. He broke it and found four cartridges unshot. He looked around; the fields were filled with silence and moonlight. He clutched the gun stiff and hard in his fingers. But, as soon as he wanted to pull the trigger, he shut his eyes and turned his head. Naw, An can't shoot wid mah eyes closed n mah head turned. With effort he held his eyes open; then he squeezed. Bloooom! He was stiff, not breathing. The gun was still in his hands. Dammit, he'd done it! He fired again. Blooooom! He smiled. Blooooom! Blooooom! Click, click. There! It was empty. If anybody could shoot a gun, he could. He put the gun into his hip pocket and started across the fields.

When he reached the top of a ridge he stood straight and proud in the moonlight, looking at Jim Hawkins' big white house, feeling the gun sagging in his pocket. Lawd, ef Ah had just one mo bullet Ah'd taka shot at tha house.Ah'd like t scare ol man Hawkins jusa little… Jusa enough t let im knowDave Saunders is a man.

To his left the road curved, running to the tracks of the Illinois Central. He jerked his head, listening. From far off came a faint hooof-hooof; hooof-hooof; hooof-hooof…. He stood rigid. Two dollahs a mont. Les see now…Tha means it'll take bout two years. Shucks! Ah'll be dam!

He started down the road, toward the tracks. Yeah, here she comes! He stood beside the track and held himself stiffly. Here she comes, erroun the ben…C mon, yuh slow poke! C mon! He had his hand on his gun; some-thing quivered in his stomach. Then the train thundered past, the gray and brown box cars rumbling and clinking. He gripped the gun tightly; then he jerked his hand out of his pocket.

Ah betcha Bill wouldn't do it! Ah betcha....The cars slid past, steel grinding upon steel. Ahm ridin yuh ternight, so hep me Gawd! He was hot all over. He hesitated just a moment; then hegrab bed, pulled atop of a car, and lay flat. He felt his pocket; the gun was still there. Ahead the long rails were glinting in the moonlight, stretching away, away to somewhere, somewhere where he could be a man...

## Notes

1. To use your hands in an awkward way when you are doing sth or looking for sth.

2. A metal or cardboard tube containing a bullet and an explosive substance.

3. Deep red.

## Questions

1. *The Man Who Was Almost a Man* is a work with modernism and naturalism. What is the naturalism element in this work?

2. What is the symbolic meaning of "gun" and "mule" in this work?

# Part VI Literature after the 2nd World War

## 1. Historical Background

The United States dominated global affairs in the years immediately after World War II. Victorious in that great struggle, and its homeland undamaged from the ravages of war, the nation was confident of its mission at home and abroad.

The Cold War was the most important political and diplomatic issue of the early postwar period. The Cold War developed as differences about the shape of the postwar world created suspicion and distrust between the United States and the Soviet Union. The Cold War and the McCarthyism in the 1950s further heightened tensions among people. Not only did the Cold War shape U.S. foreign policy, but it also had a profound effect on domestic affairs.

In the decade and a half after World War II, the United States experienced phenomenal economic growth and consolidated its position as the world's richest country. The growth had different sources. The economic stimulus provided by large-scale public spending for World War II helped get it started. Two basic middle-class needs did much to keep it going. The number of automobiles produced annually quadrupled between 1946 and 1955. A housing boom, stimulated in part by easily affordable mortgages for returning servicemen, fueled the expansion. The rise in defense spending as the Cold War escalated also played a part. Farmers—at least those with small operations—faced tough times. The West and the Southwest grew with increasing rapidity, a trend that would continue through the end of the century. As suburbs grew, businesses moved into the new areas. New highways created better access to the suburbs and its shops. Television, too, had a powerful impact on social and economic patterns. Americans of all ages became exposed to increasingly sophisticated advertisements for products said to be necessary for a good life. By 1960, three-quarters of all families owned at least one television set. In the middle of the decade, the average family watched television four to five hours a day.

Economic power at the world level continued to influence American culture through the first two postwar decades. During the 1950s, many cultural commentators pointed out that a sense of uniformity pervaded American society. A number of writers, collectively known as the "Beat Generation," went out of their way to challenge the patterns of respectability and shock the rest of the culture. Musicians and artists rebelled as well. All of these artists and authors, whatever the medium, provided models for the wider and more deeply felt social revolution of the 1960s.

In the 1950s, African Americans launched a crusade, joined later by other minority groups and women, for a larger share of the American dream. In the 1960s, politically active students protested the nation's role abroad, particularly the war in Vietnam. A youth counterculture emerged to challenge the status quo. Americans from many walks of life sought to establish a new social and political equilibrium.

By 1960, the United States was on the verge of major social change. The struggle of African Americans for equality reached its peak in the mid-1960s. After progressive victories in the 1950s, African Americans became even more committed to nonviolent direct action. However, violence accompanied militant calls for reform. Riots broke out in several big cities in 1966 and 1967. In the spring of 1968, Martin Luther King Jr. fell before an assassin's bullet. Several months later, Senator Robert Kennedy, a spokesman for the disadvantaged, an opponent of the Vietnam War, and the brother of the slain president, met the same fate. To many these two assassinations marked the end of an era of innocence and idealism. The growing militancy on the left, coupled with an inevitable conservative backlash, opened a rift in the nation's psyche that took years to heal.

During the 1950s and 1960s, increasing numbers of married women entered the labor force, but in 1963 the average working woman earned only 63 percent of what a man made. That year Betty Friedan published The Feminine Mystique, an explosive critique of middle class living patterns that articulated a pervasive sense of discontent that Friedan contended was felt by many women. The women's movement of the 1960s and 1970s drew inspiration from the civil rights movement.

The visible signs of the counterculture spread through parts of American society in the late 1960s and early 1970s. Hair grew longer and beards became common. Blue jeans and tee shirts took the place of slacks, jackets, and ties. The use of illegal drugs increased. Rock and Roll grew, proliferated, and transformed into many musical variations. The Beatles, the Rolling Stones, and other British groups took the country by storm. "Hard rock" grew popular, and songs with a political or social commentary, such as those by singer-songwriter Bob Dylan, became common. The youth counterculture reached its apogee in August 1969 at Woodstock, a three-day music festival in rural New York State attended by almost half-a-million persons. The festival, mythologized in films and record albums, gave its name to the era, the Woodstock Generation. A parallel manifestation of the new sensibility of the young was the rise of the New Left, a group of young, college-age radicals. The energy and sensibility that fueled the civil rights movement, the counterculture, and the New Left also stimulated an environmental movement in the mid-1960s.

The Nazis' Holocaust crimes against the Jews, the use of atomic bombs, and so on, all made it difficult for people to get rid of the fear and uneasiness brought about by the war. Due to the use of the atomic bomb, people felt uneasy about the success of the hydrogen bomb test in the 1950s, artificial satellite technology and other technological revolution and scientific achievements, and even suspected that technological progress could not benefit mankind. After the 1960s, a series of political events, such as the anti-war movement, civil rights movement, and women's rights movement, coupled with the increasingly serious issues like the population explosion and environmental pollution, made people's thoughts more active and chaotic.

In general, in the eyes of American writers after World War II, the historically coveted "American Dream" became a nightmare; the ideals of democracy, personal pursuits, and religious beliefs were gone. Traditional moral concepts and value systems have lost their role; the modern people lost contact with their history, have no future, and are unable to communicate their thoughts and feelings with others, therefore, they can only be in a predicament of lonely alienation forever.

## 2. Literature of the Period

All of the above is reflected in literature, producing the "Beat Generation" writers of the 1950s that rejected all cultures and values. After the 1960s, both novels and poems took the alienation of people as the theme, using exaggerated techniques and ridiculous plots. "Black humor," Theatre of the Absurd, and other schools appeared.

Generally speaking, the achievements of American novels after World War II are reflected in the following ten aspects:

First, the Beat Generation works of the 1950s. The protagonists of new novels, who do not believe in any political principles, social ideals, religious doctrines, or moral principles, are deeply sorry and upset for losing them all; they try to escape reality but always aimlessly search for something unclear. The most typical work is *On the Road* (1957), written by Jack Kerouac (1922—1969).

Second, in the 1960s, a new novel of "nonfiction," also known as "New Journalism." This kind of novel combines facts and speculation with social sensational events, blending the author's own observations and imagination. Truman Capote (1924—1984), published in *In*

*Cold Blood* (1966), was the first nonfiction novel. Norman Mailer (1923—2007), and Tom Wolfe (1931—2018) have all made great achievements in this regard. Norman's *The Armies of the Night*, which describes a march to the Pentagon in 1967 in protest of the Vietnam War, also won the Pulitzer Prize for Literature in nonfiction in 1969.

Third, the "black humor" novel. Writers use grotesque, fantasy, and exaggerated ways to reproduce the chaotic, elusive reality. Their protagonists are crazy and so is the society. This painful reality is reflected by extreme satire, and the humor turns into hysterical social interactions, with tears of laughter. The representative work of "Black Humor" is *Catch*-22 by Joseph Heller (1923—1999). Other famous black humorists are John Barth (1930— ), and Thomas Pynchon (1937— ).

Fourth, finding the "self" became the most important theme of fiction during this period. Writers asked the identity question to explore the answers to kinds of Questions: such as, "Who am I?" or "What is the essence of man?" and so on, but often draw no conclusion. The most typical work is *Invisible Man* by Ralph Ellison (1914—1994).

Fifth, fiction about the war. Works by Hemingway and others after the First World War are similar, all of which describe the poverty of military life and the tragedies of war, but no longer full of self-pity mood, but involving a wide range of aspects. Like Owen Shaw's (1913—1984) *The Young Lions* describes the psychological activities of the Nazi and the American soldiers from multiple perspectives; Mailer's *The Naked and the Dead* reflects the conflict between soldiers and officers; *From Here to the Eternity* by James Jones (1921—1977) shows the monotonous military camp life and the trampling of personal dignity by the military institutions.

Sixth, Southern literature developed rapidly in fiction. In addition to Faulkner, there was Katherine Anne Porter (1890—1980), Carson McCullers (1917—1967), Flannery O'Connor (1925—1964), Eudora Welty (1909—2001), and Robert Penn Warren (1905—1989).

Porter is one of the most accomplished American short novelists. Her works mainly describe people's loneliness and guilt, detailing the empty and poor spiritual world of the modern people by use of exquisite writing, rigorous words, and beautiful style. Her representative works include the short story collection *The Leaning Tower and Other Stories* and the novel *A Ship of Fools*. O'Connor's novels are known for being grotesque and dark. In her writing, the world is always full of violence and evil, and the traditional virtues such as diligence and integrity cannot be inherited and carried forward. O'Connor's style is slightly witty and good at using everyday spoken English. Her representative work is *A Good Man Is Hard to Find*. Welty is yet another Southern female writer who specializes in short stories. Her works are as rustic as Faulkner's, though she is not worried about the world like Faulkner was, but instead, she focuses on objectively showing human stupidity and ridiculous phenomena in life. *The Golden Apples* and *The Bride of Innisfallen* are excellent collections of her short stories. Critics generally regard Warren as the most important writer in the South after Faulkner, not only in fiction, but also as an outstanding poet and literary theorist. *All the King's Men* focuses on the central theme of Warren's work: man can only realize the corrosive effect of self and the material world through knowing oneself.

Seventh, new black writers. Ellison rose to fame with *The Invisible*. The hero of the novel finds people seeing him with a fixed eye, both in the south and in the north. He is a person without a personality in the eyes of others, and he is therefore an "invisible person." Ellison's symbols, historical allusions and myths, realism, expressionism, surrealism, and even black jazz music and blues are blended together, which makes his works brilliant from content to technique. James Baldwin (1924—1987) was active in the Civil Rights Movement for black racial equality and had a much greater political influence than Ellison. His best work is *Go Tell It on the Mountain*, which is about teenage life. Baldwin was also a brilliant essayist, writing in a sharp, passionate, and powerful style. Famous collections of essays include *Nobody Knows My Name* and *The Fire Next Time*.

Some black writers do not use the form of novels, but with a lot of facts and personal experience to reflect their oppression and pain, such as *I Have a Dream* speech by the famous pacifist Martin Luther King, Jr. (1929—1968), or *The Autobiography of Malcolm* X by Malcolm X (1925—1965).

The black writer who did much in drama was Lorraine Hansberry (1930—1965). *Raisin in the Sun* celebrates the black family's courage and strength to resist its fate, and is widely appreciated by critics. Among the best in poetry is Leroy Jones (1934—2014). He attempted to create a style and language that could only be used by blacks and only understood by blacks in order to reject traditional language, imagery, and thought, that is, the poetic character of what he called "white people."

Since the 1980s, two black female writers, Alice Walker (1944— ) and Toni Morrison (1931—2019), have become increasingly popular in the American literary world. Walker was concerned with the problems and struggles of women's movements, especially of black women. *The Color Purple* (1982), proposed how black women can care for each other, build female consciousness, and become new people with independent personalities. The novel has become a classic of American women's literature. Morrison's achievements were even greater. In 1993, Morrison was awarded the Nobel Prize for Literature, becoming the first and hitherto only black female writer to win it.

Eighth, the "Jewish literature." After the Second World War, there were many American Jewish writers, who published more and more works, forming an influential school of "Jewish literature." The most famous writers of Jewish origin are Bellow, Malamud, and Roth.

Bernard Malamud (1914—1986) specifically describes the lower-class of Jewish residents in big cities, such as small shopkeepers, miscellaneous servants, shoemakers, tailors, among others. With realistic techniques and simple and meaningful writing, he depicts the kindness and suffering of these little people, especially the discrimination and persecution of society and reformists. His story explores the Jewish relationship living in solitude to Jewish tradition. The best are *The Fixer*, *The Assistant*, *The Tenant*, and the short story collection *The Magic Barrel*.

Philip Roth (1933—2018) is a representative figure of the young generation of Jewish writers, good at describing the thoroughly Jewish American middle-class life, superficial money worship ideas, and the confusion and resistance of young people. *Goodbye, Columbus*, and *Portnoy's Complaint* describe the resistance of younger Jews against tradition and families. The trilogy *The Ghost Write, Zuckerman Unbound*, and *The Anatomy Lesson* describe the fame and loss of an enterprising young writer, which are autobiographical. Roth's novels are good for humor, but not much for sex.

Another famous Jewish writer is J. D. Salinger (1919—2010). He does not necessarily write about Jews. But his book *Catcher in the Rye* reflects the emptiness and depression of rich children, often being compared to Mark Twain's *The Adventures of Huckleberry Fin*. The difference is that the protagonist, Holden, can no longer leave the hypocritical society to seek comfort in nature.

Ninth, Chinese American literature. Strictly, Chinese American literature refers to those writers who were born, raised, and naturalized in the native country of migration and wrote in the language of the native country of migration. It is generally believed that Maxine Hong Kingston's (1940— ) autobiographical novel The Woman Warrior published in 1976 marks the beginning of the inclusion of Chinese American writers into the mainstream of American literature. Another famous Chinese American writer is Amy Tan (1952— ). Amy Tan was born in Oakland, California. Both of her parents were Chinese immigrants. She wrote four novels: *The Joy Luck Club* (1988), *The Kitchen God's Wife* (1991), *The Hundred Secret Senses* (1995), and *The Bonesetter's Daughter* (2001); two pieces of children's literature:

*The Moon Lady* (1992) and *The Chinese Siamese Cat* (1994); short stories, such as *Two Kinds* (1989), *Peanut's Fortune* (1991), and some articles and essays. Among them, *The Joy Luck Club* is considered its representative. The novel follows four mothers and daughters. The first and fourth parts of the novel are the stories of the mothers, and the second and third parts are the stories of the daughters. Its story follows the conflict between two generations and daughters, and it also includes the theme of constructing the identity of Chinese American women. The novel is a first-person retrospective narrative perspective through the use of a large number of symbolic and allegorical techniques, with an exquisite and rigorous structure.

Tenth, other trends. John Updike (1932—2009) is a versatile writer. He wrote novels as well as poems. He is a writer, an essayist, and a reviewer as well. He was also a prolific writer, composing works almost every year. His works cover a wide range of people, including how teenagers try to get rid of the shackles of small town life and try to reach a wider world, including family life, marriage problems, and relationships between people. But the most famous is the "Rabbit" saga: *Rabbit Run*, *Rabbit Redux*, *Rabbit Is Rich*, and *Rabbit at Rest*. Through the changes of the protagonist, the Rabbit books deeply reflect the characteristics of that period and the changing of the human psyche from the 1950s to the late 1980s. Many critics regard Updike as one of the most contemporary writers.

After the Second World War, American poetry has many factions and different styles, but there are some shared characteristics: it builds off the influence of Eliot's Impersonal Theory of poetry on the past's objective, implicit poetic style. Instead, it is to express the personal mind directly within the content, with personal experiences and feelings explicitly expressed by characters as they internally struggle against the mechanization and modern materialization of civilization. In form, it publicly holds opposition to English poetry, further emphasizing on the American character of poetry.

Poets who became famous after World War I, such as Stevens, Cummings, Frost, and others, remained a great influence after World War II. After World War II, many poets taught in universities and most of their poetry was considered bland, and it was not until the creation of the Beat Generation of poets that broke this dull atmosphere. In the late 50s, some young writers and poets adopted loose structures and a lot of silly language in their poetry. They opposed the American mainstream culture and value system with their decadent and indulgent lifestyles and anti-traditional literature, forming the famous "Beat Generation" literature. The poetry of the Beat Generation changed the situation of postwar poetry and began to have a strong personal autobiographical nature. Personal life events such as mental disorders, sex, divorce, and drinking became the subjects of poetry. The poet representing the movement was Allen Ginsberg (1926—1997). His poem Howl, is a scathing critique of a modern, mechanized civilization. When police charged him over its obscenity and seized the published version, Ginsberg successfully challenged the ruling in court. Life Studies, written by Robert Lowell (1917—1977), is a group of autobiographical poems that set a precedent for Confession School. Other confession poets, such as Anne Sexton (1928—1974), have written extensively about induced abortion, women's sex life, and her experiences in mental hospitals; John Berryman (1914—1972) and Sylvia Plath (1932—1963) reveal the psychology of women what causes the desire to commit suicide. Poetry from this period is also strongly political. Lowell angrily protested against the Vietnam War; Adrienne Rich (1929—2012) embraced the feminist movement; black poetess Gwendolyn Brooks (1917—2000) supported the black liberation movement; LeRoi Jones (1934—2014) further called for "black power" and even changed to a new Muslim name—Imamu Amiri Baraka (meaning Prince, a Blessed One) to show that he had abandoned his past self.

The Black Mountain poets, led by Charles Olson (1910—1970), insisted on abandoning all the formal length and normative rhythm of poetry, and even the leftside margin did not need to be uniform. They rejected all the "formal" order (form is no more than an extension of the content); New York school poets such as John Ashberry (1927—2017) and Frank O'Hara (1926—1966) were among them.

In drama, after World War II, there were four excellent American playwrights: William Inge (1913—1973), Tennessee Williams (1914—1983), Arthur Miller (1915—2005), and Edward Albee (1928—2016).

Inge is good at describing the disappointment of the little people, and his works are full of many symbolic meanings, but not too deep. His masterpieces include *Come Back, Little Sheba* and *Picnic*. Williams mainly describes the decline of the South as the frustration and pain of ordinary people, and the difficulty of pursuing happiness. He wrote a lot throughout his life, most notably *A Streetcar Named Desire*, *The Glass Menagerie*, and *Cat on a Hot Tin Roof*. Miller was the most famous American dramatist after the war. *All My Sons* is his masterpiece; but, *Death of a Salesman* is unanimously recognized as one of the best scripts after World War II. Moreover, *The Crucible* mercilessly exposes and satirizes McCarthyism's witchhunt for both real and assumed communists. Scripts such as *After the Fall* and *The Price* show that Miller is a versatile player in both subject matter and skill. Another prominent playwright was Albee. His famous works are *The Zoo Story*, *The American Dream*, and *Who's Afraid of Virginia Woolf*? Albee describes American society through symbolism, metaphors, and exaggeration. The theme is often the collapse of the American dream, and the loneliness and difficulty of pursuing self-identity.

Since the 1970s, American experimental novels, critical theories, and women's literature have also developed greatly, but that is not the focus of this book.

## 3. Representative Writers' Work

### (1) John Updike (1932—2009)

John Updike(1932—2009), is a master of American contemporary literature, a novelist, poet, playwright, essayist, and critic. He has won the Pulitzer Prize, the National Book Award, and more than a dozen awards. Born in Shillington, Pennsylvania, John Updike was an only child. His father, Wisley Updike, was a middle school math teacher, and his mother, Linda Grace Updike, was a writer. When Updike was 13, the family moved to a farmstead. There, he spent his lonely teenage years. But it was this loneliness that inspired the teenager's imagination and desire to escape loneliness. He was encouraged by his mother to begin his literary creation. He was gifted at drawing and caricature, and after graduating from Harvard in 1954, he spent a year studying art in England. Updike then returned to America and went to work for *The New Yorker*, where his first stories appeared, and to which he is still a regular contributor. Since then, Updike began to write for a living. His major works are: *Rabbit, Run* (1960), *Rabbit Redux* (1971), *Rabbit is Rich* (1981), and *Rabbit at Rest* (1990), with all part of his "Rabbit" sage. *The Centaur* (1963) and *Of the Farm* (1965) are notable among Updike's novels set in Pennsylvania.

Sex, religion, and art are the objects of Updike's lifelong pursuit, while Americans, Christians, small towns, and the middle class are the theme of Updike's unique success, making him the worthy soul-painter of the contemporary American middle class. The Rabbit saga took him 30 years to fully complete. The books are closely connected, and can be regarded as a one large book as well as separated ones. There are about 150 different vivid characters, so it becomes an epic work that fully shows the picture of the American middle class life. It deeply explores the status quo and redemption of the soul of the American middle class.

*Rabbit, Run* is the first of the Rabbit saga. It takes place between March and June of 1959. It tells the story of the young hero Rabbit Angstrom, who runs away from home due to his dissatisfaction with his dull work and family life. He represents one of the middle-class Americans whom Updike thinks is not particularly beautiful, smart, and somewhat rustic, but always willing to express himself.

The confused, emotional, and changing American society ultimately seemed suffocated by his sexual needs, religious feelings, and parenthood. In the 1950s, Eisenhower was in power, which meant the great industrial age was coming. It is a time of silence and lifelessness, but also an age of new change. The United States and the entire Western world are experiencing a spiritual crisis at this time. The shadow of the Second World War greatly affected people. Many people felt empty, distressed, confused, and anxious. Indeed, *Rabbit, Run* expresses the survival and plight of Americans in the 1950s.

The following excerpt is the first part of *Rabbit, Run*. It tells Rabbit's first escape on the road. At the beginning of the story, Rabbit, 26, climbs into the car and leaves his depressed, young wife, Janice, who is still pregnant. He heads south toward his dream place—Florida, a paradise. He occasionally stops to fuel his car or ask for directions, since he had no map, but here is a small snippet that sums up the whole of the novel, "The only way to get somewhere, you know, is to figure out where you're going before you go there." Going with the flow is not a good choice. For Rabbit, he has both the same reproductive nature as a rabbit and the same habit of leading the race but failing to win.

## Rabbit, Run (Excerption)

…

His acts take on decisive haste. In darkness he goes down another block of Jackson. He cuts up Joseph Street, runs a block, strides another, and comes within sight of his car, its grid grinning at him, parked the wrong way on this side of the street. He taps his pocket and fear hits him. He doesn't have the key. Everything depends, the whole pure idea, on which way Janice was sloppy. Either she forgot to give him the key when he went out or she never bothered to take it out of the ignition[1]. He tries to imagine which is more likely and can't. He doesn't know her that well. He never knows what the hell she'll do. She doesn't know herself. Dumb.

The back but not the front of the big Springer house is lit up. He moves cautiously in the sweet-smelling shadows under the trees in case the old lady is waiting inside the darkened living room to tell him what she thinks. He crosses around in front of the car, the '55 Ford that old man Springer with his little sandy Hitler mustache sold him for an even thousand in 1957 because the scared bastard was ashamed, cars being his business he was ashamed of his daughter marrying somebody who had nothing but a '39 Nash he bought for $125 in the Army in Texas in 1953. Made him cough up a thousand he didn't have when the Nash had just had eighty dollars' worth of work. That was the kind of thing. The Springers like to push you around. He opens the car from the passenger side, wincing at the pung of the brittle door spring and quickly ducking his head into the car. Praise be. Beneath the knobs for lights and wipers the octagon of the ignition key tells in silhouette. Bless that dope. Rabbit slithers in, closing the side door until metal touches metal but not slamming it. The front of the stucco Springer house is still unlit. It reminds him for some reason of an abandoned ice- cream stand. He turns the key through On into

Start and the motor churns and catches. In his anxiety to be secret he is delicate on the accelerator and the motor, idle for hours in the air of winter's last day, is cold, sticks, and stalls. Rabbit's heart rises and a taste of straw comes into his throat. But of course what the hell if old lady Springer does come out? The only thing suspicious is that he doesn't have the kid and he can say he's on his way to pick him up. That would have been the logical way to do it anyway.

Nevertheless he doesn't want to be put to the inconvenience of lying, however plausibly. He pulls the hand choke out a fraction, just enough to pinch his fingertips, and starts the motor again. He pumps once, and glances aside to see the Springers' living-room light flash on, and lets the clutch out, and the Ford bucks away from the curb[2].

He drives too fast down Joseph Street, and turns left, ignoring the sign saying STOP. He heads down Jackson to where it runs obliquely into Central, which is also 422 to Philadelphia. STOP. He doesn't want to go to Philadelphia but the road broadens on the edge of town beyond the electric-power station and the only other choice is to go back through Mt. Judge around the mountain into the thick of Brewer and the supper-time traffic. He doesn't intend ever to see Brewer again, that flowerpot city. The highway turns from three-lane to four-lane and there is no danger of hitting another car; they all run along together like sticks on a stream. Rabbit turns on the radio. After a hum a beautiful Negress sings, "Without a song, the dahay would nehever end[3], without a song." Rabbit wishes for a cigarette to go with his cleaned-out feeling inside and remembers he gave up smoking and feels cleaner still. He slumps down and puts one arm up on the back of the seat and glides on down the twilight pike lefthanded. "A field of corn" the Negress's voice bending dark and warm like the inside of a cello "the grasses grow" the countryside dipping around the road like a continuous dark bird "it makes no mind no how"[4] his scalp contracts ecstatically "wihithout a." The smell of parched rubber says the heater has come on and he turns the little lever to MOD[5].

"Secret Love," "Autumn Leaves," and something whose title he missed. Supper music. Music to cook by. His mind nervously shifts away from the involuntary[6] vision of Janice's meal sizzling in the pan, chops probably, the grease-tinted water bubbling disconsolately[7], the unfrozen peas steaming away their vitamins. He tries to think of something pleasant. He imagines himself about to shoot a long one-hander; but he feels he's on a cliff, there is an abyss he will fall into when the ball leaves his hands. He tries to repicture his mother and sister feeding his son, but the boy is crying in backward vision, his forehead red and his mouth stretched wide and his helpless breath hot. There must be something: the water from the ice plant running in the gutter, yellowish, the way it curled on pebbles and ran in diagonal wrinkles, waving the fragile threads of slime attached to its edges. Suddenly Janice shivers in memory on the other girl's bed in declining daylight. He tries to blot out the sensation with Miriam, Mim on his handlebars, Mim on a sled in dark snowfall being pulled up Jackson Street by him, the little kid laughing in her hood, himself the big brother, the red lights in snowfall marking the trestles[8] the town crew have used to block off the street for sledding, down, down, the runners whistling on the dark packed slick, Hold me Harry, the sparks as the runners hit the cinders spread at the bottom for safety, the scraping stop like the thump of a great heart in the dark. Once more Harry, then we'll go home, I promise Harry, please, oh I love you, little Mim only seven or so, in her dark hood, the street waxy with snow still falling. Poor Janice would probably have the wind up now, on the phone to her mother or his mother, somebody, wondering why her supper was getting cold. So dumb. Forgive me.

He accelerates. The growing complexity of lights threatens him. He is being drawn into Philadelphia. He hates Philadelphia. Dirtiest city in the world, they live on poisoned water, you can taste the chemicals. He wants to go south, down, down the map into orange groves and smoking rivers and barefoot women. It seems simple enough, drive all night through the dawn through the morning through the noon park on a beach take off your shoes and fall asleep by the Gulf of Mexico. Wake up with the stars above perfectly spaced in perfect health. But he is going east, the worst direction, into unhealth, soot, and stink[9], a smothering[10] hole where you can't move without killing somebody. Yet the highway sucks him on, and a sign says POTTSTOWN 2. He almost brakes. But then he thinks.

...

## Notes

1. The electrical system of a vehicle that makes the fuel begin to burn to start the engine; the place in a vehicle where you start this system.

2. To control or limit sth., especially sth. bad.

3. The dahay would nehever end: the days would never end.

4. It makes no mind no how: nobody knows it.

5. Middle range of the car adjustment lever.

6. Happening or done without being intended.

7. Extremely unhappily or disappointed.

8. A frame that is shaped like the letter "A," used especially for supporting a board to make a temporary table called a trestle table.

9. A very strong unpleasant smell.

10. To cover someone or something completely; to put out a fire by covering.

## Questions

1. Please analyze the psychological changes before and after Rabbit's escaping.

2. Rabbit has driven across many places, and are these places symbolic?

### （2）Allen Ginsberg (1926—1997)

Irwin Allen Ginsberg, (1926—1997) is an American poet whose poem titled *Howling and Other Poems* (1956), established his leadership in the Beat Generation, and is an "eccentric poet" in contemporary American poetry and the entire literary movement. Ginsburg was later involved in the "hippie" movement of the 1960s, and at one point he preached for the freedom to use drugs. During the Vietnam War, he was a major anti-war activist.

Ginsberg grew up in Paterson, New Jersey, where his father, Louis Ginsberg, himself a poet, taught English. Allen Ginsberg's mother, whom he mourned in his long poem *Kaddish* (1961), was confined for years in a mental hospital. His *Collected Poems*: 1947—1980 collects all of his important poems, and he won the 1974 National Book Award for his poetry collection, *The Fall of America* (1973). His poetic style inherits the tradition of the poets William Black and Walt Whitman, and is influenced by the contemporary poet William Carlos Williams. *Howl* was written in 1955 and published as part of his 1956 collection of poetry titled *Howl and Other Poems.* It is considered as an autobiography of Ginsberg up to 1955, and a brief history of the Beat Generation through its references to his relationship to other Beat artists of that time. In 1957, *Howl* attracted widespread publicity when it became the subject of an obscenity trial, as it depicted heterosexual and homosexual sex at a time when sodomy laws made homosexual acts a crime in every U.S. state. On October 3, 1957, Judge Clayton W. Horn ruled that the poem was not obscene, and *Howl* went on to become the most popular poem of the Beat Generation.

The following is the first one of the three parts. It describes scenes, characters, and situations drawn from Ginsberg's personal experiences as well as from the community of poets, artists, political radicals, jazz musicians, drug addicts, and psychiatric patients whom he encountered in the late 1940s and early 1950s. It expresses the depth of their despair when facing possible failure.

## Howl (for Carl Solomon)[1]

### I

I saw the best minds of my generation destroyed by madness, starving hys-terical naked,

dragging themselves through the negro streets at dawn looking for an angry fix,

angelheaded hipsters burning for the ancient heavenly connection[2] to the starry dynamo in the machinery of night,

who poverty and tatters and hollow-eyed and high sat up smoking in the supernatural darkness of cold-water flats floating across the tops of cit-ies contemplating jazz,

who bared their brains to Heaven under the El[3] and saw Mohammedan angels staggering on tenement roofs illuminated,

who passed through universities with radiant cool eyes hallucinating Arkan-sas and Blake-light[4] tragedy among the scholars of war,

who were expelled from the academies for crazy & publishing obscene ode s on the windows of the skull,

who cowered in unshaven rooms in underwear, burning their money in wastebaskets and listening to the Terror through the wall,

who got busted in their pubic beards returning through Laredo with a belt of marijuana for New York,

who ate fire in paint hotels or drank turpentine in Paradise Alley,[5] death, or purgatoried their torsos night after night

with dreams, with drugs, with waking nightmares, alcohol and cock and endless balls,

incomparable blind streets of shuddering cloud and lightning in the mind leaping toward poles of Canad a & Paterson,[6] illuminating all the motionless world of Time between,

Peyote solidities of halls, backyard green tree cemetery dawns, wine drunk-enness over the rooftops, storefront boroughs of (eahead joyride neon blinking traffic light, sun and moon and tree vibrations in the roaring winter dusks of Brooklyn, ashcan rantings and kind king light of mind,

who chained themselves to subways for the endless ride from Battery to holy Bronx[7] on benzedrine until the noise of wheels and children brought them down shuddering mouth-wracked and battered bleak of brain all drained of brilliance in the drear light of Zoo,

who sank all night in submarine light of Bickford's floated out and sat through the stale beer afternoon in desolate Fugazzi's, listening to the crack of doom on the hydrogen jukebox,

who talked continuously seventy hours from park to pad to bar to Bellevue[8] to museum to the Brooklyn Bridge,

a lost battalion of platonic conversationalists jumping down the stoops off fire escape s off windowsills off Empire State out of the moon,

yacketayakking screaming vomiting whispering facts and memories and anecdotes and eyeball kicks and shocks of hospitals and jails and wars, whole intellects disgorged in total recall for seven days and nights with bril-liant eyes, meat for the Synagogue cast on the pavement,

who vanished into nowhere Zen New Jersey leaving a trail of ambiguous picture postcards of Atlantic City Hall,

suffering Eastern sweats and Tangerian bone-grindings and migraines of China[9] under junk-withdrawal in Newark's bleak furnished room,

who wandered around and around at midnight in the railroad yard wondering where to go, and went, leaving no broken hearts,

who lit cigarettes in boxcars boxcars boxcars racketing through snow toward lonesome farms in grandfather night,

who studied Plotinus Poe St. John of the Cross[10] telepathy and bop kaballah[11] because the cosmos instinctively vibrated at their feet in Kansas,

who loned it through the streets of Idaho seeking visionary indian angels who were visionary indian angels,

who thought they were only mad when Baltimore gleamed in supernatural ecstasy,

who jumped in limousines with the Chinaman of Oklahoma on the impuls e of winter midnight streetlight smalltown rain,

who lounged hungry and lonesome through Houston seeking jazz or sex or soup, and followed the brilliant Spaniard to converse about America and Eternity, a hopeless task, and so took ship to Africa,

who disappeared into the volcanoes of Mexico leaving behind nothing but the shadow of dungaree s and the lava and ash of poetry scattered in fireplace Chicago, who reappeared on the West Coast investigating the FBI in beards and shorts with big pacifist eyes sexy in their dark skin passing out incomprehen-sible leaflets,

who burned cigarette holes in their arms protesting the narcotic tobacco haze of Capitalism,

who distributed Supercommunist pamphlets in Union Square weeping and undressing while the sirens of Los Alamos[12] wailed them down, and wailed down Wall,[13] and the Staten Island ferry also wailed,

who broke down crying in white gymnasiums naked and trembling before the machinery of other skeletons,

who bit detectives in the neck and shrieked with delight in policecars for committing no crime but their own wild cooking pederasty and intoxi-cation,

who howled on their knees in the subway and were dragged off the roof waving genitals and manuscripts,

who let themselves be fucked in the ass by saintly motorcyclists, and screamed with joy,

who blew and were blown by those human seraphim, the sailors, caresses of Atlantic and Caribbean love,

who balled in the morning in the evenings in rosegardens and the grass of public parks and cemeteries scattering their semen freely to whomever come who may,

who hiccupped endlessly trying to giggle but wound up with a sob behind a partition in a Turkish Bath when the blonde & naked angel cam e to pierce them with a sword,[14]

who lost their loveboys to the three old shrews of fate[15] the one eyed shrew of the heterosexual dollar the one eyed shrew that winks out of the womb and the one eyed shrew that does nothing but sit on her ass and snip the intellectual golden threads of the craftsman's loom,

who copulated ecstatic and insatiate with a bottle of beer a sweetheart a package of cigarettes a candle and fell off the bed, and continued along the floor and down the hall and ended fainting on the wall with a vision of ultimate cunt and come eluding the last gyzym of consciousness,

who sweetened the snatches of a million girls trembling in the sunset, and were red eyed in the morning but prepared to sweeten the snatch of the sunrise, flashing buttocks unde r barns and naked in the lake,

who went out whoring through Colorado in myriad stolen nightcars, N.C.,[16]

secret hero of these poems, cocksman and Adonis of Denver—joy to the memory of his innumerable lays of girls in empty lots & diner backyards, moviehouses' rickety rows, on mountaintops in caves or with gaunt wait-resses in familiar roadside lonely petticoat upliftings & especially secret gas-station solipsisms of Johns, & hometown alleys too,

who faded out in vast sordid movies, were shifted in dreams, woke on a sudden Manhattan, and picked themselves up out of basements hun-gover with heartless Tokay[17] and horrors of Third Avenue iron dreams & stumbled to unemployment offices,

who walked all night with their shoes full of blood on the

snowbank docks waiting for a door in the East River to open to a room full of steamheat and opium,

who created great suicidal drama s on the apartment cliff-banks of the Hud-son under the wartime blue floodlight of the moon & their heads shall be crowned with laurel in oblivion,

who ate the lamb stew of the imagination or digested the crab at the muddy bottom of the rivers of Bowery,[18]

who wept at the romance of the streets with their pushcarts full of onions and bad music,

who sat in boxes breathing in the darkness under the bridge, and rose up to build harpsichords in their lofts,

who coughed on the sixth floor of Harlem crowned with flame under the tubercular sky surrounded by orange crates of theology,

who scribbled all night rocking and rolling over lofty incantations which in the yellow morning were stanzas of gibberish,

who cooked rotten animals lung heart feet tail borsht & tortillas dreaming of the pure vegetable kingdom,

who plunged themselves under meat trucks looking for an egg,

who threw their watches off the roof to cast their ballot for Eternity outside of Time, & alarm clocks fell on their heads every day for the next decade,

who cut their wrists three times successively unsuccessfully, gave up and were forced to open antique stores where they thought they were grow-ing old and cried,

who were burned alive in their innocent flannel suits on Madison Avenue[19] amid blasts of leaden verse & the tanked-up clatter of the iron regiments of fashion & the nitroglycerine shrieks of the fairies of advertising & the mustard gas of sinister intelligent editors, or were run down by the drunken taxicabs of Absolute Reality,

who jumped off the Brooklyn Bridge this actually happened and walked away unknown and forgotten into the ghostly daze of Chinatown soup alley ways & firetrucks, not even one free beer,

who sang out of their windows in despair, fell out of the subway window, jumped in the filthy Passaic,[20] leaped on negroes, cried all over the street, danced on broken wineglasses barefoot smashed phonograph records of nostalgic European 1930's German jazz finished the whiskey and threw up groaning into the bloody toilet, moans in their ears and the blast of colossal steamwhistles,

who barreled down the highways of the past journeying to each other's hot-rod-Golgotha[21] jail-solitude watch or Birmingham jazz incarnation,

who drove crosscountry seventytwo hours to find out if I had a vision or you had a vision or he had a vision to find out Eternity,

who journeyed to Denver, who died in Denver, who cam e back to Denver & waited in vain, who watched over Denver & brooded & loned in Denver and finally went away to find out the Time, & now Denver is lonesome for her heroes,

who fell on their knees in hopeless cathedrals praying for each other's salvation and light and breasts, until the soul illuminated its hair for a second,

who crashed through their minds in jail waiting for impossible criminals with golden heads and the charm of reality in their hearts who sang sweet blues to Alcatraz,

who retired to Mexico to cultivate a habit, or Rocky Mount to tender Buddha or Tangiers to boys or Southern Pacific to the black locomotive or Har-vard to Narcissus to Woodlawn"[22] to the daisychain or grave,

who demanded sanity trials accusing the radio of hypnotism & were left with their insanity & their hands & a hung jury,

who threw potato salad at CCNY lecturers on Dadaism[23] and subsequently presented themselves on the granite steps of the madhouse with shaven heads and harlequin speech of suicide, demanding instantaneous lobot-omy,

and who were given instead the concrete void of insulin metrasol electricity hydrotherapy psychotherapy occupational therapy pingpong & amnesia,

who in humorless protest overturned only one sypboli c pingpong table, rest-ing briefly in catatonia,

returning years later truly bald except for a wig of blood, and tears and fin-gers, to the visible madman doom of the wards of the madtowns of the East,

Pilgrim State's Rockland's and Greystone's[24] foetid halls, bickering with the echoes of the soul, rocking and rolling in the midnight solitude-bench dolmen-realms of love, dream of life a nightmare, bodies turned to stone as heavy as the moon,

with mother finally* * * * * * *, and the last fantastic book flung out of the tenement window, and the last door closed at 4 AM and the last tele-phone slammed at the wall in reply and the last furnished room emptied down to the last piece of mental furniture, a yellow paper rose twisted on a wire hanger in the closet, and even that imaginary, nothing but a hopeful little bit of hallucination— ah, Carl,[25] while you are not safe I a m not safe, and now you're really in the total animal soup of time— and who therefore ran through the icy streets obsessed with a sudden flash of the alchemy of the us e of the ellipse the catalog the meter & the vibrating plane,

who dreamt and made incarnate gaps in Time & Space through image s jux-taposed, and trapped the archangel of the soul between 2 visual images and joined the elemental verbs and set the noun and dash of conscious-ness together jumping with sensation of Pater Omnipotens Aeterna Deus[26]

to recreate the syntax and measur e of poor human prose and stand before you speechless and intelligent and shaking with shame, rejected yet confessing out the soul to conform to the rhythm of thought in his naked and endless head,

the madman bu m and angel beat in Time, unknown, yet putting down here what might be left to say in time come after death,

and rose reincarnate in the ghostly clothes of jazz in the goldhorn shadow of the band and blew the suffering of America's naked mind for love into an eli eli lamma lamma sabacthani[27] saxophone cry that shivered the cities down to the last radio

with the absolute heart of the poem of life butchered out of their own bodies good to eat a thousand years.

## Notes

1. Ginsberg met Solomon (b.1928) while both were patients in the Columbia Psychiatric Institute in 1949 and called him "an intuitive Bronx Dadaist and prose-poet." Many details in "Howl" come from the "apocryphal history" that Solomon told Ginsberg in 1949. In "More Mishaps" (1968), Solomon admits that these adventures were "compounded partly of truth, but for the most [of] raving self-justification, crypto-bohemian boasting...effeminate prancing and esoteric aphorisms."

2. In one sense, a person who can supply drugs.

3. The elevated railway in New York City; also, a Hebrew word for God.

4. Refers to Ginsberg's apocalyptic vision of the English poet William Blake (1757 — 1827).

5. A tenement courtyard in New York's East Village; setting of Kerouac's The Subterraneans (1958).

6. Ginsberg's hometown, also the town celebrated by William Carlos Williams in his long poem Paterson.

7. Opposite ends of a New York subway line; the Bronx Zoo was the northern terminus.

8. New York public hospital to which psychiatric patients may be committed.

9. African and Asian sources of drugs.

10. Spanish visionary and poet (1542 — 1591), author of The Dark Night of the Soul. Plotinus (205 — 270), visionary philosopher. Edgar

Allan Poe (1809 — 1849), American poet and author of supernatural tales.

11. A mystical tradition of interpretation of Hebrew scripture. "Bop": jazz style of the 1940s.

12. In New Mexico, a center for the development of the atomic bomb. Union Square was a gathering place for radical speakers in New York in the 1930s.

13. Wall Street, but also alludes to the Wailing Wall, a place of public lamentation in Jerusalem.

14. An allusion to The Ecstasy of St.Teresa, a sculpture by Lorenzo Bernini (1598 — 1680 ) based on St.Teresa's (1515 — 1582) distinctly erotic description of a religious vision.

15. In Greek mythology, goddesses who determine a mortal's life by spinning out a length of thread and cutting it at the time of death.

16. Neal Cassady, hip companion of Jack Kerouac and the original Dean Moriarty, one of the leading figures in On the Road.

17. A naturally sweet wine made in Hungary.

18. Southern extension of Third Avenue in New York City; traditional haunt of derelicts and alcoholics.

19. Center of New York advertising agencies.

20. River flowing past Paterson, New Jersey.

21. The place in ancient Judea where Jesus was believed to have been crucified; also known as Calvary.

22. A cemetery in the Bronx. The Southern Pacific is a railroad company. The references in this line are to the lives of Kerouac, Cassidy, and William Burroughs (an author and fellow Beat).

23. Artistic cult of absurdity (c.1916 — 1920). "CCNY": City College of New York. This and the following incidents probably derived from the "apocryphal history of my adventures" related by Solomon to Ginsberg.

24. Three psychiatric hospitals near New York. Solomon was institutionalized at Pilgrim State and Rockland: Ginsberg's mother, Naomi, was permanently institutionalized at Greystone after years of suffering hallucinations and paranoid attacks. She died there in 1956, the year after "Howl" was written.

25. Solomon.

26. All Powerful Father, Eternal God (Latin). An allusion to a phrase used by the French painter Paul Cezanne (1839 — 1906), in a letter describing the effects of nature (1904). Ginsberg, in an interview, compared his own method of sharply juxtaposed images with Cezanne's foreshortening of perspective in landscape painting.

27. Christ's last words on the Cross: My God. my God, why have you forsaken me? (Aramaic). 1. Ginsberg's own annotation in the facsimile edition of the poem reads: " 'Moloch': or Molech, the Canaanite fire god, whose worship was marked by parents' burning their children as proprietary sacrifice. 'And thou shalt not let any of thy seed pass through the fire to Molech'[Leviticus 18:21].'"

## Questions

1. Try to make a comparison with Whitman's Song of Myself.
2. Make a further study on the Beat Generation.

### （3）Maxine Hong Kingston (b.1940)

Maxine Hong Kingston was born in Stockton, California, to parents who had emigrated from China. Her parents, feeling the fate of roulette, named their daughter Maxine after a lucky blonde gambler they knew, hoping she could bring good luck to her family. Before they emigrated, Kingston's father was a schoolteacher and a poet; her mother was a rural doctor in a profession consisting almost entirely of men. In America they took on quite different identities: her father, at times unemployed, worked in a gambling house and a laundromat; her mother raised six children, of whom Kingston was the eldest.

She graduated from the Department of British Literature at the University of California at Berkeley in 1962, and was elected a Fellow of the Humanities and Natural Sciences in 1992. She won the National Book Award for Outstanding Literary Contribution in 2008. Maxine Hong Kingston has created influential novels such as *The Woman Warrior: Memoirs of a Girlhood among Ghosts* (1976), *China Men* (1980), and *Tripmaster Monkey* (1989), which have established her position in the history of Chinese American literature.

Her works involve a wide range of themes, but from the publication of her works, main themes can be found throughout: feminism (*The Woman Warrior*), racial egalitarianism (*China Men*), building of ethnic cultural attributes (*Tripmaster Monkey*), and world pacifism (*The Fifth Book of Peace* (2004)). *The Woman Warrior: Memoirs of a Girlhood among Ghosts*, her maiden work, takes China as the background and shows the childhood life of a little girl living in a struggling Chinese circle, and the real life of the women around her through the extremely imaginative fiction and simple descriptions. The work showcases the reality of discrimination, depressive, poor, and unstable Chinese life in a Chinatown with the stories of Chinese supernatural ghosts, fairy spirits, and the heroines' battles for freedom. The expression is delicate and euphemistic, and the style is unrestrained and lucid, which impresses people with sweet enjoyment.

The following is the first section of *The Woman Warrior*, which tells the story of "my" aunt through the first-person narrator "I," hearing about the family tragedy from the mother, "My aunt married, and soon her husband went to the United States for gold. A few years later, my aunt was pregnant. She was accused of committing adultery with others and violated the taboo for women, so the whole village was angry. On the night that my aunt gave birth, they smashed her house. The aunt had nothing to do but was forced to give birth in the pigpen, and then she threw herself into the well with the baby in her arms. My aunt, the no name woman, is a typical case of oppression by male power in the feudal society."

## No Name Woman

"You must not tell anyone," my mother said, "what I am about to tell you. In China your father had a sister who killed herself. She jumped into the family well. We say that your father has all brothers because it is as if she had never been born.

"In 1924 just a few days after our village celebrated seventeen hurry-up weddings—to make sure that every young man who went 'out on the road' would responsibly come home—your father and his brothers and your grandfather and his brothers and your aunt's new husband sailed for America, the Gold Mountain. It was your grandfather's last trip. Those lucky enough to get contracts waved good-bye from the decks. They fed and guarded the stowaways and helped them off in Cuba, New York, Bali, Hawaii. 'We'll meet in California next year,' they said. All of them sent money home.

"I remember looking at your aunt one day when she and I were dressing; I had not noticed before that she had such a protruding melon of a stomach. But I did not think, 'She's pregnant,' until she began to look like other pregnant women, her shirt pulling and the white tops of her black pants showing. She could not have been pregnant, you see, because her husband had been gone for years. No one said anything. We did not discuss it. In early summer she was ready to have the child, long after the time when it could have been possible.

"The village had also been counting. On the night the baby was to be born the villagers raided our house. Some were crying. Like a great saw, teeth strung with lights, files of people walked zigzag across our land, tearing the rice. Their lanterns doubled in the disturbed black water, which drained away through the broken bunds.[1]

As the villagers closed in, we could see that some of them, probably men and women we knew well, wore white masks. The people with long hair hung it over their faces. Women with short hair made it stand up on end. Some had tied white bands around their foreheads, arms, and legs.

"At first they threw mud and rocks at the house. Then they threw eggs and began slaughtering our stock. We could hear the animals scream their deaths—the roosters, the pigs, a last great roar from the ox. Familiar wild heads flared in our night windows; the villagers encircled us. Some of the faces stopped to peer at us, their eyes rushing like searchlights. The hands flattened against the panes, framed heads, and left red prints.

"The villagers broke in the front and the back doors at the same time, even though we had not locked the doors against them. Their knives dripped with the blood of our animals. They smeared blood on the doors and walls. One woman swung a chicken, whose throat she had slit, splattering blood in red arcs about her. We stood together in the middle of our house, in the family hall with the pictures and tables of the ancestors around us, and looked straight ahead.

"At that time the house had only two wings. When the men cam e back, we would build two more to enclose our courtyard and a third one to begin a second courtyard. The villagers pushed through both wings, even your grandparents' rooms, to find your aunt's, which was also mine until the men returned. From this room a new wing for one of the younger families would grow. They ripped up her clothes and shoes and broke her combs, grinding them underfoot. They tore her work from the loom. They scattered the cooking fire and rolled the new weaving in it. We could hear them in the kitchen breaking our bowls and banging the pots. They overturned the great waisthigh earthenware jugs; duck eggs, pickled fruits, vegetables burst out and mixed in acrid torrents. The old woman from the next field swept a broom through the air and loosed the spirits-of-the-broom over our heads. 'Pig,' 'Ghost.' 'Pig,' they sobbed and scolded while they ruined our house.

"When they left, they took sugar and oranges to bless themselves. They cut pieces from the dead animals. Some of them took bowls that were not broken and clothes that were not torn. Afterward we swept up the rice and sewed it back up into sacks. But the smells from the spilled preserves lasted. Your aunt gave birth in the pigsty that night. The next morning when I went for the water, I found her and the baby plugging up the family well.

"Don't let your father know that I told you. He denies her. Now that you have started to menstruate, what happened to her could happen to you. Don't humiliate us. You wouldn't like to be forgotten as if you had never been born. The villagers are watchful."

Whenever she had to warn us about life, my mother told stories that ran like this one, a story to grow up on. She tested our strength to establish realities. Those in the emigrant generations who could not reassert brute survival died young and far from home. Those of us in the first American generations have had to figure out how the invisible world the emigrants built around our childhoods fits in solid America.

The immigrants confused the gods by diverting their curses, misleading them with crooked streets and false names. They must try to confuse their offspring as well, who, I suppose, threaten them in similar ways—always trying to get things straight, always trying to name the unspeakable. The Chines e I know hide their names;

sojourners take new name s when their lives change and guard their real name s with silence.

Chinese-Americans, when you try to understand what things in you are Chinese, how do you separate what is peculiar to childhood, to poverty, insanities, one family, your mother who marked your growing with stories, from what is Chinese? What is Chines e tradition and what is the movies?

If I want to learn what clothes my aunt wore, whether flashy or ordinary, I would have to begin, "Remember Father's drowned-in-the-well sister?" I cannot ask that. My mother has told me once and for all the useful parts. She will add nothing unless powered by Necessity, a riverbank that guides her life. She plants vegetable gardens rather than lawns; she carries the oddshaped tomatoes home from the fields and eats food left for the gods.

Whenever we did frivolous things, we used up energy; we flew high kites. We children came up off the ground over the melting cones our parents brought home from work and the American movie on New Year's Day— Oh, You Beautiful Doll with Betty Grable one year, and She Wore a Yellow Ribbon with John Wayne another year. After the one carnival ride each, we paid in guilt; our tired father counted his change on the dark walk home.

Adultery is extravagance. Could people who hatch their own chicks and eat the embryos and the heads for delicacies and boil the feet in vinegar for party food, leaving only the gravel, eating even the gizzard lining—could such people engender a prodigal aunt? To be a woman, to have a daughter in starvation time was a waste enough. My aunt could not have been the lone romantic who gave up everything for sex. Women in the old China did not choose. Some man had commanded her to lie with him and be his secret evil. I wonder whether he masked himself when he joined the raid on her family.

Perhaps she had encountered him in the fields or on the mountain where the daughters-in-law collected fuel. Or perhaps he first noticed her in the marketplace. He was not a stranger because the village housed no strangers. She had to have dealings with him other than sex. Perhaps he worked an adjoining field, or he sold her the cloth for the dress she sewed and wore. His demand must have surprised, then terrified her. She obeyed him; she always did as she was told.

When the family found a young man in the next village to be her husband, she had stood tractably beside the best rooster, his proxy,[2] and promised before they met that she would be his forever. She was lucky that he was her age and she would be the first wife, an advantage secure now. The night she first saw him, he had sex with her. Then he left for America. She had almost forgotten what he looked like. When she tried to envision him, she only saw the black and white face in the group photograph the men had had taken before leaving.

The other man was not, after all, much different from her husband. They both gave orders: she followed. "If you tell your family, I'll beat you. I'll kill you. Be here again next week." No one talked sex, ever. And she might have separated the rapes from the rest of living if only she did not have to buy her oil from him or gather wood in the same forest. I want her fear to have lasted just as long as rape lasted so that the fear could have been contained. No drawnout fear. But women at sex hazarded birth and hence lifetimes. The fear did not stop but permeated everywhere. Sh e told the man, "I think I'm pregnant." He organized the raid against her.

On nights when my mother and father talked about their life back home, sometime s they mentioned an "outcast table" whose business they still seemed to be settling, their voices tight. In a commensal tradition,[3] where food is precious, the powerful older people mad e wrongdoers eat alone. Instead of letting them start separate new lives like the Japanese, who could become samurais and geishas,[4] the Chinese family, faces averted but eyes glowering sideways, hung on to the offenders and fed them leftovers. My aunt must have lived in the same house as my parents and eaten at an outcast table. My mother spoke about the raid as if she had seen it, when she and my aunt, a daughter-in-law to a different household, should not have been living together at all. Daughters-in-law lived with their husbands' parents, not their own; a synonym for marriage in Chines e is "taking a daughter-inlaw." Her husband's parents could have sold her, mortgaged her, stoned her. But they had sent her back to her own mother and father, a mysterious act hinting at disgraces not told me. Perhaps they had thrown her out to deflect the avengers.

She was the only daughter; her four brothers went with her father, husband, and uncles "out on the road" and for some years became western men. When the goods were divided among the family, three of the brothers took land, and the youngest, my father, chose an education. After my grandparents gave their daughter away to her husband's family, they had dispensed all the adventure and all the property. They expected her alone to keep the traditional ways, which her brothers, now among the barbarians, could fumble without detection. The heavy, deep-rooted women were to maintain the past against the flood, safe for returning. But the rare urge west had fixed upon our family, and so my aunt crossed boundaries not delineated in space.

The work of preservation demand s that the feelings playing about in one's guts not be turned into action. Just watch their passing like cherry blossoms. But perhaps my aunt, my forerunner, caught in a slow life, let dreams grow and fade and after some months or years went toward what persisted. Fear at the enormities of the forbidden kept her desires delicate, wire and bone. She looked at a man because she liked the way the hair was tucked behind his ears, or she liked the question-mark line of a long torso curving at the shoulder and straight at the hip. For warm eyes or a soft voice or a slow walk—that's all—a few hairs, a line, a brightness, a sound, a pace, she gave up family. She offered us up for a charm that vanished with tiredness, a pigtail that didn't toss when the wind died. Why, the wrong lighting could erase the dearest thing about him.

It could very well have been, however, that my aunt did not take subtle enjoyment of her friend, but, a wild woman, kept rollicking company. Imagining her free with sex doesn't fit, through. I don't know any women like that, or men either. Unless I see her life branching into mine, she gives me no ancestral help.

To sustain her being in love, she often worked at herself in the mirror, guessing at the colors and shape s that would interest him, changing them frequently in order to hit on the right combination. She wanted him to look back.

On a farm near the sea, a woman who tended her appearance reaped a reputation for eccentricity. All the married women blunt-cut their hair in flaps about their ears or pulled it back in tight buns. No nonsense. Neither style blew easily into heart-catching tangles. And at their weddings they displayed themselves in their long hair for the last time. "It brushed the backs of my knees," my mother tells me." It was braided, and even so, it brushed the backs of my knees."

At the mirror my aunt combed individuality into her bob. A bun could have been contrived to escape into black streamers blowing in the wind or in quiet wisps about her face, but only the older women in our picture album wear buns. She brushed her hair back from her forehead, tucking the flaps behind her ears. She looped a piece of thread, knotted into a circle between her index fingers and thumbs, and ran the double strand across her forehead. When she closed her fingers as if she were making a pair of shadow geese bite, the string twisted together catching the little hairs. Then she pulled the thread away from her skin, ripping the hair out neatly, her eyes watering from the needles of pain. Opening her fingers, she cleaned the thread, then rolled it along her hairline and the tops of her eyebrows. My mother did the same to me and my sisters and herself. I used to believe that the expression "caught by the short hairs" meant a captive held with a depilatory string. It especially hurt at the temples, but my mother said we were lucky we didn't have to have our feet bound when we were seven. Sisters used to sit on their beds and cry together, she said, as their mothers or their slave removed the bandage s for a few minute s each night and let the blood gush back into their veins. I hope that the man my aunt loved appreciated a smooth brow, that he wasn't just a tits-and-ass man.

Once my aunt found a freckle on her chin, at a spot that the almanac said predestined her for unhappiness. She dug it out with a hot needle and washed the wound with peroxide.

More attention to her looks than these pullings of hairs and pickings at spots would have caused gossip among the villagers. They owned work clothes and good clothes, and they wore good clothes for feasting the new seasons. But since a woman combing her hair hexes beginnings, my aunt rarely found an occasion to look her best. Women looked like great sea snails—the corded wood, babies, and laundry they carried were the whorls on their backs. The Chines e did not admire a bent back; goddesses and warriors stood straight. Still there must have been a marvelous freeing of beauty when a worker laid down her burden and stretched and arched.

Such commonplace loveliness, however, was not enough for my aunt. She dreamed of a lover for the fifteen days of New Year's, the time for families to exchange visits, money, and food. She plied her secret comb. And sure enough she cursed the year, the family, the village, and herself.

Even as her hair lured her imminent lover, many other men looked at her. Uncles, cousins, nephews, brothers would have looked, too, had they been home between journeys. Perhaps they had already been restraining their curiosity, and they left, fearful that their glances, like a field of nesting birds, might be startled and caught. Poverty hurt, and that was their first reason for leaving. But another, final reason for leaving the crowded house was the never-said.

She may have been unusually beloved, the precious only daughter, spoiled and mirror gazing because of the affection the family lavished on her. When her husband left, they welcomed the chance to take her back from the in laws; she could live like the little daughter for just a while longer. There are stories that my grandfather was different from other people, "crazy ever since the little Jap bayoneted him in the head." He used to put his naked penis on the dinner table, laughing. And one day he brought home a baby girl, wrapped up inside his brown western-style greatcoat.[5] He had traded one of his sons, probably my father, the youngest, for her. My grandmother made him trade back. When he finally got a daughter of his own, he doted on her. They must have all loved her, except perhaps my father, the only brother who never went back to China, having once been traded for a girl.

Brothers and sisters, newly men and women, had to efface their sexual color and present plain miens. Disturbing hair and eyes, a smile like no other, threatened the ideal of five generations living under one roof. To focus blurs, people shouted face to face and yelled from room to room. The immigrants I know have loud voices, unmodulated to American tones even after years away from the village where they called their friendships out across the fields. I have not been able to stop my mother's screams in public libraries or over telephones. Walking erect (knees straight, toes pointed forward, not pigeon-toed, which is Chinese-feminine) and speaking in an inaudible voice, I have tried to turn myself American-feminine. Chinese communication was loud, public. Only sick people had to whisper. But at the dinner table, where the family members came nearest one another, no one could talk, not the outcasts nor any eaters. Every word that falls from the mouth is a coin lost. Silently they gave and accepted food with both hands. A preoccupied child who took his bowl with one hand got a sideways glare. A complete moment of total attention is due everyone alike. Children and lovers have no singularity here, but my aunt used a secret voice, a separate attentiveness.

She kept the man's name to herself throughout her labor and dying; she did not accuse him that he be punished with her. To save her inseminator's name she gave silent birth.

He may have been somebody in her own household, but intercourse with a man outside the family would have been no less abhorrent. All the village were kinsmen, and the titles shouted in loud country voices never let kinship be forgotten. Any man within visiting distance would have been neutralized as a lover— "brother," "younger brother," "older brother"—one hundred and fifteen relationship titles. Parents researched birth charts probably not so much to assure good fortune as to circumvent incest in a population that has but one hundred surnames. Everybody has eight million relatives. How useless then sexual mannerisms, how dangerous.

As if it cam e from an atavism[6] deeper than fear, I used to add "brother" silently to boys' names. It hexed the boys, who would or would not ask me to dance, and made them less scary and as familiar and deserving of benevolence as girls.

But, of course, I hexed myself also—no dates. I should have stood up, both arms waving, and shouted out across libraries, "Hey, you! Love me back." I had no idea, though, now to make attraction selective, how to control its direction and magnitude. If I made myself American-pretty so that the five or six Chines e boys in the class fell in love with me, everyone else—the Caucasian, Negro, and Japanese boys—would too. Sisterliness, dignified and honorable, made much more sense.

Attraction eludes control so stubbornly that whole societies designed to organize relationships among people cannot keep order, not even when they bind people to one another from childhood and raise them together. Among the very poor and the wealthy, brothers married their adopted sisters, like doves. Our family allowed some romance, paying adult brides' prices and providing dowrics so that their sons and daughters could marry strangers. Marriage promise s to turn strangers into friendly relatives—a nation of siblings.

In the village structure, spirits shimmered among the live creatures, balanced and held in equilibrium by time and land. But one human being flaring up into violence could open up a black hole, a maelstrom[7] that pulled in the sky. The frightened villagers, who depended on one another to maintain the real, went to my aunt to show her a personal, physical representation of the break she had made in the "roundness." Misallying couple s snapped off the future, which was to be embodied in true offspring. The villagers punished her for acting as if she could have a private life, secret and apart from them.

If my aunt had betrayed the family at a time of large grain yields and peace, when many boys were born, and wings were being built on many houses, perhaps she might have escaped such severe punishment. But the men — hungry, greedy, tired of planting in dry soil—had been forced to leave the village in order to send food-money home. There were ghost plagues, bandit plagues, wars with the Japanese, floods. My Chines e brother and sister had died of an unknown sickness. Adultery, perhaps only a mistake during good times, became a crime when the village needed food.

The round moon cakes and round doorways, the round tables of graduated size that fit one roundness inside another, round windows and rice bowls—these talismans had lost their power to warn this family of the law: a family must be whole, faithfully keeping the descent line by having sons to feed the old and the dead, who in turn look after the family. The villagers came to show my aunt and her lover-in-hiding a broken house. The villagers were speeding up the circling of events because she was too shortsighted to see that her infidelity had already harmed the village, that waves of consequences would return unpredictably, sometime s in disguise, as now, to hurt her. This roundness had to be mad e coin-sized so that she would see its circumference : punish her at the birth of her baby. Awaken her to the inexorable. People who refused fatalism because they could invent small resources insisted on culpability. Deny accidents and wrest fault from the stars.

After the villagers left, their lanterns now scattering in various directions toward home, the family broke their silence and cursed her. "Aiaa, we're going to die. Death is coming. Death is coming.

Look what you've done. You've killed us. Ghost! Dead ghost! Ghost! You've never been born." She ran out into the fields, far enough from the house so that she could no longer hear their voices, and pressed herself against the earth, her own land no more. When she felt the birth coming, she thought that she had been hurt. Her body seized together. "They've hurt me too much," she thought. "This is gall, and it will kill me." With forehead and knees against the earth, her body convulsed and then relaxed. She turned on her back, lay on the ground. The black well of sky and stars went out and out and out forever; her body and her complexity seemed to disappear. She was one of the stars, a bright dot in blackness, without home, without a companion, in eternal cold and silence. An agoraphobia[8] rose in her, speeding higher and higher, bigger and bigger; she would not be able to contain it; there would be no end to fear.

Flayed, unprotected against space, she felt pain return, focusing her body. This pain chilled her—a cold, steady kind of surface pain. Inside, spasmodically, the other pain, the pain of the child, heated her. For hours she lay on the ground, alternately body and space. Sometime s a vision of normal comfort obliterated reality: she saw the family in the evening gambling at the dinner table, the young people massaging their elder's backs. She saw them congratulating one another, high joy on the mornings the rice shoots came up. When these pictures burst, the stars drew yet further apart. Black space opened.

She got to her feet to fight better and remembered that old-fashioned women gave birth in their pigsties to fool the jealous, pain-dealing gods, who do not snatch piglets. Before the next spasm s could stop her, she ran to the pigsty, each step a rushing out into emptiness. She climbed over the fence and knelt in the dirt. It was good to have a fence enclosing her, a tribal person alone.

Laboring, this woman who had carried her child as a foreign growth that sickened her every day, expelled it at last. She reached down to touch the hot, wet, moving mass, surely smaller than anything human, and could feel that it was human after all—fingers, toes, nails, nose. She pulled it up on to her belly, and it lay curled there, but in the air, feet precisely tucked one under the other. She opened her loose shirt and buttoned the child inside. After resting, it squirmed and thrashed and she pushed it up to her breast. It turned its head this way and that until it found her nipple. There, it made little snuffling noises. She clenched her teeth at its preciousness, lovely as a young calf, a piglet, a little dog.

She may have gone to the pigsty as a last act of responsibility: she would protect this child as she had protected its father. It would look after her soul, leaving supplies on her grave. But how would this tiny child without family find her grave when there would be no marker for her anywhere, neither in the earth nor the family hall? No one would give her a family hall name. She had taken the child with her into the wastes. At its birth the two of them had felt the same raw pain of separation, a wound that only the family pressing tight could close. A child with no descent line would not soften her life but only trail after her, ghostlike, begging her to give it purpose. At dawn the villagers on their way to the fields would stand around the fence and look.

Full of milk, the little ghost slept. When it awoke, she hardened her breasts against the milk that crying loosens. Toward morning she picked up the baby and walked to the well.

Carrying the baby to the well shows loving. Otherwise abandon it. Turn its face into the mud. Mothers who love their children take them along. It was probably a girl; there is some hope of forgiveness for boys.

"Don't tell anyone you had an aunt. Your father does not want to hear her name. She has never been born." I have believed that sex was unspeakable and words so strong and fathers so frail that "aunt" would do my father mysterious harm. I have thought that my family, having settled among immigrants who had also been their neighbors in the ancestral land, needed to clean their name, and a wrong word would incite the kinspeople even here. But there is more to this silence: they want me to participate in her punishment. And I have.

In the twenty years since I heard this story I have not asked for details nor said my aunt's name ; I do not know it. People who can comfort the dead can also chase after them to hurt them further—a reverse ancestor worship. The real punishment was not the raid swiftly inflicted by the villagers, but the family's deliberately forgetting her. Her betrayal so maddened them, they saw to it that she would suffer forever, even after death. Always hungry, always needing, she would have to beg food from other ghosts, snatch and steal it from those whose living descendants give them gifts. She would have to fight the ghosts massed at crossroads for the buns a few thoughtful citizens leave to decoy her away from village and home so that the ancestral spirits could feast unharassed. At peace, they could act like gods, not ghosts, their descent lines providing them with paper suits and dresses, spirit money, paper houses, paper automobiles, chicken, meat, and rice[9] into eternity—essence s delivered up in smoke and flames, steam and incense rising from each rice bowl. In an attempt to make the Chinese care for people outside the family, Chairman Mao[10] encourages us now to give our paper replicas to the spirits of outstanding soldiers and workers, no matter whose ancestors they may be. My aunt remains forever hungry. Goods are not distributed evenly among the dead.

My aunt haunts me—her ghost drawn to me because now, after fifty years of neglect, I alone devote page s of paper to her, though not origamied into houses and clothes. I do not think she always means me well. I am telling on her, and she was a spite suicide, drowning herself in the drinking water. The Chinese are always very frightened of the drowned one, whose weeping ghost, wet hair hanging and skin bloated, waits silently by the water to pull down a substitute.

1976

## Notes

1. Embankments built to control the How of water, here probably irrigation water.

2. Someone or something that has the power to substitute or act for another.

3. A tradition in which people eat together at the same table.

4. In Japanese society women trained to entertain men. Samurai: the Japanese warrior elite.

5. A heavy overcoat.

6. A trait with origins farther hack than the preceding generation — a throwback.

7. A powerful, violent whirlpool.

8. An abnormal fear of open space.

9. Traditionally, offerings left at the graves of ancestors.

10. Mao Tse-Tung (1893 — 1976), head of the Chinese Communist Party and leader of China from 1949 to 1959 and 1969 to 1976.

## Questions

1. Try to analyze "my" point of view towards the sister of "my" father.

2. Do you agree that the nameless woman expressed her pursuit of freedom and the courage to fight against the feudal barriers? Why or why not?

### (4) Saul Bellow (1915—2005)

Saul Bellow (June 10,1915—April 5,2005) was an American writer, known as a spokesman for American contemporary literature. He was born in Lachine, Quebec, grew up in the Jewish ghetto of Montreal, and later moved to Chicago when he was nine. He was admitted to the University of Chicago in 1933 and transferred to Northwestern two years later, where he graduated in 1937 with a BA in Sociology and Anthropology. Bellow spent most of his time teaching in college, except briefly as an editor, journalist, and a short period of service on merchant ships.

He was made chairman of the "Social Thought Committee" at

the University of Chicago and received an honorary doctorate from Harvard University, Yale University, and Northwestern University.

During his years from 1936 to 1987, Saul Bellow published eleven novels, three novellas, four collections of short stories, and one drama in his life. In addition, he has also published three non-fiction works, including travel notes, essays, and speech collections. His early writings of *Dangling Man*(1944) and *The Victim*(1947)got high praises among the critics. In 1953, he published *The Adventure of Augie March*, which won him the National Book Award for the first time. In 1964, his *Herzog* won the National Book Award for the second time. *Mr.Sammler's Planet* (1970) allowed him to win it for the third time. In 1975, Bellow was awarded the Pulitzer Prize for *Humboldt's Gift*. In 1976, he was awarded the Nobel Prize for literature.

Saul Bellow's position in the postwar American literary world is beyond doubt, and his achievements in fiction and contributions to American literature in the 20th century may only be compared to Hemingway and Faulkner. Most of his works reveal the mental anguish of the middle-class intellectuals, and reflect the spiritual crisis of the contemporary American "rich society." Many critics see Bellow as a successor to the ideas of the American transcendentalists Emerson, Thoreau, and Whitman. Most critics believe that Bellow's novels emphasize the psychological description and have a deeper discussion of religion. In these comprehensive comments, despite different entry points and different conclusions, Bellow is considered to be an "anti-modernist" and an "affirmative humanist" among many important critics. Bellow focuses on the internal dialogue of the characters, emphasizes the protagonist's consciousness of wandering, and combines the traditional picturesque narrative mode with the modern stream of consciousness technique.

*Seize the Day* is a highly praised novella by Bellow published in 1956. Set in New York City, it describes the protagonist Tommy Wilhelm's experience in a short day of life. At the beginning of the story, Wilhelm is living at the Grorina Hotel (where his wealthy father, Doctor Edler, also lives). He was now in trapped there—he was separated from his wife, lost his job, and could not get his father's sympathy and help. He gave his last $700 to the mysterious psychologist Dr.Tamkin to invest, but, in the end, the investment failed. Both his money and Dr.Tamkin disappeared. Even worse, his father turned a deaf ear to his help again. The story ended with Wilhelm attending a stranger's funeral, full tears.

The following is selected from Chapter VI, which mainly describes how Wilhelm and Dr. Tamkin ate together in the buffet room. On their way back to the market after lunch, Tamkin was called in by Old Mr.Rappaport to buy cigars; afterwards, he returns to the market to find that Dr. Tamkin is missing, so he then goes to the hotel and toilet to look for Tamkin. In this chapter, the author mainly reveals the simplicity and helplessness of Wilhelm and Dr. Tamkin's glib and deceptive Philistine image.

## Chapter VI

Rye was still ahead when they went out to lunch, and lard was holding its own.

They ate in the cafeteria with the gilded front. There was the same art inside as outside. The food looked sumptuous. Whole fishes were framed like pictures with carrots, and the salads were like terraced landscapes or like Mexican pyramids; slices of lemon and onion and radishes were like sun and moon and stars; the cream pies were about a foot thick and the cakes swollen as if sleepers had baked them in their dreams.

"What'll you have?" said Tamkin.

"Not much. I ate a big breakfast. I'll find a table. Bring me some yogurt and crackers and a cup of tea. I don't want to spend much time over lunch."

Tamkin said, "You've got to eat."

Finding an empty place at this hour was not easy. The old people idled and gossiped over their coffee. The elderly ladies were rouged and mascaraed and hennaed and used blue hair rinse and eye shadow and wore costume jewelry, and many of them were proud and stared at you with expressions that did not belong to their age. Were there no longer any respectable old ladies who knitted and cooked and looked after their grandchildren? Wilhelm's grandmother had dressed him in a sailor suit and danced him on her knee, blew on the porridge for him and said, "Admiral, you must eat." But what was the use of remembering this so late in the day?

He managed to find a table, and Dr. Tamkin came along with a tray piled with plates and cups. He had Yankee pot roast, purple cabbage, potatoes, a big slice of watermelon, and two cups of coffee. Wilhelm could not even swallow his yogurt. His chest pained him still. At once Tamkin involved him in a lengthy discussion. Did he do it to stall Wilhelm and prevent him from selling out the rye–or to recover the ground lost when he had made Wilhelm angry by hints about the neurotic character? Or did he have no purpose except to talk?

"I think you worry a lot too much about what your wife and your father will say. Do they matter so much?" Wilhelm replied, "A person can become tired of looking himself over and trying to fix himself up. You can spend the entire second half of your life recovering from the mistakes of the first half."

"I believe your dad told me he had some money to leave you."

"He probably does have something."

"A lot?"

"Who can tell," said Wilhelm guardedly.

"You ought to think over what you'll do with it."

"I may, be too feeble to do anything by the time I get it. If I get anything."

"A thing like this you ought to plan out carefully. Invest it properly." He began to unfold schemes whereby you bought bonds, and used the bonds as security to buy something else and thereby earned twelve per cent safely on your money. Wilhelm failed to follow the details. Tamkin said, "If he made you a gift now, you wouldn't have to pay the inheritance taxes."

Bitterly, Wilhelm told him, "My father's death blots out all other considerations from his mind. He forces me to think about it, too. Then he hates me because he succeeds. When I get desperate–of course I think about money. But I don't want anything to happen to him. I certainly don't want him to die." Tamkin's brown eyes glittered shrewdly at him. "You don't believe it. Maybe it's not psychological. But on my word of honor,'A joke is a joke', but I don't want to joke about stuff like this. When dies, I'll be robbed, like. I'll have no more father."

"You love your old man?"

Wilhelm grasped at this. "Of course, of course I love him. My father. My mother–" As he said this, there was a great pull at the very center of his soul. When a fish strikes the line you feel the live force in your hand. A mysterious being beneath the water, driven by hunger, has taken the hook and rushes away and fights, writhing. Wilhelm never identified what struck within him. It did not reveal itself. It got away.

And Tamkin, the confuser of the imagination, began to tell, or to fabricate, the strange history of his father. "He was a great singer," he said. "He left us five kids because he fell in love with an opera soprano. I never held it against him, but admired the way he followed the life-principle. I wanted to do the same. Because of unhappiness, at a certain age, the brain starts to die back." (True, true! thought Wilhelm.) "Twenty years later I was doing experiments in Eastman Kodak, Rochester, and I found the old fellow. He had five more children." (False, false!) "He wept; he was ashamed. I had nothing against him. I naturally felt strange."

"My dad is something of a stranger to me, too," said Wilhelm, and he began to muse. Where is the familiar person he used to be? Or I used to be? Catherine–she won't even talk to me any more, my own sister. It may not be so much my trouble that Papa turns his back on as my confusion. It's too much. The ruins of life, and on top of that confusion–chaos and old night. Is it an easier farewell for Dad if we don't part friends? He should maybe do it angrily–"Blast you with my curse!" And why, Wilhelm further asked, should he or anybody else pity me; or why should I be pitied sooner than another fellow? It is my childish mind that thinks people are ready to give it just because you need it.

Then Wilhelm began to think about his own two sons and to wonder how he appeared to them, and what they would think of him. Right now he had an advantage,through baseball. When he went to fetch them, to go to Ebbets Field, though, he was not himself. He put on a front, but he felt as if he had swallowed a fistful of sand. The strange, familiar house, horribly awkward; the dog, Scissors, rolled over on his back and barked and whined. Wilhelm acted as if there were nothing irregular, but a weary heaviness came over him. On the way to Flatbush he would think up anecdotes about old Pigtown and Charlie Ebbets for the boys and reminiscences of the old stars, but it was very heavy going. They did not know how much he cared for them. No. It hurt him greatly and he blamed Margaret for turning them against him. She wanted to ruin him, while she wore the mask of kindness. Up in Roxbury he had to go and explain to the priest, who was not sympathetic. They don't care about individuals, their rules come first. Olive said she would marry him outside the Church when he was divorced. But Margaret would not let go. Olive's father was a pretty decent old guy, an osteopath,[1] and he understood what it was all about. Finally he said, "See here, I have to advise Olive. She is asking me. I am mostly a freethinker myself, but the girl has to live in this town." And by now Wilhelm and Olive had had a great many troubles and she was beginning to dread his days in Roxbury, she said. He trembled at offending this small, pretty, dark girl whom he adored. When she would get up late on Sunday morning she would wake him almost in tears at being late for Mass.[2] He would try to help her hitch her garters and smooth out her slip and dress even put on her hat with shaky hands; then he would rush her to church and drive in second gear in his forgetful way, trying to apologize and to calm her. She got out a block from church to avoid gossip. Even so she loved him, and she would have married him if he had obtained the divorce. But Margaret must have sensed this. Margaret would tell him he did not really want a divorce; he was afraid of it. He cried, "Take everything I've got, Margaret. Let me go to Reno. Don't you want to marry again?" No. She went out with other men, but took his money. She lived in order to punish him.

Dr. Tamkin told Wilhelm, "Your dad is jealous of you."

Wilhelm smiled. "Of me? That's rich."

"Sure. People are always jealous of a man who leaves his wife."

"Oh," said Wilhelm scornfully. "When it comes to wives he wouldn't have to envy me."

"Yes, and your wife envies you, too. She thinks, He's free and goes with young women. Is she getting old?"

"Not exactly old," said Wilhelm, whom the mention of his wife made sad. Twenty years ago, in a neat blue wool suit, in a soft hat made of the same cloth–he could plainly see her. He stooped his yellow head and looked under the hat at her clear, simple face, her living eyes moving, her straight small nose, her jaw beautifully painfully clear in its form. It was a cool day, but smelled the odor of pines in the sun, in the granite canyon. Just south of Santa Barbara, this was.

"She's forty-some years old," he said.

"I was married to a lush," said Tamkin. "A painful alcoholic. I couldn't take her out to dinner because she'd say she was going to the ladies' toilet and disappear in the bar. I'd ask the bartenders they shouldn't serve her. But I loved her deeply. She was the most spiritual woman of my entire experience."

"Where is she now?"

"Drowned," said Tamkin. "At Provincetown, Cape Cod. It must have been a suicide. She was that way–suicidal. I tried everything in my power to cure her. Because," said Tamkin, "my real calling is to be a healer. I get wounded. I suffer from it. I would like to escape from the sicknesses of others, but I can't. I am only on loan to myself, so to speak. I belong to humanity."

Liar! Wilhelm inwardly called him. Nasty lies. He invented a woman and killed her off and then called himself a healer, and made himself so earnest he looked like a bad-natured sheep. He's a puffed-up little bogus and humbug with smelly feet. A doctor! A doctor would wash himself. He believes he's making a terrific impression, and he practically invites you to take off your hat when he talks about himself; and he thinks he has an imagination, but he hasn't; neither is he smart.

Then what am I doing with him here, and why did I give him the seven hundred dollars? thought Wilhelm.

Oh, this was a day of reckoning. It was a day, he thought, on which, willing or not, he would take a good close look at the truth. He breathed hard and his misshapen hat came low upon his congested dark blond face. A rude look. Tamkin was a charlatan,[3] and furthermore he was desperate. And furthermore, Wilhelm had always known this about him. But he appeared to have worked it out at the back of his mind that Tamkin for thirty or forty years had gotten through many a tight place, that he would get through this crisis too and bring him, Wilhelm, to safety also. And Wilhelm realized that he was on Tamkin's back. It made him feel that he had virtually left the ground and was riding upon the other man. He was in the air. It was for Tamkin to take the steps.

The doctor, if he was a doctor, did not look anxious. But then his face did not have much variety. Talking always about spontaneous emotion and open receptors and free impulses, he was about as expressive as a pincushion.[4] When his hypnotic spell failed, his big underlip made him look weak-minded. Fear stared from his eyes, some times, so humble as to make you sorry for him. Once or twice Wilhelm had seen that look. Like a dog, he thought. Perhaps he didn't look it now, but he was very nervous. Wilhelm knew, but he could not afford to recognize this too openly. The doctor needed a little room, a little time. He should not be pressed now. So Tamkin went on, telling his tales.

Wilhelm said to himself, I am on his back–his back. I gambled seven hundred bucks, so I must take this ride. I have to go along with him. It's too late. I can't get off.

"You know," Tamkin said, "that blind old man Rappaport–he's pretty close to totally blind–is one of the most interesting personalities around here. If you could only get him to tell his true story. It's fascinating. This what he told me. You often hear about bigamists[5] with a secret life. But this old man never hid anything from anybody. He's a regular patriarch. Now, I'll tell you what he did. He had two whole families, separate and apart, one in Williamsburg and the other in The Bronx. The two wives knew about each other. The wife in The Bronx was younger; she's close to seventy now. When he got sore at one wife he went to live with the other one. Meanwhile he ran his chicken business in New Jersey. By one wife he had four kids, and by the other six. They're all grown, but they never have met their half-brothers and sisters and don't want to. The whole bunch of them are listed in the telephone book."

"I can't believe it," said Wilhelm.

"He told me this himself. And do you know what else?' When he had his eyesight he used to read a lot, but the only books he would read were by Theodore Roosevelt. He had a set in each of the places where he lived, and he brought his kids up on those books."

"Please," said Wilhelm, "don't feed me any more of this stuff, will you? Kindly do not—"

"In telling you this," said Tamkin with one of his hypnotic subtleties, "I do have a motive. I want you to see how some people free themselves from morbid guilt feelings and follow their instincts. Innately, the female knows how to cripple by sickening a man with guilt. It is a very special destruct, and she sends her curse to make a fellow impotent. As if she says, 'Unless I allow it, you will never more be a man.' But men like my old dad or Mr.Rappaport answer, 'Woman, what art thou to me?' You can't do that yet. You're a halfway case.[6] You want to follow your instinct, but you're too worried still. For instance, about your kids–"

"Now look here," said Wilhelm, stamping his feet. "One thing! Don't bring up my boys. Just lay off."

"I was only going to say that they are better off than with conflicts in the home."

"I'm deprived of my children." Wilhelm bit his lip. It was too late to turn away. The anguish struck him. "I pay and pay. I never see them. They grow up without me. She makes them like herself. She'll bring them up to be my enemies. Please let's not talk about this."

But Tamkin said, "Why do you let her make you suffer so? It defeats the original object in leaving her. Don't play her game. Now, Wilhelm, I'm trying to do you some good. I want to tell you, don't marry suffering. Some people do. They get married to it, and sleep and eat together, just as husband and wife. If they go with joy they think it's adultery."

When Wilhelm heard this he had, in spite of himself, to admit that there was a great deal in Tamkin's words. Yes, thought Wilhelm, suffering is the only kind of life they are sure they can have, and if they quit suffering they're afraid they'll have nothing. He knows it. This time the faker knows what he's talking about.

Looking at Tamkin he believed he saw all this confessed from his usually barren face. Yes, yes, he too. One hundred falsehoods, but at last one truth. Howling like a wolf from the city window. No one can bear it any more. Everyone is so full of it that at last everybody must proclaim it. It! It!

Then suddenly Wilhelm rose and said, "That's enough of this. Tamkin, let's go back to the market."

"I haven't finished my melon."

"Never mind that. You've had enough to eat. I want to go back."

Dr. Tamkin slid the two checks across the table. "Who paid yesterday? It's your turn, I think."

It was not until they were leaving the cafeteria that Wilhelm remembered definitely that he had paid yesterday too. But it wasn't worth arguing about.

Tamkin kept repeating as they walked down the street, that there were many who were dedicated to suffering. But he told Wilhelm, "I'm optimistic in your case, and I have seen a world of maladjustment. There's hope for you. You don't really want to destroy yourself. You're, trying hard to keep your feelings open, Wilhelm. I can see it. Seven per cent of this country is committing suicide by alcohol. Another three, maybe, narcotics. Another sixty just fading away into dust by boredom. Twenty more, who have sold their souls to the devil.

Then there's a small percentage of those who want to live. That's the only significant thing in the whole world of today. Those are the only two classes of people there are. Some want to live, but the great majority don't." This fantastic Tamkin began to surpass himself. "They don't. Or else why these wars? I'll tell you more," he said. "The love of the dying amounts to one thing; they want you to die with them. It's because they love you. Make no mistake."

True, true! thought Wilhelm, profoundly moved by these revelations. How does he know these things? How can he be such a jerk, and even perhaps an operator, a swindler, and understand so well what gives? I believe what he says. It simplifies much–everything. People are dropping like flies. I am trying to stay alive and work too hard at it. That's what's turning my brains.This working hard defeats its own end. At what point should I start over? Let me go back a ways and try once more.

Only a few hundred yards separated the cafeteria from the broker's, and within that short space Wilhelm turned again, in measurable degrees, from these wide considerations to the problems of the moment. The closer he approached to the market, the more Wilhelm had to think about money.

They passed the newsreel theater where the ragged shoeshine kids called after them. The same old bearded man with his bandaged beggar face and his tiny ragged feet and the old press clipping on his fiddle case to prove he had once been a concert violinist, pointed his bow at Wilhelm, saying, "You!" Wilhelm went by with worried eyes, bent on crossing Seventy-second Street. In full tumult the great afternoon current raced for Columbus Circle, where the mouth of midtown stood open and the skyscrapers gave back the yellow fire of the sun.

As they approached the polished stone front of the new office building, Dr. Tamkin said, "Well, isn't that old Rappaport by the door? I think he should carry a white cane, but he will never admit there's a single thing the matter with his eyes."

Mr.Rappaport did not stand well; his knees were sunk, while his pelvis only half filled his trousers. His suspenders held them, gaping.

He stopped Wilhelm with an extended hand, having, somehow recognized him' In his deep voice he commanded him, "Take me to the cigar store."

"You want me–? Tamkin!" Wilhelm whispered, "You take him."

Tamkin shook his head. "He wants you. Don't refuse the old gentleman." Significantly he said in a lower voice, "This minute is another instance of the 'here-and-now.' You have to live in this very minute, and you don't want to. A man asks you for help. Don't think of the market. It won't run away. Show your respect to the old boy. Go ahead. That may be more valuable."

"Take me," said the old chicken merchant again.

Greatly annoyed, Wilhelm wrinkled his face at Tamkin. He took the old man's big but light elbow at the bone. "Well, let's step on it," he said. "Or wait–I want to have a look at the board first to see how we're doing."

But Tamkin had already started Mr.Rappaport forward. He was walking, and he scolded Wilhelm, saying, "Don't leave me standing in the middle of the sidewalk. I'm afraid to get knocked over."

"Let's get a move on. Come." Wilhelm urged him as Tamkin went into the broker's.

The traffic seemed to come down Broadway out of the sky, where the hot spokes of the sun rolled from the south. Hot, stony odors rose from the subway grating in the street.

"These teen-age hoodlums worry me. I'm ascared of these Puerto Rican kids, and these young characters who take dope," said Mr.Rappaport. "They go around all hopped up."

"Hoodlums?" said Wilhelm. "I went to the cemetery and my mother's stone bench was split. I could have broken somebody's neck for that. Which store do you go to?"

"Across Broadway. That La Magnita sign next door to the Automat."

"What's the matter with this store here on this side?"

"They don't carry my brand, that's what's the matter."

Wilhelm cursed, but checked the words.

"What are you talking?"

"Those damn taxis," said Wilhelm. "They want everybody down."

They entered the cool, odorous shop. Mr.Rappaport put away his large cigars with great care in various pockets while Wilhelm muttered, "Come on, you old creeper. What a poky old character! The whole world waits on him." Rappaport did not offer Wilhelm a cigar, but, holding one up, he asked, "What do you say at the size of these, huh? They're Churchill-type cigars."

He barely crawls along, thought Wilhelm. His pants are dropping off because he hasn't got enough flesh for them to stick to. He's almost blind, and covered with spots, but this old man still makes money in the market. Is loaded with dough[7], probably. And I bet he doesn't give his children any. Some of them must be in their fifties. This is what keeps middle-aged men as children. He's master over the dough. Think–just think! Who controls everything? Old men of this type. Without needs. They don't need therefore they have. I need, therefore I don't have. That would be too easy.

"I'm older even than Churchill," said Rappaport.

Now he wanted to talk! But if you asked him a question in the market, he couldn't be bothered to answer.

"I bet you are," said Wilhelm. "Come, let's get going."

"I was a fighter, too, like Churchill," said the old man. "When we licked Spain I went into the Navy. Yes, I was a gob that time. What did I have to lose? Nothing. At the battle of San Juan Hill, Teddy Roosevelt kicked me off the beach."

"Come, watch the curb," said Wilhelm.

"I was curious and wanted to see what went on. I didn't have no business there, but I took a boat and rowed myself to the beach. Two of our guys was dead, layin' under the American flag to keep the flies off. So I says to the guy on duty, there, who was the sentry, 'Let's have a look at these guys. I want to see what went on here,' and he says, 'Naw,' [8] but I talked him into it. So he took off the flag and there were these two tall guys, both gentlemen, lying in their boots. They was very tall. The two of them had long mustaches. They were high-society boys. I think one of them was called Fish, from up the Hudson, a big-shot family. When I looked up, there was Teddy Roosevelt, with his hat off, and he was looking at these fellows, the only ones who got killed there. Then he says to me, 'What's the Navy want here? Have you got orders?' 'No, sir,' I says to him. 'Well, get the hell off the beach, then.'

Old Rappaport was very proud of this memory. "Everything he said had such snap, such class. Man! I love that Teddy Roosevelt," he said, "I love him!"

Ah, what people are! He is almost not with us, and his life is nearly gone, but T. R. once yelled at him, so he loves him. I guess it is love, too. Wilhelm smiled. So maybe the rest of Tamkin's story was true, about the ten children and the wives and the telephone directory.

He said, "Come on, come on, Mr.Rappaport," and hurried the old man back by the large hollow elbow; he gripped it through the thin cotton cloth. Re-entering the brokerage office where under the lights the tumblers were speeding with the clack of drumsticks upon wooden blocks, more than ever resembling a Chinese theater, Wilhelm strained his eyes to see the board.

The lard figures were unfamiliar. That amount couldn't be lard! They must have put the figures in the wrong slot. He traced the line back to the margin. It was down to 0.19, and had dropped twenty points since noon. And what about the contract of rye? It had sunk back to its earlier position, and they had lost their chance to sell.

Old Mr.Rappaport said to Wilhelm, "Read me my wheat figure."

"Oh, leave me alone for a minute," he said, and positively hid his face from the old man behind one hand. He looked for Tamkin, Tamkin's bald head, or Tamkin with his gray straw and the cocoa-colored band. He couldn't see him. Where was he? The seats next to Rowland were taken by strangers. He thrust himself over the one on the aisle, Mr.Rappaport's former place, and pushed at the back of the chair until the new occupant, a redheaded man with a thin, determined face, leaned forward to get out of his way but would not surrender the seat. "Where's Tamkin?" Wilhelm asked Rowland.

"Gee, I don't know. Is anything wrong?"

"You must have seen him. He came in a while back."

"No, but I didn't."

Wilhelm fumbled out a pencil from the top pocket of his coat and began to make calculations. His very fingers were numb, and in his agitation he was afraid he made mistakes with the decimal points and went over the subtraction and multiplication like a schoolboy at an exam. His heart, accustomed to many sorts of crisis, was now a new panic. And, as he had dreaded, he was wiped out. It was unnecessary to ask the German manager. He could see for himself that the electronic bookkeeping device must have closed him out. The manager probably had known that Tamkin wasn't to be trusted, and on that first day he might have warned him. But you couldn't expect him to interfere.

"You get hit?" said Mr.Rowland.

And Wilhelm, quite coolly, said, "Oh, it could have been worse, I guess." He put the piece of paper into his pocket with its cigarette butts and packets of pills. The lie helped him out–although, for a moment, he was afraid he would cry. But he hardened himself. The hardening effort made a violent, vertical pain go through his chest, like that caused by a pocket of air under the collar bones. To the old chicken millionaire, who by this time had become acquainted with the drop in rye and lard, he also denied that anything serious had happened. "It's just one of those temporary slumps. Nothing to be scared about," he said, and remained in possession of himself. His need to cry, like someone in a crowd, pushed and jostled and abused him from behind, and Wilhelm did not dare turn. He said to himself, I will not cry in front of these people. I'll be damned if I'll break down in front of them like a kid, even though I never expect to see them again. No! No! And yet his unshed tears rose and rose and he looked like a man about to drown. But when they talked to him, he answered very distinctly. He tried to speak proudly.

"…going away?" he heard Rowland ask.

"What?"

"I thought you might be going away too. Tamkin said he was going to Maine this summer for his vacation."

"Oh, going away?"

Wilhelm broke off and went to look for Tamkin in the men's toilet. Across the corridor was the room where the machinery of the board was housed. It hummed and whirred like mechanical birds, and the tubes glittered in the dark. A couple of businessmen with cigarettes in their fingers were having a conversation in the lavatory. At the top of the closet door sat a gray straw hat with a cocoa-colored band. "Tamkin," said Wilhelm. He tried to identify the feet below the door. "Are you in there, Doctor Tamkin?" he said with stifled anger. "Answer me. It's Wilhelm."

The hat was taken down, the latch lifted, and a stranger came out who looked at him with annoyance.

"You waiting?" said one of the businessmen. He was warning Wilhelm that he was out of turn.

"Me? Not me," said Wilhelm. "I'm looking for a fellow." Bitterly angry, he said to himself that Tamkin would pay him the two hundred dollars at least, his share of the original deposit. "And before he takes the train to Maine, too. Before he spends a penny on vacation–that liar! We went into this as partners."

## Notes

1. A person whose job involves treating some diseases and physical problems by pressing and moving the bones and muscles.

2. (especially in the Roman Catholic Church) A ceremony held in memory of the last meal that Christ had with his disciples.

3. A person who claims to have knowledge or skills that they do not really have.

4. Very vividly.

5. A person who commits the crime of bigamy, which means the crime of marrying sb. when you are still legally married to sb. else.

6. (slang) Money.

7. No.

8. A rich and powerful family.

## Questions

1. "And why, Wilhelm further asked, should he or anybody else pity me; or why should I be pitied sooner than another fellow?

It is my childish mind that thinks people are ready to give it just because you need it." what do the sentences imply?

2. "Then what am I doing with him here, and why did I give him the seven hundred dollars? thought Wilhelm." in your opinion,why did Wilhelm I give Tamkin the seven hundred dollars?

### （5）Charles Olson (1910—1970)

Charles Olson is a famous postmodern poet in America, and also the leader of the Black Mountain School which behaves actively in the twentieth century. He was born in Massachusetts in 1910. He received his Bachelor's of Arts from Wesleyan University in 1932 and taught English for two years at Clark University. He then entered Harvard University in 1936, where he completed coursework for a PhD in American civilization. In the late 1940s, he first taught then became the dean at Montenegro College in North Carolina. Rather than pursuing an academic career, Olson became active in politics. He served as the assistant chief of the foreign language section of the Office of War Information (OWI). In 1944, Olson became disillusioned with the OWI over an issue of censorship. To more fully dedicate himself to his writing, he left his job and moved to Key West, Florida, in 1945. He published his influential essay *Projective Verse* in 1950, which became the most important poetic theoretical work of Black Mountain School and a milestone in the history of modern American poetry, exerting much impact on the artistic creation of a whole generation of American poets. First, Olson advocated the revitalization of contemporary poetry through the so-called "composition by field". Secondly, as far as the form of poetry is concerned, Olsen believes that poets should give up people's normal thinking process and logical order in writing so as to exhaust the theme; in terms of the rhythm of poetry, Olson advocates arranging the cadence of the lines at the natural rhythm of breathing; the basic unit of the rhythm is not syllables, but lines. Olson wrote, "A poem is energy transferred from where the poet got it...by way of the poem itself to, all the way over to, the reader."

He began working on his often fragmentary and experimental opus, *The Maximus Poems*, in the mid-1940s. He chose Maximus (named after the second century Maximus of Tyre, as well as the itinerant 4th-century mystic, and possibly a reference to Olson's towering height) to narrate this poem, which examined the origins of American culture and life in contemporary Gloucester. *The Maximus Poems* first appeared in 1960. The volume was followed by *The Maximus Poems*, IV, V, VI (1968) and an unfinished final volume, *The Maximus Poems*, Volume Three (1975). In this set of poems, Olson uses the narrator Maximus to express his dissatisfaction and concern about reality, and for the future of mankind. Olson believes that only by studying history can one find a path to the ideal.

The following is from *The Maximus Poems*.

### Celestial Evening, October 1967

Advanced out toward the external from
the time I did actually lose space control,

here on the Fort[1] and kept turning left
like my star-nosed mole batted
on the head, not being able to
get home 50 yards as I was
from it. There is a vast

internal life, a sea or organism
full of sounds & memoried
objects swimming or sunk
in the great fall of it as,
when one further
ring of the 9 bounding
Earth & Heaven runs
into the daughter of God's
particular place, cave, palace—a tail

of Ocean whose waters then
are test if even a god
lies will tell & he or she spend
9 following years out of the company
of their own. The sounds

and objects of the great
10th within us are
what we hear see are motived by
dream belief care for discriminate

our loves & choices cares & failures unless
in this forbidding Earth & Heaven by

enclosure 9 times round plus
all that stream collecting as,
into her hands it comes: the

full volume of all which ever was which we
as such have that which is our part of it,
all history existence place s splits of moon
& slightest oncoming smallest stars at
sunset, fears & horrors, grandparents'
lives as much as we have also features
and their forms, whatever grace or ugliness our legs
etc possess, it all

come s in as also outward leads
us after itself as though then
the horn of the nearest moon was
truth. I bend my ear, as,
if I were Amoghasiddi[2] and,
here on this plain where
like my mole I have
been knocked flat, attend,
to turn & turn within

the steady stream & collect which
within me ends as in her hall and I

hear all, the new moon new in all
the ancient sky
1967　　　　　　　　　　　　　　　　1975

## Notes

1. A district in Gloucester. Massachusetts, where Olson settled after leaving Black Mountain in 1957.

2. In Tibetan Buddhism, one of the five Dhyana-Buddhas, or Buddhas of contemplation.

## Questions

1. Try to analyze the theme of the poetry based on Olson's Poetic theory.

2. Explain the rhythm of this poem.

### （6）John Berryman (1914—1972)

The poet is good at his confessional psychological poetry. He was born in Oklahoma, and at the age of 12, his father shot himself at home. The shadow of this family tragedy is often reflected in his later poems. After graduating from Columbia University, he received a scholarship to Cambridge University, and has long taught at Harvard and other universities.

He published the research book Stephen Crane in 1950. Berryman's first two collections of poems were *Poems* (1942) and *The Dispossessed* (1948). *Homage to Mistress Bradstreet*, his first experimental poetry collection, was published many years later, which earned him a reputation in 1956. This is a biographical poetry collection, praising the spiritual life of the colonial poetess Anne Bradstreet; meanwhile, associating with the present, it is written very vividly and delicately. In 1964, Berryman launched the first "Dream Songs" titled 77 *Dream Songs*. Bold in poetic skills, the poetry won the Pulitzer Prize. He later continued to write the "Dream Songs," publishing 385 songs in total, which are collected in his *His Toy, His Dream, His Rest* (1968) and *The Dream Song* (1969), which have also won the National Book Award. Each poem consists of eighteen lines, describing what the hero Henry thought and did and full of themes with a style of humor. Berryman expresses his reflection and perception of life through Henry. *Berryman's Sonnets* (1967) and *Love and Fame* (1970), which are his last two series of autobiographical poems, full of a typical Berryman-style confessional tone. Among them, the poet vowed to return to the embrace of his parents' Catholic faith. However, a return to faith did not alleviate his long mental melancholy, and in 1972, he ended his life by jumping into the frozen Mississippi River. The subsequently published autobiographical novel *Recovery* (1973) is based on his own alcoholism. His posthumous publications also included the later poetry anthologies of Delusions, etc. (1972) and the collection of stories and essays from *The Freedom of the Poet* (1976).

The followings are *From Homage to Mistress Bradstreet.*

## From Homage to Mistress Bradstreet

**17**

The winters close, Springs open, no child stirs
under my withering heart, O seasoned heart
God grudged his aid.
All things else soil like a shirt.
Simon is much away. My executive[1] stales.
T h e town cam e through for the cartway by the pales[2]
but my patience is short,
I revolt from, I am like, these savage foresters

**18**

whose passionless dicker in the shade, whose glance
impassive & scant, belie their murderous cries
when quarry seems to show.
Again I must have been wrong, twice.[3]
Unwell in a new way. Ca n that begin?
God brandishes. O love, O I love. Kin,
gather. My world is strange
and merciful, ingrown months, blessing a swelling trance.[4]

**19**

So squeezed, wince you I scream? I love you & hate

off with you. Ages! Useless. Below my waist
he has me in Hell's vise.
Stalling. He let go. Com e back: brace
me somewhere. No. No. Yes! everything down
hardens I press with horrible joy down
my back cracks like a wrist
shame I am voiding oh behind it is too late

**20**

hide me forever I work thrust I must free
now I all muscle s & bone s concentrate
what is living from dying?
Simon I must leave you so untidy
Monstcr you arc killing mc Bc surc
I'll have you later Women do endure
I can can no longer
and it passe s the wretched trap whelming and I am me.

**21**

drencht & powerful, I did it with my body!
One proud tug greens Heaven. Marvellous,
unforbidding Majesty.
Swell, imperious bells. I fly.
Mountainous, woman not breaks and will bend:
sways God nearby: anguish comes to an end.
Blossomed Sarah,[5] and I

blossom. Is that thing alive? I hear a famisht howl.

**22**

Beloved household, I am Simon's wife,
and the mother of Samuel—who m greedy yet I miss n o
out of his kicking place.
More in some ways I feel at a loss,
freer. Cantabanks & mummers,[6] nears
longing for you. Our chopping[7] score s my ears,
our costume bores my eyes.
St. George[8] to the good sword, rise! chop-logic's rife

**23**

& fever & Satan & Satan's ancient fere.[9]
Pioneering is not feeling well,
not Indians, beasts.
Not all their riddling can forestall
one leaving. Sam, your uncle has had to
go from us to live with God. 'Then Aunt went too?'

Dear, she does wait still.
Stricken: 'Oh. Then he takes us one by one.' My dear.

**24**

Forswearing it otherwise, they starch their minds.
Folkmoots[10], & blether[11], blether. John Cotton rakes[12]

to the synod of Cambridge.[13]
Down from my body my legs flow,
out from it arms wave, on it my head shakes.
Now Mistress Hutchinson rings forth a call—
should she? many creep out a broken wall—
affirming the Holy Ghost
dwells in one justified. Factioning passion blinds

## Notes

1. Power to act.

2. Stockade fence.

3. One of the several allusions to her failure to become pregnant.

4. Her first child was not born until about 1633 [Berryman's note].

5. Wife of Abraham, barren until old age, when she gave birth to Isaac (Genesis 17.19).

6. Ballad singers and mimes.

7. Disputing, snapping, haggling: axing [Berryman's note].

8. Patron saint of England, the slayer of dragons.

9. His friend Death [Berryman's note].

10. A town assembly for debate.

11. Nonsense.

12. Inclines, as a mast; bows [Berryman's note].

13. In the first synod (a body for religious debate). Cotton agreed to the condemnation and banishment of his follower Anne Hutchinson. Her heresies included a deemphasis of perfect moral conduct as evidence of the justification for Christian salvation.

## Questions

1. Who are the speakers? In what tone did they present in these lines?

2. Try to make a comparison between Mistress Bradstreet and the speaker.

### (7) Toni Morrison (b.1931)

Toni Morrison, an African American female novelist and editor, was born in Ohio and was influenced by black culture since childhood. She studied at Howard University for a Bachelor's degree and later received a master's degree from Cornell University. From 1966 to 1984, she worked at Random House as a senior editor, and then taught at the State University of New York, Princeton University, among others. She wrote in her spare time. *The Bluest Eye*(1970) was her debut novel, and the subsequent *Sula* (1973) followed the experiences of black women. *Song of Solomon* (1977) launched Morrison's national reputation, winning her the National Book Critics' Circle Award. Her most well-known work, *Beloved*, appeared in 1987 and won the Pulitzer Prize. Her other novels include *Tar Baby* (1981), *Jazz* (1992), and *Paradise* (1998). Morrison is most proud of her *Love* (2003). In addition to novels, she also writes prose and plays, and has more than 30 book reviews. *The Black Book*, edited by her, narrates more than 300 years of history of black Americans, and is known as the encyclopedia of the African American people. In 1993, Morrison became the first African American woman to receive the Nobel Prize in literature.

Morrison is a representative figure of contemporary African American literature. She not only blends black folk literature with myths and legends to render the atmosphere, but draws lessons from the techniques of magic realism as well; therefore, the environment and characters in her works are covered with a mysterious layer, depicting reality as a "modern myth." Her language is very colloquial, and the dialogue between characters is vivid. Through constantly changing of the narrative skills, the plots are often suspenseful and thrilling. Her achievements marked another peak in the history of African American literature in the 20th century after Richard Wright and Ralph Ellison, which established her as an important figure in the United States and even the broader literary world.

*Beloved* (1987) is based on real history. The story is shocking: while the female black slave, Sethe, was pursued on her way to escape, she decided to rid her child of the tragic fate of being a slave, so she resolutely cut the child's throat and buried her. The child, who died in the hands of her biological mother, was named "Beloved." In the following years, Sethe is hated and rejected by the community and endures the torture of her conscience and great loneliness. Eighteen years later, slavery was abolished, and the baby girl she killed somehow returned, making the family restless. Not only by asking for her mother's love night and day, but also seducing and pestering Paul D by fair means. During that period, the black women suffered from double oppression—race oppression and gender oppression. They are "slaves within slaves." Set in a small town of Cincinnati, Ohio, in 1873, the story shows the great spiritual crisis left behind by the practice of slavery towards African Americans.

The beginning of the story throws the reader into a closed, isolated space, "124," which has no name, only the door signs. This gray house on the Bluestone Road becomes a space where reality and ghosts coexist, where a "haunted" prank is staged. Sethe's two sons escaped from the house and Grandmother Baby Suggs died. Only the mother and daughter were left living in the house. Mother Sethe tried not to remember the past. Sadly, her mind sometimes does what it wants. When Denver and Paul D clashed over the haunting of the house, Sethe told Paul D why she did not move.

The following is an excerpted from the first section of the the first part of *The Beloved.*

## The Beloved (Excerpts)

124 WAS SPITEFUL. Full of a baby's venom. The women in the house knew it and so did the children. For years each put up with the spite in his own way, but by 1873 Sethe and her daughter Denver were its only victims. The grandmother, Baby Suggs, was dead, and the sons, Howard and Buglar, had run away by the time they were thirteen years old--as soon as merely looking in a mirror shattered it (that was the signal for Buglar); as soon as two tiny hand prints appeared in the cake (that was it for Howard). Neither boy waited to see more; another kettleful of chickpeas smoking in a heap on the floor; soda crackers crumbled and strewn in a line next to the door sill. Nor did

they wait for one of the relief periods: the weeks, months even, when nothing was disturbed. No. Each one fled at once—the moment the house committed what was for him the one insult not to be borne or witnessed a second time. Within two months, in the dead of winter, leaving their grandmother, Baby Suggs; Sethe, their mother; and their little sister, Denver, all by themselves in the gray and white house on Bluestone Road. It didn't have a number then, because Cincinnati didn't stretch that far. In fact, Ohio had been calling itself a state only seventy years when first one brother and then the next stuffed quilt packing into his hat, snatched up his shoes, and crept away from the lively spite the house felt for them.

Baby Suggs didn't even raise her head. From her sickbed she heard them go but that wasn't the reason she lay still. It was a wonder to her that her grandsons had taken so long to realize that every house wasn't like the one on Bluestone Road. Suspended between the nastiness[1] of life and the meanness of the dead, she couldn't get interested in leaving life or living it, let alone the fright of two creeping-off boys. Her past had been like her present—intolerable—and since she knew death was anything but forgetfulness, she used the little energy left her for pondering color.

"Bring a little lavender in, if you got any. Pink, if you don't."

And Sethe would oblige her with anything from fabric to her own tongue. Winter in Ohio was especially rough if you had an appetite for color. Sky provided the only drama, and counting on a Cincinnati horizon for life's principal joy was reckless indeed. So Sethe and the girl Denver did what they could, and what the house permitted, for her. Together they waged a perfunctory[2] battle against the outrageous behavior of that place; against turned-over slop jars, smacks on the behind, and gusts of sour air. For they understood the source of the outrage as well as they knew the source of light.

Baby Suggs died shortly after the brothers left, with no interest whatsoever in their leave-taking or hers, and right afterward Sethe and Denver decided to end the persecution by calling forth the ghost that tried them so. Perhaps a conversation, they thought, an exchange of views or something would help. So they held hands and said, "Come on. Come on. You may as well just come on."

The sideboard took a step forward but nothing else did.

"Grandma Baby must be stopping it," said Denver. She was ten and still mad at Baby Suggs for dying.

Sethe opened her eyes. "I doubt that," she said.

"Then why don't it come?"

"You forgetting how little it is," said her mother. "She wasn't even two years old when she died. Too little to understand. Too little to talk much even."

"Maybe she don't want to understand," said Denver.

"Maybe. But if she'd only come, I could make it clear to her."

Sethe released her daughter's hand and together they pushed the sideboard back against the wall. Outside a driver whipped his horse into the gallop local people felt necessary when they passed 124.

"For a baby she throws a powerful spell," said Denver.

"No more powerful than the way I loved her," Sethe answered and there it was again. The welcoming cool of unchiseled[3] headstones; the one she selected to lean against on tiptoe, her knees wide open as any grave. Pink as a fingernail it was, and sprinkled with glittering chips. Ten minutes, he said. You got ten minutes I'll do it for free.

Ten minutes for seven letters. With another ten could she have gotten "Dearly" too? She had not thought to ask him and it bothered her still that it might have been possible—that for twenty minutes, a half hour, say, she could have had the whole thing, every word she heard the preacher say at the funeral (and all there was to say, surely) engraved on her baby's headstone: Dearly Beloved. But what she got, settled for, was the one word that mattered. She thought it would be enough, rutting[4] among the headstones with the engraver, his young son looking on, the anger in his face so old; the appetite in it quite new. That should certainly be enough. Enough to answer one more preacher, one more abolitionist and a town full of disgust.

Counting on the stillness of her own soul, she had forgotten the other one: the soul of her baby girl. Who would have thought that a little old baby could harbor so much rage? Rutting among the stones under the eyes of the engraver's son was not enough. Not only did she have to live out her years in a house palsied[5] by the baby's fury at having its throat cut, but those ten minutes she spent pressed up against dawn-colored stone studded with star chips, her knees wide open as the grave, were longer than life, more alive, more pulsating[6] than the baby blood that soaked her fingers like oil.

"We could move," she suggested once to her mother-in-law.

"What'd be the point?" asked Baby Suggs. "Not a house in the country ain't packed to its rafters with some dead Negro's grief. We lucky this ghost is a baby. My husband's spirit was to come back in here? or yours? Don't talk to me. You lucky. You got three left. Three pulling at your skirts and just one raising hell from the other side. Be thankful, why don't you? I had eight. Every one of them gone away from me. Four taken, four chased, and all, I expect, worrying somebody's house into evil." Baby Suggs rubbed her eyebrows.

"My first-born. All I can remember of her is how she loved the burned bottom of bread. Can you beat that? Eight children and that's all I remember."

"That's all you let yourself remember," Sethe had told her, but she was down to one herself—one alive, that is—the boys chased off by the dead one, and her memory of Buglar was fading fast. Howard at least had a head shape nobody could forget. As for the rest, she worked hard to remember as close to nothing as was safe. Unfortunately her brain was devious. She might be hurrying across a field, running practically, to get to the pump quickly and rinse[7] the chamomile[8] sap from her legs. Nothing else would be in her mind. The picture of the men coming to nurse her was as lifeless as the nerves in her back where the skin buckled like a washboard. Nor was there the faintest scent of ink or the cherry gum and oak bark from which it was made. Nothing. Just the breeze cooling her face as she rushed toward water. And then sopping the chamomile away with pump water and rags, her mind fixed on getting every last bit of sap off—on her carelessness in taking a shortcut across the field just to save a half mile, and not noticing how high the weeds had grown until the itching was all the way to her knees. Then something. The plash of water, the sight of her shoes and stockings awry on the path where she had flung them; or Here Boy lapping in the puddle near her feet, and suddenly there was Sweet Home rolling, rolling, rolling out before her eyes, and although there was not a leaf on that farm that did not make her want to scream, it rolled itself out before her in shameless beauty. It never looked as terrible as it was and it made her wonder if hell was a pretty place too. Fire and brimstone all right, but hidden in lacy groves. Boys hanging from the most beautiful sycamores in the world. It shamed her—remembering the wonderful soughing trees rather than the boys. Try as she might to make it otherwise, the sycamores[9] beat out the children every time and she could not forgive her memory for that.

When the last of the chamomile was gone, she went around to the front of the house, collecting her shoes and stockings on the way. As if to punish her further for her terrible memory, sitting on the porch not forty feet away was Paul D, the last of the Sweet Home men. And although she she said, "Is that you?"

"What's left." He stood up and smiled. "How you been, girl, besides barefoot?"

When she laughed it came out loose and young. "Messed up my legs back yonder. Chamomile."

He made a face as though tasting a teaspoon of something bitter.

"I don't want to even hear about it. Always did hate that stuff."

Sethe balled up her stockings and jammed them into her pocket.

"Come on in."

"Porch is fine, Sethe. Cool out here." He sat back down and looked at the meadow on the other side of the road, knowing the eagerness he felt would be in his eyes.

"Eighteen years," she said softly.

"Eighteen," he repeated. "And I swear I been walking every one of em. Mind if I join you?" He nodded toward her feet and began unlacing his shoes.

"You want to soak them? Let me get you a basin of water." She moved closer to him to enter the house.

"No, uh uh. Can't baby feet. A whole lot more tramping they got to do yet."

"You can't leave right away, Paul D. You got to stay awhile."

"Well, long enough to see Baby Suggs, anyway. Where is she?"

"Dead."

"Aw no. When?"

"Eight years now. Almost nine."

"Was it hard? I hope she didn't die hard." Sethe shook her head. "Soft as cream. Being alive was the hard part. Sorry you missed her though. Is that what you came by for?"

"That's some of what I came for. The rest is you. But if all the truth be known, I go anywhere these days. Anywhere they let me sit down."

"You looking good."

"Devil's confusion. He lets me look good long as I feel bad." He looked at her and the word "bad" took on another meaning.

Sethe smiled. This is the way they were—had been. All of

the Sweet Home men,before and after Halle, treated her to a mild brotherly flirtation, so subtle you had to scratch for it.

Except for a heap more hair and some waiting in his eyes, he looked the way he had in Kentucky. Peachstone skin; straight-backed. For a man with an immobile face it was amazing how ready it was to smile, or blaze or be sorry with you. As though all you had to do was get his attention and right away he produced the feeling you were feeling. With less than a blink, his face seemed to change—underneath it lay the activity.

"I wouldn't have to ask about him, would I? You'd tell me if there was anything to tell, wouldn't you?" Sethe looked down at her feet and saw again the sycamores.

"I'd tell you. Sure I'd tell you. I don't know any more now than I did then." Except for the churn, he thought, and you don't need to know that. "You must think he's still alive."

"No. I think he's dead. It's not being sure that keeps him alive."

"What did Baby Suggs think?"

"Same, but to listen to her, all her children is dead. Claimed she felt each one go the very day and hour."

"When she say Halle went?"

"Eighteen fifty-five. The day my baby was born."

"You had that baby, did you? Never thought you'd make it."

He chuckled. "Running off pregnant."

"Had to. Couldn't be no waiting." She lowered her head and thought, as he did, how unlikely it was that she had made it. And if it hadn't been for that girl looking for velvet, she never would have.

"All by yourself too." He was proud of her and annoyed by her.

Proud she had done it; annoyed that she had not needed Halle or him in the doing.

"Almost by myself. Not all by myself. A white girl helped me."

"Then she helped herself too, God bless her."

"You could stay the night, Paul D."

"You don't sound too steady in the offer."

Sethe glanced beyond his shoulder toward the closed door. "Oh it's truly meant. I just hope you'll pardon my house. Come on in. Talk to Denver while I cook you something."

Paul D tied his shoes together, hung them over his shoulder and followed her through the door straight into a pool of red and undulating[10] light that locked him where he stood.

"You got company?" he whispered, frowning.

"Off and on," said Sethe.

"Good God." He backed out the door onto the porch. "What kind of evil you got in here?"

"It's not evil, just sad. Come on. Just step through."

He looked at her then, closely. Closer than he had when she first rounded the house on wet and shining legs, holding her shoes and stockings up in one hand, her skirts in the other. Halle's girl—the one with iron eyes and backbone to match. He had never seen her hair in Kentucky. And though her face was eighteen years older than when last he saw her, it was softer now. Because of the hair. A face too still for comfort; irises the same color as her skin, which, in that still face, used to make him think of a mask with mercifully punched[11] out eyes.

Halle's woman. Pregnant every year including the year she sat by the fire telling him she was going to run. Her three children she had already packed into a wagonload of others in a caravan of Negroes crossing the river. They were to be left with Halle's mother near Cincinnati. Even in that tiny shack, leaning so close to the fire you could smell the heat in her dress, her eyes did not pick up a flicker of light. They were like two wells into which he had trouble gazing. Even punched out they needed to be covered, lidded, marked with some sign to warn folks of what that emptiness held. So he looked instead at the fire while she told him, because her husband was not there for the telling. Mr.Garner was dead and his wife had a lump in her neck the size of a sweet potato and unable to speak to anyone. She leaned as close to the fire as her pregnant belly allowed and told him, Paul D, the last of the Sweet Home men. There had been six of them who belonged to the farm, Sethe the only female. Mrs.Garner, crying like a baby, had sold his brother to pay off the debts that surfaced the minute she was widowed. Then schoolteacher arrived to put things in order. But what he did broke three more Sweet Home men and punched the glittering iron out of Sethe's eyes, leaving two open wells that did not reflect firelight.

Now the iron was back but the face, softened by hair, made him trust her enough to step inside her door smack into a pool of pulsing red light. She was right. It was sad. Walking through it, a wave of grief soaked him so thoroughly he wanted to cry. It seemed a long way to the normal light surrounding the table, but he made it dry-eyed and lucky.

"You said she died soft. Soft as cream," he reminded her.

"That's not Baby Suggs," she said.

"Who then?"

"My daughter. The one I sent ahead with the boys."

"She didn't live?"

"No. The one I was carrying when I run away is all I got left. Boys gone too. Both of em walked off just before Baby Suggs died."

Paul D looked at the spot where the grief had soaked him. The red was gone but a kind of weeping clung to the air where it had been. Probably best, he thought. If a Negro got legs he ought to use them. Sit down too long, somebody will figure out a way to tie them up. Still… if her boys were gone…

"No man? You here by yourself?"

"Me and Denver", she said.

"That all right by you?"

"That's all right by me."

She saw his skepticism and went on. "I cook at a restaurant in town. And I sew a little on the sly[12]."

Paul D smiled then, remembering the bedding dress. Sethe was thirteen when she came to Sweet Home and already iron-eyed. She was a timely present for Mrs.Garner who had lost Baby Suggs to her husband's high principles. The five Sweet Home men looked at the new girl and decided to let her be. They were young and so sick with the absence of women they had taken to calves. Yet they let the iron-eyed girl be, so she could choose in spite of the fact that each one would have beaten the others to mush to have her. It took her a year to choose a long, tough year of thrashing on pallets eaten up with dreams of her. A year of yearning, when rape seemed the solitary gift of life. The restraint they had exercised possible only because they were Sweet Home men the ones Mr.Garner bragged about while other farmers shook their heads in warning at the phrase.

"Y'all got boys," he told them. "Young boys, old boys, picky boys, stropping[13] boys. Now at Sweet Home, my niggers is men every one of em. Bought em thataway, raised em thataway. Men every one."

"Beg to differ, Garner. Ain't no nigger men."

"Not if you scared, they ain't." Garner's smile was wide. "But if you a man yourself, you'll want your niggers to be men too."

"I wouldn't have no nigger men round my wife."

It was the reaction Garner loved and waited for. "Neither would I," he said. "Neither would I," and there was always a pause before the neighbor, or stranger, or peddler, or brother-in-law or whoever it was got the meaning. Then a fierce argument, sometimes a fight, and Garner came home bruised and pleased, having demonstrated one more time what a real Kentuckian was: one tough enough and smart enough to make and call his own niggers men.

And so they were: Paul D Garner, Paul F Garner, Paul A Garner, Halle Suggs and Sixo, the wild man. All in their twenties, minus women, fucking cows, dreaming of rape, thrashing[14] on pallets[15], rubbing their thighs and waiting for the new girl the one who took Baby Suggs' place after Halle bought her with five years of Sundays. Maybe that was why she chose him. A twenty-year-old man so in love with his mother he gave up five years of Sabbaths just to see her sit down for a change was a serious recommendation. She waited a year. And the Sweet Home men abused cows while they waited with her. She chose Halle and for their first bedding she sewed herself a dress on the sly.

"Won't you stay on awhile? Can't nobody catch up on eighteen years in a day."

Out of the dimness of the room in which they sat, a white staircase climbed toward the blue-and-white wallpaper of the second floor. Paul D could see just the beginning of the paper; discreet flecks of yellow sprinkled among a blizzard of snowdrops all backed by blue. The luminous white of the railing and steps kept him glancing toward it. Every sense he had told him the air above the stairwell was charmed and very thin. But the girl who walked down out of that air was round and brown with the face of an alert doll.

Paul D looked at the girl and then at Sethe who smiled saying, "Here she is my Denver. This is Paul D, honey, from Sweet Home."

"Good morning, Mr.D."

"Garner, baby. Paul D Garner."

"Yes sir."

"Glad to get a look at you. Last time I saw your mama, you were pushing out the front of her dress."

"Still is," Sethe smiled, "provided she can get in it."

Denver stood on the bottom step and was suddenly hot and shy. It had been a long time since anybody (good-willed white woman, preacher, speaker or newspaperman) sat at their table, their sympathetic voices called liar by the revulsion in their eyes. For twelve years, long before Grandma Baby died, there had been no visitors of any sort and certainly no friends. No colored people. Certainly no hazelnut man with too long hair and no notebook, no charcoal, no oranges, no Questions. Someone her mother wanted to talk to and would even consider talking to while barefoot. Looking, in fact acting, like a girl instead of the quiet, queenly woman Denver had known all her life. The one who never looked away, who when a man got stomped to death by a mare right in front of Sawyer's restaurant did not look away; and when a sow began eating her own litter did not look away then either. And when the baby's spirit picked up Here Boy and slammed him into the wall hard enough to break two of his legs and dislocate his eye, so hard he went into convulsions[16] and chewed up his tongue, still her mother had not looked away. She had taken a hammer, knocked the dog unconscious, wiped away the blood and saliva, pushed his eye back in his head and set his leg bones. He recovered, mute and off-balance, more because of his untrustworthy eye than his bent legs, and winter, summer, drizzle or dry, nothing could persuade him to enter the house again.

Now here was this woman with the presence of mind to repair a dog gone savage with pain rocking her crossed ankles and looking away from her own daughter's body. As though the size of it was more than vision could bear. And neither she nor he had on shoes. Hot, shy, now Denver was lonely. All that leaving: first her brothers, then her grandmother—serious losses since there were no children willing to circle her in a game or hang by their knees from her porch railing. None of that had mattered as long as her mother did not look away as she was doing now, making Denver long, downright long, for a sign of spite from the baby ghost.

"She's a fine-looking young lady," said Paul D. "Fine-looking. Got her daddy's sweet face."

"You know my father?"

"Knew him. Knew him well."

"Did he, Ma'am?" Denver fought an urge to realign her affection.

"Of course he knew your daddy. I told you, he's from Sweet Home."

Denver sat down on the bottom step. There was nowhere else gracefully to go. They were a twosome, saying "Your daddy" and "Sweet Home" in a way that made it clear both belonged to them and not to her. That her own father's absence was not hers. Once the absence had belonged to Grandma Baby—a son, deeply mourned because he was the one who had bought her out of there. Then it was her mother's absent husband. Now it was this hazelnut stranger's absent friend. Only those who knew him ("knew him well") could claim his absence for themselves. Just as only those who lived in

Sweet Home could remember it, whisper it and glance sideways at one another while they did. Again she wished for the baby ghost—its anger thrilling her now where it used to wear her out. Wear her out.

"We have a ghost in here," she said, and it worked. They were not a two some anymore. Her mother left off swinging her feet and being girlish. Memory of Sweet Home dropped away from the eyes of the man she was being girlish for. He looked quickly up the lightning-white stairs behind her.

"So I hear," he said. "But sad, your mama said. Not evil."

"No sir," said Denver, "not evil. But not sad either."

"What then?"

"Rebuked. Lonely and rebuked."

"Is that right?" Paul D turned to Sethe.

"I don't know about lonely," said Denver's mother. "Mad, maybe, but I don't see how it could be lonely spending every minute with us like it does."

"Must be something you got it wants."

Sethe shrugged. "It's just a baby."

"My sister," said Denver. "She died in this house."

Paul D scratched the hair under his jaw. "Reminds me of that headless bride back behind Sweet Home. Remember that, Sethe? Used to roam them woods regular."

"How could I forget? Worrisome…"

"How come everybody run off from Sweet Home can't stop talking

about it? Look like if it was so sweet you would have stayed."

"Girl, who you talking to?"

Paul D laughed. "True, true. She's right, Sethe. It wasn't sweet and it sure wasn't home." He shook his head.

"But it's where we were," said Sethe. "All together. Comes back whether we want it to or not." She shivered a little. A light ripple of skin on her arm, which she caressed back into sleep. "Denver," she said, "start up that stove. Can't have a friend stop by and don't feed him."

"Don't go to any trouble on my account," Paul D said.

"Bread ain't trouble. The rest I brought back from where I work. Least I can do, cooking from dawn to noon, is bring dinner home. You got any objections to pike?"

"If he don't object to me I don't object to him."

At it again, thought Denver. Her back to them, she jostled the kindlin and almost lost the fire. "Why don't you spend the night, Mr.Garner? You and Ma'am can talk about Sweet Home all night long."

Sethe took two swift steps to the stove, but before she could yank Denver's collar, the girl leaned forward and began to cry.

"What is the matter with you? I never knew you to behave this way."

"Leave her be," said Paul D. "I'm a stranger to her."

"That's just it. She got no cause to act up with a stranger. Oh baby, what is it? Did something happen?"

But Denver was shaking now and sobbing so she could not speak. The tears she had not shed for nine years wetting her far too womanly breasts.

"I can't no more. I can't no more."

"Can't what? What can't you?"

"I can't live here. I don't know where to go or what to do, but I can't live here. Nobody speaks to us. Nobody comes by. Boys don't like me. Girls don't either."

"Honey, honey."

"What's she talking 'bout nobody speaks to you?" asked Paul D.

"It's the house. People don't— "

"It's not! It's not the house. It's us! And it's you!"

"Denver!"

"Leave off, Sethe. It's hard for a young girl living in a haunted house. That can't be easy."

"It's easier than some other things."

"Think, Sethe. I'm a grown man with nothing new left to see or do and I'm telling you it ain't easy. Maybe you all ought to move. Who owns this house?"

Over Denver's shoulder Sethe shot Paul D a look of snow. "What you care?"

"They won't let you leave?"

"No."

"Sethe."

"No moving. No leaving. It's all right the way it is."

"You going to tell me it's all right with this child half out of her mind?"

Something in the house braced, and in the listening quiet that followed Sethe spoke.

"I got a tree on my back and a haint[17] in my house, and nothing in between but the daughter I am holding in my arms. No more running—from nothing. I will never run from another thing on this earth. I took one journey and I paid for the ticket, but let me tell you something, Paul D Garner: it cost too much! Do you hear me? It cost too much. Now sit down and eat with us or leave us be."

Paul D fished in his vest for a little pouch of tobacco—concentrating on its contents and the knot of its string while Sethe led Denver into the keeping room that opened off the large room he was sitting in. He had no smoking papers, so he fiddled with the pouch and listened through the open door to Sethe quieting her daughter. When she came back she avoided his look and went straight to a small table next to the stove. Her back was to him and he could see all the hair he wanted without the distraction of her face.

"What tree on your back?"

"Huh." Sethe put a bowl on the table and reached under it for flour.

"What tree on your back? Is something growing on your back? I don't see nothing growing on your back."

"It's there all the same."

"Who told you that?"

"White girl. That's what she called it. I've never seen it and never will. But that's what she said it looked like. A chokecherry tree. Trunk, branches, and even leaves. Tiny little chokecherry leaves. But that was eighteen years ago. Could have cherries too now for all I know."…

## Notes

1. Spite,meanness,malice,viciousness,cruelty.

2. Done as a duty or habit, without real interest, attention or feeling.

3. To cut or shape wood or stone with a chisel,a tool with a sharp

flat edge at the end, used for shaping wood, stone or metal. Unchisel is its opposite.

4. In a time of sexual activity.

5. Paralysis (= loss of control or feeling in part or most of the body), especially when the arms and legs shake without control.

6. To make strong regular movements or sounds.

7. To wash sth. with clean water only, not using soap.

8. A plant with a sweet smell and small white and yellow flowers. Its dried leaves and flowers are used to make tea, medicine, etc.

9. A large spreading plane tree with lobed leaves, round spiked fruit clusters, and flaking bark.

10. To move gently up and down in the shape of waves on the ocean.

11. To hit sb/sth hard with your fist (= closed hand).

12. Acting or done in a secret or dishonest way, often intending to trick people.

13. A piece of leather used for keeping the blade of a razor sharp; a very bad mood when you are annoyed about sth.

14. To hit a person or an animal many times with a stick, etc. as a punishment/ to move or make sth. move in a violent or uncontrolled way.

15. A heavy wooden or metal base that can be used for moving or storing goods.

16. A sudden shaking movement of the body that cannot be controlled.

17. Haunt.

## Questions

1. Try to analyze the symbolic meaning of "124"?
2. What is Sethe like? Are you sympathetic with her?

### (8) Joseph Heller(1923—1999)

Joseph Heller is a famous Jewish American writer, who gained world fame with his satirical, anti-war novel *Catch*-22 (1961), set in WWII Italy. Heller is widely regarded as one of the best post-World War II satirists. Born in Brooklyn, New York, into a Russian-Jewish family, he lost his father early on and lived a hard life. He served in the United States Air Force during World War II and performed 60 bombing missions as a bombardier in Europe. After retiring from the army, he successively attended New York University, Columbia University, and Oxford University. Then he taught at the university for two years. From 1954, he served successively as an advertising writer for *Time* and *Look*, and as a marketing manager for the magazine McCall. During this time, he wrote his first novel, *Catch*-22 (1961), in his spare time. In 1963, he began teaching how to write stories and plays in college. Several of his later works also sold well, but all failed to surpass *Catch*-22. Through the use of Black Humor, *Something Happened* (1974) exposes the dark side of contemporary American social life and distorted relationships among people due to their selfish desires; *In Good as gold*(1979), the protagonist Bruce Gold tries to regain the Jewishness he has lost. *God Knows* (1984) was a modern version of the story of King David and an allegory of what it is like for a Jew to survive in a hostile world. *Closing time*(1994)is a sequel to *Catch*-22. Heller also writes plays. His play-within-a-play, *We Bombed in New Haven* (1968), was written in part to express his protest against the Vietnam War. In his novels, the plots are almost absurd, against the logic of life. They include a morbid sense of humor. His doubts about the absurd American society as well as his satire and philosophical exploration of life are also presented vividly. He is also good at using reverse tone and irrelevant words to achieve an ironic and humorous effect. The narrative technique of combining reality and fantasy is another feature of his work. Reality and fantasy permeate alternately in his descriptions, which creates a confusing scene and shows the panic of the characters in a certain environment. Moreover, his works are often full of cynical attitudes, nihilistic tendencies, and pessimistic moods.

Black humor appeared in the 1960s and is one of the most important literary genres in contemporary American literature. Writers of this genre highlight the absurdity of the world around the characters and the social oppression of individuals. By using a magnifying glass and a distorting mirror, they exaggerate this absurdity and oppression, which, through distortion and deformation, makes them become more absurd and ridiculous, more abnormal and unreasonable, and therefore, ugly and despised. Undoubtedly, the characters' helplessness and painful mood are obvious, so some people call black humor "humor under the gallows."

*Catch*-22 is not only a war novel, but also a novel about people's lives in peaceful times. This novel attacked the dehumanization of all contemporary institutions and corruptions of individuals who gain power in said institutions. The armed-forces are viewed as one of the most outrageous examples of the two evils.

The following text is selected from chapter five of the novel. The events within are mainly broken down into three segments: first, a story between Chief White Halfoat and Chief White Halfoat; second, Yossarian pretending to be insane again; and third, the description of their mission on B-25 bombers. Through these seemingly chaotic narratives, the author explains the *Catch*-22 incisively and vividly, which creatively shows the morbid reality of the United States and the mental state of the people in its society.

## Chapter 5 Chief White Halfoats

Doc Daneeka lived in a splotched[1] gray tent with Chief White Halfoat, whom he feared and despised.

'I can just picture his liver,' Doc Daneeka grumbled.

'Picture my liver,' Yossarian advised him.

'There's nothing wrong with your liver.'

'That shows how much you don't know,' Yossarian bluffed[2], and told Doc Daneeka about the troublesome pain in his liver that had troubled Nurse Duckett and Nurse Cramer and all the doctors in the hospital because it wouldn't become jaundice[3] and wouldn't go away.

Doc Daneeka wasn't interested. 'You think you've got troubles?'

he wanted to know. 'What about me? You should've been in my office the day those newlyweds walked in.'

'What newlyweds?'

'Those newlyweds that walked into my office one day. Didn't I ever tell you about them? She was lovely.' So was Doc Daneeka's office. He had decorated his waiting room with goldfish and one of the finest suites of cheap furniture. Whatever he could he bought on credit, even the goldfish. For the rest, he obtained money from greedy relatives in exchange for shares of the profits. His office was in Staten Island in a two-family firetrap just four blocks away from the ferry stop and only one block south of a supermarket, three beauty parlors, and two corrupt druggists. It was a corner location, but nothing helped. Population turnover was small, and people clung through habit to the same physicians they had been doing business with for years. Bills piled up rapidly, and he was soon faced with the loss of his most precious medical instruments: his adding machine was repossessed, and then his typewriter. The goldfish died. Fortunately, just when things were blackest, the war broke out.

'It was a godsend[4],' Doc Daneeka confessed solemnly. 'Most of the other doctors were soon in the service, and things picked up overnight. The corner location really started paying off, and I soon found myself handling more patients than I could handle competently. I upped my kickback fee with those two drugstores. The beauty parlors were good for two, three abortions a week. Things couldn't have been better, and then look what happened. They had to send a guy from the draft board around to look me over. I was Four-F[5]. I had examined myself pretty thoroughly and discovered that I was unfit for military service. You'd think my word would be enough, wouldn't you, since I was a doctor in good standing with my county medical society and with my local Better Business Bureau. But no, it wasn't, and they sent this guy around just to make sure I really did have one leg amputated[6] at the hip and was helplessly bedridden with incurable rheumatoid arthritis.[7]Yossarian, we live in an age of distrust and deteriorating spiritual values. It's a terrible thing,' Doc Daneeka protested in a voice quavering with strong emotion. 'It's a terrible thing when even the word of a licensed physician is suspected by the country he loves.' Doc Daneeka had been drafted and shipped to Pianosa as a flight surgeon, even though he was terrified of flying.

'I don't have to go looking for trouble in an airplane,' he noted, blinking his beady, brown, offended eyes myopically[8]. 'It comes looking for me. Like that virgin I'm telling you about that couldn't have a baby.'

'What virgin?' Yossarian asked. 'I thought you were telling me about some newlyweds.'

'That's the virgin I'm telling you about. They were just a couple of young kids, and they'd been married, oh, a little over a year when they came walking into my office without an appointment. You should have seen her. She was so sweet and young and pretty. She even blushed when I asked about her periods. I don't think I'll ever stop loving that girl. She was built like a dream and wore a chain around her neck with a medal of Saint Anthony hanging down inside the most beautiful bosom I never saw. "It must be a terrible temptation for Saint Anthony," I joked—just to put her at ease, you know. "Saint Anthony?" her husband said. "Who's Saint Anthony?" "Ask your wife," I told him. "She can tell you who Saint Anthony is." "Who is Saint Anthony?" he asked her. "Who?" she wanted to know. "Saint Anthony," he told her. "Saint Anthony?" she said. "Who's Saint Anthony?" When I got a good look at her inside my examination room I found she was still a virgin. I spoke to her husband alone while she was pulling her girdle back on and hooking it onto her stockings. "Every night," he boasted. A real wise guy, you know. "I never miss a night," he boasted. He meant it, too. "I even been puttin' it to her mornings before the breakfasts she makes me before we go to work," he boasted. There was only one explanation. When I had them both together again I gave them a demonstration of intercourse with the rubber models I've got in my office. I've got these rubber models in my office with all the reproductive organs of both sexes that I keep locked up in separate cabinets to avoid a scandal. I mean I used to have them. I don't have anything any more, not even a practice. The only thing I have now is this low temperature that I'm really starting to worry about. Those two kids I've got working for me in the medical tent aren't worth a damn as diagnosticians. All they know how to do is complain. They think they've got troubles? What about me? They should have been in my office that day with those two newlyweds looking at me as though I were telling them something nobody'd ever heard of before. You never saw anybody so interested. "You mean like this?" he asked me, and worked the models for himself awhile. You know, I can see where a certain type of person might get a big kick out of doing just that. "That's it," I told him. "Now, you go home and try it my way for a few months and see what happens. Okay?" "Okay," they said, and paid me in cash without any argument. "Have a good time," I told them, and they thanked me and walked out together. He had his arm around her waist as though he couldn't wait to get her home and put it to her again. A few days later he came back all by himself and told my nurse he had to see me right away. As soon as we were alone, he punched me in the nose.'

'He did what?'

'He called me a wise guy and punched me in the nose. "What are you, a wise guy?" he said, and knocked me flat on my ass. Pow! Just like that. I'm not kidding.'

'I know you're not kidding,' Yossarian said. 'But why did he do it?'

'How should I know why he did it?' Doc Daneeka retorted with annoyance.

'Maybe it had something to do with Saint Anthony?' Doc Daneeka looked at Yossarian blankly. 'Saint Anthony?' he asked with astonishment. 'Who's Saint Anthony?'

'How should I know?' answered Chief White Halfoat, staggering inside the tent just then with a bottle of whiskey cradled in his arm and sitting himself down pugnaciously[9] between the two of them.

Doc Daneeka rose without a word and moved his chair outside the tent, his back bowed by the compact kit of injustices that was his perpetual burden.. He could not bear the company of his roommate.

Chief White Halfoat thought he was crazy. 'I don't know what's the matter with that guy,' he observed reproachfully. 'He's got no brains, that's what's the matter with him. If he had any brains he'd grab a shovel and start digging. Right here in the tent, he'd start digging, right under my cot. He'd strike oil in no time. Don't he know how that enlisted man struck oil with a shovel back in the States? Didn't he ever hear what happened to that kid—what was the name of that rotten rat bastard pimp of a snot nose back in Colorado?'

'Wintergreen.'

'Wintergreen.'

'He's afraid,' Yossarian explained.

'Oh, no. Not Wintergreen.' Chief White Halfoat shook his head with undisguised admiration. 'That stinking little punk wise-guy son of a bitch ain't afraid of nobody.'

'Doc Daneeka's afraid. That's what's the matter with him.'

'What's he afraid of?'

'He's afraid of you,' Yossarian said. 'He's afraid you're going to die of pneumonia.'

'He'd better be afraid,' Chief White Halfoat said. A deep, low laugh rumbled through his massive chest. 'I will, too, the first chance I get. You just wait and see.' Chief White Halfoat was a handsome, swarthy[10] Indian from Oklahoma with a heavy, hard-boned face and tousled black hair, a half-blooded Cree from Enid who, for occult reasons of his own, had made up his mind to die of pneumonia. He was a glowering, vengeful, disillusioned Indian who hated foreigners with names like Cathcart, Korn, Black and Havermeyer and wished they'd all go back to where their lousy ancestors had come from.

'You wouldn't believe it, Yossarian,' he ruminated[11], raising his voice deliberately to bait Doc Daneeka, 'but this used to be a pretty good country to live in before they loused it up with their goddam piety.' Chief White Halfoat was out to revenge himself upon the white man. He could barely read or write and had been assigned to Captain Black as assistant intelligence officer.

'How could I learn to read or write?' Chief White Halfoat demanded with simulated belligerence, raising his voice again so that Doc Daneeka would hear. 'Every place we pitched our tent, they sank an oil well. Every time they sank a well, they hit oil. And every time they hit oil, they made us pack up our tent and go someplace else. We were human divining rods.. Our whole family had a natural affinity for petroleum deposits, and soon every oil company in the world had technicians chasing us around. We were always on the move. It was one hell of a way to bring a child up, I can tell you. I don't think I ever spent more than a week in one place.' His earliest memory was of a geologist.

'Every time another White Halfoat was born,' he continued, 'the stock market turned bullish. Soon whole drilling crews were following us around with all their equipment just to get the jump on each other. Companies began to merge just so they could cut down on the number of people they had to assign to us. But the crowd in back of us kept growing. We never got a good night's sleep. When we stopped, they stopped. When we moved, they moved, chuckwagons, bulldozers, derricks, generators. We were a walking business boom, and we began to receive invitations from some of the best hotels just for the amount of business we would drag into town with us. Some of those invitations were mighty generous, but we couldn't accept any because we were Indians and all the best hotels that were inviting us wouldn't accept Indians as guests. Racial prejudice is a terrible thing, Yossarian. It really is. It's a terrible thing to treat a decent, loyal Indian like a nigger, kike[12], wop[13] or spic[14]. Chief White Halfoat nodded slowly with conviction.

'Then, Yossarian, it finally happened—the beginning of the end. They began to follow us around from in front. They would try to guess where we were going to stop next and would begin drilling before we even got there, so we couldn't stop. As soon as we'd begin to unroll our blankets, they would kick us off. They had confidence in us. They wouldn't even wait to strike oil before they kicked us off. We were so tired we almost didn't care the day our time ran out. One morning we found ourselves completely surrounded by oilmen waiting for us to come their way so they could kick us off. Everywhere you looked there was an oilman on a ridge, waiting there like Indians getting ready to attack. It was the end. We couldn't stay where we were because we had just been kicked off. And there was no place left for us to go. Only the Army saved me. Luckily, the war broke out just in the nick of time, and a draft board picked me right up out of the middle and put me down safely in Lowery Field, Colorado. I was the only survivor.' Yossarian knew he was lying, but did not interrupt as Chief White Halfoat went on to claim that he had never heard from his parents again. That didn't bother him too much, though, for he had only their word for it that they were his parents, and since they had lied to him about so many other things, they could just as well have been lying to him about that too. He was much better acquainted with the fate of a tribe of first cousins who had wandered away north in a diversionary movement and pushed inadvertently into Canada. When they tried to return, they were stopped at the border by American immigration authorities who would not let them back into the country. They could not come back in because they were red.

It was a horrible joke, but Doc Daneeka didn't laugh until Yossarian came to him one mission later and pleaded again, without any real expectation of success, to be grounded. Doc Daneeka snickered once and was soon immersed in problems of his own, which included Chief White Halfoat, who had been challenging him all that morning to Indian wrestle, and Yossarian, who decided right then and there to go crazy.

'You're wasting your time,' Doc Daneeka was forced to tell him.

'Can't you ground someone who's crazy?'

'Oh, sure. I have to. There's a rule saying I have to ground anyone who's crazy.'

'Then why don't you ground me? I'm crazy. Ask Clevinger.'

'Clevinger? Where is Clevinger? You find Clevinger and I'll ask him.'

'Then ask any of the others. They'll tell you how crazy I am.'

'They're crazy.'

'Then why don't you ground them?'

'Why don't they ask me to ground them?'

'Because they're crazy, that's why.'

'Of course they're crazy,' Doc Daneeka replied. 'I just told you they're crazy, didn't I? And you can't let crazy people decide whether you're crazy or not, can you?' Yossarian looked at him soberly and tried another approach. 'Is Orr crazy?'

'He sure is,' Doc Daneeka said.

'Can you ground him?'

'I sure can. But first he has to ask me to. That's part of the rule.'

'Then why doesn't he ask you to?'

'Because he's crazy,' Doc Daneeka said. 'He has to be crazy to keep flying combat missions after all the close calls he's had. Sure, I can ground Orr. But first he has to ask me to.'

'That's all he has to do to be grounded?'

'That's all. Let him ask me.'

'And then you can ground him?' Yossarian asked.

'No. Then I can't ground him.'

'You mean there's a catch?'

'Sure there's a catch,' Doc Daneeka replied. 'Catch-22. Anyone who wants to get out of combat duty isn't really crazy.' There was only one catch and that was Catch-22, which specified that a concern for one's own safety in the face of dangers that were real and immediate was the process of a rational mind. Orr was crazy and could be grounded. All he had to do was ask; and as soon as he did, he would no longer be crazy and would have to fly more missions. Orr would be crazy to fly more missions and sane if he didn't, but if he was sane he had to fly them. If he flew them he was crazy and didn't have to; but if he didn't want to he was sane and had to. Yossarian was moved very deeply by the absolute simplicity of this clause of Catch-22 and let out a respectful whistle.

'That's some catch, that Catch-22,' he observed.

'It's the best there is,' Doc Daneeka agreed.

Yossarian saw it clearly in all its spinning reasonableness. There was an elliptical precision about its perfect pairs of parts that was graceful and shocking, like good modern art, and at times Yossarian wasn't quite sure that he saw it at all, just the way he was never quite sure about good modern art or about the flies Orr saw in Appleby's eyes. He had Orr's word to take for the flies in Appleby's eyes.

'Oh, they're there, all right,' Orr had assured him about the flies in Appleby's eyes after Yossarian's fist fight with Appleby in the officers' club, 'although he probably doesn't even know it. That's why he can't see things as they really are.'

'How come he doesn't know it?' inquired Yossarian.

'Because he's got flies in his eyes,' Orr explained with exaggerated patience. 'How can he see he's got flies in his eyes if he's got flies in his eyes?' It made as much sense as anything else, and Yossarian was willing to give Orr the benefit of the doubt because Orr was from the wilderness outside New York City and knew so much more about wildlife than Yossarian did, and because Orr, unlike Yossarian's mother, father, sister, brother, aunt, uncle, in-law, teacher, spiritual leader, legislator, neighbor and newspaper, had never lied to him about anything crucial before. Yossarian had mulled[15] is newfound knowledge about Appleby over in private for a day or two and then decided, as a good deed, to pass the word along to Appleby himself.

'Appleby, you've got flies in your eyes,' he whispered helpfully as they passed by each other in the doorway of the parachute tent on the day of the weekly milk run to Parma.

'What?' Appleby responded sharply, thrown into confusion by the fact that Yossarian had spoken to him at all.

'You've got flies in your eyes,' Yossarian repeated. 'That's probably why you can't see them.' Appleby retreated from Yossarian with a look of loathing bewilderment and sulked in silence until he was in the jeep with Havermeyer riding down the long, straight road to the briefing room, where Major Danby, the fidgeting group operations officer, was waiting to conduct the preliminary briefing with all the lead pilots, bombardiers and navigators. Appleby spoke in a soft voice so that he would not be heard by the driver or by Captain Black, who was stretched out with his eyes closed in the front seat of the jeep.

'Havermeyer,' he asked hesitantly. 'Have I got flies in my eyes?' Havermeyer blinked quizzically. 'Sties?[16]' he asked.

'No, flies,' he was told.

Havermeyer blinked again. 'Flies?'

'In my eyes.'

'You must be crazy,' Havermeyer said.

'No, I'm not crazy. Yossarian's crazy. Just tell me if I've got flies in my eyes or not. Go ahead. I can take it.' Havermeyer popped another piece of peanut brittle into his mouth and peered very closely into Appleby's eyes.

'I don't see any,' he announced.

Appleby heaved an immense sigh of relief. Havermeyer had tiny bits of peanut brittle adhering to his lips, chin and cheeks.

'You've got peanut brittle crumbs on your face,' Appleby

remarked to him.

'I'd rather have peanut brittle crumbs on my face than flies in my eyes,' Havermeyer retorted.

The officers of the other five planes in each flight arrived in trucks for the general briefing that took place thirty minutes later. The three enlisted men in each crew were not briefed at all, but were carried directly out on the airfield to the separate planes in which they were scheduled to fly that day, where they waited around with the ground crew until the officers with whom they had been scheduled to fly swung off the rattling tailgates of the trucks delivering them and it was time to climb aboard and start up. Engines rolled over disgruntedly on lollipop-shaped hardstands, resisting first, then idling smoothly awhile, and then the planes lumbered around and nosed forward lamely over the pebbled ground like sightless, stupid, crippled things until they taxied into the line at the foot of the landing strip and took off swiftly, one behind the other, in a zooming, rising roar, banking slowly into formation over mottled treetops, and circling the field at even speed until all the flights of six had been formed and then setting course over cerulean water on the first leg of the journey to the target in northern Italy or France. The planes gained altitude steadily and were above nine thousand feet by the time they crossed into enemy territory. One of the surprising things always was the sense of calm and utter silence, broken only by the test rounds fired from the machine guns, by an occasional toneless, terse remark over the intercom, and, at last, by the sobering pronouncement of the bombardier in each plane that they were at the I.P.[17] and about to turn toward the target. There was always sunshine, always a tiny sticking in the throat from the rarefied air.

The B-25s they flew in were stable, dependable, dull-green ships with twin rudders and engines and wide wings. Their single fault, from where Yossarian sat as a bombardier, was the tight crawlway separating the bombardier's compartment in the plexiglass nose from the nearest escape hatch. The crawlway was a narrow, square, cold tunnel hollowed out beneath the flight controls, and a large man like Yossarian could squeeze through only with difficulty. A chubby, moon-faced navigator with little reptilian eyes and a pipe like Aarfy's had trouble, too, and Yossarian used to chase him back from the nose as they turned toward the target, now minutes away. There was a time of tension then, a time of waiting with nothing to hear and nothing to see and nothing to do but wait as the antiaircraft guns below took aim and made ready to knock them all sprawling into infinite sleep if they could.

The crawlway was Yossarian's lifeline to outside from a plane about to fall, but Yossarian swore at it with seething antagonism, reviled it as an obstacle put there by providence as part of the plot that would destroy him. There was room for an additional escape hatch right there in the nose of a B-25, but there was no escape hatch. Instead there was the crawlway, and since the mess on the mission over Avignon he had learned to detest every mammoth inch of it, for it slung him seconds and seconds away from his parachute, which was too bulky to be taken up front with him, and seconds and seconds more after that away from the escape hatch on the floor between the rear of the elevated flight deck and the feet of the faceless top turret gunner mounted high above. Yossarian longed to be where Aarfy could be once Yossarian had chased him back from the nose; Yossarian longed to sit on the floor in a huddled ball right on top of the escape hatch inside a sheltering igloo of extra flak suits that he would have been happy to carry along with him, his parachute already hooked to his harness where it belonged, one fist clenching the red-handled rip cord, one fist gripping the emergency hatch release that would spill him earthward into the air at the first dreadful squeal of destruction. That was where he wanted to be if he had to be there at all, instead of hung out there in front like some goddam cantilevered goldfish in some goddam cantilevered goldfish bowl while the goddam foul black tiers of flak were bursting and booming and billowing all around and above and below him in a climbing, cracking, staggered, banging, phantasmagorical, cosmological wickedness that jarred and tossed and shivered, clattered and pierced, and threatened to annihilate them all in one splinter of a second in one vast flash of fire.

Aarfy had been no use to Yossarian as a navigator or as anything else, and Yossarian drove him back from the nose vehemently each time so that they would not clutter up each other's way if they had to scramble suddenly for safety. Once Yossarian had driven him back from the nose, Aarfy was free to cower on the floor where Yossarian longed to cower, but he stood bolt upright instead with his stumpy arms resting comfortably on the backs of the pilot's and co-pilot's seats, pipe in hand, making affable[18] small talk to McWatt and whoever happened to be co-pilot and pointing out amusing trivia in the sky to the two men, who were too busy to be interested. McWatt was too busy responding at the controls to Yossarian's strident instructions as

Yossarian slipped the plane in on the bomb run and then whipped them all away violently around the ravenous pillars of exploding shells with curt, shrill, obscene commands to McWatt that were much like the anguished, entreating nightmare yelpings of Hungry Joe in the dark. Aarfy would puff reflectively on his pipe throughout the whole chaotic clash, gazing with unruffled curiosity at the war through McWatt's window as though it were a remote disturbance that could not affect him. Aarfy was a dedicated fraternity man who loved cheerleading and class reunions and did not have brains enough to be afraid. Yossarian did have brains enough and was, and the only thing that stopped him from abandoning his post under fire and scurrying back through the crawlway like a yellow-bellied rat was his unwillingness to entrust the evasive action out of the target area to anybody else. There was nobody else in the world he would honor with so great a responsibility. There was nobody else he knew who was as big a coward. Yossarian was the best man in the group at evasive action, but had no idea why.

There was no established procedure for evasive action. All you needed was fear, and Yossarian had plenty of that, more fear than Orr or Hungry Joe, more fear than Dunbar, who had resigned himself submissively to the idea that he must die someday. Yossarian had not resigned himself to that idea, and he bolted for his life wildly on each mission the instant his bombs were away, hollering, 'Hard, hard, hard, hard, you bastard, hard!' at McWatt and hating McWatt viciously all the time as though McWatt were to blame for their being up there at all to be rubbed out[19] by strangers, and everybody else in the plane kept off the intercom, except for the pitiful time of the mess on the mission to Avignon when Dobbs went crazy in mid-air and began weeping pathetically for help.

'Help him, help him,' Dobbs sobbed. 'Help him, help him.'

'Help who? Help who?' called back Yossarian, once he had plugged his headset back into the intercom system, after it had been jerked out when Dobbs wrested the controls away from Huple and hurled them all down suddenly into the deafening, paralyzing, horrifying dive which had plastered Yossarian helplessly to the ceiling of the plane by the top of his head and from which Huple had rescued them just in time by seizing the controls back from Dobbs and leveling the ship out almost as suddenly right back in the middle of the buffeting layer of cacophonous flak from which they had escaped successfully only a moment before. Oh, God! Oh, God, oh, God, Yossarian had been pleading wordlessly as he dangled from the ceiling of the nose of the ship by the top of his head, unable to move.

'The bombardier, the bombardier,' Dobbs answered in a cry when Yossarian spoke. 'He doesn't answer, he doesn't answer. Help the bombardier, help the bombardier.'

'I'm the bombardier,' Yossarian cried back at him. 'I'm the bombardier. I'm all right. I'm all right.'

'Then help him, help him,' Dobbs begged. 'Help him, help him.' And Snowden lay dying in back.

## Notes

1. Marked,stained,spotted.

2. Be full of bravado.

3. A medical condition in which the skin and the white parts of the eyes become yellow.

4. It was a good chance.

5. A classification of conscription in the United States. It refers to those who are not suitable for military service both physically and mentally.

6. To remove someone's arm, leg, hand, finger, or toe in a medical operation.

7. A disease that gets worse over a period of time and causes painful swelling and permanent damage in the joints of the body, especially the fingers, wrists, feet and ankles.

8. Narrow-minded.

9. Aggressively.

10. Dark complexion.

11. Contemplate;be lost in thought.

12. Jews.

13. Black skin Southern Europeans moving to the United States.

14. (American slang) (derogatory) Hispanic Americans.

15. Pondered over.

16. An infection of the eyelid(= the skin above or below the eye) which makes it red and sore.

17. I.P., bomb point.

18. Pleasant, friendly and easy to talk to.

19. Bombed.

## Questions

1. "Fortunately, just when things were blackest, the war broke out." Illustrated the writing skill of the sentence.

2. Try to explain the implied meaning of *Catch*-22.

# References

[1] Bureau of International Information Programs U.S. Department of State. Outline of U.S. History[EB/OL].(2005)[2022-10-01].http://usinfo.state.gov/.

[2] BAYM N.The Norton Anthology of American Literature [M]. shorter 6th ed.New York:W.W.Norton & Company,Inc.,2002.

[3] MORRISON T.The Beloved[M].New York:Plume,1998.

[4] ED.REIDHEAD J.The Norton Anthology of American Literature[M].9th ed.New York:W.W.Norton & Company,Inc.,2013.

[5] V.REMINI Robert.A Short History of the United States[M].New York:Harper Collins Publishers Ltd., 2008.

[6] TAO Jie.Selected Readings in American Literature[M].third ed.Beijing: Higher Education Press, 2018.

[7] UPDIKE J.Rabbit, Run[M].New York:Ballantine Books, 1996.

[8] 百度百科 . 理查德・赖特 . https://baike.baidu.com/item/%E7%90%86%E6%9F%A5%E5%BE%B7%C2%B7%E8%B5%96%E7%89%B9/5493263?fromtitle=Richard%20Wright&fromid=5460537&fr=Aladdin.

[9] 英文阅读网 . 英文小说 : 嘉莉妹妹 - 磁性相吸：各种力的摆布 [EB/OL].(2007-02-12)[2022-10-01].http://www.enread.com/mobile/?mid=3&aid=10321 SISTER CARRIE.

[10] Poets.org: charles-olson[EB/OL].[2022-10-01].https://poets.org/poet/charles-olson.

[11] 百度文库 .The-Outcasts-of-Poker-Flat[EB/OL].[2022-10-01].https://wenku.baidu.com/view/455ae389f5ec4afe04a1b0717fd5360cbb1a8d35.html?fixfr=eBXRbW%252FFEq8VLW1xPELy7g%253D%253D&fr=income2-wk_go_searchX-search.

[12] 百度文库 .Local Color[EB/OL].[2022-10-10]. https://wenku.baidu.com/view/5adef523bcd126fff7050b57.html.

[13] 百度文库 .Mark Twain( 英文简介 ) [EB/OL].[2022-10-13]. https://wenku.baidu.com/view/da1c5a92ef06eff9aef8941ea76e58fafbb0452e.htm（marktwain）.

[14] 百度文库 . 美国 文学 Theodore Dreiser[EB/OL].[2022-10-15].https://wenku.baidu.com/view/dea1cecba1c7aa00b52acbe6.html?fixfr=YZg%252FJmSrBPcawOxYxBEz3w%253D%253D&fr=income1-wk_go_search-searchDREISER.

[15] Britannica.Arts & Culture:John Updike[EB/OL].[2022-10-20].https://www.britannica.com/biography/John-Updike.

[16] Britannica.Arts & Culture: Mark Twain[EB/OL].[2022-11-10].https://www.britannica.com/biography/Mark-Twain.

[17] Britannica.Arts & Culture: Theodore Dreiser[EB/OL].[2022-11-13].https://www.britannica.com/biography/Theodore-Dreiser.

[18] Poetry Foundation:Stephen Crane[EB/OL].[2022-11-20]. https://www.poetryfoundation.org/poets/stephen-crane.